Minorities and Reconstructive Coalitions

As with Muslims today, Catholics were once suspected of being antidemocratic, oppressive of women, and supportive of extremist political violence. By the end of the twentieth century, Catholics were considered normal and sometimes valorized as exemplary citizens. Can other ethnic, racial, and religious minorities follow the same path? *Minorities and Reconstructive Coalitions* provides an answer by comparing the stories of ethnic Catholics' political incorporation in Australia, Canada, and the United States. Through comparative and historical analysis, the book shows that reconstructive coalitions, such as labor and pan-Christian moral movements, can bring Catholics and Protestants together under new identities, significantly improving Catholic standing. Not all coalitions are reconstructive or successful, and institutional structures such as regional autonomy can enhance or inhibit the formation of these coalitions. The book provides overviews of the history of Catholics in the three countries, reorients the historiography of Catholic incorporation in the United States, uncovers the phenomenon of minority overrepresentation in politics, and advances unique arguments about the impact of coalitions on minority politics.

Willie Gin received his doctorate in political science from the University of Pennsylvania and is currently an assistant professor at Xavier University of Louisiana. His main areas of research interest are in minority incorporation, American political development, and how current technology affects both racial and income inequality. He has recently published in journals such as *Politics and Religion*.

Routledge Studies in Nationalism and Ethnicity
Series Editor: William Safran
University of Colorado Boulder, USA

This new series draws attention to some of the most exciting issues in current world political debate: nation-building, autonomy and self-determination; ethnic identity, conflict and accommodation; pluralism, multiculturalism and the politics of language; ethnonationalism, irredentism and separatism; and immigration, naturalization and citizenship. The series will include monographs as well as edited volumes, and through the use of case studies and comparative analyses will bring together some of the best work to be found in the field.

Nationalism, Ethnicity and Boundaries
Conceptualising and Understanding Identity through Boundary Approaches
Edited by Jennifer Jackson and Lina Molokotos-Liederman

Minorities and Reconstructive Coalitions
The Catholic Question
Willie Gin

Minorities and Reconstructive Coalitions
The Catholic Question

Willie Gin

LONDON AND NEW YORK

First published 2017
by Routledge
2 Park Square, Milton Park, Abingdon, Oxon OX14 4RN

and by Routledge
711 Third Avenue, New York, NY 10017

Routledge is an imprint of the Taylor & Francis Group, an informa business

© 2017 Willie Gin

The right of Willie Gin to be identified as author of this work has been asserted by him in accordance with sections 77 and 78 of the Copyright, Designs and Patents Act 1988.

All rights reserved. No part of this book may be reprinted or reproduced or utilized in any form or by any electronic, mechanical, or other means, now known or hereafter invented, including photocopying and recording, or in any information storage or retrieval system, without permission in writing from the publishers.

Trademark notice: Product or corporate names may be trademarks or registered trademarks, and are used only for identification and explanation without intent to infringe.

British Library Cataloguing in Publication Data
A catalogue record for this book is available from the British Library

Library of Congress Cataloging in Publication Data
Names: Gin, Willie, author.
Title: Ethnic minority incorporation and reconstructive coalitions : the Catholic question / Willie Gin.
Description: 1 [edition]. | New York : Routledge, 2017. | Series: Routledge studies in nationalism and ethnicity | Includes bibliographical references and index.
Identifiers: LCCN 2016058395| ISBN 9781138283237 (hardback) | ISBN 9781315270364 (e-book)
Subjects: LCSH: Church and minorities. | Catholic Church–Doctrines. | Christianity and politics–Catholic Church–History–20th century. | Protestant churches–Relations–Catholic Church. | Catholic Church–Relations–Protestant churches.
Classification: LCC BV639.M56 G56 2017 | DDC 305.6/82–dc23
LC record available at https://lccn.loc.gov/2016058395

ISBN: 978-1-138-28323-7 (hbk)
ISBN: 978-1-315-27036-4 (ebk)

Typeset in Times New Roman
by Wearset Ltd, Boldon, Tyne and Wear

Printed and bound in Great Britain by
TJ International Ltd, Padstow, Cornwall

Contents

	Series editor's foreword	vi
	Acknowledgments	vii
1	The multiplicity of the Catholic past	1
2	Transubstantiating the body politic: a theory of reconstructive coalitions	14
3	Catholic incorporation from 1890 to the mid-twentieth century	25
4	Working with Catholicism in Australia	46
5	Catholicism at arm's length in the United States	65
6	Provincializing Catholicism in Canada	89
7	Catholic standing in the latter half of the twentieth century	109
8	Realigning Catholicism and Protestantism at the turn of the twentieth century in the United States	131
9	The limits of pan-Christian coalitions in Australia and Canada	151
10	The Catholic past as prologue? The future of ethnic, racial, and religious minority incorporation	175
	Appendices	194
	Selected bibliography	198
	Index	215

Series editor's foreword

This book explores the connection between religion and ethnicity. It shows that religion, no matter how universal in its aspirations, is usually cloaked in an ethnonationally specific garb, and members of religious communities, like those of ethnic ones, are objects of stereotypes. There is a Polish and an Irish Catholicism, just as there is a Greek and a Russian Eastern Orthodoxy, and an Arab, Indonesian, Bengali, and Iranian Islam. Religious identity may be transformed into an ethnic one, as in Bosnia; and in some cases, such as those of Jews, Armenians, and Sikhs, the two identities have been intertwined.

The treatment of minorities is nationally differentiated, ranging from stigmatization and exclusion to toleration, valorization, representation, and incorporation into the political system and process. It is based on the size of the subcommunity, its internal texture, and its economic function as well as on the structure of the polity and the institutional setting. These factors influence the strategies adopted by minorities; if they wish to maintain their distinct identities, they engage in lobbying and coalition building, at least in democracies marked by interparty competition, where ethnic and religious subcommunities behave like political or class based ones. The emphasis in this study is on the United States, where minority incorporation is examined chronologically and in depth and comparison with Canada, Australia, and, to a lesser extent, South Africa. These countries share a number of features: they are English-speaking, democracies, and have a Protestant majority; they are settler states, and are therefore more receptive to immigrants and more open to the incorporation of minorities.

This thoroughly documented case study provides an examination of assimilationist, pluralist, and other theories concerning the behavior of citizens in complex societies, the place of interests versus ideology, and the political strategies of ethno-religious minorities in pursuit of acceptance. It is an important contribution to the study of the politics of ethnic and religious minorities.

William Safran
University of Colorado at Boulder

Acknowledgments

I am particularly grateful to my advisors at the Department of Political Science at the University of Pennsylvania who first oversaw this project: Rogers Smith, Marie Gottschalk, and Anne Norton. Thanks for the patience, the excellent advice, and the occasional free lunch (next one's on me). I would also like to thank the School of Arts and Sciences at the University of Pennsylvania; the Democracy, Citizenship, and Constitutionalism program at the University of Pennsylvania; and the United States Studies Centre in Sydney for providing me financial and material resources to support my research. Several people deserve thanks for providing visa support, spare couches, storage space, and useful information for a clueless American, including: Kim Yi, John Porter, Annie Ng, Anne-Marie D'aoust, David Grondin, Sarah van Beurden, and Michael Jackson. The staff at Van Pelt Library, the National Library of Canada, Carleton Library, the State Library of New South Wales, Fisher Library at the University of Sydney, the National Library of Australia in Canberra, the New York Public Research Library, and the anonymous, super-efficient elves of interlibrary loan all deserve much appreciation for dealing with my many requests. Many other people contributed to improving the book through reading versions of chapters or listening to presentations, including Richard Johnston, Michael Hogan, Rodney Smith, Brendan O'Leary, my fellow graduate students at Penn, and two anonymous reviewers. I am especially appreciative of my current academic home, Xavier University of Louisiana, for support in completing the publishing of book manuscript. For successfully guiding the manuscript to publication, I would also like to thank William Safran, Claire Maloney, Ann King, Amy Ekins-Coward, Matthew Twigg, and the other members of the editorial and production teams at Routledge and Wearset who worked on the manuscript.

I am grateful Vicky Hattam, David Plotke, and Mary Prophet for being my earliest academic supporters before this book even existed. One cannot get through academia without people outside of it, so I'm also thankful for the companionship of Kim Yi, Edmund Fong, and Albert Lowe.

Most importantly, I thank my parents, Lilly and Jin, for decades of unfailing love and support. Both of you will never read this book, but nevertheless, I hope that somehow you understand that it all was made possible by the both of you.

1 The multiplicity of the Catholic past

> Growing up in a small Ohio town in the 1950s, I knew the religion of just about every kid in my 600-person high school. [...] When my children attended high school in the 1980s, they didn't know the religion of practically anyone. It simply didn't matter. [...] In my lifetime, Americans have deconstructed religion as a basis for making decisions. Why can't we do the same thing with other types of diversity?
>
> Robert Putnam[1]

Catholic political incorporation has been forgotten. Perhaps the best marker for the unremembered histories of Catholic political incorporation is the film *V for Vendetta* (2006). In the film, a disfigured revolutionary wearing a Guy Fawkes mask fights a futuristic totalitarian government, chanting, "Remember, remember, the fifth of November." Unknown to many of the film's viewers, the chant references the Gunpowder Plot of 1605, in which Fawkes and his fellow Catholic conspirators planned to blow up Parliament and assassinate the Protestant king, James I. In the past, the ditty to "Remember the fifth of November" invited listeners to recall Catholic treason. During the colonial era in America, celebrations of Guy Fawkes Day featured burnings of the Pope in effigy. Yet, at the turn of the twenty-first century, the makers of *V for Vendetta* treated the Fawkes mask as a symbol of heroic resistance from tyrannical government, and this association crossed over into real social movements. Protestors donned the grinning visage of Guy Fawkes in the Occupy Wall Street movement of 2011. Use of the mask spread among pro-democratization movements throughout the world, compelling authoritarian governments in the Middle East to ban the mask and its transgressive smirk.

How did a symbol of Catholic treason become a worldwide symbol of resistance against authoritarian government? It is not likely that the Fawkes mask has been taken up because of a perception of the link between Catholicism and freedom. Many of the Occupy protesters, for instance, would probably object to the Catholic Church's stance on abortion and homosexuality. It is more likely that the connection of the Fawkes mask to Catholicism has simply been forgotten. This forgetting is reflected in the fact that there is no name or term readily at hand to describe the once prolific discourse about Catholic fitness for democratic

2 Multiplicity of the Catholic past

life. In the nineteenth and early twentieth century, "the Jewish Question" marked the supposed "problem" of Jewish citizens as political subjects. Today, scholars use "the Muslim Question" to describe the problem of integrating Muslims into liberal democracies. The African American scholar W.E.B. Du Bois famously mused, "How does it feel to be a problem?" in response to "the Negro problem." That there is no comparable remembrance or reflection on "the Catholic question" or "the Catholic problem" points to a significant absence in both scholarship and America's collective conscience.

This forgetting is surprising because of the powerful hold anti-Catholicism once had in Anglo-American discourse. Nearly every stereotype and suspicion leveled against Muslims today had previously been used against Roman Catholics. Like contemporary Muslim stigma, anti-Catholic discourse was based on ethnic, racial, and religious grounds.[2] Compared with Protestants who tended to originate in Northwestern Europe, Catholics tended to have ethnic origins in Southern and Eastern Europe. Even Catholics from Northwestern Europe like the Irish and the French were sometimes seen as a different race from Anglo Saxons, with race and ethnicity often conflated in nineteenth- and early twentieth-century discourse. These perceived ethnoracial differences were often seen as parallel to deeper religious pathologies. Many Protestants accused Catholics of being hierarchical, antidemocratic, and unpatriotic, subject to a Pope who was considered "infallible." Catholics appeared to have strange, almost pagan beliefs, such as that Mary was born without sin, and that bread and wine taken during communion really did "transubstantiate" into the blood and body of Christ. Max Weber famously argued in *The Protestant Ethic and the Spirit of Capitalism* that Catholics tended to not be as economically prosperous as Protestants, and Catholic entrepreneurial and intellectual stagnation was often attributed to their insularity, separatism, and insistence upon educating their children in their own schools. Catholics were also accused of being oppressive of women, and *The Awful Confessions of Maria Monk*, an almost pornographic story of abuse of a woman at the hands of priests, became one of the nineteenth century's bestsellers, despite later being revealed to be a fabrication. Political terror became associated with Catholics, in the form of the savagery of the Inquisition, the treason of the Gunpowder Plot's attempt to assassinate King James I in 1605, and the guerrilla violence conducted by the Irish Republican Army in their struggles against Protestants in Northern Ireland.[3] It was as if Catholics and Protestants constituted two distinct cultures – the original clash of civilizations.

Yet, by the end of the twentieth century, the civilizational clash between Protestantism and Catholicism had receded, and Catholics were mostly considered respectable members of the community, and in some cases valorized as exemplary citizens. This is the most likely reason why most don't remember Catholic stigmatization today. Just as the "losers" of history often get written out of the textbooks, so too do the "winners" – at least, how they got to be "winners." How Catholic stigmatization was overcome has been obscured, the field left open to myth making.

Precisely because anti-Catholicism has been overcome in democratic societies, however, makes it a valuable case to study. One of the most important developments in the twenty-first century will be the increase in ethnic, racial, and religious diversity of many liberal democracies. The United States, among other countries, is experiencing levels of diversity not seen in its history. White Christians no longer constitute a majority in the United States, and whites may no longer be a majority by the 2040s.[4] These developments raise questions about whether newer and older minority groups in liberal democracies will integrate easily into the mainstream or be subject to various forms of unequal citizenship and restricted capacities. The more typical story of minority relations is one of frustration and disappointment. The predominant narrative in the academic and mainstream literature is that the relationship between diversity and democracy is deeply problematic, if not outright inimical.[5] In the United States, race remains a point of deep contention, and the most sophisticated social and political sciences demonstrate that the country is not a "post-racial" society.[6] In Europe, bans on the veil and minarets, the rise of nativist parties, and the exclusivist reaction to refugees from the Middle East show that diversity and democracy is a problem not limited only to the United States.

Histories, not history

A few commentators have sought general lessons from the overcoming of anti-Catholicism. Ross Douthat, a Catholic writer for the *New York Times*, suggested that a history of bigotry and prejudice in the United States actually helped speed up Catholic assimilation. Without such pressure, Catholics would have remained more distinct and separatist.[7] In a blog for the *New York Review of Books*, historians John T. McGreevey and R. Scott Appleby argued very nearly the opposite, stating that Catholics needed to do more than appear respectable and quietly fit in as "lace curtain" Irish: "If the Catholic experience in the United States holds any lesson it is that becoming American also means asserting one's constitutional rights, fully and forcefully, even if that assertion is occasionally taken to be insulting."[8] Nicholas Kristof, another *New York Times* columnist, suggested that Catholic behavior was not crucial, and argued that "we have a more glorious tradition intertwined in American history as well, one of tolerance, amity and religious freedom. Each time, this has ultimately prevailed over the Know Nothing impulse."[9] Something in American institutions, ideology, and character, Kristof implied, lent itself to a progressive narrative of religious freedom and ethnic incorporation.

The temptation to derive lessons from the U.S. Catholic experience exists not only in the op-ed pages of the nation's newspapers, but also in academia. The political scientist Robert Putnam, in concluding his study showing that greater diversity tends to be associated with lower social capital, wondered whether the contemporary incorporation of minorities would follow the path of Catholics in the twentieth century.[10] The epigraph at the start of this chapter is from that study. Just a few years later, Putnam and David E. Campbell wrote *American*

Grace, which, among many other things, sought to answer why the religious tensions between Protestants, Catholics, and Jews had disappeared by the end of the twentieth century. One answer Putnam and Campbell found was that increasing social contact and intermarriage accounted for a great deal of the disappearance in tension among religions. Many families, Putnam and Campbell noted, were interreligious, and this would prevent conflicts from erupting along these lines again.[11] Other attempts to understand the overcoming of anti-Catholicism comes from whiteness scholars such as David Roediger. Roediger focuses not so much on religion as on race, arguing that it was the ability of Irish, Italian, and other Southern and Eastern Europeans' ability to assimilate as whites that led to their eventual acceptance.[12]

These attempts to learn from the American Catholic experience, insightful on many points, have several limitations. One is that they look only at the experience of Catholics in the United States. Once one looks outside the United States, one finds not one, but multiple stories of Catholic political incorporation. In the nineteenth and early twentieth century, ethnic Catholics of Irish, French, and Southeastern European origin constituted significant minorities in Australia, Canada, and the United States, prompting conflicts with Protestants with Northwestern European origins.[13] Despite this similarity, the trajectories of ethnic Catholics in these countries diverged, yielding three important comparative stories: about descriptive representation and policies, about the role of parties in incorporating Catholics, and how political incorporation can contribute to the political development of a country.

Looking at differences in the descriptive representation of Catholics and policies associated with religion in Australia, Canada, and the United States helps unlock these multiple stories of political incorporation.[14] There are two broad patterns of variation that need to be explained. The first pattern consists of the trajectory of Catholic political incorporation from 1890 to about the mid-twentieth century. By the time of the Great Depression, Catholic political incorporation had proceeded much more favorably in Australia than in the United States or Canada. By 1929 Catholics were overrepresented in the prime ministership, cabinet positions, and the House of Representatives – a striking feat for a minority group that trailed Protestants in income and wealth. Catholics achieved this feat largely as members of the Labor party, and this success prompted competing parties to be more favorable toward Catholics as well. As early as 1940, Robert Menzies, who later became leader of the center-right Liberal–Country party coalition, indicated his willingness to break with long-standing commitments not to fund Catholic schools with state money, and during his prime ministership in the 1950s he helped orchestrate incremental steps in providing federal funding to Catholic schools, leading to the breakthrough in 1963, when state aid for parochial schools for science education was passed.

By contrast, in the United States, a Catholic president was not elected until 1960 and Catholics did not constitute nearly as large a percentage of cabinet positions even during the Great Depression, when Catholics comprised a substantial part of the New Deal Democratic coalition. Catholics did reach relative

Multiplicity of the Catholic past 5

population parity in the House of Representatives during the New Deal, but there was not as significant overrepresentation as in Australia. Polls revealed that the South remained significantly anti-Catholic, even though Southerners were united with Catholics in the Democratic coalition. In terms of policy, literacy tests in voting made it more difficult for more recent and foreign-born populations of Catholics (such as Italians and other Eastern European groups) to vote. In terms of funding of parochial schools, many state-level Blaine amendments forbid state governments from directly providing funding to religious educational institutions. Supreme Court decisions like *Everson* v. *Board of Education* also made direct funding constitutionally difficult, though some indirect public funding for parochial schools came in 1965 with the passage of the Elementary and Secondary Education Act.

Catholic incorporation in Canada by 1960 also does not compare favorably with Australia. Canadian Catholics have constituted 40 to 45 percent of the Canadian population, approximately double that of Australian Catholics. In the late nineteenth and early twentieth century, Canadian Catholics were doing better in descriptive representation compared to Australia and the United States. Catholics were chosen as prime ministers and constituted much more significant blocs of both cabinet members and lower house parliamentarians than in the other two countries. State funding of Catholic schools existed in Quebec and in some of the other provinces. Despite this more favorable start, Catholic political incorporation stalled, with Catholic representation in cabinets and the House of Commons remaining slightly underrepresentative, especially in the western provinces and Ontario. Australian and U.S. Catholic representation in the lower legislative chambers surpassed that of Canada by the 1930s. By 1963, state funding for parochial schools was not available to all Canadian provinces, whereas such funding existed in all Australian states.

The politics concerning Catholic minorities did not stop after achieving population proportionality in descriptive representation. For both Australia and the United States, Catholic incorporation was driven largely through representation in the Labor and Democratic parties. It was only much later that Catholics achieved population proportionality in right-leaning parties. In addition to this lag between the parties, a second distinctive feature of contemporary Catholic political incorporation is the existence of valorization of Catholic identities. The politics of minority standing does not end with normalization but can continue if that minority becomes overrepresented and is praised and elevated to a position of symbolic privilege. Conservative Catholics and Protestants have often accused left-leaning Catholic political candidates of not being Catholic enough on such questions as abortion. More recently, liberal groups have often pointed to the statements of Pope Francis for validation on issues of poverty, inequality, and climate change. Accounts of Catholic political incorporation have to consider both the integration of Catholics into center-right parties and the potential path from normalization to valorization.[15]

The second broad empirical puzzle concerns patterns of Catholic representation and valorization during the period from 1960 to the present, particularly in

6 *Multiplicity of the Catholic past*

the United States and Australia. During this period, Catholic political incorporation has not continued in any straightforward linear fashion from the previous period. In particular, the situation between the United States and Australia flips. At the end of the twentieth and the start of the twenty-first century, Catholics find themselves overrepresented in many political offices in the United States, including the House, the Supreme Court, and governorships. Catholic overrepresentation has been moderate in Australia, particularly in recent Liberal/National cabinets and in those candidates which Labor has fielded for parliamentary elections. In Canada, there has been overrepresentation of Catholics in the prime ministership, but there is not enough evidence to evaluate their overrepresentation in other offices.[16] Looking specifically at Catholic representation in right-leaning parties also seems to show that Catholic incorporation on the right occurs more quickly in the United States. Catholics in the United States reached proportionality in the House Republican caucus in the 1980s. It was only in the 1990s that the Liberal Party in Australia started boasting of heavy Catholic representation. Data limitations prevent a full consideration for Canada, but the evidence that does exist suggests that it was only after 2006 – well after the United States and Australia – that an overarching conservative religious coalition representing Protestants and Catholics was able to capture office in Canada.

This quick summary of data on descriptive representation and policies shows not only intercountry differences, but also differences in Catholic incorporation over time, party, and geography within each country. Those venturing a guess about the demise of anti-Catholicism in the United States might have marked the election of John F. Kennedy – the first time a Catholic was chosen as president in the United States – as the end of Catholic stigmatization in that country. Others may have chosen Vatican II, when the Church sought to modernize its teachings and became closer to Protestantism. Yet, as shown above, Catholics achieved proportional representation in the House many decades earlier, namely in the 1930s. But the 1930s does not serve as an adequate marker of the end of stigmatization either. Significant regional differences remained, with anti-Catholicism still vibrant in the South. In addition, it was only in the 1980s that Catholics achieved proportional representation in the Republican Party.

These patterns of Catholic descriptive representation across time, space, and party open a window onto deeper questions about the relationship between party and minority political incorporation, the second important story to be gleaned from looking at the multiple histories of Catholic incorporation. Catholics and white southerners were allied together in the Democratic Party during the New Deal period, yet the white South was the most anti-Catholic region of the United States in the 1960s, despite the fact that white Southerners were largely Democratic voters. Similarly, Catholics were key constituents of the Liberal Party in Canada, one of the most successful parties in a democracy in the twentieth century. Yet this political coalition of Protestants and Catholics did not do much to increase Catholic standing in Canada relative to the United States and Australia. Mere affiliation in a successful electoral party alone does not seem to transform Catholic stigmatization. What is different about the Labor Party in

Australia in the mid-twentieth century, which was not as successful as the Canadian Liberal party? What is it about the political coalitions in the late twentieth century in the United States and Australia that have allowed for more drastic transformation of Catholic standing in right-wing parties?

Looking beyond descriptive representation and coalition formation, Catholic minority incorporation in these three countries also reveals interesting differences in political development, the third important story to be learned from the Catholic experience. Quebec, the stronghold of French Catholic political power and once one of the more economically conservative provinces, has become one of the more liberal provinces in Canada. Taking the long view and looking at political development comparatively, one can see that Canadian Catholic identity has evolved differently than it has in Australia or the United States. In the 1960s, during the Quiet Revolution, Quebec dramatically secularized, leading to much more substantial drops in Catholic churchgoing than in the other two countries. Why did this transformation of Catholic identity take place in Canada, but not to such an extent in Australia and the United States? One of the most important differences in political incorporation in the three countries is that group rights to schools and language were more readily recognized in Canada than they were in the other two countries. This allows a unique opportunity to see how the granting of group rights can affect the development of identities in liberal democracy.

The value of studying Catholic political incorporation comparatively

This brief summary of the differing stories of Catholic political incorporation already challenges several potential misconceptions:

1   that the experience of American Catholics is representative;
2   that overrepresentation of a stigmatized minority is not possible;
3   that Catholic political incorporation follows from single big events and diffuses evenly everywhere;
4   that the politics of minority political valuation ends after proportional representation is achieved;
5   that political coalitions easily transform Catholic valuation among coalition partners;
6   that Catholic identity evolves similarly across liberal democracies.

Focusing on these variations of descriptive representation, party incorporation, and political development over place and time in these three particular countries is valuable in providing as close to a laboratory setting as possible to show which factors really matter to improving minority standing. Political scientists like to look for natural experiments, in which one factor is changed while all other factors are held constant among the subjects. In this situation, any subsequent change in the experimental subjects must be due to the one factor that was changed. Countries do not provide the controlled conditions of a laboratory. However, if one can find very similar countries, one might get close to an experimental setting, and supplement this comparison with other forms of evidence.

The particular countries in this study – the United States, Canada, and Australia – are ideal for this comparative study of Catholic incorporation because of their similarities. All three are traditionally grouped as relatively similar democracies. All three countries were early democratizers, which gets at the key question of this book: what happens to stigmatized minorities in democratic societies? All three share a British heritage, and the populations in each are majority white and (at least for the earlier period) majority Protestant, thus setting up similar conflicts between Protestants and Catholics. There are enough similarities among the three countries to provide a fairly controlled comparison to tease out what factors are important in explaining the divergences in Catholic political incorporation. The differences that do exist allow potential explanations to be evaluated.

A second compelling reason for this comparative approach is that there are limited opportunities for the study of minority political incorporation in democratic contexts. Comparative historical study has been hampered by scarcity. There have been few long-lived liberal democracies (multiple decades of fairly extensive provision of rights) with significant minority populations (over 15 percent of the population, and upward to 45 percent). Studies of minorities in liberal democracies have typically focused on situations where those minorities are in a position of being outright dominated by the majority groups.[17] Studies of more numerically significant minority populations have typically featured countries where civil war is imminent and liberal democracy is tenuous or nonexistent.[18] Studies where minorities are beginning to constitute fairly heavy population proportions of liberal democratic countries are particularly important, because this is where many liberal democracies are heading, and the main question is not the presence or lack of civil war and a stable state, but the degree to which rights, opportunities, influence, and capabilities are extended to minorities. Catholics are a relatively large minority group, ranging from 15 to 45 percent of national populations in the three cases and time periods chosen for study in this book. Given the paucity of potential comparisons, scholars should jump at any opportunity to increase the number of cases with which minority political incorporation can be compared.

A third compelling reason for this particular study is the sheer variety of experiences of Catholics. Catholics are ideal for a study of minority incorporation because they have passed from underrepresentation to normalized representation to overrepresentation, and not necessarily in a straightforward, linear fashion. Over the course of the twentieth century, Catholics have also passed through various phases of stigmatization, normalization, and valorization, categories that do not map one-to-one with underrepresentation, proportional representation, and overrepresentation.

There have been times when both parties in two-party systems competed for their votes to times when one party captured their votes. Catholics have passed through different phases of church–state relations (e.g., whether or not there has been strict separation of church and state) and international order (e.g., whether Roman Catholics have been considered an opponent or ally of the most powerful international actors). The rich variety of these transformations provides much material for a comparativist to seek similarities and differences.

One potential objection is that Catholics never experienced as harsh discrimination as other minorities, such as African Americans, Native Americans, and aboriginal groups, so this study would not tell researchers much about the politics of minority incorporation when the minority is heavily stigmatized. Despite a vigorous discourse questioning Catholic fitness for republican and democratic citizenship, explicit denial of citizenship rights to Catholics was relatively rare after the mid-nineteenth century. Many of the actual policy battles between Protestants and Catholics focused on church–state issues (state funding going to Catholic institutions), control of Catholic behavior (Catholic education, convent inspection), the prevention of Catholic politicians from being elected, and informal bans on hiring Catholics.

However, it could be argued that it is an advantage of this study that discrimination against Catholics was never as harsh as that directed against other minorities. That Catholics have been successfully incorporated helps expand thinking about minority political incorporation. Looking at how this status transformation occurred, as well as its limits, is likely to yield insights into how status transformation can take place within democratic political and social structures. The example of Catholics may be particularly beneficial for understanding today's politics of minority incorporation because contemporary status orderings are trending away from direct legal ascription to "softer" kinds of exclusion. Containing Catholics has historically relied on operations in the political, social, and economic markets, as well as at the edges of Catholic identity, where regulating Catholicism overlapped with the regulation of more stigmatized identities (such as Southern and Eastern European ethnicity). This can shed light on the formation of contemporary status orders, which have moved away from direct legal ascription, yet preserve inequalities through mechanisms in civil society.

Yet another advantage of studying Catholics is that it can illuminate the interplay of race, ethnicity, and religion. Latinos in the United States and Muslims in Western Europe similarly occupy multiple positions on race, ethnicity, and religion. The kinds of coalitions that can emerge when there are significant crosscutting lines in ethnicity, race, and religion are likely to be different than the ones that emerge where racial, ethnic, and religious diversity overlap perfectly. The Catholic case is instructive in capturing this complicated interplay.

In addition, the hierarchical nature of the Church provides some methodological advantages. Since the Pope is central to defining moral authority on core religious values, differences that develop among Catholics in various national contexts are likely to stem largely from differences in the local context in which Catholics find themselves rather than doctrinal differences.

In short, the possibility of studying what happens to a minority group constituting fairly substantial population proportions in democratic societies in a fairly controlled manner is a rare historical opportunity. At the same time, it is likely

10 *Multiplicity of the Catholic past*

that over the course of the twenty-first century minority groups of this size will increasingly become the norm. The analogies and comparisons are never going to be perfect. Still, studying the cases that do exist in the historical record can at least advance the process of concept formation that may lead to greater insight into minority political incorporation.

Argument and plan of the book

Explaining the variations in political incorporation of Catholics in two time periods in these three countries is the goal of this book. What need to be explained are the timing of the transformations; the extent of the transformation (from underrepresentation to overrepresentation); the transformation's geographical and partisan diffusion within each country; and intercountry differences.

The book opens by arguing that reconstructive coalitions explain transformation of minority status and the variations in Catholic political incorporation. Improvements in minority standing occur when majority groups are united with minority groups in a coalition that is not merely designed for electoral victory, but which also espouses a broader umbrella identity that subsumes both the majority and minority identities. Coalitions that have this ideological dimension – a reconstructive coalition in this book's terminology – will produce more change in the standing of the minority than coalitions that lack it. Examples of reconstructive coalitions include the early twentieth-century labor movement (organizing Protestants and Catholics under the umbrella of a class identity) and late twentieth-century conservative moral movements (organizing many believers under the umbrella of a conservative religious identity). Such reconstructive coalitions are more likely to occur when the minority is central (either organizationally or symbolically) to the coalition, and when the institutional context makes both the majority and minority groups dependent on an umbrella identity to advance their interests. Institutional contexts such as significant regional or provincial autonomy can inhibit the formation of reconstructive coalitions and lead to coalitions of convenience that do not substantially change coalition partners' standing to each other.

The evidentiary strategy of the book includes looking at the broad differences among the countries, the timing of increases in Catholic political representation, and the diffusion of improvements to Catholic standing in geographical regions and across political parties, to see in particular whether the strength of reconstructive coalitions predicts transformations in Catholic standing. The book also traces the processes by which Catholic standing is changing by examining how central Catholics are to particular coalitions, what types of coalitions spark change, whether reconstruction under a broader identity is taking place, and which groups are leading such reconstruction.

Chapter 2 outlines the theory of reconstructive coalitions in the transformation of minority standing. Subsequently, the book is divided into two parts: the first looking at transformation around the Great Depression, the latter at transformation associated with the rise of Christian conservative movements in the late twentieth century. Chapter 3 presents evidence on the timing and intercountry differences in transformation of Catholic standing in the three countries starting around 1930, and why other theories do not account for this transformation. Domestically, differences in the ability of Catholics to enter certain kinds of coalitions mattered. Chapters 4, 5, and 6 supplement the comparative evidence by looking in depth at how Catholics interacted with labor politics in these three countries, and the degree to which institutional factors such as regional identities impeded reconstructive coalitions centered on labor.

Chapter 7 documents the shift in Catholic standing in response to the rise of Christian conservative movements from 1960 to the late twentieth century, and shows variations in the degree to which there is overrepresentation and the degree to which religiousness in general mattered to politics in the late twentieth century. Chapters 8 and 9 supplement the comparative by looking in depth at the success of Christian conservative coalitions in the United States (Chapter 8) and how institutional factors affected the formation of Christian conservative coalitions in Australia and Canada (Chapter 9).

Chapter 10 concludes with an answer to the epigraph from Putnam that leads this study: why can't we deconstruct our current ethnic, religious, and racial tensions as we deconstructed Catholic–Protestant tensions in the past? The conclusion begins to map out how Catholic political incorporation might compare to the incorporation of Muslims in Western Europe, and African, Latino, Jewish, and Mormon Americans in the United States.

Notes

1 Robert D. Putnam, "*E Pluribus Unum*: Diversity and Community in the Twenty-First Century," *Scandinavian Political Studies* 30, no. 2 (2007): 160.
2 As a shorthand, throughout the book "Catholic" will refer specifically to the Roman Catholic denomination. Orthodox, Greek, Eastern, or Ukrainian Catholics will be designated by their full appellation.
3 The connection between Catholicism and past acts of terrorism was recently made during Representative Peter King's congressional hearings in 2011 on extremists in U.S. mosques. Critics pointed out that King had once supported the Irish Republican Army, which targeted innocent civilians. King responded that the IRA was different because they did not attack Americans. Scott Shane, "For Lawmaker Examining Terror, a Pro-IRA Past," *New York Times*, March 8, 2011, A1.
4 Ruy Teixiera, "New Progressive America: Twenty Years of Demographic, Geographic, and Attitudinal Changes across the Country Herald a New Progressive Majority." Report for the Center for American Progress, March 11, 2009. Available at www.americanprogress.org/issues/2009/03/progressive_america.html.
5 Alberto Alesina and Edward Glaeser, *Fighting Poverty in the US and Europe: A World of Difference* (New York: Oxford University Press, 2004), ch. 6; Putnam, "*E Pluribus Unum*."
6 Michael Tessler, *Post-Racial or Most-Racial? Race and Politics in the Obama Era* (Chicago, IL: University of Chicago Press, 2016).
7 Ross Douthat, "Islam in Two Americas," *New York Times*, August 15, 2010.
8 John T. McGreevey and R. Scott Appleby, "Catholics, Muslims, and the Mosque Controversy," *New York Review of Books* blog, August 27, 2010. Available at www.nybooks.com/blogs/nyrblog/2010/aug/27/catholics-muslims-mosque-controversy/.

12 *Multiplicity of the Catholic past*

9   Nicholas Kristof, "America's History of Fear," *New York Times*, September 4, 2010.
10 Putnam, "*E Pluribus Unum*," 160.
11 Robert D. Putnam and David E. Campbell, *American Grace: How Religion Divides and Unites Us* (New York: Simon & Schuster, 2012).
12 David Roediger, *Working Toward Whiteness: How America's Immigrants Became White – The Strange Journey from Ellis Island to the Suburbs* (New York: Basic Books, 2006).
13 In this book the reference to Catholics as minorities in Canada is used strictly in a numerical sense. It does not mean that French Catholics should not be considered coequals in the founding of Canadian society. Anti-Catholicism as used in this book means those philosophies, ideologies, and policies that are motivated by an explicitly ascriptive critique of the fitness of Catholics for citizenship or as representing dangers to the fundamental workings of liberal democracy. It is not used in the sense that some contemporary writers attempt to use it, as meaning opposing the political positions of Catholics. Opposing the Catholic Church's positions on abortion, contraception, gay marriage, the death penalty, or pre-emptive war do not count as anti-Catholicism within the narrower scope of this book.
14 Political incorporation is distinct from social and economic incorporation. Economic incorporation refers to interaction in labor and capital markets. Social incorporation refers to interaction in social relationships, and may be detected in intermarriage, degree of intermixing in social clubs, and segregation indices in residential patterns. By contrast, political incorporation refers to the participation and influence in the governance of society. Even with this broad definition of political incorporation, different scholars will include different elements. Wong's definition of political incorporation, for example, includes the following elements: (1) symbolic representation through elected and appointed officials; (2) influence over policy agendas and policy formulation; and (3) attempts to mobilize the vote of previously politically disenfranchised members by the dominant institutions in society. Janelle Wong, "Thinking About Immigrant Political Incorporation," Workshop on Immigrant Incorporation, Mobilization, and Participation, Campbell Public Affairs Institute, Maxwell School of Syracuse University, December 6, 2002. Available at https://web.archive.org/web/20060223172950/www.maxwell.syr.edu/moynihan/programs/iiwg/pdfs/Wong.pdf. I would include discourse about the group's fitness for citizenship, and the patterning of the group's political allies and enemies; that is, how broad are the political coalitions with which the group is allied, and how broad are the coalitions that oppose the group. As one recent literature review has found, there is no one standard definition of political incorporation. See the introduction to Jennifer Hochschild, Jacqueline Chattopadhyay, Claudine Gay, and Michael Jones-Correa (eds), *Outsiders No More? Models of Immigrant Political Incorporation* (New York: Oxford University Press, 2013), 7–8. In this book I focus on dimensions (descriptive representation, coalition formation, discourses of democratic fitness of Catholics) that contribute to political incorporation, without claiming to have exhausted all possible elements of political incorporation.
15 With stigmatization, the minority is seen as civically deficient compared to other groups. With normalization, the minority is seen as not civically distinctive from other groups. With valorization, the minority is seen as exemplifying civic traits that are considered desirable.
16 Religious affiliation of contemporary political representatives in Canada is very difficult to acquire, though this may indicate the relative lack of care of politicians to broadcast one's religious identity. Religious affiliation of contemporary political representatives in Australia is also difficult to determine, though one can point to instances where political representatives, such as Prime Minister John Howard, trumpeted the number of Catholics in their coalition.

17 Any study of minorities in the United States, as well as minorities in Britain, France, and Germany, would fall into this category. Comparative studies of immigration are much more abundant, but these studies tend to focus on different kinds of questions such as social and economic incorporation, as opposed to political incorporation and political influence.
18 The countries that rank highest on measures of ethnolinguistic fractionalization tend to be in Africa and Asia, and tend to be nondemocratic and/or not economically developed. Diverse countries that are both democracies and economically developed include countries that Arend Lijphart classified as consociational democracies (Belgium, the Netherlands, and Switzerland).

2 Transubstantiating the body politic
A theory of reconstructive coalitions

A variety of theories have been advanced that attempt to explain the rise and fall of minority standing. These include how assimilated the minority is to the majority's norms; how many resources a minority controls; what types of coalitions can minorities join; what political opportunities and events might occur to enhance attention to minority issues; and how political institutions might enhance or detract from minority power. It would be hopeless to think that there is one factor which could cover all cases of minority incorporation. Even if there were such a model, it would likely be so vague or abstract as to be useless.[1] The intention of this book is not to find such an overarching, universal model. Rather, the purpose is to find processes that may have been missed in previous explanations.

In particular, the Catholic case shows the need for an account of overrepresentation of minorities – an understandable gap, since underrepresentation is more common for stigmatized minorities. Related to this first point, the second thing a new theory of minority incorporation needs is an account of positive change in the standing of minorities. Most of the extant literature focuses on continuing stigmatization. Third, a new theory needs to adequately account for the problem of identity. Since many majority and minority groups are cross-cut by multiple potential identities along ethnic, racial, religious, class, and regional lines, how can one tell which identity gets prioritized? If assimilation is important, which identity is most important to be similar around: race, class, or religion? Are minorities assimilating as whites, workers, or Christians? If the resources of a minority are important, then those resources of the minority are going to vary based again on the identity of the minority (e.g., as ethnic Irish and Italians, or as common European Catholic immigrants). Italian immigrants are going to have far fewer resources than a united European Catholic immigrant bloc. Similarly, the effect of political opportunities and institutions is dependent on the boundaries of identity of the majority and minority group. In short, many of these other theories cannot get started until an account of how identity is fixed or changed is first given. This chapter looks to how coalitions can potentially prioritize and reconstruct identities, and how historical institutionalist legacies shape what kinds of coalitions are available to determine political identities.

Reconstructive coalitions and minority incorporation

One of the puzzles of Catholic incorporation in the three countries was why successful Catholic–Protestant coalitions in the United States and Canada were not as transformative of Catholic status as in Australia at the time of the Great Depression. The investigation of coalitions has long preoccupied scholars of minority political incorporation, for the simple reason that minorities often do not have enough population or wealth on their own to influence society. Researchers in the U.S. context have found that alliances with liberal whites or alliances between minorities were key to electing minority representatives in local urban governments, though these coalitions were often unstable.[2] Much of the literature on coalitions and minorities focuses on what makes a coalition possible. Black power theorists, for instance, argued that coalitions must form based on concrete interests, rather than conscience.[3]

Even when there are electable majority–minority coalitions, these may not be sufficient for status change. Paul Frymer has noted that African Americans were reliable partners in the Republican coalition prior to the New Deal, and with the subsequent Democratic coalition, but these parties were not responsive to African American interests. For Frymer, African Americans are a captured minority, because of their small size and because the median voter tends to be anti-black. Under these conditions, competing parties feel no need to appeal to their vote, and the party with which African Americans are aligned takes the minority's vote for granted. Frymer envisions substantive change emerging once the minority group is no longer captive, perhaps when the minority group is larger, or when cross-cutting issues put their vote into play.[4] This study goes beyond Frymer in arguing that coalitions matter not just in whether the minority is captive or not, but also in whether the coalition is reconstructive or not in shaping identities. What explains the patterns of Catholic incorporation in the three countries is the success of reconstructive coalitions.

Coalitions can change minority status and identities in a variety of ways. Coalitions can bring people together from different backgrounds, creating greater trust, more dense social networks, and enhanced norms of reciprocity – the elements of what Putnam has called social capital.[5] Just as participation in civic groups like Masons, Elks, and bowling clubs can create bridging capital among members of different backgrounds, so can participation in political movements – parties, interest groups, protest movements – create bridging capital. Second, coalitions can persuade leaders of that coalition to reduce stigmatization to make the coalition as large as possible. This reduction can happen if the leaders of the coalition decide to be silent about a minority group's status, reducing the salience of a stigmatized identity. The movement's broader goals take precedence over previous identities, displacing them in significance. Leaders of coalitions may go further and actively articulate new identities that transform old identities, bringing them under the umbrella of a new identity. This ideological redefinition may take place on both majority and minority groups' identities. The previously valorized majority identity may be redefined so that it is less starkly opposed to the minority identity. The previously stigmatized minority identity may be rearticulated so that claims which antagonize the majority are reduced. The efforts of political leaders and activists in rearticulating identities may play an especially important role in mass public opinion. Some recent research on polarization, for instance, has shown how the more extreme positions of party elites and activists can filter into the mass public, causing the masses to become more polarized over time. Most ordinary citizens lack the time and resources to fully educate themselves on issues. Political elites and activists serve as important cues for ordinary citizens.[6]

When any of the rearticulating mechanisms described above take place, that coalition may be said to be reconstructive.[7] A strong labor movement, for instance, may prioritize a class identity over other kinds of identity. Pan-Christian moral movements at the end of the twentieth century may emphasize a broad religious identity over denominational identities. Reconstruction of identities goes along with this broader fight against secularism and atheism, as when a "Judeo-Christian" tradition is emphasized.

Not all coalitions are reconstructive. Parties and coalitions may be marriages of convenience, in which the goal is electoral victory and not necessarily a programmatic implementation of policy based on a singular identity of that party and coalition. Instead, when such "brokerage" or "catchall" parties achieve political power, they may implement policies that advance in piecemeal fashion the various interests comprising that alliance. These coalitions may capture electoral office, be long-lasting, and even contribute to political stability. Yet they may not actually lead to an increase in recognition of the standing of coalition partners. Black power and racial realist theorists' suggestion that coalitions built on interest are superior to those built on ideology may miss this side-effect of coalitions that do have an ideological component. Brokerage coalitions, when built only on bare interest, may invoke "toleration" rather than real empathy with coalition partners. Political theorists have noted that toleration actually presupposes that the group tolerated remains unappealing, unassimilable, and indigestible – a maintenance of stigma, rather than an overcoming.[8]

A coalition which is based on a common enemy, for instance, may or may not be reconstructive. It depends on the depth to which bridging capital is created and the degree to which the coalition rearticulates older identities into a larger umbrella identity. A coalition built around "religious freedom" is less likely to be reconstructive than coalitions in which the groups in the coalition share a common ideology beyond toleration (e.g., seeing in each religious doctrine a common definition of the natural order of gender, family, and sex roles).

The degree of reconstruction of any particular coalition may be thought of as falling along a spectrum. A coalition that builds more social capital among members of different backgrounds would be more reconstructive than one that builds less. A coalition that involves active rearticulation of old identities into new, broader identities would be more reconstructive than a coalition that only promotes silence about the stigmatized minority identity.

As an example, one can predict that the capacity for building social capital in the labor movement is greater than in just an electoral coalition. Labor movements may require workers to participate with other workers in potential strike actions. The level of trust involved may be high, since the consequences of defection from a strike could be disastrous. Electoral coalitions may not involve as much cross-group participation and social capital. Each group instead may be focused on mobilizing its particular members to the polls. This may be even more true today with sophisticated data-heavy turnout operations, which rely on already existing Facebook networks to mobilize neutral voters.[9] In general, one would expect social movement organizations to build more capital and engage in more rearticulation of identity than purely electoral mobilizations, since these types of movements engage in more sustained protest and action than electoral movements.

The same electoral parties may also differ in their degree of ideological cohesiveness and convenience over time. Some preliminary evidence for the usefulness of believing there is an important difference for minorities in coalitions on whether parties are ideologically coherent or parties of convenience comes from the work of Noel, who has argued that the contemporary Democratic and Republican parties are distinct in that they are ideologically polarized, compared to Democratic and Republican parties in the early twentieth century that were built for electoral victory and the deliverance of patronage.[10] The distinction corresponds approximately to the reconstructive/coalition-of-convenience distinction I have drawn here. What is interesting is that another scholar has noted that contemporary Republican and Democratic views on race seem to be polarizing. As Tesler notes, more Democrats are falling into line with African American views on issues like police brutality or whether the Confederate flag is racist, while the reverse is happening for Republicans.[11] The ideological cohesiveness of the contemporary parties has pulled Democrats closer to African Americans, and Republicans further away.

At one end of the spectrum would be a pure coalition of convenience which may not even last beyond the next election, and at the other end a purely reconstructive coalition which espouses an encompassing identity that is enduring. Labor and pan-Christian moral movements are typically not completely reconstructive. However, they do reconstruct identities to some degree. A successful labor agenda may require workers to organize into unions, build social capital with each other, trust each other enough to engage in strikes together, and to display a willingness to not let differences in identity get in the way of collective bargaining and action. Similarly, pan-Christian moral movements are often associated with ecumenical discussions, as well as theorizations of the essence of a "Judeo-Christian" tradition (or sometimes, more broadly, a religious tradition) that often contrasts itself with an atheistic form of thinking.

How a single coalition bridges majority and minority groups affects how competing coalitions respond. If Coalition A is reconstructive and manages to capture political power, then a competing coalition, Coalition B, will have less success in trying to break up that coalition through further stigmatization of the minority that is allied with Coalition A. Given the success of Coalition A in capturing political power, the incentive will shift for Coalition B to revalue their opinion of that minority and compete for some of that minority's affiliation and votes. By contrast, if Coalition A is not reconstructive, then Coalition B may seek instead to try to win back political power by appealing to prejudiced elements of Coalition A that may be receptive to stigmatization of the minority group.

This analysis may be reframed in terms of median voter logic. In Frymer's conceptualization of competition for a minority's vote, a minority is captive when its affiliation is concentrated in one party and the median voter is prejudiced against the minority. In this situation, there is little incentive for the coalition that contains the minority or the competing coalition to substantially assert the interests of that minority because the median voter is discriminatory. A reconstructive coalition can transform this calculus. If a coalition containing the minority group is politically successful, then the median voter and the minority group are now paired in a winning coalition. If that coalition is also reconstructive, there is the possibility that the median voter is convinced to be no longer as discriminatory against the minority. The calculus will shift for the opposing coalitions to pay greater attention to the minority's vote, since the median voter is no longer as receptive to stigmatization of the minority. Opposing parties may not seek full reconstruction of the minority's stigmatization to attract the minority's vote; they may only seek to attract fractions of the minority's vote. Still, this would mark an improvement on previous attitudes of the opposing party to the minority.

If this analysis is correct, then, counterintuitively, it is possible for one-party political incorporation to advance minority political incorporation better than two-party competition for a minority. It is often assumed that a minority's political influence is enhanced when many parties are competing for their vote. Some minority leaders may advocate partisan neutrality to try to stimulate this competition for the minority's affiliation. The problem with such a concept is that parties may compete for a minority's vote based not on ending stigmatization of that minority, but on appealing to fractions of the minority based on narrower identities and delivering patronage to those fractions in a non-reconstructive manner. Rather than appealing to Catholics as a whole, a competing coalition may appeal to wealthy Catholics, urban Catholics, or a particular ethnic fragment of Catholics. Both the creation of bridging capital and the level of ideological rearticulation of hostilities will be limited in such a case. In Frymer's logic, the median voter may not be induced to end their stigmatization of the minority group.

One-party incorporation, when it is reconstructive, can be more transformative than fragmentary competition. Because much of the minority's affiliation is concentrated in one party and the party is heavily reliant on the minority's support, there is a greater likelihood of dealing with the group as a whole, rather than with particular fragments of the group. Under these conditions, the bridging capital that is created will be more extensive. The ideological rearticulations will be more extensive and encompassing.

In addition, overrepresentation of the minority may occur in this situation. When there is one-party incorporation of a stigmatized minority (say, in party

A), it is likely that opposition parties have taken advantage of the minority's stigmatization to appeal to members of the majority that might otherwise be attracted to party A. This is the danger of one-party incorporation; it causes members of the majority to defect to other parties. However, this also means that the minority becomes particularly concentrated in party A, and the minority's proportion in party A is likely to be higher than their population proportion. This means that if party A wins control of the legislature, the minority is likely to be overrepresented in the legislature relative to their population proportion.

One-party incorporation, when it is reconstructive, can initiate processes that make some competition for the minority possible, as described above. More generally, what matters for the standing of a minority is the kind of competition for a minority's vote. Competition between two coalitions, both of which are non-reconstructive, is not likely to transform minority status and contribute to underrepresentation. Competition between one coalition that is reconstructive and another that is non-reconstructive is only likely to lead to sustained change if the reconstructive coalition is successful. Competition between two coalitions, both of which are reconstructive, will likely be the most transformative of minority status, perhaps leading to valorization of the minority. The latter situation may be another instance in which overrepresentation of the minority is possible.

An institutionalist account of reconstructive coalitions

If reconstructive political coalitions are an important medium through which minority groups achieve political incorporation, then what needs to be explained is why reconstructive coalitions appear in some contexts but not in others. Historical institutionalist theory can shed light on this question. Historical institutionalists have sought to understand where identities, values, and preferences originate.[12] Historical institutionalists are predisposed not to think in terms of universal political behavior but to see how context produces politics, and to explicate how these contexts change over time. For historical institutionalists these contexts are produced based on choices made in the past. The path-dependency school in historical institutionalism, for instance, has argued that preferences and identities come from previous policy battles.[13] More recently, another approach in historical institutionalism has sought change in intercurrence, or the clash of multiple institutional orders.[14] Institutional orders affect later politics in several ways. Institutional orders can affect the perception of later actors, such as the invisible order of tax breaks, which disguises the true extent of state welfare provision and contributes to the idea of a "non-productive" class that leeches off the productive class.[15] There may be policy feedback. Positive feedback can lead to shoring up support for the institutional order, for instance, as in the growth of interest groups that support Social Security, making it the untouchable "third rail" of U.S. politics. Negative feedback may occur when people become frustrated with the institutional order, leading to new rounds of social mobilization.[16] When institutional orders fail to achieve their original purposes they may be subject to displacement, layering, drift, conversion, and exhaustion.[17]

These institutional legacies shape how countries respond to exogenous shocks to the political system. Previous theorists of minority political incorporation are not wrong in identifying political opportunities as important transformative events in majority–minority relations. Common political opportunities that arose in each of the countries to potentially transform Catholic–Protestant relations include the Great Depression, World War II, the Cold War, and secularization leading to the rise of the religious right. How these countries responded to these events and how these events affected Catholic political incorporation, however, were channeled by each country's particular institutional history into different coalitional possibilities.

One way in which historical institutionalists attempt to explain political phenomena is by parsing the context into a series of "orders." An order has been defined by Orren and Skowronek as "a constellation of rules, institutions, practices, and ideas that hang together over time, a bundle of patterns."[18] For example, there could be a "presidential order," which constitutes the governing authority available to the president at any given time. At one point in time that may include significant executive unilateral power; at other times it may not. It all depends on the particular rules, institutions, practices, and ideas that exist at a particular time. Presidents like Bush and Obama may occupy a different presidential order than presidents like Washington and Jefferson. Similarly, one might speak of a "Jim Crow" order composed of the rules, institutions, practices, and ideas that contributed to limiting African Americans in the South from around the turn of the twentieth century to 1965. This order may encompass laws on school segregation, miscegenation, and voting; norms about who is to show deference in walking on the street; and ideas about racial superiority. For this book's study, one can envision a Catholic–Protestant order in each of the three countries which is focused on laws preventing the spread of state funding to separate Catholic institutions; norms of residential and job segregation, and the desirability of electing Catholic representatives; and ideas about the inferiority of Catholics and the superiority of Protestants. One can envision a class order composed of laws on collective bargaining, unionization, and government welfare and insurance programs; norms about fraternization with union supporters and communists; and ideas about how a country maintains its economic productivity and what free labor means.

The usefulness of the order concept is that it allows us to see how a country's political development emerges from the interaction of orders – whether orders work with or against each other.[19] In the case of minority incorporation, the status of the minority is likely to change when there is significant overlap in transforming the order of majority–minority relations with another institutional order. In early twentieth-century politics there was a great deal of potential overlap between transforming Catholic–Protestant order and transforming class order. Catholics tended to earn less than Protestants, and they were often leaders of union movements in the three countries. Because Catholics are overrepresented in the working class, transformation of the class order will require cooperation from Catholics, and the potential transformation of Catholic–Protestant order. The overlap contributes to the likelihood of a reconstructive coalition. Another way of saying this is that Catholics are organizationally central to a coalition seeking transformation in the order of class.

In the late twentieth century, one can describe a church–state order in which religious considerations are increasingly excised from the public sphere, funding is decreased to religious institutions, and abortion and same-sex marriage liberalized. Catholics may be particularly useful allies in challenging this order because Catholics have many separate schools, Catholic doctrine is opposed to abortion and same-sex marriage, and Catholic doctrine encourages greater deference to authority. The overlap between changing church–state order and Catholic identity contributes to the likelihood of a reconstructive coalition. Another way of stating this is that Catholics are both organizationally and symbolically central to a coalition seeking to reinstall a conservative vision of gender, sex, religious schooling, and morals. They are organizationally central because they comprise a large proportion of the potential activists and voters in this coalition. They are symbolically central because of the ideological value of their particular doctrinal stances and position within the church–state order.

The degree of potential overlap and centrality of the minority to change/maintenance of another order may vary. Where the overlap or centrality is particularly strong one can expect not just significant transformation of the minority's status within the coalition, but also the possibility of overrepresentation. If Catholics are concentrated in the working class and then a working-class party comes into power, one would expect Catholics to be overrepresented among political representatives. The overrepresentation of Catholics in the working-class party will be exacerbated if non-Catholics are driven away from the working-class party due to anti-Catholicism; that will enhance the dependence of the working-class party on Catholics. A similar mechanism can explain the phenomenon of valorization. Christian conservative coalitions may rely heavily on Catholics because the situation of Catholics presents advantageous elements for Christian conservative discourse. The heavy reliance of the Catholic Church on parallel private institutions (schools, colleges, hospitals) makes it exemplary and crucial in debates about the appropriate boundaries of church and state, as in the school voucher debate or the debate about whether Obamacare can require insurance plans to include coverage of abortions. Other features of the Catholic Church also make it exemplary in Christian conservative discourse, particularly the role of Pope John Paul II in resisting "atheistic" communism and the role of authority and natural rights in the Catholic Church, which gives Christian conservatives a ready ideological support against abortion and same-sex marriage.

The overlap between transforming one political order and transforming minority standing may also be weak. All parties and coalitions are likely to have fissures. Where such fissures are very large, reconstructive change is unlikely. Even if a minority group is part of a winning electoral coalition, members of its coalition who represent a societal majority group may not moderate their positions toward the minority. Several factors may make lack of overlap likely. Previous policies may make it difficult for coalition partners to come together. Frymer, for instance, has argued that firmer alliances between white unions workers and African Americans were prevented because of court decisions that pitted the two against each other.[20]

In addition, provincial or regional autonomy makes it less likely that coalition partners accede to a common identity espoused by the electoral coalition. If groups have significant provincial, regional, or state autonomy, and a distinctive identity dependent on that local autonomy, then there is less necessity for them to join national coalitions. They will be less likely to agree to broader policies that might lead to a more overarching identity because of the distinctive prerogatives of protecting their regional identity. This is one of the supposed advantages of federalism. In slowing down policy change and allowing for more institutional veto points, federalism prevents a transformative change occurring in one area from rapidly spreading and relaying throughout the country. It is inherently a less nationally reconstructive institution. Nationwide reconstruction may only take place if the various regions are united behind a common political identity.

The difference in overlap in political orders helps explain the differing strengths of reconstructive coalitions for Catholics in the two time periods for the three countries considered in this book. Prior to the mid-twentieth century, the labor movement was much stronger in Australia than in the other two countries, so Australian Catholics had an advantage in using class as a way to spread positive discourses about Catholics. One finds that the strength of reconstructive coalitions is limited by the attachment to racial order in the South in the United States, and the attachment to provincial autonomy in Quebec. When one looks at the strength of pan-Christian moral movements at the end of the twentieth century, one finds that they are strongest in the United States and weakest in Canada, where again one finds that concerns about provincial autonomy in Quebec trump concerns over religious moral order.

This perspective also more fully captures the role of minority incorporation in political development. Transformation in the order of a particular minority is likely to be associated with transformations in other orders with which it overlaps. When one pulls on the string of one order, one can see how interwoven it is with the tapestry of other elements.

To summarize this section, one way to distinguish this theory from others is to specify the empirical observations that would be consistent with the theory.

1 Transformation of minority groups will be sparked in the political realm through reconstructive coalitions that bridge the identities of the majority and the minority.
2 Mere electoral success of a coalition between the majority and the minority group does not guarantee increase in political standing of the minority. Such a coalition may not transform prejudiced attitudes among the majority in the coalition. It depends on whether the coalition is reconstructive.

3 Reconstruction and transformations in standing may occur in one party, multiple parties, or no parties.
4 One-party incorporation, when that coalition is reconstructive, may improve minority standing within the coalition. It may also change the calculus of competing coalitions on the value of continued stigmatization, though not necessarily leading to full reconstruction in these opposing coalitions.
5 Two-party competition for a minority's votes and resources may not lead to transformation in minority standing when both parties are non-reconstructive, or when only one is reconstructive but not politically successful.
6 Overrepresentation may occur when there is heavy dependence of a transformative coalition on a minority group, even when the minority group is lacking in economic resources or has not been assimilated along other lines of identity.
7 Reconstructive coalitions at the national level will be hindered by the presence of strong regional identities. The geographical dispersion of reconstruction depends on the degree of regional autonomy and identity.
8 The timing of transformation in minority standing will be related to the presence of reconstructive coalitions.
9 Differences among countries in minority standing will correspond to the potential of reconstructive coalitions that depend on the minority.
10 Differences in minority incorporation will be associated with differences in the political development of particular countries because transformation of minority status is tied in with other transformative projects.

These empirical predictions either go beyond what previous theories have attempted to predict, or specify predictions that are in opposition to what other theories predict. Assimilation, power resources, coalition, opportunity, and institutional theories do not predict that degree of reconstruction of a coalition matters, and none of the theories predicts the particular patterns of diffusion of minority incorporation among parties, time, and geography envisioned here. This theory considers more explicitly the role of political movements and parties rather than just general societal changes in the transformation of minority group standing. The effectiveness of this theory in the Catholic case in comparison with other explanations will be tested in the following chapters by looking at whether its empirical predictions line up with improvements in Catholic standing in Australia, Canada, and the United States around the time of the Great Depression and the birth of Christian conservative political movements.

Notes

1 For a similar argument, see Jennifer L Hochschild and John H. Mollenkopf, "Modeling Immigrant Political Incorporation," in Jennifer L. Hochschild and John H. Mollenkopf, *Bringing Outsiders In: Transatlantic Perspectives on Immigrant Political Incorporation* (Ithaca: Cornell University Press, 2009), 15.
2 Rufus P. Browning, Dale Rogers Marshall, and David H. Tabb, *Protest Is Not Enough* (Berkeley: University of California Press, 1984); Raphael Sonensheim, *Politics in*

Black and White: Race and Power in Los Angeles (Princeton, NJ: Princeton University Press, 1993); Rufus P. Browning, Dale Rogers Marshall, and David H. Tabb (eds), *Racial Politics in American Cities*, 3rd edn (New York: Longman, 1997).
3. Kwame Ture and Charles Hamilton, *Black Power: The Politics of Liberation* (New York: Vintage, 1992), 75. Other "racial realists" also argue that interests are fundamental in successful coalitions. Derrick Bell, *Faces at the Bottom of the Well: The Permanence of Racism* (New York: Basic Books, 1993).
4. Paul Frymer, *Uneasy Alliances* (Princeton, NJ: Princeton University Press, 2010).
5. Robert Putnam, *Bowling Alone: The Collapse and Revival of American Community* (New York: Touchstone, 2001), 18–19.
6. Matthew Levendusky, *The Partisan Sort: How Liberals Became Democrats and Conservatives Became Republicans* (Chicago, IL: University of Chicago Press, 2009), chs 5–6.
7. The terminology of "reconstruction" is borrowed from Skowronek's well-known work which classifies presidents as either reconstructive, articulators, pre-emptive, or disjunctive. Stephen Skowronek, *The Politics Presidents Make: Leadership from John Adams to Bill Clinton* (New York: Belknap Press, 1997).
8. Wendy Brown, *Regulating Aversion: Tolerance in the Age of Identity and Empire* (Princeton, NJ: Princeton University Press, 2006), 26, 44–47.
9. Jim Rutenberg, "Data You Can Believe In," *New York Times Magazine*, June 20, 2013.
10. Hans Noel, *Political Ideologies and Political Parties in America* (New York: Cambridge University Press, 2014).
11. Michael Tesler, "Donald Sterling Shows the Separate Realities of Democrats and Republicans," Monkey Cage blog, May 1, 2014. Available at www.washingtonpost.com/blogs/monkey-cage/wp/2014/05/01/donald-sterling-shows-the-separate-realities-of-democrats-and-republicans-about-race/; Michael Tesler, "Democrats Increasingly Think the Confederate Flag Is Racist, Republicans Don't," Monkey Cage blog, July 9, 2015. Available at www.washingtonpost.com/blogs/monkey-cage/wp/2015/07/09/democrats-increasingly-think-the-confederate-flag-is-racist-republicans-dont/.
12. See, e.g., Victoria Hattam, *Labor Visions and State Power: The Origins of Business Unionism in the United States* (Princeton, NJ: Princeton University Press, 1993).
13. Paul Pierson, "Increasing Returns, Path Dependence, and the Study of Politics," *American Political Science Review* 94, no. 2 (June 2000): 251–267.
14. Karen Orren and Stephen Skowronek, *The Search for American Political Development* (New York: Cambridge University Press, 2004).
15. Suzanne Mettler, *The Submerged State: How Invisible Government Policies Undermine American Democracy* (Chicago, IL: University of Chicago Press, 2011).
16. James Morone, *Hellfire Nation: The Politics of Sin in American History* (New Haven, CT: Yale University Press, 2004).
17. Wolfgang Streeck and Kathleen Thelen, "Introduction: Institutional Change in Advance Political Economies," in Wolfgang Streeck and Kathleen Thelen (eds), *Beyond Continuity: Institutional Change in Advanced Political Economies* (New York: Oxford University Press, 2005), 1–39.
18. Orren and Skowronek, *The Search for American Political Development*, 14–15.
19. In Orren and Skowronek's terminology, "intercurrence" (ibid.: 113–114).
20. Paul Frymer, *Black and Blue: African Americans, the Labor Movement, and the Decline of the Democratic Party* (Princeton, NJ: Princeton University Press, 2007).

3 Catholic incorporation from 1890 to the mid-twentieth century

In 1928 Al Smith, the first Catholic American to run for the U.S. presidency, was resoundingly defeated at the polls, receiving only 87 out of 531 electoral votes. Democrats had fared poorly against Republicans in the early twentieth century – the only Democrat elected during this period, Woodrow Wilson, won because of a split in the Republican Party. Smith's defeat, however, was not mere "politics as usual." Catholic voters, comprising approximately 16 percent of the population, flocked to the Smith campaign, many registering to vote for the first time. A substantial proportion of Catholics had previously voted Republican.[1] Meanwhile, formerly solid Democratic strongholds in the South did not turn out as strongly for the Democrats as in previous elections, reflecting their concerns that the roots of the country were not only white, but Protestant. Although many Southern elected officials publicly supported Smith, deeming preservation of segregation more important than preservation of a Protestant order, five former Confederate states supported the Republican candidate, Herbert Hoover. The United States would have to wait another 32 years before it would elect its first and only Catholic president, which it would do by the thinnest of margins.

Half a world away and just one year after Smith's defeat, James Scullin became the first Catholic prime minister of Australia, a position he served in for a little over two years. Historians noted that his rise to the prime ministership as head of the Labor Party did not ignite nearly as much widespread suspicion of his Catholic heritage as did Al Smith.[2] An editorial in a Catholic periodical wrote that even though "the Federal elections were fought with the gloves off [...] sectarianism played a very small part in the conflict, and that very few candidates had anti-Catholic fanatics behind them."[3] Australian Catholic Archbishop Daniel Mannix even suggested that the election of a Catholic to the prime ministership could serve as a lesson to the United States.[4] The relative acceptance of Catholics on all sides of the political spectrum was also reflected in the fact that the opposition Nationalist Party joined with the Catholic Joseph Lyons, a former minister within Scullin's government, to lead a new party, the United Australia Party. Lyons became Scullin's successor from 1932 to 1939. Another practicing Catholic, Ben Chifley, served as prime minister from 1945 to 1949. The end of the Chifley prime ministership book-ended a run in which Catholics were prime ministers for 14 out of 20 years, an impressive achievement for a group that constituted approximately 20 percent of the population from the 1920s through the 1940s.

Given that Catholics made up a formidable 40 percent of the population in Canada and constituted one of the nation's "founding groups," one might have expected Catholics to do well there. At the same time, because of the deep rift between the French and English in that country, which has also played out as a rift in religion (Protestant and Catholic) and region (Quebec and other provinces), one might also have reasonably expected a more difficult time for Catholics in that country. Canada elected a Catholic, Sir John Thompson, as its prime minister in 1892, nearly 40 years ahead of Australia and 70 years ahead of the United States. Unlike Smith and Kennedy in the United States, and Scullin and Chifley in Australia, who were all representatives of left parties, Thompson was a member of a Conservative coalition united behind high tariffs and an industrial policy for Canada. A Methodist who converted to Catholicism when he married, Thompson was also an English Catholic, representing a middling figure between Canada's two founding cultures.[5] Thompson was later succeeded by Sir Wilfred Laurier, who was Canada's first French Catholic prime minister and heralded a dramatic shift in allegiances of Catholics from the Conservative Party to the Liberal Party. After Laurier's government ended in 1911, Canada would not select another French Catholic for prime minister until 37 years later, with Louis St. Laurent (1948–1957).

These three countries present three very different stories of Catholic incorporation at the highest levels of government in the early twentieth century. Presidential and prime ministerial politics, subject as they are to the vagaries of personalities and events, may not be adequate representations of the general state of Catholics in each country. Yet the basic story presented above at the time of the Great Depression – mixed incorporation in the United States, fuller incorporation in Australia, and stalled incorporation in Canada – applies as a basic difference between the three countries when one looks at other indicators of Catholic incorporation, including appointed and elected officials at lower levels of government. After canvassing these indicators, the chapter considers how these divergences compare with ideas about how minority political incorporation takes place.

Other indicators of divergence

Catholic appointed officials

In Australia, Scullin noted that eight of the 18 members of his Cabinet – nearly 45 percent – were Catholics.[6] This prompted the Catholic newspaper *The Advocate* to argue that Catholics should take pride in this accomplishment.[7] Various Protestant religious newspapers recognized the overrepresentation of Catholics in Scullin's cabinet and bureaucratic appointments as well.[8] A letter to the editor in the Adelaide *Advertiser* complained,

Catholic incorporation: 1890 to 1950s 27

Is it not a fact that the appointments made by the Scullin Government are a glaring and pitiful application of the aphorism, "the spoils to the victor," when the bulk of the appointments are of the same persuasion [i.e., Catholic]?[9]

This pattern of Catholic overrepresentation continued during Chifley's government (1945–1949), with over half of his ministers Catholic.[10]

Scullin's cabinet may be compared with Franklin Roosevelt's, which, as with many cabinets at the time, was a carefully balanced cross-section of the population.[11] Roosevelt appointed one Catholic, James Farley, as postmaster general, to go along with the one prominent Jewish American in Roosevelt's cabinet, Henry Morgenthau, and one woman, Frances Perkins. After Farley became disenchanted with the New Deal and ran against Roosevelt in the 1940 election, Roosevelt continued to include Catholics in his cabinet, appointing Frank Murphy as his attorney general, and Frank Walker as his postmaster general. The number of Catholics in Roosevelt's cabinets never exceeded Catholic population proportions, and did not even look distinctive compared with earlier Republican presidents: McKinley had appointed one, and Theodore Roosevelt two.[12]

In comparison, substantial Catholic representation in Canadian ministries occurred early in Canadian history, reflecting the necessity for any mass electoral Canadian party to secure Catholic votes. The MacDonald cabinet after Confederation reserved five positions for Ontario, two for each of the Maritimes, and four for Quebec, with three of those from Quebec likely to be Roman Catholic, since one had to be English speaking.[13] The *Canadian Parliamentary Guide* gives information on the religion of most Members of Parliament from approximately 1910 to 1990, and these data are summarized in Figure 3.1. The low point of Catholic representation in ministries occurred in the tenth ministry (1917–1920), when Roman Catholics constituted 10.6 percent of the ministry.[14] Pearson's government from 1963 to 1968 had the most Catholic senior officials of any government up until that time, with Catholics represented at 45.7 percent, approximately the Catholic population proportion. In between these two periods, Catholic representation in ministries ranged from about 24 to 35 percent. In summary, despite the advantage in numbers Canadian Catholics possessed, they were never overrepresented to the degree that Australian Catholics were in the Scullin, Curtin, and Chifley governments.

Parliament and the House of Representatives

Political office holding at lower levels confirms the above patterns. Joan Rydon has assembled data on the religious backgrounds of members of the House of Representatives in Australia from 1901 to 1972, which is summarized in Figure 3.2. These data show that in the first 14 years from the founding of the Australian federation in 1901, Roman Catholics were highly underrepresented, with between three and seven members in the 75-member House. There is a significant leap in Roman Catholic representation starting with the Scullin

28 *Catholic incorporation: 1890 to 1950s*

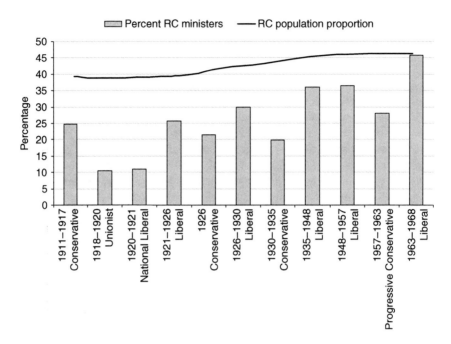

Figure 3.1 Percentage of Catholics in Canadian ministries, 1911–1968.

Source: Canadian Parliamentary Guide.

Note

Figures represent percentage of total months during a ministry in which a Catholic served in the position. I include all ministers listed on the Government of Canada Privy Council Office website at www.pco-bcp.gc.ca/index.asp?lang=eng&page=information&sub=publications&doc=min/table-eng. htm (accessed April 28, 2009). Ministers without portfolio were not included in the calculation. Those members for whom a religion was not listed in the *Guide* are excluded in the denominator. The calculation for the short eleventh ministry is likely to be inaccurate owing to the large sample of those ministers not listing their religious affiliation.

government in 1929, with 18 Catholic representatives in a body of 75. In the Chifley government, there were 31 Catholic representatives. In short, during the Labor governments between 1929 and 1949, Catholics were overrepresented in the Australian House of Representatives by nearly double their population proportion of about 20 percent.[15]

It is unclear from Rydon's data how often these parliamentarians with Catholic backgrounds attended church. Some were most likely non-practicing. Responses to Census questions indicate that only a tiny proportion of the population were willing to label themselves as having no religion. Even if there were a substantial number of lapsed Catholics in the Labor Party, it is unclear whether the average Protestant could tell the difference between lapsed and practicing Catholics. The success of Catholics in the federal legislature mirrored what had happened previously in state legislatures, and Protestant papers reacted with some alarm to this earlier development. When Labor won control of the

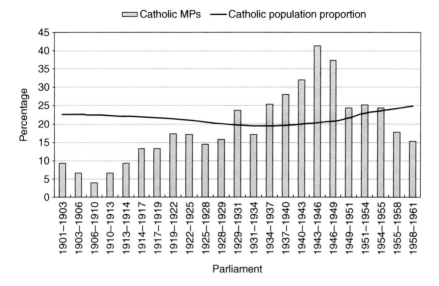

Figure 3.2 Percentage of Catholics in the Australian House of Representatives, 1901–1961.

Source: Joan Rydon, *A Biographical Register of the Commonwealth Parliament, 1901–72*. Canberra: Australian National University Press, 1975.

Note
Data show only Roman Catholic percentage at start of the parliamentary session.

government in New South Wales in 1920, the *Methodist* estimated that at least 30 of the 45 members of the Labor caucus were Roman Catholics and pointed out the overrepresentation of Catholics in the New South Wales ministry. The newspaper concluded that Catholics had "so captured the Labour movement as to have a dominating influence and an altogether disproportionate share of representation in it."[16] The *Australian Christian World* echoed that statement, writing that "the capture of the Labor Party by the Irish Romanist element is more or less an accomplished fact" because of "the devious and unscrupulous trickery" of Irish Catholic priests, an "ever restless force which is undermining the security and happiness of the people of this continent."[17]

Information on U.S. Congresses prior to the 1930s is difficult to obtain. In 1911 Catholic Archibishop John Ireland estimated that there were three or four Catholic senators and 15 or 16 Catholic representatives.[18] An anti-Catholic pamphleteer estimated that there were 24 members of the House in 1920 that were Catholic or had a Catholic background, with about two-thirds of these being Republicans.[19] The anti-Catholic publication *The Menace* estimated that there were 38 Catholics in the House in 1925.[20] Although none of these sources can be taken as precisely accurate, they do at least concur in giving a picture of substantial underrepresentation of Catholics prior to the New Deal.

30 Catholic incorporation: 1890 to 1950s

More reliable information is available starting in the 1930s. Democrat John J. O'Connor, in assessing a run for the Speakership of the House, provided an estimate of 74 Catholics in 1936, with about 95 percent of these being Democrats.[21] Surveys show that in the seventy-seventh and seventy-eighth Congresses (1941–1945), Roman Catholic representatives constituted about 20 percent of the House and 11 percent of the Senate, so that Roman Catholics, who comprised about 18 percent of the population, had reached parity, perhaps even slight overrepresentation, in the House by this time (see Figure 3.3).[22] Since 1963, there has been more regular information. It was only in the 1990s that Catholic representation in the Senate approached parity, while Roman Catholic representation in the House tracked Roman Catholic population percentages up until the 1980s, when it began to outstrip the population proportion.

By comparison, Catholic representation in the lower legislative chamber in Canada never achieved population proportionality in the first half of the twentieth century. Figure 3.4 summarizes the Roman Catholic composition of the House of Commons in the Canadian Parliament, based on information from the *Canadian Parliamentary Guide*. This percentage has stayed relatively constant between 1911 and 1972, fluctuating between 28 and 39 percent, which is slightly under the Catholic percentage of the population for this period (between 40 and 45 percent).[23]

The countries may also be compared to show the representation of Catholics from particular provinces and states. An index of representation may be constructed taking the proportion of Catholic representatives in a particular legislative body and dividing it by the population proportion of Catholics in that

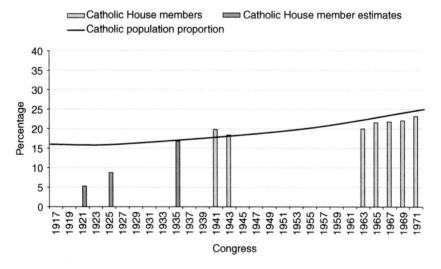

Figure 3.3 Percentage of Catholics in U.S. House, 1921–1971.

Source: Nations, *Rome in Congress* (n. 20); *The Menace*; John O'Connor manuscript collection, Lilly Library, Indiana University, Bloomington; surveys from Madge M. McKinney (n. 23); *Congressional Quarterly Almanac*.

Catholic incorporation: 1890 to 1950s 31

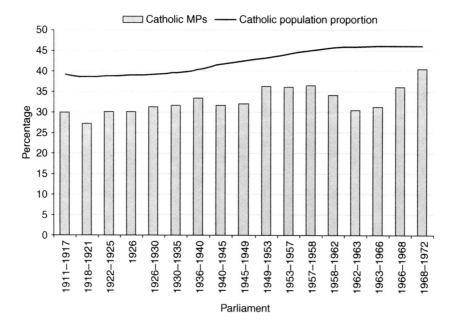

Figure 3.4 Percentage of Catholics in the Canadian House of Commons, 1911–1972.
Source: Canadian Parliamentary Guide.

Note
Figures include members elected during by-elections, and is not adjusted for "time served." Rather, each elected member counts as one data point. Even if those members not stating a religion were treated as missing data and excluded from the denominator in the calculations, there would still be Catholic underrepresentation up until the 1960s.

legislative body's territory (for a breakdown of Catholic population percentages in states and provinces in the three countries, see Appendices 1–3). An index of representation under one indicates underrepresentation, while an index of over one indicates overrepresentation. As may be seen in Table 3.1, Catholics are only proportionally represented in Quebec and New Brunswick from 1936 to 1962. Most of the underrepresentation of Canadian Catholics comes from Ontario and the western provinces. By contrast, in Australia, Catholics are overrepresented in all the states from 1930 to 1960 with the exception of Victoria, where Roman Catholics have been somewhat underrepresented (Table 3.2). In the United States (Table 3.3) there is overrepresentation in several states as well, but not to the same degree as in Australia.

Perhaps the best way to judge Catholic incorporation is to look at electoral districts where Catholics hardly ever constituted a majority and have to attract significant non-Catholic votes. Achieving electoral victories in such conditions represents a greater level of acceptance. Catholic representatives were elected above their population proportion in Australian states with the lowest Catholic population percentages (e.g., Tasmania). In Canada Catholics at similar

Table 3.1 Percentage of Catholics in Provincial Delegations to the Canadian House of Commons, 1911–1962

		Alberta	BC	Manitoba	Ontario	Sask	NB	NS	PEI	Quebec
1911–1935	RC MPs (%)	5	1	7	10	1	31	26	25	82
	RC percentage of population, 1911 (%)	17	15	16	19	18	41	29	45	86
	Index of representation	**0.31**	**0.09**	**0.41**	**0.51**	**0.07**	**0.75**	**0.88**	**0.56**	**0.95**
1936–1962	RC MPs (%)	8	9	12	12	8	47	27	18	88
	RC percentage of population, 1941 (%)	19	13	19	23	22	48	33	45	87
	Index of representation	**0.40**	**0.68**	**0.63**	**0.53**	**0.33**	**0.98**	**0.83**	**0.40**	**1.02**

Source: Data from *Canadian Parliamentary Guide*.

Note
An index of representation of 1 equals proportionate representation; below 1 indicates underrepresentation; above 1 indicates overrepresentation. Catholic representation is measured at the start of each parliamentary session and does not include data from by-elections.

Table 3.2 Percentage of Catholics in State Delegations to Australian House of Representatives, 1901–1961

		NSW	QLD	SA	TAS	VIC	WA
1901–1929	RC MPs (%)	13	7	8	0	13	26
	RC population (%)	25	24	14	17	22	22
	Index of representation	**0.50**	**0.31**	**0.56**	**0.00**	**0.58**	**1.18**
1929–1961	RC MPs (%)	33	36	23	18	15	22
	RC population (%)	24	23	15	16	22	21
	Index of representation	**1.38**	**1.53**	**1.53**	**1.12**	**0.66**	**1.06**

Source: Joan Rydon, *A Biographical Register of the Commonwealth Parliament, 1901–1972*.

Note
An index of representation of 1 equals proportionate representation; below 1 indicates underrepresentation; above 1 indicates overrepresentation. Catholic representation is measured at the start of each parliamentary session, and is summed over the two time periods. By-elections are not included in the figures.

Table 3.3 Percentage of Catholics in U.S. State Delegations to 74th Congress (1935–1937)

State	Catholic representatives from state (%)	Catholic percentage of population, 1926	Index of representation
CA	30	16	1.90
WI	40	24	1.69
MO	23	15	1.57
IL	30	19	1.54
NY	32	27	1.18
MN	22	19	1.16
MI	22	20	1.12
LA	33	30	1.10
MD	17	15	1.10
PA	24	23	1.01
MA	40	40	1.00
CT	33	37	0.89
OH	12	16	0.73
NJ	21	29	0.73
RI	33	50	0.66
AVG	27	25	1.16

Source: John O'Connor manuscripts, Lilly Library; U.S. Bureau of the Census, *Census of Religious Bodies, 1926*.

Note
An index of representation of 1 equals proportionate representation; below 1 indicates underrepresentation; above 1 indicates overrepresentation. States with only one or two representatives are excluded. Population figures for 1926 are used owing to collection problems with the 1936 Census during the Great Depression.

population proportions were not electorally successful. This indicates an increase in Catholic standing in Australia relative to Canada.

Explaining the divergence

The evidence reveals information about the timing, depth, and relative movement of Catholic descriptive representation. In Australia, the most significant increase occurred around the Great Depression. The available evidence indicates that the same occurred in the United States, whereas in Canada the Great Depression had little effect on Catholic representation. Second, Australian Catholics became not just proportionally represented; they become overrepresented. Third, Australian Catholic descriptive representation exceeded that of the United States and Canada during the Great Depression.

These three observations are even more striking when considered together with the fact that Australian Catholics were poorer than Protestants in the 1920s (evidence for this will be shown below). It is not often in the history of liberal democracies that a stigmatized, economically disadvantaged minority group can achieve proportional descriptive representation, much less overrepresentation.

The remainder of this chapter will use these four observations to sort through potential alternative explanations for Catholic incorporation. This section assesses a variety of explanations, including assimilation, power resources, coalitions, and institutions. Those readers who are not interested in examining the details of these alternative explanations and wish to see how the reconstructive coalition argument works in explaining the patterns may skip ahead to Chapters 4, 5, and 6, which looks at each country in more depth.

Assimilation explanations

Assimilation theories of immigrant incorporation argue that immigrants will be politically incorporated as they drop their most distinctive characteristics (such as language) and "melt" into the mainstream. Social and economic incorporation will generally tend to precede political incorporation.

A greater proportion of the Catholic population in Australia had been rooted for more generations than Catholics in the United States, so one might think that with greater generational tenure Australian Catholics were more likely to be wealthier, better educated, and more politically engaged. However, Canadian Catholics had as deep roots as Australian Catholics, so the differing trajectories between these two countries suggest that a generational perspective is incomplete.

In addition, it does not appear that Australian Catholics' generational tenure benefited them that significantly. They were not particularly wealthy. Using the 1933 Census data, one can estimate an average breadwinner income for Protestants and Roman Catholics.[24] For Protestants the average was £160. For Catholics the average was £130, so Catholics were making 81 percent of what Protestants were making. The average Catholic family also had more dependent children than the average Protestant family: 2.41 to 2.17. Depending on how much it costs to raise a dependant, the average Catholic individual was surviving on between 76 to 81 percent of the income of the average Protestant.[25] Two other factors heightened inequality between the two groups. First, Roman Catholics devoted some of their income to send their children to private schools. The Australian census shows that 56 percent of young Catholics were in private schools in 1921, increasing to 61 percent in 1933.[26] Second, accumulated wealth favored Protestants. The 1915 War Census, for instance, revealed that persons in higher income brackets (in which Protestants were overrepresented) had a much lower ratio of income to assets.[27]

There are no comparable figures on wealth and income for Catholics in the United States and Canada during the same time period, so it is possible that Australian Catholics were relatively better off than Catholics compared to Protestants in the other two countries. Even if this is true, the fact that Australian Catholics could become overrepresented in descriptive representation while being worse off than Protestants casts doubt on economic assimilation as the source of Australian Catholic gains.

Irish Catholics constituted a larger part of the Catholic population in Australia than in Canada (where the French predominated) or the United States (where there were substantial German, Spanish, and French Catholics). Perhaps the Irish assimilated to a greater degree and became less foreign than other ethnic Catholics. This explanation is doubtful however. Irishness was as much a source of tension with English Protestants as any other ethnicity, because of the conflict over Ireland in relation to the British Empire. In addition, some studies indicate that from the middle of the nineteenth to the early twentieth century, Irish Americans' resort to distinct ethnic claims increased rather than decreased, which does not suggest a particular propensity among Irish Catholics to assimilate.[28]

One might focus on French ethnicity in Canada and argue that it was French difference, especially in language, that made Catholic political incorporation more difficult. In addition to underestimating differences between Gaelic and English, this potential explanation also does not account for the timing of Catholic political incorporation in Australia and the United States (around the Great Depression) nor intracountry geographic distribution (limitations of Catholic incorporation in the American South).

The distance between Catholics and Protestants may also be driven by differing commitments to the British Empire. Hartz and other authors in *Founding of New Societies* have argued that the British fragment that founded Australia was a radical fragment, composed to a greater degree of radical Chartists and others hostile to the wealthy. Hartz believed that the English settlers to both the United States and Canada were part of a liberal fragment, though the influence of the American Revolution and the movement of some Loyalists to Canada may have made English Canadians more "whiggish" in character.[29] It could be that Canada may have been more tied to British identity than the other two countries considered here, and, since Protestant–Catholic conflicts were often centered on the British Empire, ties to the British Empire may explain variations in Protestant–Catholic tensions.[30] But the historical record does not show that Canadians were more invested in British imperial identity. For example, Australia's financial contributions to the Crimean War outstripped all others.[31] Australia also contributed approximately 16,000 men to the Boer War, while Canada contributed about 7,400, despite the fact that Australia's population was substantially lower than that of Canada's at the time.[32] Despite Protestant Australians' huge commitment to the British Empire, Australian Protestants during the Great Depression trusted Catholics to a greater degree than in Canada.

The variations in Catholic incorporation are also not well explained by differences in potential economic competition between Protestant and Catholics in the three countries. Alba has argued that assimilation is aided when such assimilation is not likely to lead to zero-sum conflict between the majority and minority groups. Alba notes that the assimilation of Southern and Eastern European immigrant groups in the United States occurred primarily after World War II, when the expansion of the economy made it relatively easier for Southern and Eastern European groups to take up well-paying jobs without threatening the prerogatives of older stock Americans.[33] However, as is shown in this comparison, significant Catholic political incorporation occurred in both Australia and the United States during the Great Depression, precisely when potential economic competition between Catholic new immigrant groups and older stock Protestants was intense.

Secularization may be thought of as a species of assimilation theory, because Catholics and Protestants may simply have stopped caring about religion. One Australian scholar has argued that

> one of the main reasons for the marked decline in sectarian hostilities between Catholic and Protestant by the mid-1920s was the realization by leaders on both sides that the great mass of the Australian population cared very little about church matters.[34]

There is some evidence that religious adherence was lower in Australia than in Canada and the United States at the end of the nineteenth century,[35] but one doesn't have to be Protestant to be anti-Catholic. In the nineteenth century, despite lower religious adherence, Australia matched the United States and Canada in anti-Catholic policies, for example, by reversing state aid to religious schools.[36] Similarly, one can point to current conflicts over Muslims in many Western and Northern European nations to show that societies in which religious influence has waned can be just as anxious about religious minorities.

Even if one believed that secularization was more advanced in Australia, this would not explain why the period immediately before Scullin was chosen as prime minister in Australia saw some of the bitterest struggles between Protestants and Catholics.[37] World War I sparked debates over conscription of soldiers, with Catholics largely opposed and Protestants generally in favor. The period during World War I also saw the formation of the Catholic Federation, a group that sought to endorse political candidates to support Catholic issues such as state aid to schools. This prompted the formation of the Protestant Federation, and in New South Wales in the 1920s Protestant political candidates endorsed by the Protestant Federation won control over the lower legislature under Premier George Fuller. One of the main goals of the Fuller government was to enact legislation to make promulgation of the *Ne Temere* and *Motu Proprio* decrees of the Catholic Church illegal. *Ne Temere* (1908) declared that any marriage of a Catholic not sanctified by the Catholic Church was not a marriage, and *Motu Proprio* (1917) suggested that Catholic Canon Law superseded civil law. Although the Fuller government's efforts were blocked by the Legislative Council in New South Wales, the effort to pass those laws indicated the continuing significance of religious issues to politics.[38]

Other potential measures of secularization include literacy rates, education, and urbanization, which may be associated with the growth of more cosmopolitan norms. Australia was more urbanized than the other two countries, and there is some evidence of higher Australian literacy rates. Only 1.6 percent of those over the age of ten could not read in Australia, compared to 6 percent in the United States and 5.1 percent in Canada in the period immediately before the Great Depression.[39] There is no evidence of greater Australian higher educational attainment. Enrollment in colleges and universities was fairly low in all three countries, with 18- to 24-year-olds enrolled in colleges and universities between 3 and 10 percent from 1911 to World War II in the United States, up to 1 percent in Australia, and about 2.3 percent in Canada.[40] The slight difference in literacy seems an unlikely candidate to explain why Australian overrepresentation in the House could be nearly double the rate of their population proportion. In addition, high literacy and urbanization did not prevent the outbreak of sectarian conflict between Catholics and Protestants in Australia during World War I and the 1920s in New South Wales.

If assimilation theory cannot explain the intercountry divergences, it also cannot explain the timing or extent of increase in descriptive representation. There was no sudden change in Catholic indicators on wealth or education around the Great Depression. Assimilation theory also predicts that with the decline of social differences there should be proportionate representation of Catholics rather than overrepresentation.

Power resources

Might differences in power resources explain the divergence? The above discussion has already shown that Australian Catholics tended to have less money and wealth than Protestants. In addition, the size of the Catholic population does not correlate with the divergences in political incorporation. Catholics constituted a greater proportion of the population in Canada, and this may have mattered further back in Canadian history. In particular, Laurier failed to extend separate schools in Manitoba in 1896, but succeeded in extending the separate school system to Alberta and Saskatchewan in 1905. Other provinces had to resort to more covert measures. However, by the 1930s, Catholics seem to have done better in some respects in Australia than in Canada.

38 *Catholic incorporation: 1890 to 1950s*

In the 1920s, Australia's Catholic population proportion (around 22 percent) was slightly larger than the U.S. Catholic population proportion (around 16 percent), yet the difference is not that great. Australian Catholics may have had some advantages in power resources relative to U.S. Catholics because a greater proportion of Australian Catholics existed in the country since its founding, which may have given them a head start on political mobilization. Still, one should not exaggerate these deeper roots. Self-government wasn't introduced in Australia until the mid-nineteenth century. Even as suffrage was introduced, there were still property qualifications and other kinds of restrictions, including plural votes, for both the Lower and Upper House, serving to lessen the effective power of Catholics. As shown in Figure 3.2, if Australian Catholics had a head start relative to U.S. Catholics, it was not by much. In the first decade of the twentieth century, Australian Catholics were still heavily underrepresented in the Australian House.

Looking at individual Australian states also does not indicate that size of the Catholic population determined levels of Catholic representation. Table 3.2 shows representation of Catholics in the states, ordered from left to right according to the degree of overrepresentation during the period 1929 to 1961. South Australia, with a proportion of Catholics similar to the United States, experienced significant Catholic overrepresentation to the same degree as states (New South Wales, Queensland) with larger proportions of Catholics. Catholic representation is better correlated with success of the ALP. Similarly, Table 3.3 shows that during the New Deal, Catholic overrepresentation existed in some U.S. state delegations to the House. This overrepresentation is not tied to the size of the Catholic population in those states.

Perhaps it may be thought that the size of the Canadian Catholic population makes them more of threat and thus prevents better Catholic–Protestant relations. But if fear of size is an important factor, one would wonder why the actual representation of so many Catholics in the Australian Parliament in the 1930s and 1940s did not likewise provoke a sense of threat. In addition, Catholics in several northeastern states in the United States were between 30 to 40 percent of the population, yet Catholics were well represented in those states (Table 3.3).

Another difference in the three countries' Catholic populations is that Australia's was evenly spread out among provinces and was both rural and urban, while the Catholic population in the United States was concentrated in northeastern cities and certain sections of the Midwest. This may explain some of the divergence between the United States and Australia.[41] With Catholics "packed" into particular U.S. regions, perhaps some Catholic votes were wasted in single-member districts. Yet Catholics were sometimes overrepresented in some U.S. states, just as Australian Catholics were in Australian states. This does not indicate that packing was a barrier to Catholic representation. Even if packing does explain some of the differences between the two countries, it does not explain the timing of the transformation of Catholic representation around the Great Depression; Catholics did not suddenly become "unpacked" in the United States at this time. Moreover, packing predicts underrepresentation because of wasted votes; but Catholics in the United States achieved proportionate representation in the 1930s. The packing explanation also runs into difficulties in explaining the divergence between Canada and Australia. In both countries the Catholic population was not simply confined to cities, and in both countries Catholics had substantial presence in all provinces.

Coalition and pluralist theories

Do coalitions of Catholics with Protestant majorities explain the patterns of Catholic incorporation described above? What is striking from the case of Catholic political incorporation is that in all three countries Catholics were allied with Protestants in parties that managed to capture government during the Great Depression. Despite successful electoral coalitions with Protestants, Catholic descriptive representation varied substantially among the three counties. The mere fact of coalition does not predict the level of descriptive representation of Catholics.

What about pluralism? Pluralist theories of minority incorporation suggest either that diversity should lead to more flexible, cross-cutting coalitions and greater minority incorporation, or that greater diversity tends to make the majority population feel besieged and treat minority populations with greater suspicion. Diversity is a difficult concept to measure, partly because the concept has multiple dimensions. In the field of ecology, for instance, diversity as richness is typically distinguished from diversity as evenness. Richness refers to the number of different groups within a society. A society including whites, blacks, and Latinos would be "richer" than a society comprising only whites and blacks. Evenness refers to the proportion of each of the groups in a society. Imagine that Society A is half white and half black and Society B is three-quarters white and one-quarter black. If one were to randomly draw two people from those two societies, the probability of picking a white–black pair would be greater in Society A than in Society B. Hence, one can say that Society A is more diverse in terms of evenness.

Australia, Canada, and the United States were all diverse societies, though in differing combinations of richness and evenness. Australia's Catholic population has been larger than in the United States; thus in terms of religious evenness Australia is more diverse. However, Australia's Catholic population has been largely Irish, whereas the Catholic population in the United States has been much more diverse, with Irish in the northeast, Germans in the Midwest, French in the northeast and Louisiana, and Latinos in the southwest; thus in terms of religious richness the United States may be said to be more diverse. Canada is religiously diverse in terms of both evenness and richness. Not only was there greater evenness between Catholics and Protestants, but Catholics in Canada were also differentiated into distinct French and Irish fragments.

Since all three societies were diverse, it is hard to see how theories of pluralism could account for differences in the decline of Catholic–Protestant tensions. Let us look first from a "diversity is good for minorities" perspective. If one were looking only at richness, Australia was the least diverse, yet

40   Catholic incorporation: 1890 to 1950s

Catholics fared better there in the first half of the twentieth century. If one were only looking at diversity as evenness, Australia is more diverse than the United States, which may explain why Catholics in Australia fared better, but Canada is more diverse in terms of evenness than Australia, and Catholics did worse there in the first half of the twentieth century. The same considerations plague a "diversity is bad for minorities" perspective, since each country's relative position to each other in terms of diversity as richness and evenness is mixed.

More simply, pluralist theory does not predict the timing of Catholic overrepresentation (there was no sudden increase or decrease in the demographic composition of the countries in the 1930s) and fails to explain the phenomenon of overrepresentation. Greater pluralism should lead to no group controlling politics and no significant overrepresentation of a group, particularly a stigmatized, economically disadvantaged one like Catholics. Yet that is precisely what happens in Australia and, to lesser extent, in the United States.

Political opportunities

The political opportunity of war does not seem to explain the patterns. Although a good case can be made that World War II increased the standing of U.S. Catholics, particularly with Hollywood depictions of tri-faith platoons fighting together against the Nazis and Japanese, overrepresentation of Catholics in Australia, and to a lesser degree the United States, preceded World War II. In addition, World War I increased tensions between Catholics and Protestants in Australia and Canada, since Protestants in both of those countries were particularly interested in supporting the British Empire.

The racial structure may form another important political opportunity for groups attempting incorporation. Roediger and Jacobson, among others, have suggested that the presence of an even more stigmatized non-white group may help the incorporation of "in-between" groups.[42] Neither explicitly says that larger black populations are correlated with a higher degree of acceptance of whites of questionable status. Their analysis of the documentary record indicates to them only that these groups affirmed themselves as white in the process of becoming Americans. Yet it seems a reasonable extrapolation that where a more stigmatized group is more populous, less stigmatized groups may be able to position themselves favorably against that group. One might think of the way Asian Americans have been sometimes considered a "model minority" in comparison to blacks and Latinos.

One could argue the reverse and state that instead of aiding Catholic incorporation, the presence of blackness in the United States may have hurt "ambiguous" whites. The script applied to blacks and Asians readily translated into application against ambiguous whites. This possibility seems more plausible when one considers that the most antiblack region of the United States, the South, also expressed vociferous anti-Catholicism in the 1910s and 1920s.

Neither of these two explanations fits the patterns of Catholic incorporation. Of the three countries considered, the United States had by far the largest non-white (in terms of today's classification schema) population, yet fell somewhere in between Australia and Canada in terms of Catholic descriptive representation. The racial explanation also does not explain the timing of the increase of Catholic representation around the Great Depression, since there was no sudden increase or decrease in the racial composition of the countries at this time.

Finally, one may look at the political opportunity of the Great Depression itself. Perhaps by increasing the salience of class, religious tensions between Catholics and Protestants declined. This may explain the timing of the increase in Catholic representation in Australia and the United States, but it does not explain why Canada lagged behind the other two countries despite also experiencing the Great Depression. Something more was required to turn the political opportunity of the Great Depression into a sustained increase in Catholic standing.

Institutional explanations

Scholars of minority and immigrant incorporation have argued that major political institutions matter in incorporation outcomes.[43] In the lower legislative chambers, all three countries share majoritarian "winner-take-all" electoral systems, although Australia has instant runoff voting with its preferential voting system. Preferential voting encourages the formation of smaller parties in Australia, but it is unclear why this would lead to greater representation of Catholics; one would expect greater polarization between Protestants and Catholics if smaller third parties representing religious interests were organized.

With regard to the executive, the United States has a presidential system compared with a parliamentary system in Australia and Canada. Perhaps it is easier to get a majority of elected representatives in a parliamentary system to select a Catholic as prime minister than getting a majority of the population to vote for a Catholic president. However, the fact that both the ALP and the UAP selected Catholic prime ministers at this time does not suggest a slim majority supporting Catholics; instead it suggests a broader consensus toward acceptability of Catholics. In addition, the divergence between Australia and Canada, despite their common parliamentary system, demonstrates that this factor is not determinative.

With cabinet appointments, there is the need for Senate confirmation in the United States, and the possibility of a filibuster, so more political elites have to support Catholics to get Catholic appointments. However, at the time of the New Deal, 64 of 96 votes were needed to stop a filibuster in the Senate, and Democrats had filibuster-proof majorities from 1935 to 1943, so barring intraparty division; Democrats should have been able to reward their coalition partners accordingly. In addition, this factor does not explain the divergence between Australia and Canada, since both have similar methods of selecting cabinet members.

In addition, all three countries had no established church, but the three countries have different church–state boundaries. The United States has come closest to the separation of church and state, though what this separation entails is a continuing matter of constitutional debate. Australia and Canada, by contrast, have historically come closer to the British practice where constitutionality is more amorphous and the legislature has great primacy in constitutional questions. The church–state boundary has been much more fluid in these two countries. Despite this similarity, there have still been significant divergences between Australia and Canada, which means that formal church–state boundaries are not the explanatory variable either.

More broadly, none of these institutional differences explains the timing of Catholic political incorporation in these two countries. There were no great institutional changes in the three countries in the 1930s in electoral procedures or structure of government that explain the diverging pattern of Catholic incorporation. Nor do institutional structures explain the fact of major overrepresentation in the Australian context.

Conclusion

A preliminary comparison among the three countries shows that existing theories of minority political incorporation do not easily fit in with the patterns of Catholic political incorporation in the three countries. The following three chapters will argue that differences in the strength of reconstructive labor coalitions in the three countries explain the variations in the first half of the twentieth century. Each country was subjected to an exogenous shock, namely the Great Depression, which had the potential to bring Catholics and Protestants together and transform Catholic representation. Yet each country responded differently to this shock. Previous developments conditioned how these three countries reacted and whether transformation in the economic order could simultaneously lead to transformations in the order of Catholic–Protestant relations. The broad patterns cited in this chapter are reinforced by a more in-depth look at how the different trajectories of incorporation led to different policies, institutions, and identities, transforming each country's democratic, class, and religious orders.

Notes

1 George J. Marlin, *The American Catholic Voter: 200 Years of Political Impact* (South Bend, IN: St. Augustine's Press, 2004), 130–131, 161, 164, 171, 188. Although there were no polls to determine how many Catholics voted for Republicans at this time, one can look at vote results from predominantly Catholic cities and counties, keeping in mind problems of ecological fallacy.
2 Roger C. Thompson, *Religion in Australia: A History* (Melbourne: Oxford University Press, 1994), 68. John Robertson, *J.H. Scullin: A Political Biography* (Nedlands, Western Australia: University of Western Australia Press, 1974), 210.
3 *Freeman's Journal*, October 24, 1929, 24.
4 "Mr. Scullin Establishes Record," *Advertiser* (Adelaide, South Australia), October 28, 1929, 19.
5 James Watt, "Anti-Catholic Nativism in Canada: The Protestant Protective Association," *Canadian Historical Review* 48, no. 1 (March 1967): 49.

6 "Broadminded Australia," *Mercury* (Hobart, Tasmania), December 17, 1930, 12.
7 *The Advocate*, cited in "The Progress of Rome," *The Mercury* (Hobart, Tasmania), October 29, 1929.
8 *Methodist*, November 9, 1929, 3; December 7, 1929, 3; *Australian Christian World*, December 6, 1929, 9.
9 "Sectarianism in Politics," *Advertiser* (Adelaide), December 2, 1931, 18.
10 Thompson, *Religion in Australia*, 122; Joan Rydon, *A Federal Legislature: The Australian Commonwealth Parliament 1901–1980* (Melbourne: Oxford University Press, 1986), 143.
11 Roosevelt's cabinet was balanced religiously with two Episcopalians, three Presbyterians, and two Methodists. Geographically, it included three New Yorkers, three Southerners, two Midwesterners, and two Westerners. See "Roosevelt's Ten," *Time*, March 6, 1933. Available at www.time.com/time/printout/0,8816,745236,00.html.
12 Franklin Roosevelt may have been more generous in his judicial appointments. According to one scholar, approximately 25 percent of federal judicial posts were filled by Catholics during the Roosevelt and Truman administrations, compared with 4 percent during the three Republican administrations that preceded them. Prendergast, *Catholic Voter*, 113.
13 Douglas V. Verney, *Three Civilizations, Two Cultures, One State: Canada's Political Traditions* (Durham, NC: Duke University Press, 1986), 232.
14 This figure, a decline of more than 50 percent from Catholic representation in the previous ministry, reflected widespread discontent with Canadian Catholics' refusal to support conscription to help Britain in World War I.
15 Rydon has a slightly different way of presenting the same data, by looking at the percentages of Catholics of members elected for the first time. From 1901 to 1909, Roman Catholics constituted 9.5 percent of members of the Federal Parliament of Australia elected for the first time, despite the fact that for most of the nineteenth century Catholics constituted approximately 25 percent of the population. The period from 1910 to 1916 seems to mark the moment in Australian politics when Roman Catholics achieved near parity with their population percentage. In that time frame, Roman Catholics constituted 20.6 percent of federal parliamentarians while making up 22.7 percent of the population in 1901 and 21.6 percent in 1921. From 1931 to 1948, Roman Catholics exceeded their population percentage, constituting approximately 30.6 percent of parliamentarians. This number dropped back down to around 20 percent in the three decades following, which is slightly less than the 25 percent of the population claiming Roman Catholic heritage from 1960 to 1980. See Rydon, *Federal Legislature*.
16 *Methodist*, April 10, 1920, 7; April 17, 1920, 7.
17 "The Vagaries of Father O'Reilly," *Australian Christian World*, April 29, 1921, 9.
18 *Life*, March 9, 1911. Prendergast has said that there were 20 Catholics in Congress in 1890 and 1892. William B. Prendergast, *The Catholic Voter in American Politics: The Passing of the Democratic Monolith* (Washington, DC: Georgetown Press, 2004), 72. Unfortunately, Prendergast does not cite his source.
19 Gilbert O. Nations, *Rome in Congress* (The Protestant, 1922).
20 "Religion and Politics," *Menace*, March 21 and 28, 1925, 1. Prendergast has stated that there were 42 Catholics in Congress in 1923, all but seven of whom were Democrats, but his source is uncited. Prendergast, *The Catholic Voter in American Politics*, 95.
21 "Catholic Senate and House, 1936," John O'Connor Manuscripts Collection, Collection No. LMC 1945, Box 25, Lilly Library, Indiana University-Bloomington. In the document, Martin A. Brenner has been taken as a misspelling of Martin A. Brennan, a representative from Illinois; Patrick Boland has been incorrectly listed as a representative from New York rather than from Pennsylvania.

44 Catholic incorporation: 1890 to 1950s

22 Madge M. McKinney, "The Personnel of the Seventy-Seventh Congress," *American Political Science Review* 36, no. 1 (February 1942): 67–75; Madge M. McKinney, "Religion and Elections," *The Public Opinion Quarterly* 8, no. 1 (spring 1944): 110–114.
23 Data from the Netherlands and Germany (both of which have Catholic populations comprising from 35 to 40 percent of the population, show that the Canadian representation levels are about the same as in those two countries. See Heinrich Best and Maurizio Cotta (eds), *Parliamentary Representatives in Europe: 1848–2000: Legislative Recruitment and Careers in Eleven European Countries* (New York: Oxford University Press, 2000).
24 The average for the lower and upper income brackets was calculated using the assumptions of Ian McLean and Sue Richardson, "More or Less Equal? Australian Income Distribution in 1933 and 1980," *Economic Record* 62 (March 1986): 67–82.
25 The inequality between working-class Protestants and Catholics may be exaggerated by the heavy tilt of the topmost income bracket, but even leaving that out one would still find Catholic individuals living on approximately 85 to 87 percent of that of Protestants.
26 *Census of the Commonwealth of Australia Taken for the Night Between the 3rd and 4th April 1921, Part VI – Religion* (Melbourne: H.J. Green), 398–399. *Census of the Commonwealth of Australia 30th June, 1933, Part XVI – Religion* (Canberra: L.F. Johnston), 1074.
27 Australian Bureau of Statistics, *The Private Wealth of Australia and Its Growth as Ascertained by Various Methods, Together with a Report of the War Census of 1915. Prepared under Instructions from the Minister of State for Home and Territories by G.H. Knibbs, Commonwealth Statistician* (Melbourne: McCarron, Bird, and Co., 1918), 59.
28 James J. Connolly, *The Triumph of Ethnic Progressivism: Urban Political Culture in Boston, 1900–1925* (Cambridge, MA: Harvard University Press, 1998); Philip J. Ethington, *The Public City: The Political Construction of Urban Life in San Francisco, 1850–1900* (New York: Cambridge University Press, 1994).
29 For similar arguments about differences between the United States and Canada, see Seymour Martin Lipset, *Continental Divide: The Values and Institutions of the United States and Canada* (Toronto: C.D. Howe Institute and National Planning Association, 1989).
30 One should note however that McRae, in a footnote to *Founding of New Societies* stated that "hyperloyalism" to the British empire "would appear to be far more deeply if less belligerently felt in the single-fragment societies of Australia and New Zealand" compared to the "dual fragment" society of Canada, which contained not only an English fragment, but a French one as well. Kenneth D. McRae, "The Structure of Canadian History," in Louis Hartz (ed.), *Founding of New Societies: Studies in the History of the United States, Latin America, South Africa, Canada, and Australia* (New York: Harcourt, Brace, & World, 1964), 239. Still, one would wonder if the presence of a French fragment in Canada might not make the English fragment more anxious and more insistent on maintaining a British identity.
31 James Winter, "English Democracy and the Example of Australia," *The Pacific Historical Review* 35, no. 1 (February 1966): 67–81.
32 Laurie Field, *The Forgotten War: Australia and the Boer War* (Carlton, Victoria: Melbourne University Press, 1995), 193–196. Carman Miller, *Painting the Map Red: Canada and the South African War, 1899–1902* (Montreal: Canadian War Museum and McGill-Queen's, 1993).
33 Richard Alba, *Blurring the Color Line: The New Chance for a More Integrated America* (Cambridge, MA: Harvard University Press, 2009), ch. 3.
34 Michael Hogan, *The Sectarian Strand: Religion in Australian History* (Ringwood, Victoria: Penguin, 1987), 204.

Catholic incorporation: 1890 to 1950s   45

35 David Hilliard, "Australia: Towards Secularisation and One Step Back," in Callum G. Brown and Michael Snape (eds), *Secularisation in the Christian World* (Burlington, VA: Ashgate, 2010), 78; Roger Finke and Rodney Stark, *The Churching of America, 1996–2005: Winners and Losers in Our Religious Economy* (New Brunswick, NJ: Rutgers University Press, 2005). There is no direct measure of religious attendance in Canada at the end of the nineteenth century, but Canada in 1946 had the highest rate of religious attendance of all three countries, with two-thirds of the population claiming to have gone to church in the past week; Reginald Bibby, *Fragmented Gods: The Poverty and Potential of Religion in Canada* (Toronto: Irwin, 1987), 17. Census data on churches also seem to show similar seating capacity for the United States and Canada at the turn of the twentieth century; Peter Beyer, "Religious Vitality in Canada: The Complementarity of Religious Market and Secularization Perspectives," *Journal for the Scientific Study of Religion* 36, no. 2 (June 1997): 276; US Census, *Abstract of the Eleventh Census, 1890* (New York: Arno, 1976), 240; Bureau of the Census, *Religious Bodies, 1906, Part I: Summary and General Tables* (Washington, DC: Government Printing Office, 1910), 34.
36 Hogan, *Sectarian Strand*, ch. 4; Ronald Manzer, *Educational Regimes and Anglo-American Democracy* (Toronto: University of Toronto Press, 2003), 40–45, 69–70.
37 Hogan has called the 1922 election in New South Wales "probably the high point of sectarian politics in Australia" (*Sectarian Strand*, 190).
38 Ibid., 194.
39 The Australian literacy rate from the 1921 Census is listed in Dominion of Canada, Dominion Bureau of Statistics, *Illiteracy and School Attendance in Canada: A Study of the Census of 1921 with Supplementary Data* (Ottawa: F.A. Acland, 1926), 30; *Historical Statistics of the United States: Colonial Times to 1970, Part I* (Washington, DC: Bureau of the Census, U.S. Department of Commerce, 1975), 382; *Canada Year Book, 1927–28*, 139.
40 Wray Vamplew (ed.), *Australians: Historical Statistics* (New South Wales: Fairfax, Syme, and Weldon Associates, 1987), 36–37; *Australia Year Book*; *Historical Statistics of the United States*, 10, 383; M.C. Urquhart (ed.), *Historical Statistics of Canada* (Toronto: Macmillan., 1965), 601.
41 In a contrary perspective, Patrick O'Farrell believes that even dispersion was an impediment, weakening Irish Catholic influence, though he admits the possibility of less stigmatization. See *The Irish in Australia: 1788 to the Present* (Notre Dame, IN: Notre Dame University Press, 2000), 116.
42 David R. Roediger, *Working toward Whiteness: How America's Immigrant Became White – The Strange Journey from Ellis Island to the Suburbs* (New York: Basic Books, 2005); Matthew Frye Jacobson, *Whiteness of a Different Color: European Immigrants and the Alchemy of Race* (Cambridge, MA: Harvard University Press, 1998).
43 Christina Wolbrecht and Rodney E. Hero (eds), *The Politics of Democratic Inclusion* (Philadelphia, PA: Temple University Press, 2005).

4 Working with Catholicism in Australia

The Australian Labor Party was founded in 1891, and by 1910 Australia ranked among the most progressive countries in the world in terms of the strength of its labor movement and the development of legislation to ensure social welfare.[1] This is even more startling, given that there were significant Protestant–Catholic tensions during this time. According to an increasingly influential view of the relationship between diversity and political development, Protestant–Catholic diversity should make social democratic welfare outcomes more difficult.[2]

Catholic political representation also advanced, and Catholics remained integral to the Labor Party until the 1950s when Catholic support for the Labor Party was split by a group of Catholics concerned about the influence of communism among unions. This heralded a realignment of Catholic votes away from the left and led to greater competition for Catholic votes. Thus, in the 1960s, when Kennedy became the first Catholic president in the United States and faced some anti-Catholic sentiment, one sees the Australian right making appeals to the Catholic vote by supporting state funding for parochial schools. One survey also found that among the Australian public only about 11 to 12 percent of the population held negative feelings toward Catholics.[3]

A reconstructive labor coalition contributed to the transformation of Catholic standing in Australia. This coalition was reconstructive and not simply a coalition of convenience for several reasons. Catholics were concentrated in the working class, making them organizationally important to the labor movement. The development of compulsory voting ensured that attempts to try to restrict the Catholic influence became impossible. In addition, the lack of severe regional differences as in the United States and Canada meant that the reconstruction of Catholic–Protestant relations could diffuse more effectively throughout the nation. Thus, when issues of class rose in salience as a result of the political opportunity of the Great Depression, Catholics could be turned to as dependable allies. It was at this moment of the crisis of capitalism that Catholic representation dramatically increased, and labor leaders' emphasis that Catholics and Protestants were similar had the greatest success. Faced with an electorally successful reconstructive coalition, opposing parties increased their attempts to appeal to Catholics, solidifying a more general increase in the standing of

Catholics. Successful one-party incorporation into a reconstructive coalition sparked competing parties to adjust their attitudes toward the minority group.

The institutional context of coalition formation: the strength of the labor movement

Compared with the United States and Canada, Australia's union movement was far larger and more encompassing. Compulsory arbitration quickly took hold in Australia. Union membership in Australia increased to a degree not seen before in the United States and Canada. In 1901, only 6.1 percent of employees were members of unions. By 1911, this had increased to 27.9 percent of employees; by 1916, the number of union members comprised nearly half of the Australian workforce.[4] By contrast, the unionization rate was approximately 10 percent in the United States and Canada before the Great Depression. Compulsory arbitration and pattern bargaining in Australia meant that workers outside of unions were often covered under these arbitration agreements. State-sanctioned wage levels covered up to 80 percent of all workers, with minimum wages determined based on cost-of-living analyses by the Commonwealth Statistician.[5]

The development of a relatively large union movement was also correlated with the emergence of a viable labor party. At the federal level, the Australian Labor Party first captured government from 1910 to 1913. The Australian Labor Party received an average of 43 percent of the vote in 16 elections in the early twentieth century, making it one of the most successful labor parties in the world at the time.[6] The electoral threat of Labor helped enact broad welfare state legislation in advance of the United States, such as means-tested old-age pensions and non-means-tested maternity allowances, both adopted by 1912.[7] Although many of these reforms would stall, making Australia look more like the stingy "Anglo-American" welfare state by the 1950s, unionization rates would remain high, helping to tamp down on inequality, and potentially lowering the distance between more well-off Protestants and somewhat poorer Catholics. Castles has called Australia an early manifestation of the "wage earner's welfare state."[8]

Various explanations have been forwarded in accounting for Australia's union development. One scholar has argued that it is primarily because of the relatively quicker closure of the frontier in Australia that explains why there was a more cohesive union movement in Australia.[9] In 1901 the proportion of the Australian population residing in urban areas was 49.4 percent. In comparison, in 1900 approximately 39.6 percent of the United States population resided in urban areas, and has typically been about 7 to 10 percentage points lower than the Australian urban proportion throughout the twentieth century. In Canada in 1901 approximately 37 percent of the population resided in urban areas, and its growth approximately tracks that of the United States.[10]

Australia's agricultural sector was also distinct in that cattle and sheep ranching predominated, leading to larger landowners and the proletarianization of agricultural labor. The sheep-shearing sector was one of the first to experience widespread unionization.[11] Still, this difference can be exaggerated, as agrarian radicalism was high in the United States during the populist movements of the 1880s and 1890s. Canada's agricultural sector in the prairie west was home to some of Canada's most radical parties in the 1920s and a base for the social democratic Cooperative Commonwealth Federation in the 1930s.

Tighter labor markets and higher wages may also explain the more advanced union development in Australia.[12] The distance of Australia from Europe coupled with the "white Australia" policy of the government to prevent extensive immigration from Asia meant that the labor market in Australia was comparatively tighter than in the United States and Canada. Tighter labor markets lead to higher wages, and one scholar has claimed that in the 1870s Australia had the highest per capita income in the world.[13] Commenting on the degree of economic opportunity in Australia, the novelist Henry Kingsley described Australia as a "workingman's paradise."[14] This may have accorded labor greater power to achieve its political goals, though one may wonder why relative prosperity did not make labor more accepting of the status quo, if laborers were already doing well under an unregulated system.[15] Moreover, by the 1890s, Australia's status as a "workingman's paradise" had diminished owing to economic depression.

A more equal income distribution may have had a greater effect on the kind of labor movement that developed, rather than on the overall strength of the labor movement. Reitz has pointed out that immigrants to countries with high economic inequality are typically going to do worse, since immigrants tend to get slotted into the lowest paying positions in the economic structure. A less stratified economy means that immigrants have a better chance of climbing the economic ladder, and that there is likely less of a gap between skilled and unskilled labor.[16] Thus, there may have been less of an opportunity to play off immigrant versus non-immigrant and skilled versus unskilled labor against each other, as in the development of craft unions in the United States.

In addition to these factors, the relative unity of the Australian Catholic population most likely helped in the development of a cohesive, broad union movement. Restriction of immigration from Southern and Eastern Europe helped ensure that the Catholic population in Australia was mostly Irish, and thus there was no easy way to divide the Catholic vote along ethnic lines. As Buckley and Wheelwright have stated, "The task of trade union organizers was much easier in Australia than in the USA, where the problems of uniting workers of many different nationalities, languages, and culture were overwhelming, and immigrants were repeatedly used as strikebreakers."[17] Several analyses of the U.S. labor movement have noted how racial and ethnic diversity undermined labor organizing.[18]

In summary, there were several potential reasons why the labor movement in Australia at the turn of the century was one of the most vigorous in the world. The institutionalization of a particular kind of class order with high levels of unionization, pattern bargaining, and a "wage earner's welfare state" meant that conditions were particularly ripe for a Catholic and labor alliance to lead to gains in Catholic standing, particularly when events like the Great Depression increased the salience of class.

The institutional context for coalition formation: compulsory voting

A further institutional advantage in promoting a reconstructive Catholic–Protestant working-class coalition was the development of compulsory voting, which prevented the tactic of weakening Catholic importance to working-class Protestants by disenfranchising Catholics. Compulsory registration and compulsory voting passed at both the state and the federal level, whereas in the United States and Canada there were no significant movements to expand voter turnout.

Lack of Catholic ethnic diversity as well as the high mobilization of Catholics through Labor may have contributed to the emergence of compulsory voting. Following the Australian Federation in 1901, there was an attempt to establish a common roll for federal elections. This task was entrusted to the police, but became a huge administrative burden. To ease the administrative task, the electoral office recommended that people be given the onus of reporting themselves to the appropriate electoral office. The Fisher Labor government introduced compulsory registration in 1911.[19] With compulsory enrollment established, the move to compulsory voting was made easier. But unlike compulsory registration, it was primarily Nationalist governments introducing compulsory voting. The only time a Labor Party was in power when compulsory voting was passed was Western Australia in 1936.

Queensland was the first province to adopt compulsory voting in 1915. Compulsory voting was introduced by a Nationalist backbencher at the federal level in 1924 with barely any debate.[20] Most of the rest of the states followed in the next five years. The effect of compulsory voting was immediate. In the federal House, participation in the elections between 1917 and 1922 had ranged between 59 and 78 percent. Beginning in 1925, participation increased to over 90 percent. Similar increases occurred when Victoria adopted compulsory voting for its legislative assembly in 1927 (a bump in participation of 30 percentage points); New South Wales in its 1930 elections; and Tasmania with its 1928 electoral act (an increase of over 12 percentage points).[21]

Parties in power face complicated incentives on the expansion of the vote. On the one hand, the party in power has already won under the rules of the status quo. A coalition that is in power may be more receptive to vote expansion if it can target the expansion precisely to those groups that favor it. A party in power, though, also has the option of increasing its probability of victory through vote restriction, by measures such as literacy tests and onerous registration requirements. Vote restriction rather than vote expansion may on average be more palatable for parties of the more well-off because the well-off tend to have more resources to deploy in election contests. For instance, in contemporary U.S. politics, the less educated and those making less money tend to turn out at lower levels than those in higher occupational strata.[22] Compulsory voting would reduce the role of resources in electoral mobilization because there is no longer a need to launch get-out-the-vote efforts. Since middle- and upper-class groups have more resources, they would need very compelling reasons to adopt compulsory voting.

The history of the adoption of compulsory voting in Australia tracks the history of the adoption of proportional voting in Western European countries. As several scholars have noted, where labor parties have had a strong chance of winning government, proportional representation was often adopted by right-leaning coalitions as a means of preserving the influence of the more well-off.[23] If labor parties are extremely well organized and turn out at higher rates than more privileged classes, then there would be an incentive to adopt compulsory voting to drive up the turnout of the privileged classes.

Religion may have helped play some role in the passage of compulsory voting. Relatively ethnically homogeneous Catholics were well organized into the Labor Party and helped account for its electoral success. This high degree of Catholic organization, participation, and voting for Labor fits into preconceived Protestant stereotypes of Catholic automatons following the bidding of their priests and the Pope. Thus, for some militant Protestants, the passage of compulsory registration and voting laws reflected a concerted effort to protect Protestant hegemony. For instance, a 1923 editorial in the *Protestant World* of New South Wales argued that Labor was winning because Protestants weren't turning out to vote at the same rate as Catholics:

> So many lazy and indifferent Protestants neglect their duty. [...] Why is it that Roman Catholics, who number less than 25 percent of the community, wield so much influence and political power? [...] Their masters [...] see to it that their followers are not too tired to go to the ballot box.[24]

Hence, the compulsory vote was seen by some Protestants as a way of maximizing Protestant turnout to equal the Catholic vote. Although the article cited above called only for greater debate among Protestants on forcing citizens to vote, the analysis given in the article suggested that the *Protestant World* was in favor of it. Similar types of arguments were used in the *Watchman* and the Adelaide *Advertiser*.[25] Although militant Protestants were probably not in a majority in Australia, they did have the capacity to shape public opinion, as in earlier campaigns against state aid to parochial schools. Thus one could at least say that lack of Protestant mobilization against the issue made compulsory voting easier to pass.

A brief comparison with the United States helps illustrate the importance of the Catholic–Labor mobilization. In the United States, compulsory registration and voting laws had been contemplated by some who had worried that it was the upper classes and the higher races who didn't vote, as they didn't resort to the "machine politics" through which the thronging masses were organized.[26] Yet in the United States these alternatives were never successful, because there was an easier way to preserve Protestant hegemony: disenfranchise or dilute the vote of fragments of the Catholic population. Since this option was not available in Australia owing to the relative ethnic homogeneity of the Catholic population and Catholics' heavy identification with Labor, the second-best option was to make sure that Protestants continued to participate at the maximum level and hope that the superior numbers of Protestants over Catholics might contribute to policies that were more favorable to Protestants.

Regardless of how one interprets the development of compulsory voting in Australia – whether it was due to Protestant fears of Catholic mobilization or for some other reason – the institutionalization of compulsory voting meant that the power of the Catholic minority in Australia could not be lessened through vote restriction. This institutional development preserved the possibility of the centrality of Catholics to the emerging Labor coalition.

The centrality of Catholics to Labor

Roman Catholics made up a substantial proportion of the Australian Labor Party during this period. Starting from Federation in 1901, politicians with Catholic backgrounds had steadily increased their numbers in the Labor Party, constituting over 40 percent of all Labor parliamentarians from 1931 to 1954 (see Figure 4.1). There is also some evidence that districts where Catholics exceeded their average population percentage were crucial in getting Labor parliamentarians elected.[27]

The organizational importance of Catholics to Labor was accelerated by World War I and the conscription crisis. Catholics largely opposed conscription of Australian men to support the British war effort, partly due to the controversy of British rule over Ireland. The Labor Party adopted the same anti-conscription position. The opposition Nationalist Party supported the British Empire's war effort and took

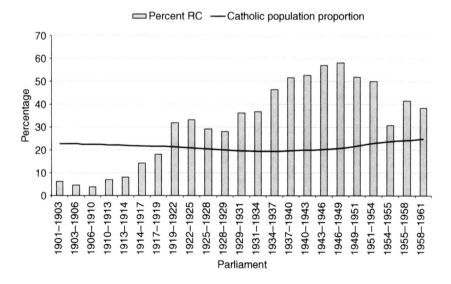

Figure 4.1 Percentage of Catholics among Australian Labor MPs.

Source: Joan Rydon, *A Biographical Register of the Commonwealth Parliament, 1901–72*. Canberra: Australian National University Press, 1975. Those without a religion listed in Rydon are included in the denominator for calculation.

advantage of anti-Catholic sentiment to attract non-Catholic Labor members. As a result, Catholics came to constitute about 18 percent of all Labor Party representatives during World War I, and this trend increased in the 1920s when Catholic Labor MPs constituted between a quarter and one-third of all Labor MPs.

Reconstruction: toward a laborist concept of Catholic autonomy

The labor movement had a significant effect on Catholics, and Catholic–Protestant relations. This class coalition was a natural fit because Catholics were generally economically less well-off than Protestants. A census from New South Wales in the early twentieth century showed evidence of occupational stratification along Catholic and Protestant lines, with Catholics overrepresented in unskilled laborer categories and the unemployed, and underrepresented among employers.[28] In 1933 the Roman Catholic unemployment rate was nearly 3 percentage points higher than that of Anglicans, and 4 to 6 percentage points higher than that of other Protestant denominations. The previous chapter showed how Australian Catholics earned substantially less than the average Australian Protestant. Although one scholar has argued that there was a substantial Catholic middle class and even upper class by the 1930s, there were still strong reasons from an economic standpoint for the average Catholic family to support the Labor Party over more conservative alternatives.[29]

Contact through the union meant that in contrast to the United States and Canada, Australian Catholics and Protestants were building "bridging social capital." The Australian poet and writer Henry Lawson celebrated the way in which the labor movement was bringing Protestants and Roman Catholics together, writing, "They tramp in mateship side by side –/The Protestant and Roman –/They call no biped lord or sir,/And touch their hat to no man!"[30]

Although there was a fit between Catholics and Labor, the relationship was initially ambivalent. The papal encyclical *Rerum Novarum*, delivered in 1891, lent some support to the union movement and labor parties, with Pope Leo XIII stating that it was legitimate to critique the excesses of capitalism. This provided some symbolic centrality of Catholics to the labor movement. *Rerum Novarum*, however, also condemned socialism. Catholic Church leaders were committed anti-communists and sought to position the Catholic Church as between both communism and laissez-faire capitalism. It was only when substantial socialist leadership was removed from the Australian union movement and the Labor Party that Catholics started to move away from their traditional affiliation with Protectionist parties to Labor.[31]

The incorporation of Catholics into the Labor Party affected the identity of the party, as Cardinal Moran's efforts to purge the Labor Party of extreme socialist elements shows. At the same time, the Labor Party had an effect on Catholic identity. The effect was more noticeable among the Catholic laity than among church leaders. Church leaders maintained their distance from the Labor Party. On several occasions the Labor Party's failure to include a plank supporting state aid for Catholic parochial schools motivated Catholic Church leaders to establish independent Catholic parties to try to serve as a crucial swing vote between the Labor and more conservative governments. Catholic Church leaders thought that by withholding complete identification with Labor, two-party competition for the Catholic vote would increase Catholic influence.

Tensions between Catholic Church leaders and Labor never disappeared completely. In 1914 the ALP refused to negotiate with the Catholic Federation on state aid to parochial schools. But instead of suffering an electoral penalty, Labor subsequently increased the number of seats it won in the 1914 election. Following the election, the Labor Party in Victoria banned the Catholic Federation from membership. The following year, Catholics organized the Victorian Catholic Workers' Association to try to transform the Labor Party from within, which was successful in diluting the membership ban on the Catholic Federation, but did little to change the ALP's stance on state aid to education.[32]

Independent Catholic parties ultimately did not prove workable in Australia's single-member electoral system. When presented with the choice between supporting the Labor Party or an independent party, most Catholics sided with the Labor Party. Incorporation into parties and unions gave Catholics other avenues by which to think through the meaning of Catholicism and the Catholic agenda. For example, in defending Labor's lack of support for state funding for parochial schools, James Scullin argued that Labor's overall agenda would benefit Catholics and that splitting with the Labor party would not lead to the conservative parties offering state aid to parochial schools: "Catholic educational claims [...] would undoubtedly divide men and women who are otherwise agreed on economic principles which have been a greater gain to Catholic workers than twenty grants such as is being asked for would be."[33] Scullin affirmed that the labor agenda was simultaneously a class and a religious agenda.

One way in which the labor agenda was simultaneously a religious agenda was in increasing Catholic representation. By the turn of the century, Catholic political candidates were winning elections. Under the Progressive state government in New South Wales in 1901, Catholics counted for one-third of Labor MPs. In reaction to these events, Presbyterian leader Dill Macky urged the formation of the Protestant Defence Association (PDA). The PDA allied with the Free Trade Party under the Reform Party in subsequent elections, and won control of the New South Wales government in 1903, yet lost control in 1907. The *Catholic Press* responded, "The elections will be memorable for the downfall of Orangeism."[34] The success of Labor governments in 1910 in New South Wales and other provinces led to even more Catholic parliamentarians.

Class helped moderate religious cleavages, as may be seen in the timing of increases in Catholic representation. Other kinds of cleavages besides class could still gain great salience at moments of crisis, such as World War I. Roman Catholic representation in Parliament also rose immediately prior to the Great Depression (see Figure 3.3). James Scullin was selected as prime minister in an election in which the major issue was the defense of the industrial arbitration system.[35] Scullin's government did not last long, in part because the crash of Wall Street and the global Great Depression occurred immediately after he took office. Although the United Australia Party was able to capitalize on the misfortunes of the Scullin government during the early part of the Great Depression, the success of Catholic parliamentary candidates began to increase again, starting with the 1934 elections and continuing to increase through the rest of the economic crisis.

Protestant defection from Labor during the conscription crisis set up Catholic overrepresentation, in that Catholics increasingly became the backbone of the Labor Party. As a result, when Labor came to power under Scullin, Curtin, and Chifley, Catholics, who were already overrepresented among Labor members (see Figure 4.1), were also overrepresented nationally.

The increase in the representation of Catholics was not driven by party competition for Catholics. Figure 4.2 shows that over the first half of the twentieth century the trend in the proportion of Catholic MPs that were non-Labor declined. This trend did not reverse itself until about 1963. At times, the Catholic Church in Australia considered whether or not to be too closely allied with one particular party. The data show that increase in Catholic representation was actually compatible with greater membership in one party.

Catholic representation at the state level also demonstrates how the fortunes of the Labor Party contributed to Catholic representation, particularly in considering the difference between the state of Victoria against the other Australian states. Catholic overrepresentation bears some correlation with the success of the federal Labor Party. From 1929 to 1961, the federal Labor Party performed the worst in Victoria, the state where Catholics were least well represented relative to their population proportion (see Table 4.1). In the other states the ALP did better, and Catholic representation tended to be better as well.[36]

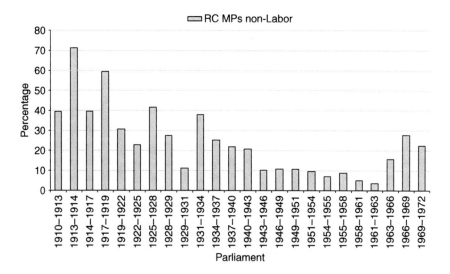

Figure 4.2 Percentage of non-Labor MPs among Catholic MPs.

Source: Joan Rydon, *A Biographical Register of the Commonwealth Parliament, 1901–1972.*

Table 4.1 Australian states and Catholic representation in the House

		NSW	QLD	SA	TAS	VIC	WA
1901–1929	RC MPs (%)	12.5	7.3	7.8	0.0	12.6	25.5
	RC population (%)	24.9	23.8	14.0	17.1	21.6	21.6
	Index of representation	**0.50**	**0.31**	**0.56**	**0.00**	**0.58**	**1.18**
1929–1961	RC MPs (%)	32.8	35.6	22.7	18.3	14.6	22.2
	RC population (%)	23.8	23.3	14.8	16.4	22.0	21.0
	Index of representation	1.38	1.53	1.53	1.12	0.66	1.06
	Percentage of Catholic MPs in ALP (%)	54.5	87.5	26.7	19.2	32.7	35.5
	State's federal Labor MPs (%)	46.3	38.5	47.8	48.1	34.3	40.4
	ALP percentage of vote at state parliamentary level (%)	46.7	45.9	43.3	49.8	39.0	43.5
	ALP percentage of seats at state parliamentary level (%)	49.7	56.8	35.6	51.2	33.3	52.0

Source: Joan Rydon, *A Biographical Register of the Commonwealth Parliament, 1901–1972*; Wray Vamplew (ed.), *Australians, Historical Statistics* (Broadway, NSW: Fairfax, Syme, & Weldon Associates, 1987).

Note
Catholic representation measured at start of each parliamentary session and summed over the two time periods. By-elections not included in the table.

Another way to judge the relative strength of labor among the Australian states is to look at Labor Party control of state governments. Victoria and South Australia experienced relatively low ALP representation. South Australia appears anomalous from this perspective owing to the "playmander," named after Thomas Playford. The infamous malapportionment of districts heavily favored rural over urban districts in state government, allowing the Liberal and Country League to stay in power for three decades despite sometimes losing the overall popular vote.[37] As already discussed, at the federal level the ALP did relatively well in South Australia. Hence, if either labor representation in the federal Parliament or labor control of state governments is used to measure strength of labor in the various Australian states, Victoria consistently has weaker labor representation than the other states, which correlates with weaker Catholic representation.

The difference between Victoria and the other Australian states was not driven by a significantly different distribution of Catholics among electoral districts. Rough estimates of the Catholic population in electoral districts in Victoria indicate that more than 75 percent of the districts in Victoria had Catholic populations of above 14 percent, the rate at which Catholic MPs appear in Victoria from 1929 to 1961 (see Appendix 4).

The state-level data also show the reconstructive effect of labor on Catholic representation in Australia. States with small and large Catholic populations experience gains in Catholic representation. From a power resources perspective, one would expect that Catholic representation would fare better in states where the Catholic population is large. Yet the data in Table 4.1 show that it is not the case that New South Wales and Queensland, both with the highest proportions of the population that are Catholic (around 26 percent from 1933 to 1961, and closer to 30 percent at the turn of the twentieth century) are the only states experiencing Catholic overrepresentation. Catholics were overrepresented to the greatest degree in South Australia, where Catholics constituted only 16.9 percent of the population from 1933 to 1961, the lowest among the six Australian states considered here. In addition, Catholics comprised a significant component of the Victorian population, yet were underrepresented owing to the weakness of Labor there.

The experience of South Australia lends support to the reconstructive interpretation of the Catholic–Labor alliance. It may be argued that the overrepresentation of Catholics in Labor was not particularly reconstructive of Protestant–Catholic relations because the most anti-Catholic Protestants were being driven into the arms of non-Labor parties. However, as may be seen in Appendix 4, it is likely that Catholics did not number more than 15 percent of the population in any South Australian electoral district. This means that a larger proportion of the Protestant population was supporting Catholic candidates in South Australia than in states like New South Wales, where Catholics might constitute a majority of Labor voters in particular electoral districts.

Not only did Labor aid in Catholic representation, but Labor also helped other Catholic interests. Catholic institution building fared well under a laborist

Working with Catholicism in Australia 57

concept of Catholic freedom. There was improvement in the ability of Australian Catholics to send their children to Catholic schools. New South Wales has collected data on the number of Catholic children in public schools versus private schools. By 1905, 58 percent of all Catholic children attending school were attending private schools. This continued to increase until the 1950s, when about 72 percent of all Catholic children attending school were going to parochial institutions, despite minimal state aid to religious schools.[38] There was also improvement throughout Australia. The Census shows that 56 percent of young Catholics were attending private schools in 1921, increasing to 62 percent in 1933.

There is also evidence that parochial schools developed more quickly in Australia than in Canada. The data from Australia can be made comparable to data from Ontario (which is approximately the size of Australia) by recalculating the figure as the proportion of the Catholic population aged five to 19 (see Figure 4.3).[39] When one looks at the rate of increase of enrollment of Catholic students in Catholic schools from 1900 to 1933, one sees that the rate of increase is actually greater in Australia than in Canada, despite the fact that state funding for Catholic primary schools has existed in Ontario as a matter of right since Canadian Confederation in 1871.

The comparison is complicated by the split in Ontario between French- and English-speaking Catholics. This may have prompted English-speaking

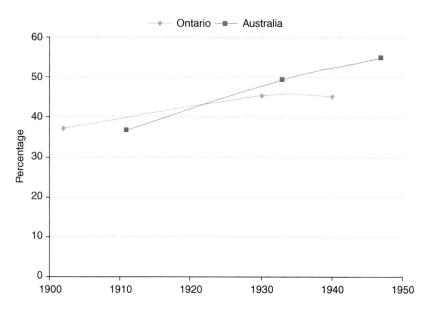

Figure 4.3 Ratio of Catholics in parochial schools to Catholic population, age 5 to 19, select years, in Ontario and Australia.

Sources: Data for Australia from Census, and Wray Vamplew (ed.) *Australians*. Data for Ontario from Ontario Census file and various editions of the *Report of the Minister of Education, Province of Ontario* (n. 39).

Ontarians with a Catholic upbringing to assimilate into a secular or non-Catholic Canadian identity to a greater degree than French-speaking Catholics. Still, although there were differences between English- and French-speaking Catholics in Ontario, there was never any indication that English-speaking Catholics sought to give up their Catholicism. English-speaking Catholic leaders wanted to maintain Catholic schools as much did as French-speaking Catholic leaders. Given this potential complication, at the very least one can say that the "worker's welfare state" in Australia was consistent with an increase in Catholic institution building. It is also likely that the "worker's welfare state" in Australia did at least as well as, if not better than, the Canadian "state aid" model in building up Catholic institutions.

This analysis points to how the class issue and the religious issue can be intertwined. Some of the debate in the literature has tried to segregate the issues. But in fact, supporting Catholic incomes works to support Catholic religious institution building, since individuals with more resources can choose to deploy those resources for whatever purposes they see fit. This analysis supports Scullin's evaluation: economic equality contributed to some forms of religious freedom.

Spurring competition for Catholic votes: state aid to parochial schools

Successful one-party incorporation stimulated competition for Catholic votes. This may be seen as early as in the 1930s, when the United Australia Party chose the Catholic Joseph Lyons to lead the party. Lyons later treasured the Bible upon which he swore the oath of office as prime minister, noting the act of inclusion in having a Roman Catholic prime minister sworn in by a Jewish governor general over a Protestant version of the Bible, namely the King James edition.[40]

John Cramer, who was elected in 1949 in the New South Wales district of Bennelong and was the sole Roman Catholic member of the Liberal Party in the 1950s, noted in his memoir, "I was aware of course that I was something of a freak, as it had seemed in the whole of Australia almost impossible for a Catholic to win preselection for a safe seat in the Liberal Party."[41] During preselection, Cramer was asked whether he owed "allegiance to the Pope or the King." As Cramer notes in his memoir, the chairman "immediately disallowed the question and asked me not to answer it." Cramer answered the question anyway, replying that his Catholicism "had nothing whatever to do with the Liberal Party or with politics," an answer he claimed was greeted with applause.[42]

Catholic integration within the Liberal and Country Parties was only sporadic. In 1966, for instance, the Catholic Phillip Lynch believed that it would be wise to not advertise his religious affiliation when he ran successfully as a Liberal for a seat in Flinders, Victoria.[43] In part, the Liberal and Country Party coalitions did not have to fully integrate Catholics into the party. The split in the Labor Party between the ALP and the DLP over the issue of communism ensured that enough conservative Catholics in the DLP were throwing their second-preference votes to the Liberal–Country coalition.

However, successful Catholic political incorporation did eventually lead to reversals in the Liberal and Country Parties in their support for state aid for denominational schools in 1963. A dual system of denominational and national schools prevailed in the mid-nineteenth century, with two schools boards, one for the denominational schools and one for the national schools. By the 1860s, it was increasingly clear that Catholics were benefiting the most from this situation. One 1867 report in Victoria noted that 55 percent of Catholic children were in denominational schools, while only 38 percent of Anglicans, 33 percent of Methodists, and 20 percent of Presbyterian children were being educated in denominational schools.[44] Politicians like Henry Parkes successfully exploited fears of Catholicism to pass legislation ending state aid to denominational schools and consolidating control over schools in unitary school boards. All political parties and all the major Protestant bodies supported state schools. This development in Australia was not that dissimilar to the United States, where public funding for parochial schools was also limited.

If one were looking at a simple power analysis, one might have expected state aid to occur in the United States rather than in Australia. Tri-faith rhetoric expanded in the United States during World War II, and more religious rhetoric appeared in presidential speeches in the United States during the Cold War period than in comparable Australian governor general speeches.[45] Yet it was in Australia that Robert Menzies, who later helped found the Liberal Party in Australia, broke with long-standing opposition to state aid for religious schools and, in a broadcast address on February 19, 1943, called for such aid in the post-war period as necessary to preserve morality as the basis of civilization. That speech and an additional speech in 1945 were lauded by the Australian *Catholic Weekly*.[46]

If one were looking to secularization or modernization theories to explain state aid in Australia, one might expect to see a society-led drive for state aid. Public opinion polls indicated some transformation of mass opinion after World War II in favor of state aid.[47] Even so, throughout the 1950s most Protestant denominations issued resolutions opposing state aid. The drive for state aid for denominational schools was led by politicians rather than by the churches. In addition, the campaign to extend state aid was orchestrated by the right, seeking to attract Catholic voters. The Labor Party incorporated some planks that could be interpreted as favorable to state aid in 1951, but in 1955 the party advocated against such aid.[48] It was the Liberal Menzies government that started incrementally trying to provide state money to parochial schools, through measures such as tax breaks for education expenses and interest relief for capital construction of non-state schools in Canberra.[49]

The break of the Democratic Labor Party (DLP) from the ALP in 1956 and the opportunity for the right to win the second-preference votes of Catholics contributed to the realignment of the right on the state aid issue. Concerned about communist influence within the trade union movement and the Labor Party, the DLP was formed as an alternative for Catholics. To attract DLP second-preference votes in Australia's instant runoff elections, the Country Party adopted state aid as part of its political platform in the early 1960s, followed by a combined plank on state aid by the Liberal and Country coalition in 1962.[50] The transformation of the Liberal platform followed an extremely close election in 1961, when a Liberal–Country majority was won by a margin of one seat, in Moreton, which was decided by only 110 votes.[51] More generally, the second-preference votes of the DLP helped decide the election for Liberal–Country. Labor responded in 1963 by proposing means-tested scholarships paid to parents for use at either government or non-government schools, while the Liberal Party offered direct assistance to non-government schools.[52]

That political elites led this reconstructive movement is clear from opposition by Protestant Church leaders. At almost every step along the incremental move to full-fledged state aid to denominational schools in the form of grants to support science education, Protestant Church leaders largely opposed the reforms. Some churches supported tax breaks to parents for educational expenses, but majorities in every church opposed direct state aid to church schools. Every general conference or synod of the Church of England, Presbyterians, Methodists, and Baptists in the 1950s passed resolutions opposing state aid. In the late 1950s the Australian Council of the World Council of Churches, a pan-Christian group founded after World War II and somewhat similar to the U.S. Federal Council of Churches, collected opinions from its member churches, and found opinion to be mostly against.[53] Shortly after the passage of full-fledged state aid, the Presbyterian Public Questions Committee surveyed its dioceses in 1964. Of these, 21 Presbyteries were against state aid, five were explicitly for, and ten recommended no action in response to the government's state aid program, being undecided, suggesting alternative courses of protest, or requesting more time to discuss the issue.[54] In 1967 the New South Wales Council of Churches and the Council for the Defence of Government Schools launched a legal suit against state aid based on Section 116 of the Constitution and supported anti-state aid candidates in the election of 1969.

During the 1960s campaign to extend state aid to parochial schools, Menzies framed his support as a way of solving a practical problem. Fears of Soviet advances in science and technology gave impetus to support science education. In addition, Australia's post-World War II immigration boom prompted an increase in the Catholic population, and parochial school budgets were strained. However, Menzies's answer should not be taken at face value. He had already stated during World War II that he supported state aid to church schools because they formed the foundation for morality in society. In addition, state aid was withdrawn in the late nineteenth century partly due to budgetary crises, as it was found that the costs of each denomination having its own schools was higher than having a uniform state school system.[55]

B.A. Santamaria, a strong intellectual influence on the Democratic Labor Party, believed that the play for second-preference votes of the DLP was a key factor in the politician-led drive to provide state aid to church schools.[56] The Roman Catholic Liberal member Cramer saw it in much the same way as Santamaria. As he put it, Menzies believed the independent schools had a good case and he also saw in the issue a very considerable political advantage. [...] There was naturally much sectarian opposition to the matter, and Menzies got himself criticized by anti-Catholic sections of the community. He stuck to his guns, however, and got a good political following for his effort.[57]

The DLP often gave its second-preference votes to the Liberal Party over the following two decades. Although a majority of Catholics continued to vote Labor, the peeling off of some 10 to 15 percent of Catholics to the DLP helped pave the way for rule by the Liberal Party. During the period from 1950 to 1980, the ALP governed for only three years. The experience of the DLP shows how important the coalition between Catholics and Labor was to each side. Catholic overrepresentation disappeared, and Australia's once progressive social welfare states became much less generous.

Conclusion

The fundamental orientation of party politics in Australia around class helped lead to the incorporation of Catholics, and Catholic representation in political office significantly increased in times of great salience of class. In contrast to theories which suggest that the majority and stigmatized minorities would find it difficult to cooperate owing to lack of trust, the Australian case shows that in some circumstances these barriers could be overcome. Catholics embraced a concept of Catholic freedom as laborers' autonomy, which moderated Catholic appeals for measures that may have alienated Protestant voters. Protestants supported Catholics in the Labor Party because Catholics were central to that coalition. Support for Labor was less alienating to Protestants because unionization, where one has a claim to greater benefits as a result of work, are not as stigmatizing as other redistributive measures such as means-tested welfare, where the claim to benefits is not tied to work. Successful one-party incorporation helped pave the way for opposition parties to become reconstructive as well.

The next chapter focuses on the United States, where class development was delayed compared to Australia. Class consciousness was also not as encompassing, with labor and unions faring particularly poorly in the South. As a result, the reconstruction of Catholic–Protestant relations both within and across parties was not as thoroughgoing.

Notes

1 Francis G. Castles, *Working Class and Welfare: Reflections on the Political Development of the Welfare State in Australia and New Zealand, 1890–1980* (Sydney; London: Allen & Unwin, 1985), 12–17.
2 See, e.g., Rodney E. Hero and Caroline J. Tolbert, "A Racial/Ethnic Diversity Interpretation of Politics and Policy in the States of the U.S.," *American Journal of Political Science* 40, no. 3 (August 1996): 851–871; Robert C. Lieberman, *Shifting the Color Line: Race and the American Welfare State* (Cambridge, MA: Harvard

University Press, 1999), 235–250; Alberto Alesina, Reza Baqir, and William Easterly, "Public Goods and Ethnic Divisions," *Quarterly Journal of Economics* 114 (November 1999): 1243–1284; Alberto Alesina and Edward L. Glaeser, *Fighting Poverty in the US and Europe: A World of Difference* (New York: Oxford University Press, 2004).
3 Hans Mol, *Religion in Australia: A Sociological Investigation* (Melbourne: Thomas Nelson, 1971), 69.
4 Kenneth F. Walker, "Australia," in Walter Galenson (ed.), *Comparative Labor Movements* (New York: Russell and Russell, 1968), 185.
5 Alastair Grieg, Frank Lewins, and Kevin White, *Inequality in Australia* (Port Melbourne: Cambridge University Press, 2002), 192; Castles, *Working Class and Welfare*, 14.
6 Castles, *Working Class and Welfare*, 21.
7 Ibid., 16, 22.
8 Ibid., 103. The main weak point of the system was that one needed to secure employment first and that full employment conditions had to be maintained.
9 A.H. Birch, *Federalism, Finance, and Social Legislation in Canada, Australia, and the United States* (Oxford: Clarendon Press, 1955), 205.
10 Australian figures from Wray Vamplew (ed.), *Australians: Historical Statistics* (Broadway, New South Wales, Australia: Fairfax, Syme, and Weldon Associates, 1987), 40. U.S. figures from www.census.gov/population/censusdata/table-4.pdf; note differing definitions of urban in the U.S. Census. Canadian figures from www12.statcan.ca/english/census06/analysis/popdwell/Subprov1.cfm. One should also note that despite the similarity of urban proportions in Canada and the United States, the labor movement in Canada, in terms of union membership, exceeded that of the United States in the post-World War II period, so it is likely that other factors besides number of freeholders and yeoman farmers play a role in trade union development.
11 Mark Hearn, *One Big Union: A History of the Australian Workers Union, 1886–1994* (New York: Cambridge University Press, 1996), 4–6, 23–40.
12 Verity Burgmann, "Capital and Labour," in A. Curthoys and A. Markus (eds), *Who Are Our Enemies? Racism and the Working Class in Australia* (Neutral Bay, Australia: Hale and Iremonger, 1978).
13 Archer notes that up until the depression of the 1890s, "Australia was the most prosperous country in the world." Robin Archer, *Why Is There No Labor Party in the United States* (Princeton, NJ: Princeton University Press, 2007), 24–27. See also Francis G. Castles, *Australian Public Policy and Economic Vulnerability: A Comparative and Historical Perspective* (Sydney: Allen & Unwin, 1988).
14 Lewins and White, *Inequality in Australia*, 169.
15 Foner has noted that one of the popular explanations of why there hasn't been socialism in the United States is that United States workers were more prosperous than European workers. He notes, however, that the evidence in support of this contention is weak. Eric Foner, "Why Is There No Socialism in the United States?" *History Workshop Journal* 17 (spring 1984): 57–80.
16 Jeffrey G. Reitz, *Warmth of the Welcome: The Social Causes of Economic Success for Immigrants in Different Nations and Cities* (Boulder, CO: Westview Press, 1998), ch. 5.
17 Ken Buckley and Ted Wheelwright, *No Paradise for Workers: Capitalism and the Common People in Australia, 1788–1914* (Melbourne: Oxford University Press, 1988), 153.
18 Gwendolyn Mink, *Old Labor and New Immigrants in American Political Development: Union, Party, And State, 1875–1920* (Ithaca, NY: Cornell University Press, 1986); Lizabeth Cohen, *Making a New Deal: Industrial Workers in Chicago, 1919–1939* (New York: Cambridge University Press, 1991).
19 John Hirst, *Australia's Democracy: A Short History* (Crows Nest, NSW: Allen & Unwin, 2002), 321–323.

20 Ibid., 323–324.
21 See appropriate editions of the *Year Book Australia*.
22 Steven J. Rosenstone and John Mark Hansen, *Mobilization, Participation, and Democracy in America* (New York: Macmillan, 1993), 46–49.
23 For an argument that proportional representation was adopted by the right to contain left-wing power, see Carles Boix, "Setting the Rules of the Game: The Choice of Electoral Systems in Advanced Democracies," *American Political Science Review* 93, no. 3 (1999): 609–624.
24 *Protestant World*, February 15, 1923, 3.
25 "Political Machines," *Watchman*, June 26, 1919, 4; R.A. Withers, "Will It Speak," *Watchman*, December 11, 1919, 4; "Saturday's Duty," *Watchman*, March 23, 1922, 4.; "The Machine Curse," *Watchman*, September 1, 1921; "Political Machines," *Watchman*, June 26, 1919, 4; "The Church and Labor," *Watchman*, January 26, 1922, 4; Will Sky-Line, "State Rolls," *Watchman*, April 23, 1925, 3; "Flying Shots," *Watchman*, June 11, 1925, 1, 4; "Australia and Empire: A Loyalist's Fears," *Advertiser* (Adelaide, SA), April 17, 1930.
26 Alexander Keyssar, *The Right to Vote: The Contested History of Democracy in the United States* (New York: Basic Books, 2000), 128; Ward E.Y. Elliott, *The Rise of Guardian Democracy; the Supreme Court's Role in Voting Rights Disputes, 1845–1969* (Cambridge, MA: Harvard University Press, 1974), ch. 4.
27 R.N. Spann, "The Catholic Vote in Australia," in Henry Mayer (ed.), *Catholics and the Free Society* (Melbourne: F.W. Cheshire, 1961), 119, n. 16, citing Cecelia Hamilton, "Irish Catholics of New South Wales and the Labor Party, 1890–1910," *Historical Studies* 8, no. 31 (November 1958): 265.
28 Richard Broome, *Treasure in Earthen Vessels: Protestant Christianity in New South Wales Society, 1900–1914* (St. Lucia, Queensland: University of Queensland, 1980), xiii.
29 See Judith Brett, *Australian Liberals and the Moral Middle Class: From Alfred Deakin to John Howard* (New York: Cambridge University Press, 2003), ch. 3.
30 Robin Archer, *Why Is There No Labor Party in the United States?* (Princeton, NJ: Princeton University Press, 2007), 202.
31 Patrick Ford, *Cardinal Moran and the ALP: A Study in the Encounter between Moran and Socialism, 1890–1907 – Its Effects Upon the Australian Labor Party: The Foundation of Catholic Social Thought and Action in Modern Australia* (New York: Cambridge University Press, 1966), 222.
32 Hogan, *Sectarian Strand*, 184; Patrick O'Farrell, *The Catholic Church and Community: An Australian History* (Kensington: New South Wales University, 1985), 211.
33 Patrick O'Farrell (ed.), *Documents in Australian Catholic History, Volume II: 1884–1968* (Melbourne: Geoffrey Chapman, 1969), 240.
34 Ford, *Cardinal Moran and the ALP*, 277.
35 Andrew Frazer, "Parliament and the Industrial Power," in Geoffrey Lindell and R.L. Bennett (eds), *Parliament: The Vision in Hindsight* (Annandale, NSW: Federation, 2001), 123.
36 The proportion of Catholics in the Queensland Labor Party may seem extreme, but at least one newspaper article noted that in 1937, looking at the state's Parliament, 27 out of 43 members of the ALP were Catholic, or nearly 63 percent. "Protestant Labor Party Formed," *Townsville Daily Bulletin* (Queensland), December 9, 1937, 7, Trove online newspaper collection.
37 Wilfrid Prest, Kerrie Round, and Carol S. Fort, *Wakefield Companion to South Australian History* (Kent Town, South Australia: Wakefield, 2001), 57.
38 See appropriate editions of the *New South Wales Statistical Register*.
39 This is presentist, in that not all children aged five to 19 years old would be expected to be in school at this time, yet it is necessary to allow comparisons between Australia

and Ontario, given the age categories available in the Census. It is likely that for many students, primary school was deemed enough education, and high school unnecessary. This explains why these percentages give lower estimates for the number of Catholic children enrolled in Catholic schools than what may be calculated from the Australian statistical registers and censuses, which simply list the numbers of Catholics in parochial schools and public schools. Data for Australia from Census, and Wray Vamplew (ed.), *Australians, Historical Statistics* Data for Ontario from Ontario Census file, available at the United Kingdom Data Archive, and various editions of the *Report of the Minister of Education, Province of Ontario* (Toronto: Legislative Assembly of Ontario).

40 Dame Enid Lyons, *Among the Carrion Crows* (Adelaide: Rigby, 1972), image opposite 81.
41 John Cramer, *Pioneers, Politics and People: A Political Memoir* (Sydney: Allen & Unwin, 1989), 102.
42 Ibid., 101.
43 Richard Yallop, "Catholics Cross the Floor," *The Australian*, September 27, 2002, 11.
44 Hogan, *Sectarian Strand*, 92.
45 More detailed analysis of this is given in Chapters 9 and 10 (this volume).
46 "Menzies Sees Threat to Church Schools, Advocates State Aid," *Catholic Weekly*, February 25, 1943, 1, 5; "Religion in Education Upheld," *Catholic Weekly*, August 2, 1945, 1. Menzies also made a statement deploring sectarian strife at this time. See "Sectarian Strife Denounced," *Sydney Morning Herald*, July 4, 1942, 8.
47 Michael Hogan, "The Catholic Campaign for State Aid to Non-state Schools in NSW and ACT" (Ph.D. dissertation, University of Sydney, 1977), 91.
48 Ibid., 95–98; Ian R. Wilkinson, Brian J. Caldwell, R.J.W. Selleck, Jessica Harris, and Pam Dettman, *A History of State Aid to Non-government Schools in Australia* (Department of Education, Science and Training, Commonwealth of Australia, 2007), 32. See also Ronald Fogarty, *Catholic Education in Australia, 1806–1950*, vol. 2 (Melbourne: Melbourne University Press, 1959), 465 on a vote in 1950 that nearly made a plank of outright endorsement of state aid in the ALP.
49 Hogan, "The Catholic Campaign," 110–115.
50 Ibid., 120–122.
51 That result in Moreton was partially decided on the second-preference votes of Communist Party voters going to the Liberal Party, rather than to the Catholic candidate in Moreton. Ross Fitzgerald, *The Pope's Battalions: Santamaria, Catholicism, and the Labor Split* (St. Lucia, Queensland: University of Queensland Press, 2003), 188.
52 Wilkinson et al., *A History of State Aid*, 31–32.
53 Havery L. Perkins, "State Aid to Denominational Schools," Report to the Australian Council of Churches, 1961, 4–6, MS 7645, Box 69, National Library of Australia. "Official Pronouncements of the Churches in Australia Regarding State Aid," Special Committee's Report to the 1961 Sydney Diocesan Synod, MS 7645, Box 69, National Library of Australia.
54 *Minutes of the Proceedings of the General Assembly of the Presbyterian Church of Australia* (Sydney, September 1964), Thirtieth Session. See *Public Questions Committee Report*, starting on 189.
55 Fogarty, *Catholic Education in Australia*, ch. 6.
56 B.A. Santamaria, *"State Aid" in Perspective* (Melbourne: Hawthorn Press, 1966), 2–3.
57 Cramer, *Pioneers, Politics and People*, 136.

5 Catholicism at arm's length in the United States

Less than a week before the 1884 presidential election pitting James Blaine against Grover Cleveland, the Reverend Samuel D. Burchard remarked at a pro-Republican gathering of Protestant ministers that the Democrats were the party of "rum, Romanism, and rebellion," associating Catholics with immorality and treason. Democrats and Catholics pounced on the statement as confirmation of the religious bias of the Republican Party. Blaine, who had a Catholic mother, rejected the statement a few days before the election, stating, "I should esteem myself of all men the most degraded if […] I could […] make a disrespectful allusion to that ancient faith in which my revered mother lived and died."[1] Despite Blaine's damage control, Burchard's remark was interpreted by some observers at the time as costing the Republicans and Blaine the presidential election.[2] Catholics had increased in the electorate, and they were already winning office at the local level, which led many Republicans to tone down anti-Catholic rhetoric that had been much more common from the end of the Civil War up until 1884. In the pivotal state of New York, where Catholics probably comprised close to 20 percent of the population, Blaine lost to Cleveland by fewer than 1,200 votes. If those votes had swung the other way, Blaine would have received New York's 36 electoral votes and won the election. Although it is now impossible to assess whether that single remark really won Cleveland the election, the fact that some Republicans believed that it did most likely reinforced the weight the Catholic vote already had in Republican minds.[3]

For the next 70 years the national political parties, recognizing the potential power of the Catholic vote, trod lightly around the subject of anti-Catholicism in the face of recurrent waves of nativist sentiment and suspicion. Particularly up until the 1930s the two parties competed for Catholics, but Catholic–Protestant relations were not significantly reconstructed. Even after the 1930s, when Catholics were part of the electorally successful New Deal coalition, anti-Catholicism continued to exist, though typically expressed by movements outside the parties. Why, given dramatic examples of the influence of Catholics to particular elections in the United States, was Catholic standing not as deeply transformed?

Two-party competition in some circumstances can lead to the parties attempting to outbid each other for support of Catholics. One sees this dynamic at work in the Australian case, when the opposition United Australia Party appointed a

Catholic leader in 1931, or when Liberal leader Menzies started to support state aid to religious schools in the 1940s. Two-party competition for Catholic votes in the United States did not lead to as transformative changes in Catholic standing because the reconstructive element in those coalitions were not as strong. Two institutional factors contributed to the weakness of this reconstructive coalition. First, the labor movement was not as developed in the United States compared with Australia. A stronger labor movement would have more effectively united Protestants with Catholics on the left. Second, the South was committed to supporting a Jim Crow racial order and state-level autonomy. As a result, class issues had a lower chance of reconstructing Catholic–Protestant relations at a national level.

This chapter starts by examining the national parties' attempts to deal with anti-Catholic sentiment from around 1890 to 1960, showing stalemate on the issue up until the 1930s and then mixed progress afterwards. This section reinforces the finding in Chapter 3's look at descriptive representation that Catholic political incorporation was stalled relative to Australia. The section also confirms the theoretical prediction from Chapter 2 that two-party competition for Catholic votes does not necessarily transform Catholic standing if that competition is not based on reconstructive coalitions.

The importance of reconstructive coalitions in ideologically binding Catholics and Protestants under a broader class identity is demonstrated in the middle section of this chapter by an in-depth look at liberal Protestants in the social gospel movement and in the New Deal coalition working with Catholics on class issues. Just as in Australia, the Great Depression's renewed focus on class helped Catholics in the United States gain political representation owing to Catholic centrality to the labor movement. Yet the institutional factors cited above (weakness of the labor movement, southern regional differences) made this process of reconstruction less thoroughgoing, as will be showm in the final section of this chapter. The Democratic Party acted more like a brokerage and catchall party rather than like a reconstructive party. It failed to successfully bring its constituent members under the umbrella of a new overarching identity, partly because of prior commitments to identities and institutions.

The parties and Catholicism

Although Catholics had existed in the United States from colonial times, Catholic immigration increased substantially following the Civil War, causing the Catholic population to quadruple from three million in 1860 to 12 million in 1900 and leaving the parties in a quandary about how to approach this now substantial voting bloc. At the beginning of this Catholic population explosion, from 1868 to 1880, anti-Catholicism had picked up where it had left off from the Know Nothing movement in the 1850s. Republicans pushed the issue, in many cases leading to state amendments barring the use of government funds for sectarian schools.[4] After the Burchard gaffe in 1884, however, Republicans began to less explicitly endorse anti-Catholicism, realizing that heavy immigration was making the United States more diverse. In 1892, for instance, the Republican National Committee selected a Catholic, Thomas H. Carter, as its chairman, and included in its platform support for Irish nationalism, support for people of all faiths, and a carefully worded statement recognizing the contributions of private schools but not suggesting that any public money would ever be directed to such private schools.[5]

Republican commitment to this strategy was tested during the economic depression from 1893 to 1897. The recession fueled nativist suspicion of Catholics and foreigners, and contributed to the growth of the American Protective Association (APA), which reached an estimated membership of over half a million.[6] Close competition between the national parties meant conflicted responses to the rise of anti-Catholic nativism. The Republican Party refused to include a plank critical of the APA in 1894. Attempts by the APA to get a provision in the Republican convention confirming prohibition of state support for sectarian schools failed.[7]

William McKinley, a rising star in the Republican Party, had refused support of the APA in his state political career.[8] In his run for the Ohio governorship in 1891, McKinley sought to include both new and old immigrants in his coalition, arguing that his policy centerpiece, the protective tariff, could minimize job competition and mute ethnic and religious conflict.[9] As governor, McKinley appointed Catholics to prominent public positions; obtained the support of Catholics such as Archbishop Ireland of St. Paul; and criticized the nativist faction of the Republican Party led by Joseph Foraker.[10]

In his run for the presidency, McKinley continued to court Catholic voters. During the 1896 presidential campaign a Jewish rabbi led the prayers to open the Republican national convention, which one scholar has interpreted as a signal to voters that the party was not solely committed to maintaining Protestant hegemony.[11] Other acts of symbolic religious inclusion were advanced on foreign policy issues rather than domestic issues that would affect constituents more readily. The Republican platform included support for Irish home rule and the end of the persecution of Jews in Russia.[12] McKinley's open courtship of Catholics led the APA to forgo endorsing him, though the APA continued to support the Republican Party.[13] Across the border in Canada, the *Sentinel*, an anti-Catholic publication, judged that the Republican party was as beholden to Catholics as were the Democrats.[14]

Democrats tried to portray Republicans as anti-Catholic and associated the gold standard with a "British policy," perhaps to sway Irish Catholics against the Republicans.[15] However, the Democrats suffered from their own image problems. Bryan's support of immigration restriction and his heavy emphasis on evangelical Protestantism may have turned some Catholics off from his candidacy.[16]

Republican hegemony from 1896 to 1932 was most likely aided by doing better with a fragment of Catholic voters.[17] Since many Catholics were concentrated in urban areas, Republican tariff and monetary policies privileging urban over rural interests would have appealed to them. A study of the relationship between the size of the Catholic population in a county and that county's Democratic presidential vote shows a correlation from 1876 to 1892. However, from 1900 to 1928 this correlation weakens, which could mean greater success in Republicans attracting Catholic votes, although in terms of absolute numbers most Catholics continued to support the Democratic Party.[18] At the very least, Republican presidents believed that their support from Catholics had increased. In recognition of what he believed to be his increased share of the Catholic vote, McKinley appointed as his attorney general Joseph McKenna – the first Catholic cabinet member in 50 years.[19] Theodore Roosevelt believed that he received "a greater proportion of the Americans of Irish birth or parentage and of the Catholic religion than any previous republican candidate," and Taft expressed similar sentiments.[20]

The rise of the Ku Klux Klan (KKK) in the 1910s and 1920s provided another test of the response of the parties to anti-Catholicism. As the KKK grew larger in the 1920s, reaching a membership of perhaps three million, anti-Catholicism became a much more prominent theme in the organization, especially because in many of the Midwestern states in which the KKK flourished the African American population was small and Catholics were considered a greater threat.[21] Both of the national parties were hesitant in dealing with this renewed anti-Catholicism. The response both for and against the KKK at the state level was much stronger than the response at the federal level.[22]

The inability of the parties to address the Ku Klux Klan was evident at the party's national conventions in 1924. The June 1924 Republican convention featured a plank to condemn the Klan by name, but the plank never had enough support to come to a vote. As a presidential candidate, Calvin Coolidge also never condemned the organization.[23] A similar plank was introduced at the 1924 Democratic convention.[24] The three leading Democratic presidential candidates staked out differing positions on the Klan. William G. McAdoo, a lawyer from Los Angeles and treasury secretary during Woodrow Wilson's presidency, did not denounce the Ku Klux Klan, and was actively supported by Klan members.[25] Al Smith, the Catholic governor from New York, supported the plank. Thomas Walsh, a senator from Montana, waffled, stating, "I would vote for a very strong straight religious freedom plank, and think we should adopt one, but would not name the Ku Klux Klan."[26] The religious liberty plank failed by one vote at the Democratic convention. The breakdown of the state delegate votes is highly correlated with the size of the Catholic population of the states (see Table 5.1).[27]

Significant Catholic support for Republicans led Democrats to believe that if they nominated a Catholic they could use symbolic politics to mobilize more of those voters to return to the Democratic Party. In 1924 the Democrats nearly nominated either Walsh or Smith, both Catholics, but the convention reached deadlock because Walsh supported Prohibition and Smith did not. Eventually John W. Davis emerged as a compromise candidate. The Catholic John J. Raskob was selected as chair of the Democratic National Committee.

After Smith's nomination in 1928, significant anti-Catholicism surfaced. Articles in magazines and publications that were critical of potential Catholic

Table 5.1 Delegate votes on religious liberty plank at 1924 Democratic convention

Catholic proportion of home state of Democratic delegation	Yes	No	Not voting	Percentage voting against
Below 10 percent Catholic	57	254.5	7.5	79.8
Between 10 and 20 percent Catholic	191	210	1	52.2
Over 20 percent Catholic	271.5	66.5	2	19.6

Source: Richard C. Bain, *Convention Decisions and Voting Records* (Washington, DC: Brookings Institution, 1960).

influence on Smith included the *Atlantic Monthly*, the *New Republic*, *Current History*, and the *Christian Century*.[28] J. Thomas Heflin, a Democratic senator from Alabama, opposed Smith's nomination and spread rumors that the Pope was inciting Mexico and Nicaragua into war against the United States.[29] Even some supporters of Smith seemed to accept Smith not because he was inherently a good candidate, but as the lesser of two evils. As Mississippi governor Theodore Bilbo put it, he "would swallow the Pope and the whole dern Vatican than vote for Herbert Hoover and negro supremacy in the South."[30]

Republicans at the highest levels continued to be careful not to invoke anti-Catholicism. Presidential candidate Herbert Hoover did not make mention of Smith's religion.[31] When Willie W. Caldwell, a Republican committeewoman in Virginia, distributed a letter stating that the United States needed to be saved from "being Romanized and rum-ridden" – almost identical to Burchard's statement in 1884 – the Republican Party denounced the letter.[32] Yet at the lower levels of the party, the party did not rein in anti-Catholicism. As one scholar has put it, "The party organization neither disciplined those who pandered to religious bigotry nor attempted to police their activities."[33] Smith ended up losing many Southern states that had previously voted Democratic.

Because both national parties did not want to seem either too pro-Catholic or too anti-Catholic up until 1928, attempts to "contain" Catholicism often succeeded only when the religious motivation was submerged and arguments invoking other categories of ascription were highlighted. The literacy test for immigration passed in 1917, for instance, emphasizing language over religion. The Johnson–Reed Act limiting immigration established quotas based on country of origin, privileging countries who had sent immigrants to the United States prior to the great wave of immigrants from Southern and Eastern Europe at the end of the nineteenth century. Immigration restriction was not primarily couched in terms of limiting Catholics, but in terms of limiting particular national "racial" groups such as Italians and Southern and Eastern Europeans that were seen as inferior.

There were also efforts to restrict voting, largely through the imposition of more literacy tests. The period between approximately the 1890s and the 1920s is the most productive and sustained in terms of the enactment of literacy requirements for the vote, with ten states outside the South passing such laws.[34] The legislative debates concerning literacy requirements often did not explicitly mention religious considerations. In debating a literacy requirement in New York's constitutional convention in 1915, for example, the main sponsor of the amendment pointed specifically to the problem of Southern and Eastern European races.[35] Although Catholic power would be indirectly affected, passing the bill required focusing on other kinds of stigmatized categories.

In the 1930s and 1940s, with the success of the Democratic Party and Catholic participation in World War II, Catholics increased their representation in office. However, significant anti-Catholic sentiments continued to exist. In the 1940s and 1950s several bills considered federal aid to parochial schools, which led to a public debate between Eleanor Roosevelt and Cardinal Spellman over the merits.[36] Attempts to provide federal funding to schools failed. In 1948, 1949, and 1950 there were several bills that left it up to states to decide whether to allocate funding for the auxiliary expenses of parochial schools. These bills were defeated in committee in the House.[37]

The complicated mixture of both pro- and anti-Catholic sentiment among potentially Democratic constituencies influenced Democratic electoral strategy. In the 1950s Theodore Sorenson penned the Bailey Memorandum, which argued that a Democratic Catholic presidential candidate would be aided by his Catholicism rather than hindered. Sorenson argued that Al Smith brought immigrant voters into the ranks of Democrats, and Kennedy could do something similar with Catholic voters in critical states.[38] Sorenson believed that though Kennedy would lose votes among Protestants, many of whom were in the South, these would likely not be enough to affect the electoral votes that Democrats would win in the South, because racial order would continue to deliver much of the South to the Democrats. Meanwhile, the mobilization of Catholics in the Northeast and Midwest could potentially win Democrats electoral votes in crucial swing states.

Recent scholarship has shown that the Republican candidate, Richard Nixon, did not want to explicitly associate himself with anti-Catholicism, though he did want to take advantage of anti-Catholic sentiment against Kennedy. A Gallup poll taken in 1959, for instance, showed that 28 percent of respondents indicated that they would not vote for a "well-qualified" Catholic presidential candidate.[39] Nixon relied on proxies to attempt to organize Protestant hostility toward Kennedy's Catholicism.[40]

True to Bailey's prediction, Kennedy did win the electoral votes of crucial swing states while holding on to much of the South. Kennedy did nearly lose Texas, however. Had Kennedy lost Texas he would have lost the election, which shows that the strategy outlined in the "Bailey Memorandum" was not a foolproof strategy and that anti-Catholic sentiment could come close to providing the margin to tip the election in Nixon's favor.

To sum up: up until the 1930s the national parties largely avoided the issue of Catholicism, and even when Democrats won office with the Great Depression, significant changes in Catholic standing did not filter through the entire Democratic coalition, leading to continuing questions about Catholicism up until Kennedy's election. What explains the parties' inability to reconstruct Catholic–Protestant relations in the United States to enhance Catholic standing, even though Catholics constituted a sizable proportion of the population and both of the national parties competed for their votes? Part of the answer has to do with the way in which class issues were not as salient in the United States compared with Australia.

Class and the reconstruction of religion

Before delving into the institutional limits of a class-based reconstructive coalition, it is important to show the potential of class to reconfigure Catholic–Protestant relations in various parts of the United States, if not to the same degree as in Australia. Today, it is generally recognized that denominational differences have declined and that the liberal versus conservative cleavage across all denominations plays a more significant role.[41] One stream that contributed to this goes back to the early twentieth century. Concern for the working class prompted some Protestants to reconsider religious toleration, join interfaith efforts to combat social problems, and sometimes institutionalize a public culture of antidiscrimination and pluralism.

The ability of class issues to reconstruct Protestant–Catholic relations and merge the two religions into a common identity was evident at the beginning of the social gospel movement. Washington Gladden, one of the intellectual forebears of the movement, wrote "The Christian League of Connecticut," a fictionalized account of how churches in that state decide to put aside their sectarian differences and work toward Christianizing society. When one character in the story asks if the movement should include Roman Catholics, a supporter of the movement notes, "Any church that makes its teachings conform to the Apostles' Creed is orthodox enough for me."[42] The fictionalized account became the most popular story Gladden ever penned. Despite supporting public schools and being worried about the potential for Catholics in office to abuse their position in certain municipal governments where Catholics constituted a large part of the population, Gladden defended Catholics during the rise of the APA in the 1890s and the Ku Klux Klan in the 1910s, calling Pope Leo XIII "the most enlightened and the most progressive pontiff who has ever occupied that throne" and specifically citing his position on "the social question" as manifesting "a large intelligence and quick human sympathy." Gladden also cited a need for all conservative forces to unite against "the greed" of the nation's "spoilers."[43]

Other figures in the social gospel movement also defended Catholics. Lyman Abbott criticized the APA.[44] Richard T. Ely, despite not supporting state aid to religious schools, argued that Protestants could learn from Roman Catholics. Claiming that fully Christianizing America required an ethic of self-renunciation and a spirit of self-sacrifice, Ely noted that "The Roman Catholic Church provides opportunities for self-renunciation the most complete." Protestants, Ely advised, should build up orders of "deaconesses, brotherhoods, sisterhoods, and associations of lay worshipers" to channel appropriately the spirit of self-sacrifice.[45] Those in the Anglican/Episcopalian tradition, which emphasizes church ritual to a greater degree than other Protestant denominations, also found commonality with Catholics. Vida Scudder, for instance, believed that Protestantism was too individualist, and that the more social nature of Catholicism could aid social gospel efforts.[46]

As is evident from Gladden's story, many social gospelers de-emphasized doctrinal differences because of their emphasis on social reforms to help the poor and disadvantaged. The emphasis on "factory acts, educational laws, laws for the establishment of parks and of playgrounds for children, laws securing honest administration of justice, laws rendering the courts accessible to the poor as well as the rich" could form an overlapping consensus for Christians of all stripes.[47] Many, though by no means not all, social gospelers were proponents of liberal theology, accepting of modern scholarship that questioned the infallibility of the Bible as God's revealed truth, and accepting the use of science, method, and human reason to solve social problems. The de-emphasis on doctrinal differences meant that Protestants could downplay differences among Protestant denominations. It was only a small leap to apply this to Protestant–Catholic and Protestant–Jewish differences as well.

Interfaith movements had both stronger and weaker versions. The stronger form envisioned a universal religion; the weaker versions called for coexistence and cooperation. On a spectrum of reconstruction of Catholic–Protestant relations the interfaith movement did not promise total reconstruction, but at least greater acceptance and realization of common goals. To the extent that left-wing social gospelers were seeking allies in the fight to create the kingdom of heaven on earth, Catholics were organizationally central: they tended to be overrepresented in the working class and made up a substantial part of the union movement.[48] In addition, the labor movement tended to be supported by the Catholic Church. Papal encyclicals, while condemning communism, also approved of unions and wages that supported working-class families. The church hierarchy supported the establishment of Catholic labor schools and the nurturing of Catholic labor priests.[49]

Earlier ecumenical movements, such as the Evangelical Alliance of Protestants, achieved unity in part through opposition to Catholics; yet by the turn of the century some Protestants began to reach out. The leading organization in the Protestant ecumenical movement was the Federal Council of Churches (FCC). The commitment of the FCC to greater toleration is reflected in its early history. The conference held in 1905 to establish the FCC included an anti-Catholic statement. By 1908 that statement had been removed.[50]

Stronger evidence for the FCC's commitment to religious toleration and cooperation emerged in the 1920s, after the mobilization of World War I had shown how each of the three church traditions – Protestant, Catholic, and Jewish – were willing to support mobilization for the war and social welfare efforts for when the troops returned home. When the Ku Klux Klan revived its activities in the 1920s, the FCC formed the Goodwill Committee to oppose the Klan.[51] The Goodwill movement featured numerous events in which representatives of the Protestant, Catholic, and Jewish faiths traveled together on goodwill trips.[52] The FCC also opposed the questioning of Al Smith's Catholicism during his presidential run in 1928.

Although Pius XI warned against interfaith efforts in his encyclical *Mortalium Animus* in 1928 and though some Catholic bishops barred Catholics from participation in interfaith congresses, other Catholic organizations expressed sympathy, including the Calvert Association, the Knights of Columbus, the National Catholic Welfare Conference, and the liberal Catholic journal *Commonweal*.[53] Initially there were some concerns that the Protestant Goodwill movement was a way to improve the Protestant image to make it easier to convert non-Protestants.[54] To make the interfaith organizations less explicitly Protestant, the National Council of Christians and Jews was established in 1928, which included members from the three Judeo-Christian religions. Members of the group from each of the three faiths regularly proclaimed that they were not interested in seeking converts.[55]

Publications of the NCCJ make clear its left-leaning social gospel orientation. A pamphlet by the NCCJ noted that "on the basis of our common religious principles" both Catholics and Protestants "can work for decent social and living conditions, for racial justice, for the checking of juvenile delinquency, and for the building of a better world order based on fair treatment of all men and nations."[56] Another work sponsored by the NCCJ noted that Protestants, Catholics, and Jews were agreed on social insurance, rights of unions and collective bargaining, living wages, broad participation in management of work and industry, international economic cooperation, promotion of cooperatives, and opposition to racism. The president of the NCCJ, Everett Clinchy, noted that these commonalities were the result not of contingency and convenience, but because

> from their faith in God is derived their estimate of man and their conception of the divine purpose for mankind. Out of these basic convictions stem all their ideals for society. [...] Cooperation on the part of the three faiths in social education and action is not only permissible; it is imperatively necessary.[57]

Leaders of the Democratic Party eagerly advanced this tri-faith rhetoric. In his presidential election campaign in 1932, Franklin Delano Roosevelt argued that the "ideal of social justice" he advocated was "accepted by the moral leadership of all the great religious groups of the country [...] Protestant, Catholic, and Jewish," and he quoted passages from the Federal Council of Churches, papal encyclicals, and the chairman of the Social Justice Commission of the Central Conference of American Rabbis.[58]

In 1934, the NCCJ helped launch two more initiatives to institutionalize the interfaith movement. The first was the Religious News Service, which provided religious news about the three faiths. The second effort was the formation of Brotherhood Day, which provided another opportunity to deploy tri-faith rhetoric. Again, Roosevelt was an eager participant in solemnizing Brotherhood Day, calling it "an experiment in understanding" and a "venture in neighborliness."[59] Roosevelt's "Good Neighbor" speech was followed by the organization of the Good Neighbor League. On the Sunday before Labor Day in 1936, the

League arranged for religious leaders of the major faiths (including John Ryan, a leader in the Catholic social justice tradition) to speak in praise of the economic policies of Roosevelt's first term. The League also widely distributed the pamphlet "The Social Ideals of the Churches and the Social Program of the Government," which claimed that the government had practically instantiated the churches' common stance on economics.[60]

"Trialogues" featuring representatives of the three religions became such a familiar event that in 1939 alone it was estimated that there were over 10,000 such events conducted in 2,000 communities across the United States. A review conducted in 1941 also estimated that there were 200 local roundtables of the NCCJ in large cities, and over 2,000 more less formal affiliates in smaller areas.[61]

The Temple of Religion at the 1939 New York's World Fair perfectly symbolized the hegemony of the tri-faith rhetoric being deployed by the NCCJ and the Democratic Party. Representatives of Catholicism, Protestantism, and Judaism helped raise $300,000 for the austere, cylindrical structure to be used by all faiths to discuss all things spiritual.[62] Tri-faith rhetoric and the Judeo-Christian idea gained even more momentum during World War II. The dramatic example of chaplains of each faith who decided to go down with the troop ship *Dorchester* captured the way in which the three religions were being seen as quintessentially American.[63] In the movies, Catholics were being portrayed in a more positive light.[64]

Efforts to build a culture of pluralism continued in the 1940s, especially in antidiscrimination efforts linking religious discrimination with racial discrimination. The NCCJ supported various educational efforts on racial equality.[65] In the February 1942 celebration of National Brotherhood Week, the NCCJ emphasized beliefs held in common by Protestants, Catholics, and Jews, including belief in a republican form of government and rejection of theories of race.[66] The rejection of theories of race is significant because the belief that inferior races tended to follow inferior religions had historically been one stream of anti-Catholicism. Catholic Interracial Councils supported civil rights legislation and Monsignor Francis J. Hass chaired the federal Fair Employment Practice Committee (FEPC) during World War II.[67] The Ives–Quinn antidiscrimination bill in New York passed in 1945, with all Democrats supporting the bill.[68]

Similar FEPC bills passed in New Jersey (1945), Massachusetts (1946), Connecticut (1947), Rhode Island (1949), and Pennsylvania (1955). One scholar has found a mild statistical relation between size of Catholic population and passage of state-level fair employment legislation.[69] The state fair employment bills were sometimes framed as not just helping blacks, but also religious minorities. In Pennsylvania, the Governor's Committee on Industrial Race Relations issued a report in February 1953 noting "significant discrimination against Jews" and "bias against Italians, Catholics, and other religious groups." In addition, Governor Fine noted on one of the earlier versions of the fair employment bills that "we need to strike a body blow against communist agitators who make a big issue about job discrimination in America." This framing would attract

Catholics, since the Vatican was particularly vehement about opposing communism.[70] This is not to minimize significant opposition to racial integration by people of faith outside the South when the black civil rights struggle gained more momentum there. However, there should at least be some recognition that liberal Christians and Jews outside the South were making some halting steps toward dismantling an exclusivist white Protestantism and creating a public norm of a culture of equality.[71]

One should not overestimate the reach of the FCC, the NCCJ, and ecumenicism. Even after the war, liberal Protestant publications questioned the fitness between Catholicism and democracy, including a prominent multipart series in the *Christian Century*.[72] Class issues did not eliminate tensions between Catholics and Protestants, and in many cases differences emerged among denominations on fundamental class issues. The Catholic Church hierarchy's antipathy of anticommunism often lent Catholic working-class politics a conservative cast, particularly after the end of World War II, when the threat of communism increased in salience, and the Catholic Church was pivotal in leading to the expulsion of the most left-leaning unions in the CIO.[73] Zeitz has argued that the New Deal coalition of Jews and Catholics in New York City was breaking up prior to the 1960s partially as a result of differences over communism and labor.[74]

What is important is not so much Protestant and Catholic unanimity on a labor agenda, but that class issues contributed to splits within both denominations such that liberal Protestants and liberal Catholics could find themselves in agreement. Splits between conservatives and liberals within the Catholic Church often aided liberal Protestants' evaluation of the potential of alliances with liberal Catholics. John Coleman Bennett, one of the co-founders of the journal *Christianity and Crisis*, approved of liberal Catholic journals like *Commonweal* and *America*, and celebrated the contributions of radical Catholics such as Dorothy Day. *Christianity and Crisis* outgrew its own suspicions of Catholics and in the 1950s published articles by such liberal Catholics as Gustave Weigel and Daniel Callahan, as well as thinkers from other faiths who supported greater acceptance of Catholics, including Will Herberg. One writer went so far as to suggest that Protestants should accept the Pope as a spiritual leader.[75] *Christianity and Crisis* also notably refused to engage in debate about whether John Kennedy's Catholicism posed a question for his ability to be president, and Bennett became one of the first well-known Protestants to support using public funds for Catholic parochial schools.[76]

In summary, then, a detailed look at the development of the social gospel and interfaith efforts in the United States shows that class had the potential to reconfigure religious relations in the United States as it did in Australia. Because the official Catholic hierarchy often frowned upon ecumenical efforts, unions and parties were particularly important in uniting Catholics and Protestants on a common action agenda. The difference between Australia and the United States emerges partly because class was not as strong a basis for political action. By 1929 in Australia, there had been a long association between Catholics and the Labor Party and a much stronger union movement. By contrast, the United

States lacked a labor party and the union movement was far weaker. This helps explain the discrepancy between the reception of Scullin versus the reception of Smith, in 1929 and 1928 respectively. The relative lack of salience of class meant that Catholics often ended up splitting their votes. In the early twentieth century, two-party competition for Catholic votes did not have to appeal to Catholics *qua* Catholics. Instead, differences among Catholics could be used to mobilize support for Catholics for the Republican Party.

Only when economic catastrophe struck and the class issue gained in salience did Catholic representation in the United States significantly improve. Catholics moved strongly back to the Democratic Party with the Great Depression, highlighting the importance of the economic dimension to Catholic voters. Splits among Catholics mattered less because of the economic crisis and social changes. As may be seen in Figure 3.4, by the 1940s Catholics had achieved representation in the House relatively proportional to their actual population proportion. The boost to the Democratic Party's political fortunes as a result of the Great Depression simultaneously elevated Catholic political fortunes. But even after 1932, Catholic–Protestant relations would be less transformed relative to Australia because the nature of the Democratic coalition in the United States differed from the nature of the Labor coalition in Australia.

The institutional limits of religious reconstruction

While Gallup polls showed a greater willingness by the public to vote for Catholic presidential candidates from the 1930s to the 1960s, anti-Catholic attitudes remained vigorous in the white South. Data from American National Election Studies (ANES) show that churchgoing Protestants in the South tended to give lower "feeling thermometer" scores to Catholics up until the 1970s (see Table 5.2).[77] Southerners were also distinctive in their willingness to vote for Kennedy in 1960.[78] This constitutes one of the puzzles of understanding Catholic–Protestant relations in the United States. Why were white Southerners in the 1960s so anti-Catholic, given that both Southerners and Catholics were nominally allied together in the Democratic Oarty?

Reconstruction of Catholic–Protestant relations did not proceed as thoroughly because the Democratic coalition more closely resembled a coalition of convenience rather than a reconstructive coalition, stemming from the lack of a strong

Table 5.2 Feeling thermometer means towards Catholics, by region, 1964–1968

	Regular churchgoing Protestants	All Protestants	All non-Catholics
Northeast	65.1	64.7	63.8
North Central	63.8	63.4	63.3
West	60.8	59.1	59.2
South	57	57.6	57.6

Source: ANES.

labor identity in the South. In 1964, for instance, the 11 Southern states in the Confederacy on average had about 15 percent of the non-agricultural workforce unionized, compared to 29 percent for all states.[79] The weak development of the labor movement in the South and the failure of Operation Dixie to unionize the South in 1946 were related to the distinctive racial order that had developed in that region, in which concerns about preserving white hegemony trumped concerns over issues like class.

The relative weakness of the labor movement and weakness of identification with class in the white South led to less of concern with the social gospel and with national ecumenical efforts. As three scholars of Southern religion have put it, "Until recent times, the South has not hosted many major events or produced ecumenical leadership to give it much eminence in the chronicles of the ecumenical movement in North America." The Southern Baptist and Southern Presbyterian denominations rejected joining the Federal Council of Churches in 1908 because of the organization's concern with the economic problems associated with industrialization. Southern Presbyterians joined the ecumenical effort only in the mid-twentieth century, when the FCC became the National Council of Churches, while Southern Baptists continued to stand apart.[80] To the extent that the social gospel mattered to white Southern religionists, they were more likely to focus on questions of temperance rather than on economic order.

This did not mean that the white South was always anti-Catholic. More often than not, concerns about racial order conditioned responses to Catholicism in the South, and religious reconstruction followed a different path. Sectional animosity could hinder anti-Catholicism, as during the Civil War, when the South began looking toward Catholic countries, including France, Spain, and Mexico, as potential allies against the North. When racial order was secured again in the South with the establishment of Jim Crow, anti-Catholic movements had a freer hand to express themselves because the South did not need Catholic allies, nor would the passage of anti-Catholic policies threaten to undermine practices associated with preserving Southern racial order.

Historian Eugene Genovese called the South in the early nineteenth century "the least anti-Semitic and anti-Catholic region of the United States, as a long list of Jews and Catholics certified. [...] Convent burning disgraced the cities of the Northeast, not those of the South."[81] As the Know Nothing movement gained momentum in the 1850s, Southern states participated, despite the fact that Catholic immigration was concentrated in the Northern states. Yet even during the height of the Know Nothing movement, sectional interests often trumped Southern interests in constructing a national Protestant institutional order. Discussion of Catholicism was often connected to discussion of its relation to slavery. The Catholic Church could appear threatening, being identified with universalism and miscegenation, particularly because the Catholic Church held sway over so much of Latin America, where whites were severely outnumbered.[82] At the same time Southerners often found Catholicism a useful ally in the fight to justify slavery.[83] In search of philosophies to justify hierarchy and inequality, some Southerners looked to the Catholic Church for inspiration, seeing the Middle Ages as a golden age against the democratic and liberal excesses embodied in the North.[84] Many Northerners saw inherent connections between Catholicism and slavery as well. Some antislavery proponents blamed Roger Taney's Catholicism for his decision in *Dred Scott* to bar federal regulation of slavery in the territories.[85] Antislavery proponents also attempted to link the hierarchical organization of Catholicism with the hierarchical relationship in slavery.[86] These ideologies increased the symbolic centrality of Catholicism to protection of racial order.

Concerns about protecting slavery affected not only Catholics but also other religious minorities. Early attempts to limit polygamy in the Utah territory failed in 1854, 1856, and 1860, with most Southern political elites voting against such regulation. Southern politicians worried that if federal action were justified for regulating polygamy, then federal action might also be justified for regulating concubinage with slaves in the South.[87] Southerners also potentially feared that anti-Catholicism might serve as a basis for hostility toward other Protestant minority sects, many of which were found in the South. As Alexander Stephens of Georgia put it, "If we discriminate to-day against Mormons, to-morrow, perhaps, we shall be asked to discriminate against Baptists, Methodists, Presbyterians, or Catholics."[88] In the failed 1860 vote on banning polygamy, Southern representatives were equally split on the issue, but of the 60 votes against the bill 34 were Southerners, with representatives from the Deep South much more likely to vote against the bill than border states.[89] The bill failed to reach a vote in the Senate, and a similar bill, the Morrill Act, passed in 1862 only after secession and the Civil War had reduced Southern representation in the federal legislature. Two decades later, southern representatives also largely opposed the Edmunds Act in 1882, which made polygamy a felony and revoked the right of polygamists to vote and serve on juries.[90]

The eventual splits in the Know Nothing movement along sectional and slavery divisions confirmed that nativism could not be the primary cleavage in politics. Although the Know Nothing party platform called for a continuation of the status quo on the question of slavery, the 1856 elections indicated that more voters were willing to vote for Republicans or Democrats on the slavery issue than for the Know Nothings on the nativism issue.

When the Civil War broke out, both the North and the South became more inclusive of minorities in seeking support for their causes. With the Emancipation Proclamation, Lincoln gradually moved toward expanding the Republican coalition to include African Americans. The South also became more inclusive, but toward religious minorities.[91] The Confederate government was the first in American history to include a tri-faith cabinet. While Lincoln's inaugural cabinet included Episcopalians, Presbyterians, a Quaker, and a Unitarian, Jefferson Davis's cabinet included Presbyterians, Methodists, an Episcopalian, a Baptist, a Roman Catholic, and a Jew. Catholic Stephen Mallory, of Florida, was appointed secretary of the Navy, while the Jewish Southerner Judah Benjamin held positions as the Confederate attorney general, secretary of war, and secretary of state. Three of Davis's cabinet were also foreign-born, and the Confederate constitution, unlike the U.S. Constitution, signaled its religious inclusiveness by including a reference to God.[92] As a marker of the controversial nature of the appointments, some abolitionists derided them as confirmation that the Confederacy was driven by a conspiratorial Roman Catholic and Jewish plot.[93]

Southern Catholics were among the primary participants in the war. Catholic father Abram Ryan became a regionally admired poet and chaplain in the Confederate Army, as well as a friend of the family of Jefferson Davis.[94] Pierre Gustave Toutant Beauregard, the Southern general who fired on Fort Sumter in 1861, was a Catholic.[95] The Confederate government's openness to Catholics was at least partly motivated by efforts to acquire the aid of Catholic powers France, Spain, and Mexico.[96]

After the end of the war, the Republican Party revived the anti-Catholic themes of the Know Nothing movement. In 1867 Congress voted to stop funding a diplomatic mission in the Vatican. In Ohio, after the Geghan Law passed in 1874 allowing prisoners to see Catholic priests, a Republican administration oversaw the law's repeal. In 1875 Ulysses Grant stated in a public speech that no public money should go to sectarian schools, and warned that if "we are to have another contest in the near future for our national existence, the dividing-line will not be the Mason and Dixon's, but between patriotism and intelligence on one side and superstition, ambition, and ignorance on the other."[97] The 1876 and 1880 Republican platforms subsequently included support for passage of the Blaine Amendment, a constitutional amendment calling for prohibition of any public funds to support parochial schools.[98]

There were many factors that would have made the white South receptive to anti-Catholicism. In response to reconstruction, religious defenses of the South became more prominent.[99] The small proportion of Catholics in the South also made exclusive Protestantism a latent possibility. The South's embrace of race could lend support to exclusivist religion, because proper religious identity could be seen as a manifestation of ethnoracial identity. However, the interests of white Southern political elites continued to rub up against attempts to construct a national Protestant moral majority. In the House a weak version of the Blaine Amendment passed 180 in favor, seven against, 98 abstaining.[100] A stronger Senate version failed to achieve the two-thirds vote needed to send the amendment for ratification to the states: 28 senators voted for, 16 against, and 27 abstained, largely along partisan lines.[101] The only Southern senators to support the amendment were Republicans. During debate Southerners complained that it would increase federal authority over education issues.[102]

After the failure to pass a federal constitutional amendment, momentum shifted to altering state constitutions to include the Blaine Amendments. The vast majority of these were passed after reconstruction ended, from 1875 to as late as 1959. Militant Protestants also demanded that new territories admitted as states to the union adopt Blaine-style amendments in their state constitutions.[103]

As late as the 1890s, Southerners continued to be unenthusiastic about anti-Catholicism. The American Protective Association in the 1890s did not attract much Southern support, with Southerners viewing it as an attempt by the Republican Party to gain more power. Worse, the APA sought support among

African Americans, further fueling Southern suspicion of the movement.[104] As the twentieth century neared, Congress gradually reduced the amount of funding it granted Catholic missions to operate contract Indian schools. Those who did not support contracting out Indian education to Catholic groups were overwhelmingly Northern, with only three Southern Congressmen joining the list of 57 Congressmen the APA would later call the "roll of honor."[105]

The decline in the saliency of sectional divisions between North and South after the end of reconstruction opened up the possibility of a renewed political anti-Catholicism in the South, as Catholicism became less central to protecting a well-entrenched racial order. With the abdication of Northern responsibility for reconstruction, and with the establishment of Jim Crow, the "shadow" of sectional controversy over the future declined. By the 1890s the South had weathered attempts by liberal Republicans to impose any sort of racial equality in the South. By the turn of the century, the South had also weathered populist agrarian attempts to transform its economic system. Hence, white Southerners could be more confident of their place in the national system. As Jim Crow became more stable, Southerners became increasingly more nativist and anti-Catholic. The shift is notable in the political leader Tom Watson. Initially envisioning a coalition of lower class blacks and whites to overturn the economic system, the failure of economic populism led Watson to embrace a more religiously based populism that was more anti-Catholic and white supremacist in tone.[106]

In the early twentieth century, the South became a hotbed of anti-Catholicism. As one *Nation* article put it in 1920, anti-Catholicism "stands second only to the hatred of the Negro as the moving passion of entire Southern communities."[107] Anti-Catholicism was embraced by Thomas E. Kilby in his successful gubernatorial run in Alabama, and led to a convent inspection law. Kilby also instituted Bible reading in schools.[108] True Americans gained control of local government in Birmingham, Alabama in 1920 and got rid of Catholic municipal employees apart from two policemen.[109] Tom Watson, editor of the anti-Catholic *Watson's Jeffersonian Magazine*, helped orchestrate the Veazey Act in Georgia in 1916 that allowed for convent inspection, which was not repealed until 1966.[110] During his 1920 campaign to become senator of Georgia, Watson also opposed the League of Nations as a Papist conspiracy and also spread rumors that President Wilson was being controlled by the Pope.[111] In Florida, three Catholic sisters were arrested in 1916 for violating a 1913 law that prohibited whites from teaching blacks in white schools.[112] The surprise election of Sidney Catts in the gubernatorial election in Florida in 1916 as a member of the Prohibitionist Party led to a convent inspection law in 1917 that was only repealed in 1935.[113] The South was also becoming much more anti-immigrant, at a time when immigration from Southern and Eastern Europe was predominant. In a literacy bill of 1912, 16 out of 17 Southern senators and 68 out of 73 Southern representatives voted for the measure. Just 14 years earlier, 15 out of 18 Southern senators had voted against a literacy bill.[114]

The relationship between racial order and religious order is apparent in the voting patterns of Southern states for Al Smith and John F. Kennedy. Several Southern states – Tennessee, Florida, North Carolina, Texas, and Virginia – voted

Catholicism at arm's length in the U.S. 81

for Hoover in 1928. Political scientist V.O. Key has noted that where blacks comprised a higher proportion of the population, Southerners were more likely to vote for Al Smith. Where blacks were not as high a proportion of the population, more white Southerners voted for the Republican candidate in 1928.[115] Hence, where blacks presented the most threat to whites, Southerners tended to stay with the Democratic Party and vote for the Catholic Smith. Where blacks did not present as large a threat, Southerners were freer to express their anti-Catholicism with a vote for Hoover.[116]

Similar patterns are found in the Kennedy election. As with the 1928 election there is a relationship between size of black population and vote for Kennedy in the South. States in the South with over 20 percent of the population black went 53 to 45 percent for Kennedy (Louisiana and Mississippi are excluded from the analysis because a substantial proportion of voters in those two states went for independents, and in Mississippi the Independent Democratic candidate actually won). Southern states with a black population of under 20 percent actually broke for Nixon: 51 to 48 percent (see Table 5.3). Bryce Harlow, who served in a

Table 5.3 Black population and vote for president, southern states, 1960

	Black 1960 (%)	Vote Republican (%)	Vote Democratic (%)
West Virginia	4.8	47.3	52.7
Oklahoma	6.6	59	41
Kentucky	7.1	53.6	46.4
Texas	12.4	48.5	50.5
Tennessee	16.5	52.9	45.8
Maryland	16.7	46.4	53.6
Florida	17.8	51.5	48.5
Average of southern states with black population under 20 percent		**51.3**	**48.4**
Virginia	20.6	52.4	47
Arkansas	21.8	43.1	50.2
North Carolina	24.5	47.9	52.1
Georgia	28.5	37.4	62.5
Alabama	30.0	41.7	56.8
South Carolina	34.8	48.8	51.2
Average of southern states with black population above 20 percent		**45.2**	**53.3**
Louisiana*	31.9	28.6	50.4
Mississippi*	42.0	24.7	36.3

Source: *Statistical Abstract of the United States*, 1961; Alice V. McGillivray, Richard M. Scammon, and Rhodes Cook, *America at the Polls 1960–2000: John F. Kennedy to George W. Bush – A Handbook of American Presidential Election Statistics* (Washington, DC: CQ Press, 2001).

Note
* Louisiana and Mississippi are excluded from summation because these states voted for independent states of electors as well.

variety of positions in the Eisenhower administration, attributed Nixon's defeat to "a maldistribution of bigots."[117]

The cross-cutting issue of race delayed attempts to extend funding to parochial schools. Southern opposition to federal education bills was based primarily on race, especially following the Brown decision in 1954. Even when there wasn't "poison pill" Powell Amendments stipulating that schools had to be classified as desegregated before they could be eligible for federal aid for schools, influential committee chairs blocked parochial school funding, evident in the bills from 1946 to 1954, and in the bills John F. Kennedy attempted to pass. Some federal aid to parochial schools came only with the Elementary and Secondary Education Act in 1965, which included a compromise to allow aid for lower income students in Catholic parochial schools. The compromise pushed forward only when there was a large concurrent Democratic majority in Congress that minimized the influence of Southern Democrats on the party and simultaneously pushed through reform in race.

Conclusion

The Australian case showed how an ideologically coherent national coalition centering around labor could pull differing regions into alignment with each other. Australian states that had not elected many Catholic representatives in proportion to the Catholic population percentage eventually started to do so by the 1930s. The United States experienced much more diverse regional development because of prior Southern commitments to states' rights and protection of racial order. The discourse of anti-Catholicism in national elite political tactics could diverge from the discourse of anti-Catholicism at the regional and local levels. Southern interests in protecting racial order shaped the South's attitude toward Catholics, despite the fact that Catholics only constituted negligible proportions of the Southern population. By the 1910s, Catholics were not central to protecting racial order in the South. One scholar has argued that once racial order began to be challenged in the South again during the civil rights movement, Southerners began to look for allies in their support for segregation and became more open to Catholics.[118]

The next chapter considers a case in which Catholics constituted a much larger proportion of the population. There it is also found that the degree of centrality of Catholics to particular coalitions and institutional factors made reconstructive coalitions harder and help explain why transformations in Catholic standing did not proceed to the same degree as in Australia and the United States. In the United States, regional order made white Southerners less willing to reconstruct Catholic–Protestant relations along class lines; in Canada, regional order made French Catholics less willing to reconstruct Catholic–Protestant relations along class lines.

Notes

1 Mark Wahlgren Summers, *Rum, Romanism, and Rebellion: The Making of a President, 1884* (Chapel Hill: University of North Carolina Press, 2000), 285.
2 Arthur Pue Gorman, a Maryland Democrat involved in the Cleveland campaign, noted, "If anything will elect Cleveland these words will do it. The advantages are now with us" (Summers, *Rum, Romanism, and Rebellion*, 283). Referring to Burchard, one Republican Party operative stated, "The election was all safe [...] until that miserable, pusillanimous, canting, hypocritical, double-dyed traitor [...] made his speech" (Summers, *Rum, Romanism, and Rebellion*, 285). Blaine: "I should have carried New York by 10,000 if the weather had been clear on election day and Mr. Burchard had been doing missionary work in Asia Minor or Cochin China" (William B. Prendergast, *The Catholic Voter in American Politics* (Washington, DC: Georgetown University Press, 1999), 77).
3 David G. Farrelly, "'Rum, Romanism and Rebellion' Resurrected," *The Western Political Quarterly* 8, no. 2 (June 1955): 262–270.
4 Prendergast, *The Catholic Voter in American Politics*, 73–75.
5 Ibid., 72, 79.
6 John Higham, *Strangers in the Land: Patterns of American Nativism* (New York: Atheneum, 1967), 68, 80–81.
7 Prendergast, *The Catholic Voter in American Politics*, 82, 84.
8 Lew Daly, "In Search of the Common Good," *Boston Review*, May/June 2007. On Ohio APA and McKinley's refusal to concede to their demands, see Daniel Tichenor, *Dividing Lines: The Politics of Immigration Control in America* (Princeton, NJ: Princeton University Press, 2002), 74.
9 Gwendolyn Mink, *Old Labor and New Immigrants in American Political Development: Union, Party, and State, 1875–1920* (Ithaca, NY: Cornell University Press, 1990), 137.
10 Quentin R. Skrabec, Jr., *William McKinley, Apostle of Protectionism* (New York: Algora, 2008), 146. Kevin Phillips, *William McKinley* (New York: Times Books, 2003), 79.
11 Tichenor, *Dividing Lines*, 75.
12 Mink, *Old Labor and New Immigrants in American Political Development*, 137.
13 Skrabec, *William McKinley, Apostle of Protectionism*, 147; Phillips, *William McKinley*, 79.
14 *Sentinel* (Toronto), December 29, 1892, 1.
15 Skrabec, *William McKinley, Apostle of Protectionism*, 139; Prendergast, *The Catholic Voter in American Politics*, 78.
16 Skrabec, *William McKinley, Apostle of Protectionism*, 139.
17 Kevin Phillips estimates that up to 45 percent of Catholics voted for McKinley (*William McKinley*, 79). Tichenor notes that McKinley did well among all immigrant groups apart from Irish Catholics (Tichenor, *Dividing Lines*, 75). Mink argues that new immigrants sided with the Republican Party while unionists tended to side with the Democratic Party in the election of 1896 (Mink, *Old Labor and New Immigrants in American Political Development*, 35, 117).
18 Paul Kleppner, *Continuity and Change in Electoral Politics, 1893–1928* (New York: Greenwood Press, 1987), 220–222.
19 Prendergast, *The Catholic Voter in American Politics*, 90.
20 Ibid., 88. Further evidence of the Republican Party's successful appeal to religious minorities in urban areas is the fact that many Jewish representatives in Congress prior to the New Deal were Republican. See Kurt F. Stone, *The Jews of Capitol Hill: A Compendium of Jewish Congressional Members* (Lanham, MD: Scarecrow Press, 2011), 632–634.
21 Higham, *Strangers in the Land*, 292, 297.

22 When Peter Tague, a representative from Massachusetts, and David Walsh, a senator from Massachusetts, pressed the Republican Harding administration to act against Klan activity, the attorney general claimed that it was a state matter not a federal one. David M. Chalmers, *Hooded Americanism: The First Century of the Ku Klux Klan, 1865–1965* (Garden City, NY: Doubleday, 1965), 198.
23 Chalmers, *Hooded Americanism*, 214.
24 The plank read:

> We condemn political secret societies of all kinds as opposed to the exercise of free government and contrary to the spirit of the Constitution of the United States. We pledge the Democratic Party to oppose any effort on the part of the Ku Klux Klan or any organization to interfere with the religious liberty or political freedom of any citizen, or to limit the civic rights of any citizen or body of citizens because of religion, birthplace, or racial origin.

25 Rory McVeigh, "Power Devaluation, the Ku Klux Klan, and the Democratic National Convention of 1924," *Sociological Forum* 16, no. 1 (March 2001): 5.
26 Thomas J. Carty, *A Catholic in the White House? Religion, Politics, and John F. Kennedy's Presidential Campaign* (New York: Palgrave Macmillan, 2004), 24.
27 Votes of the delegates from Richard C. Bain, *Convention Decisions and Voting Records* (Washington, DC: Brookings Institution, 1960), Appendix D.
28 Carty, *A Catholic in the White House?*, 29, 33.
29 Ibid., 30.
30 Ibid.
31 Ibid., 29.
32 Ibid., 32.
33 Prendergast, *The Catholic Voter in American Politics*, 110.
34 See Alexander Keyssar, *The Right to Vote: The Contested History of Democracy in the United States* (New York: Basic Books, 2000); Cybelle Fox, *Three Worlds of Relief: Race, Immigration and the American Welfare State from the Progressive Era to the New Deal* (Princeton, NJ: Princeton University Press, 2013), 34–35.
35 The sponsor noted that the new immigrants were valuable, but that their culture posed a threat to US institutions. *Revised Record of the Constitutional Convention of the State of New York*, April 6 to September 10, 1915, Vol. III (Albany, NY: JB Lyon Company, Printers, 1916), 3012.
36 See Carty, *A Catholic in the White House?*, 69.
37 Diane Ravitch, *The Troubled Crusade: American Education, 1945–1980* (New York: Basic Books, 1983), ch. 1.
38 Carty, *A Catholic in the White House?*, 44.
39 Shaun A. Casey, *The Making of a Catholic President: Kennedy vs. Nixon 1960* (New York: Oxford University Press, 2009), 24.
40 Ibid., chs 4 and 5.
41 Robert Wuthnow, *Restructuring of American Religion: Society and Faith Since World War II* (Princeton, NJ: Princeton University Press, 1988).
42 Washington Gladden, "The Christian League of Connecticut," in Robert T. Handy (ed.), *The Social Gospel in America 1870–1920* (New York: Oxford University Press, 1966), 75.
43 Washington Gladden, "The Anti-Catholic Crusade," *Century Illustrated Magazine* XLVII, no. 5 (March 1894): 789; "The Mischief of the A.P.A.," *Century Illustrated Magazine* LII, no. 1 (May 1896): 156.
44 "Catholics and the Schools," *New York Times*, October 15, 1894.
45 "The Social Law of Service," in Handy (ed.), *The Social Gospel in America 1870–1920*, 234.
46 Gary Dorrien, *The Making of American Liberal Theology: Idealism, Realism, and Modernity, 1900–1950* (Louisville: Westminster John Knox, 2003), 137. Other

social gospelers remained suspicious of Catholics. Walter Rauschenbaush, for instance, continued to critique the Catholic Church for its opposition to liberalism and democracy. More conservative social gospelers focused on moral vices such as liquor, an issue that increased alienation with many Catholics, since Catholics tended to be against prohibition. Dorrien, *The Making of American Liberal Theology*, 6, 136, 525–526; Walter Rauschenbusch, *Christianity and the Social Crisis* (New York: Macmillan, 1908), 320; James Morone, *Hellfire Nation: The Politics of Sin in American History* (New Haven, CT: Yale University Press, 2004), 338, 340.

47 Handy, *The Social Gospel in America*, 249.
48 On Catholics constituting the largest group in the union movement and being overrepresented among union leaders, see Seymour Martin Lipset and Gary Marks, *It Didn't Happen Here: Why Socialism Failed in the United States* (New York: Norton, 2001), 149.
49 Steve Rosswurm, "The Catholic Church and the Left-led Unions: Labor Priests, Labor Schools, and the ACTU," in Steve Rosswurm (ed.), *The CIO's Left-led Unions* (New Brunswick, NJ: Rutgers University Press, 1992), 121–124.
50 Eric Kaufmann, *The Rise and Fall of Anglo-America* (Cambridge, MA: Harvard University Press, 2004), 124.
51 Ibid., 127–128; Lance J. Sussman, "'Toward Better Understanding': The Rise of the Interfaith Movement in America and the Role of Rabbi Isaac Landman," *American Jewish Archives* 34 (April 1982): 38.
52 Kaufmann, *Rise and Fall of Anglo-America*, 127–130.
53 Sussman, "'Toward Better Understanding'," 40–41.
54 Benny Kraut, "Jews, Catholics, and the Goodwill Movement," in William R. Hutchison (ed.), *Between the Times: The Travail of the Protestant Establishment in America, 1900–1960* (New York: Cambridge University Press, 1989), 201.
55 Kevin M. Schultz, *Tri-faith America: How Catholics and Jews Held Postwar America to Its Protestant Promise* (New York: Oxford University Press, 2011), 32.
56 John H. Elliott, *Building Bridges Between Groups that Differ in Faith, Race, Culture* (New York: National Conference of Christians and Jews, 1947), 20.
57 Benson Y. Landis (ed.), *Religion and the Good Society: An Introduction to Social Teachings of Judaism, Catholicism, and Protestantism* (New York: National Conference of Christians and Jews, 1942), 6–7, 39–62.
58 Franklin D. Roosevelt, "Campaign Address at Detroit, Michigan," October 2, 1932, American Presidency Project. Available at www.presidency.ucsb.edu/ws/index.php?pid=88393.
59 Franklin D. Roosevelt, "Radio Address on Brotherhood Day," February 23, 1936, American Presidency Project. Available at www.presidency.ucsb.edu/ws/index.php?pid=15250.
60 Donald R. McCoy, "The Good Neighbor League and the Presidential Campaign of 1936," *Western Political Quarterly* 13, no. 4 (December 1960), 1015–1016. See also Stanley Hugh, "I Vote for Roosevelt," *Christian Century*, September 16, 1936, 1219.
61 Schultz, *Tri-faith America*, 40–41.
62 "Meaningless Temple," *Time*, April 11, 1938.
63 A mural depicting the sacrifice of the chaplains is at Faith Baptist Temple, Philadelphia, Pennsylvania.
64 Colleen McDaniel, *Catholics in the Movies* (New York: Oxford University Press, 2008), 59–126.
65 Thomas J. Sugrue, *Sweet Land of Liberty: The Forgotten Struggle for Civil Rights in the North* (New York: Random House, 2008), 216, 219, 245.
66 William R. Hutchison, *Religious Pluralism in America: The Contentious History of a Founding Ideal* (New Haven, CT: Yale University Press, 2003), 197.
67 William J. Collins, "The Political Economy of State Fair Housing Laws Before 1968," *Social Science History* 30, no. 1 (spring 2006), 28.

68 Hasia R. Diner, *The Jews of the United States, 1654–2000* (Berkeley: University of California Press, 2004), 206; Anthony Chen, "'The Hitlerian Rule of Quotas': Racial Conservatism and the Politics of Fair Employment Legislation in New York State, 1941–1945," *Journal of American History* 92, no. 4 (March 2006): 1259.
69 William J. Collins, "The Political Economy of State-level Fair Employment Laws, 1940–1964," *Explorations in Economic History* 40, no. 1 (January 2003): 24–51. The study finds a stronger association with size of Jewish population, union, and NAACP members. This same scholar has found no relation between state-level fair housing laws and size of the Catholic population. William J. Collins, "The Political Economy of State Fair Housing Laws Before 1968," *Social Science History* 30, no. 1 (spring 2006): 15–49.
70 The Philadelphia Council for Equal Jobs Opportunity included a Catholic interracial committee. See Eric Ledell Smith and Kenneth C. Wolensky, "A Novel Public Policy," *Pennsylvania History* 69, no. 4 (fall 2002): 498, 510–511, 512.
71 Not all Catholics viewed the FEPC favorably. Roman Catholic Louisiana Senator Allen Ellender's comments in reaction to the federal Fair Employment Practices Committee are revealing: it would force businesses to hire "so many colored people, so many Catholics, so many Protestants." Cited in Adam Fairclough, *Race and Democracy: The Civil Rights Struggle in Louisiana 1915–1972* (Athens: University of Georgia Press, 1999), 148.
72 See the series "Can Catholicism Win America?" in the *Christian Century* starting on November 29, 1944, and ending on January 17, 1945, followed by the series "Can Protestantism Win America?" starting on April 3, 1946, and ending on July 3, 1946.
73 Rosswurm, "The Catholic Church and the Left-led Unions," 128–137.
74 Joshua Zeitz, *White Ethnic New York: Jews, Catholics, and the Shaping of Postwar Politics* (Chapel Hill: University of North Carolina Press, 2007).
75 Mark Hulsether, *Building a Protestant Left:* Christianity and Crisis *Magazine, 1941–1993* (Knoxville: University of Tennessee Press, 1999), 64–65.
76 Ibid., 64; Dorrien, *The Making of American Liberal Theology*, 528.
77 David W. Moore, "Little Prejudice Against a Woman, Jewish, Black or Catholic Presidential Candidate," Gallup News Service, June 10, 2003. Available at www.gallup.com/poll/8611/little-prejudice-against-woman-jewish-black-catholic-presidenti.aspx.
78 Robert Wuthnow, *Red State Religion: Faith and Politics in America's Heartland* (Princeton, NJ: Princeton University Press, 2012), 211.
79 Barry T. Hirsch, David A. Macpherson, and Wayne G. Vroman, "Estimates of Union Density by State," *Monthly Labor Review*, July 2001, 52.
80 Samuel S. Hill, Charles H. Lippy, and Charles Regan Wilson, *Encyclopedia of Religion in the South* (Macon, GA: Mercer University Press, 2005), 273. Hill et al. note that in 1980, Southern Baptists constituted 20 percent of the population of the South, while churches affiliated with the National Council of Churches constituted about 12 percent of the population of the South; much of the latter were African American denominations that joined the NCC in 1950.
81 Eugene D. Genovese, *The Southern Front: History and Politics in the Cultural War* (Columbia: University of Missouri Press, 1995), 249–250. Hill has also argued that "Nativism surfaced in the South much later than it had in the Northeast and Midwest" because of low immigration to the South. Samuel S. Hill, *Religion in the Southern States* (Macon, GA: Mercer University Press, 1983), 67.
82 Thomas F. Haddox, *Fears and Fascinations: Representing Catholicism in the American South* (New York: Fordham, 2005), 8, ch. 1.
83 For an example, see article in *Southern Standard* (New Orleans), June 3, 1855, excerpted in Kenneth J. Zanca (ed.), *American Catholics and Slavery: 1789–1866 – An Anthology of Primary Documents* (New York: University Press of America,

1994), 105; also an article from the *Richmond Dispatch*, March 8, 1861,on page 106 of the same collection.
84 Thomas Haddox, *Fears and Fascinations: Representing Catholicism in the American South* (New York: Fordham, 2005), 8. See also Chapter 2. Catholic polities had resorted to slavery. Even Bartolome de Las Casas, who protested treatment of Native Americans in the New World, thought it appropriate to force Indians to labor. On the other hand, the Papal encyclical *In Supremo Apostolatus* in 1839 condemned the slave trade. Zanca, *American Catholics and Slavery*, 23, 27. Zanca (p. 127) notes that most Catholic periodicals did not condemn slavery outright, though some Northern Catholics supported the Civil War to preserve the union at the start of the war.
85 Carty, *A Catholic in the White House?*, 17.
86 Ibid.
87 Gaines M. Foster, *Moral Reconstruction: Christian Lobbyists and the Federal Legislation of Morality, 1865–1920* (Chapel Hill: University of North Carolina Press, 2002), 15–17.
88 Foster, *Moral Reconstruction*, 15–16.
89 *Congressional Globe*, Thirty-sixth Congress, First Session: 1559.
90 David Buice, "A Stench in the Nostrils of Honest Men: Southern Democrats and the Edmunds Act of 1882," *Dialogue: A Journal of Mormon Thought* 21, no. 3 (1988): 100–113; David T. Smith, *Religious Persecution and Political Order in the United States* (New York: Cambridge University Press, 2015), 71–72.
91 Lincoln also moved in a direction of religious inclusion, linking Catholic freedom with the anti-slavery issue. See Jay P. Dolan, *In Search of an American Catholicism: A History of Religion and Culture in Tension* (New York: Oxford University Press, 2003), 57.
92 See Jason D. Berggren, "Jefferson Davis, Religion, and the Politics of Recognition," *White House Studies* 5, no. 2 (March 22, 2005): 231–242.
93 Ibid.
94 Zanca, *American Catholics and Slavery*, 188–189.
95 Patrick Foley, "Catholics of the South: Historical Perspectives," *Catholic Social Science Review* 13 (2008): 78.
96 Berggren notes that Pope Pius IX was the only international leader to address Jefferson Davis as "the Illustrious and Honorable [...] President of the Confederate States of America" (Berggren, "Jefferson Davis, Religion, and the Politics of Recognition").
97 Joseph Moreau, *Schoolbook Nation: Conflicts over American History Textbooks from the Civil War to the Present* (Ann Arbor: University of Michigan Press, 2003), 98.
98 Prendergast, *The Catholic Voter in American Politics*, 75.
99 Daniel W. Stowell, *Rebuilding Zion: The Religious Reconstruction of the South, 1863–1877* (New York: Oxford University Press, 1998); Edward J. Blum, *Reforging the White Republic: Race, Religion, and American Nationalism, 1865–1898* (Baton Rouge: Louisiana State Press, 2005).
100 *Congressional Record* (1876), 5191. This version of the amendment prohibited funds specifically appropriated for schools from being used to support sectarian schools, but left open the possibility that general treasury funds could be used for such support. Noah Feldman, *Divided by God: America's Church-State Problem – and What We Should Do About It* (New York: Farrar, Straus, & Giroux, 2005), 78.
101 *Congressional Record* (1876), 5595.
102 Mark Edward Deforrest, "An Overview and Evaluation of State Blaine Amendments: Origins, Scope, and First Amendment Concerns," *Harvard Journal of Law & Public Policy* 26 (2003): 569–570.
103 Kyle Duncan, "Secularism's Laws: State Blaine Amendments and Religious Persecution," *Fordham Law Review* 72 (December 2003): 493.

104 Higham, *Strangers in the Land*, 81, 86.
105 Donald L. Kinzer, *An Episode of Anti-Catholicism: The American Protective Association* (Seattle: University of Washington Press, 1964), 259–260.
106 C. Vann Woodward, *Tom Watson: Agrarian Rebel* (New York: Oxford University Press, 1963), ch. 22.
107 Charles P. Sweeney, "Leo Frank and Bigotry in the South," *Nation*, November 24, 1920. Available at www.thenation.com/article/leo-frank-and-bigotry-south/.
108 Higham, *Strangers in the Land*, 292.
109 Ibid.; Sweeney, "Leo Frank and Bigotry in the South."
110 Rita H. Delorme, "Recalling an Epic Battle: Bishop Keiley, Sisters, and the Catholic Laymen's Association versus the Veazey Law," *Southern Cross* (Roman Catholic Diocese of Savannah), July 20, 2006, 3. Available at https://diosav.org/sites/all/files/archives/S8626p03.pdf.
111 Higham, *Strangers in the Land*, 292.
112 Hill, *Religion in the Southern States*, 68. See David P. Page, "Bishop Michael J. Curley and Anti-Catholic Nativism in Florida," *Florida Historical Quarterly* XLV, no. 2 (October 1966): 110–111. The Florida circuit court judge for St. Johns County ruled that private schools were not subject to the law, arguing that just as private white citizens could refuse services to blacks, so could private Catholic citizens offer those same services. In other words, the judge invoked the protection of racial order to justify toleration in the religious order.
113 Page, "Bishop Michael J. Curley and Anti-Catholic Nativism in Florida," 116. Page does note resistance to anti-Catholicism; the argument here is not that anti-Catholicism became universal in the South, only that its latitude for expression was increased because of greater confidence in racial order.
114 Higham, *Strangers in the Land*, 167.
115 V.O. Key, *Southern Politics in State and Nation* (New York: Alfred A. Knopf, 1950), 318–320.
116 Since most blacks were disenfranchised, concerns about ecological fallacy are less applicable here. The ecological fallacy is the attempt to infer individual voting behavior from county-level (or higher-level) data of voting behavior. For instance, knowing that counties with higher white population proportions vote in higher proportions for party A does not mean that whites supported party A. It could be that black and white support for party A varies with how large each group is. But if blacks are significantly restricted from voting at all, concerns about ecological fallacy are diminished.
117 Prendergast, *The Catholic Voter in American Politics*, 145.
118 Andrew S. Moore, *The South's Tolerable Alien: Roman Catholics in Alabama and Georgia, 1945–1970* (Baton Rouge: Louisiana State University Press, 2007). See also "White Clergymen Urge Local Negroes to Withdraw from Demonstrations," *Birmingham News*, April 13, 1963.

6 Provincializing Catholicism in Canada

In Canada the capacity of the class issue to realign religion and potential nativism is exemplified in James Shaver Woodsworth (1874–1942), a founding father of the social democratic movement in Canada in the 1920s and 1930s. Early in his career at the turn of the twentieth century, Woodsworth embraced an identity as a Protestant culture warrior. In 1907 Woodsworth became the superintendent of All Peoples' Mission, a Methodist church in Winnipeg, and a year later the church bought the mortgage of the Polish Catholic church in the city. Woodsworth schemed to allow the Catholic congregation to continue to come to the church and hold services mostly as they had before, but also to have a Methodist minister slowly introduce Protestant thinking to the congregants.[1] Woodsworth also authored *Strangers Within Our Gates* in 1909, which expressed alarm at the growing multicultural diversity within Canadian society stemming from heavy immigration at the start of the twentieth century. Fearing that the Anglo Saxon Protestant element that had contributed to modernity and freedom would be swamped by Catholics, Woodsworth advocated assimilation and English-only education, and opposed separate schools.[2]

In 1918 Woodsworth left the Methodist church, citing war and dominance of the church by the wealthy as his reasons.[3] His commitment to laborers and the poor ultimately redefined his thinking about nativism and his relation to British imperialism:

> If on this continent we can learn how diverse people may live together in peace we will contribute a thousand fold more to the world's peace than either building a "tin pot navy" or contributing the money for three British Dreadnoughts.[4]

This was important because Canada's relationship to British imperialism contributed to Protestant–Catholic tensions in the country. Later, Woodsworth would become the founding father of the Cooperative Commonwealth Federation (subsequently the New Democratic Party) in Canada, the closest thing to a democratic socialist or labor party in the Canadian context. Woodsworth maintained that his labor politics was not Marxist, but simultaneously British, Protestant, and Catholic, consonant with the ideals of social Catholicism expressed in the papal encyclicals *Rerum Novarum* and *Quadragesima Anno*.[5]

Woodsworth's social democratic politics inclined him and the Cooperative Commonwealth Federation to favor greater centralization of power in Ottawa. These policies would put him at odds with the interests of Quebec. Canadian Catholics, particularly in Quebec, favored provincial autonomy over incorporation into a class-based movement. This had not always been the case. At the time of Confederation, the idea of having a relatively powerful centralized government was accepted by a cross-ethnic, cross-religious, and cross-regional coalition of Conservatives. Yet, over time, provincial autonomy became more important.

The privileging of provincial autonomy helps explain the divergence in Catholic incorporation in comparison with Australia and the United States. Catholic incorporation in Canada is a particularly interesting case because, of the three countries in this study, Canada has the highest Catholic proportion of population. The balance of power between Protestants and Catholics was much more even. Given their size and the majoritarian electoral system in Canada, both parties needed Catholic votes to achieve sustained electoral success. One might have expected greater competition for Catholic votes and dampening of Protestant hostility. Yet Catholics were often underrepresented in political office, and they did not do better than Australian or U.S. Catholics, with Canadian Catholics being particularly underrepresented in the western provinces and Ontario.

Canada is also the only country of the three in this study in which a Catholic majority controlled a major province. The presence of a Catholic majority in one province, as well as Catholics being a large enough minority to influence the composition of the federal legislature, meant that Catholics could exert significant pressure to reinforce provincial prerogatives. Rather than conceiving of religious freedom as capabilities exercised at the level of the individual worker as in Australia, French Catholics in Quebec were encouraged to conceive of religious freedom as provincial autonomy, with Catholics in control of all major state institutions in that province. This made more difficult the formation of the cross-national coalition that developed in Australia, which could simultaneously increase Catholic capabilities and standing. In the Australian case, a national coalition around class emerged, helping to suppress the importance of the religious dimension. In the United States and Canada, national coalitions typically did not center on one dimension of identity, and acted more like catchall parties than ideologically cohesive parties. Such coalitions were more amenable to preserving the status quo, rather than transforming and reconstructing identity. Canada is similar to the United States in that "class voting" in Canada has been low.[6]

The following section will describe the Confederation agreement and what might be considered unique in structuring Catholic–Protestant relations in Canada compared with Australia and the United States. Subsequent sections show how federal politics led to a patchwork of compromises across the provinces in the policies of schools and language, setting the stage for the privileging of provincial autonomy. The final section considers how this trend toward greater decentralization made more difficult the formation of a cross-national labor coalition and conditioned how the political opportunity of the Great Depression affected Catholic–Protestant relations.

Institutional context to Catholic political incorporation

The British North America (BNA) Act established Canadian confederation in 1867, and the terms of this institutional settlement helped shape the future of Catholics and Protestants. In the first decades after Confederation, religious suspicion did not prevent electoral coalitions between Catholics and Protestants. The Conservative Party coalition that emerged as the dominant force in Canadian politics from 1867 to 1890 attempted to unite elements from Ontario and Quebec, English and French, and Protestant and Catholic. Led by John MacDonald and George-Etienne Cartier, the coalition centered on development of the Canadian west; construction of a transcontinental railroad; protectionist policies to promote industrialization; autonomy for French Quebec; and limited expansion of democratic rights. Opposed to the Conservatives were an assorted group of anti-Confederationists (mainly in the Maritime provinces); free traders and those wanting a more laissez-faire economic approach; liberals wanting more expansion of democratic rights and accountable legislatures; and Rougists in Quebec who wanted greater separation of church and state.[7] The Conservative coalition hoped to bridge ethnic and religious groups and reduce their importance to party politics. As John MacDonald put it, "If a British-Canadian desires to conquer, he must 'stoop to conquer.' He must make friends of the French without sacrificing the status of his race or his religion. He must respect their nationality."[8] The cabinets of Conservative governments up until 1890 were quasi-consociational, including significant Catholic representation, well in advance of both Australia and the United States. The Conservative Thompson ministry, for instance, included eight Protestants and six Catholics.[9]

Although the Conservative coalition that implemented Confederation was stable for several decades, several factors contributed to its unraveling. The first was ambiguity about state aid to Catholic schools. The BNA Act established that provincial legislatures had sovereignty over education, but Section 93 also dictated that provinces could not eliminate the right to Catholic and Protestant public schools that were in existence "by law" at the time of Confederation. For example, there were Protestant schools in Quebec and Catholic schools in Ontario. If provincial governments attempted to ban these separate schools, the federal Parliament had the power to "disallow" such legislation.

The BNA Act left several unanticipated questions unresolved. Did the phrase "by law" rule out protection for separate schools that had been established by informal arrangements rather than by legislative decree? Did the phrase rule out protection of separate schools in new provinces that did not exist at the time of Confederation? Since high school education became entrenched only after Confederation, did the guarantee of separate schools mean that there should be separate high schools as well? What did the guarantee of separate schools mean in terms of the divvying up of various taxes for public and separate schools? Did the "spirit" of the Confederation agreement in which French-language rights were preserved in the legislature translate into "rights" for the teaching of the French language in schools?

The schools issue was embedded in a second, larger issue concerning the character of new territories in the west as they became incorporated as Canadian provinces. Just as the addition of new territories in the United States contributed to animosity between North and South over the issue of slavery, so did the expansion of the Canadian frontier lead to arguments about the letter versus the spirit of the British North America Act.[10] Migrants to the west were primarily non-Catholic and non-French. Some anti-Catholic Protestants saw the west as a way to dilute the importance of Quebec in the Canadian Confederation and secure Canada as a Protestant, English-speaking country aligned with the British Empire.

The third destabilizing force was the commitment to the British Empire. Beginning with the Boer War and culminating in the conscription crisis during World War I, the demands of maintaining a connection with the British Empire began to increase. Protestants and Catholics, British and French debated the merits of how much Canada needed to remain tied to the British Empire.

These unanticipated developments contributed to the outbreak of major conflicts between Protestants and Catholics up until the end of the British Empire, leading to a cascade of mistrust between Protestants and Catholics. The expansion of Anglo Protestants into the frontier led to the Red River uprising in 1869/1870 and the Northwest Rebellion of 1885, both led by Louis Riel, a Catholic Métis. The Métis were defeated in 1885, and the eventual execution of Riel outraged French Catholics in Quebec. A more stridently nationalist government emphasizing French Catholic distinctiveness was elected in Quebec, led by Honoré Mercier. Mercier's government passed the Jesuit Estates Act in 1888, which provided compensation for lands that had been taken from Jesuits by the British colonial government in 1800.[11] This in turn prompted outrage among Protestants outside Quebec, and led to the formation of the Equal Rights Association, led by D'Alton McCarthy: McCarthy was one of the "Noble Thirteen" who voted for the federal Parliament to annul the Jesuit Estates Act. He also later led the Protestant Protective Association in the 1890s, which sought to reduce the influence of Catholicism in Canadian politics.[12]

Some of these stressors were distinct from those existing in Australia and the United States; others were not. Concerns about ties to the British Empire do not explain differences in Catholic incorporation between Canada and Australia, which also experienced severe Protestant–Catholic conflict over the Boer War and conscription in World War I. The schools issue was also not that distinctive. Australian and American Catholics continued to advocate for separate schools or ways of providing funding to separate schools. One might argue that Canadian Catholics were more likely to feel aggrieved because the British North America Act could be interpreted as upholding the right to separate schools. In Australia, there was no parallel sense of constitutional aggrievement because there was no ambiguous constitutional language to battle over, but Catholics in Australia often felt they were being "double taxed" for maintaining separate schools. Catholics in the United States also often felt constitutionally wronged over prevention of funding to religious schools, since allegedly non-denominational religious instruction often continued in public schools in many states, and the Catholic hierarchy considered such "general" religious instruction to be Protestant education.

In comparison with the United States and Australia, one of the most distinctive features of Canada was that it had a province, Quebec, in which a majority Catholic and French population ruled. Quebec's distinctiveness was aided by the majoritarian first-past-the-post electoral system. For instance, after 1896, when Quebec Catholics became more resistant to vote for Conservatives, Conservatives could win between 15 and 25 percent of the vote in Quebec, yet typically only win under 10 percent of the seats.[13] This made it harder for Conservatives to win seats in Quebec and reduced the number of French Catholic representatives within the Conservative coalition. Similarly, the Liberal Party, which Catholics started to favor after 1896, could poll between 26 and 40 percent of the vote in Protestant-dominated Ontario, yet often win less of a percentage of the seats in that province.

This large Catholic population in Canada and a heavy concentration in Quebec has meant two things. First, Catholics have been in a better position to win concessions from Protestants in Canada, due to their numbers. The concentration of Catholics in Quebec has also meant that Quebec Catholics will often pursue policies that will increase their provincial autonomy rather than other kinds of policies. As a result, the ability of Catholics and Protestants to engage in significantly reconstructive coalitions is diminished. This dynamic was evident in the two biggest policy battles affecting Catholics during this period: schools and language. Policies on religious schooling ranged from completely non-sectarian to dual confessional school systems. In language policy, French-language instruction and use received significantly less protection.

At least initially, Catholics in Canada did do better in these two policy regimes than in the United States and Australia, having achieved at least some state support for Catholic schools and French-language teaching in certain provinces in the early twentieth century. But further gains for Catholics in these areas generally stalled after this.

Religious schools

Unlike in Australia and the United States, the struggle over state aid to schools was not decided in favor of separation of church and state in the nineteenth century. At the federal level, there was no equivalent to the U.S. Constitution's establishment clause, barring state funds to religious schools. In addition, no province (save for British Columbia) had a written constitution, so there were no attempts to pass Blaine-style amendments in the provinces.[14] As Wiseman has put it, most English Canadians identified with British practices, which meant "parliamentary supremacy, judicial deference to legislative enactments, and an understanding of prescriptive rights as variable with evolving circumstances in accordance with English common law tradition."[15] In Canada the state aid issue was resolved through a series of compromises that left an uneven legacy of state aid in some provinces but not in others.

Section 93 of the BNA Act guaranteed the rights to separate denominational schooling in those provinces where such schooling existed "by law" at the time of Confederation. Since Catholic and Protestant school boards and schools existed in Ontario and Quebec, Catholic schools were preserved in those two provinces. Ontario set up primarily non-denominational public schools, with the option of having separate schools for Catholics, and Quebec established concurrent endowment of denominational schools. The situation was more ambiguous in the Maritimes. Prior to Confederation, in New Brunswick the Parish School Act of 1858 set up explicitly non-denominational schools, but as a matter of informal compromise there were about 250 schools operated by Roman Catholics with public support. The New Brunswick legislature abolished Catholic separate schools in the Commons School Act 1871. Controversy erupted over whether the federal government should disallow this act of the provincial legislature. The federal government did not do so, and tensions over schools led Catholics to stop paying school taxes, which prompted the provincial government to seize the property of Catholics as tax payments. Later that year, following electoral controversies and violence between opposing sides, a new compromise was brokered. The Catholic Church could certify teachers; textbooks would be edited or annotated to avoid giving religious offense; and religious instruction could be offered after school hours in the schools.[16] Similar informal agreements were achieved in Nova Scotia and Prince Edward Island.

The schools question was even more explosive for those territories in the west incorporated as provinces following Confederation. British Columbia joined the Confederation in 1871 and established non-denominational public schools. Manitoba joined the Confederation in 1870, but Catholics constituted a more politically influential group than in British Columbia. In 1871 Manitoba was 45 percent Catholic, and under section 22 of the Manitoba Act a system of Catholic separate schools funded by the state was established. Due to heavy Protestant migration, however, Manitoba became only 18.5 percent Catholic by 1881. In 1890, the English and Protestant majority in Manitoba successfully abolished Catholic separate schools.[17] Catholics argued that this reneged on agreements in the British North America Act, and sought to have the federal government overturn the provincial government's decision.

The issue of whether or not to disallow the Manitoba legislation split the Conservative coalition, with many Ontario Conservatives supporting no action and Quebec Conservatives supporting the intervention of the federal government to restore Catholic separate schools. The leader of the Liberal Party, Wilfrid Laurier, did not want to use the federal power of disallowance to overturn the Manitoba legislation, appealing to the fears of French Catholics about the precedent this might set for use of that power against Quebec. Some in the Catholic hierarchy saw Laurier's tentativeness to use disallowance as a reason to oppose him. However, Quebec Catholics had been shifting to the Liberal Party from the Conservative Party throughout the 1880s in response to both the economic distress of the 1880s and the handling of the Riel issue. Laurier and the Liberals ended up winning 49 of 65 seats in Quebec, a gain of 14 seats. Quebec's representatives constituted a substantial proportion of the 118-to-88 margin the Liberals held over the Conservatives in Parliament.

Subsequently, Laurier negotiated the Laurier–Greenway compromise to end the Manitoba schools crisis. Under the compromise, no separate denominational schools were established. Instead, in urban schools where there were at least 40 Catholic families, or in rural schools where there were ten, Catholic teachers were to be employed, though they were to follow the public school curriculum. At the request of ten families, there could also be a half hour of religious instruction in the schools at the end of the school day in the faith of the families making the request.[18] The solution of allowing Catholic instruction after school hours was reminiscent of "released-time programs" achieved in many U.S. localities from 1913 to 1947.[19] Some French Catholics remained dissatisfied with this compromise, arguing that it ignored the special status of French Catholics in the BNA Act.

The schools question again created tension with the question of the admission of Saskatchewan and Alberta as full-fledged provinces, both of which had been governed as one unit, the North-West Territories. Under the terms of the North-West Territories Act of 1875, the federal government made provision for Catholic separate schools in the western territories. An 1884 law in the territorial legislature allowed a minority in any district to have a separate school. This legislation was modeled after Quebec's dual confessional system. The Catholic members of the school board would have authority over curriculum, teacher training standards, and inspection in Catholic schools, with some limitations, including the restriction of religious instruction to outside normal school hours.[20] In 1892 control over all schools in the territories came under the Council of Public Instruction, which included religious representatives, though these representatives did not have any voting power, meaning that Catholics lost control over inspection. In 1901 the territorial government passed a school ordinance that did not give Catholics significant powers.[21] Laurier, in contrast with his handling of the Manitoba crisis, introduced legislation guaranteeing the existence of separate schools in Alberta and Saskatchewan initially under terms closer to the 1875 law.

In sum, the Liberals at the national level adopted a middling strategy toward resolving church–state issues, never fully implementing what the most conservative Catholics desired but avoiding a completely secular public school system.[22] The Liberal Party did not have to be too aggressive on the schools issue at the national level, since they could rely on other issues – such as emphasizing Canadian nationalism over British Empire, and on protecting Quebec's autonomy – to attract Catholic votes. This left widely disparate solutions to the issue of state funding to Catholic schools across Canadian provinces.

School issues would continue to surface in subsequent decades, but primarily at the provincial level, with the federal government playing a minor role. One problem with the school settlement in Saskatchewan and Alberta was that minority groups (either Protestant or Catholic) had to number a minimum amount before a separate school could be requested. As a result, there were inevitably a few cases where Protestants were being educated in majority Catholic districts without recourse to a separate school, and vice versa. These exceptions could serve as lightning rods for criticism from both Protestants and Catholics.[23]

Tensions between Catholics and Protestants also flared up over the division of corporate and business taxes, and whether a portion of these should be set aside for Catholic schools. This was an issue for Saskatchewan's first premier Thomas Walter Scott, a Liberal who advocated splitting the taxes equitably in 1913, which created an uproar among Protestants up until Scott's resignation in 1916 due to health issues.[24] Catholics raised the tax issue in Ontario after the Catholic Taxpayers Association helped elect the Liberal government led by Mitchell Hepburn in 1934. Hepburn introduced legislation divvying up corporate and business taxes for Catholic separate schools but later withdrew the measure, in part because of the negative results of a by-election in East Hastings.[25]

High schools did not exist at the time of Confederation, so it was also ambiguous whether the guarantee to support funding Catholic schools that existed at the time of Confederation applied only to primary schools, or to primary schools and high schools. Up until 1925, the Ontario provincial government did not support such funding. This lack of funding was contested in the Tiny Township case. In 1928, the Judicial Committee of the Privy Council ruled that grades 9 and 10 of Catholic schools were entitled to public funding, but that grades beyond that were not, though the provincial government could stipulate state funding under normal democratic processes.

In short, the institutionalization of the compromise over education, rather than settling the question for all time, continued to keep Protestant–Catholic tensions on a slow burn, as ambiguities and issues of implementation at the provincial level continued to surface.

Language policy

As with schools, language policy also varied greatly among the Canadian provinces. Unlike the schools issue, which was framed explicitly as a religious question, the removal of bilingual education in the provinces proceeded to a greater degree. Rights to education in French gradually disappeared in many more provinces, reflecting the fact that English speaking outnumbered French speaking to a much greater degree than Protestants outnumbered Catholics. The situation is comparable to the United States, where racial and ethnic identities were highlighted over religious identities in the policy fields of immigration and voting rights restriction. Framing the issues around linguistic and ethnic identities provided much more favorable coalitional possibilities for those seeking to contain Catholic power. Where religion piggybacked on race in the U.S. context, the containment of Catholicism piggybacked on language and ethnicity in the Canadian context.

For many Canadians, there was no separation between issues of language and religion. Both issues were connected. Militant Protestant newspapers asserted that the language issue was simultaneously a religious issue, because getting the French to learn English could weaken the power of the Catholic Church.[26] The *Sentinel*, the largest Protestant publication in Canada, often made distinctions between English Catholics and French Catholics, with English-speaking Catholics seen as preferable to French-speaking Catholics.[27] Moreover, with English the dominant language in North America, a "natural" progression toward English was seen as occurring.[28]

French Canadian Catholics also saw preservation of language as key to maintaining religious identity. The French Canadians, like the German Catholics in the United States, were more inclined to argue that there was a crucial link between language and religion. The discourse on "survivance" posited that French-language use and Roman Catholic practice were tied together. If the French started speaking English, they would be more inclined to drop Catholicism as well.[29] Assimilation was blamed for what the French described as the loss of 25 million Irish to the faith in United States.[30] The different positions of the French and the English over the relation of culture/race and religion carried over into arguments about how best to deal with new immigrants. The French were philosophically inclined to support native language retention and bilingualism while Anglophone Catholics were inclined to support assimilation to English.[31]

English-speaking Catholics also saw language and religion as intertwined. Some believed that promoting English would help English Catholics convert English Protestants.[32] Ties of language often found Ontarian Irish Catholics allied with English non-Catholics. As with the Irish in the United States, Irish Canadian Catholics were more inclined to support a policy of assimilation and integration with the Canadian mainstream. John Joseph Lynch, Irish Catholic prelate and later Archbishop of Ontario, early on envisioned a complementary relationship between the Irish and the English:

> Ireland was subdued [...] in order the more effectively to amalgamate the inhabitants with the English nation. [...] They resisted but were compelled by force to learn the language. God has his designs in this. Little did Irish children suspect when they were whipped in school for not knowing the English lesson that God destined the English language in their mouths to spread the true faith of the Divine Son throughout the greater part of the world.[33]

Lynch favored English-speaking Catholicism because this would help lead to conversions of English. He believed that Quebec remained stuck "in the thirteenth century" and likened Quebec Catholics to the Cajuns in Louisiana, believing that they "will not leave a single permanent mark on this country."[34] He did not support Louis Riel, nor did he support the educational claims of Catholic minorities in New Brunswick.[35] Lynch wanted to halt French immigration to Ontario to preserve the Anglophone character of Catholicism there.[36]

The language in the BNA Act provided for greater protections for religion than for language, so there was greater opportunity to deny official French-language use. Up until the early twentieth century, bilingual policy followed the same contours as Catholic separate school policy. In 1871 Section 23 of the Manitoba Act decreed that the proceedings of the Manitoba legislature and courts were to be in French and English. In 1890 Manitoba's provincial government ended the use of French in records of the legislature and courts, along with ending Catholic separate schools. The Laurier–Greenway agreement in Manitoba led to the compromise that if there were at least ten students of a non-English language in that school, then instruction should be bilingual. The incorporation of Alberta and Saskatchewan as provinces in 1905 allowed that local school boards could permit teaching in French.[37]

After 1905, language and Catholic separate school policy began to diverge. In Ontario in 1912, under a Conservative provincial government, Regulation 17 was passed mandating instruction in English and allowing French instruction only up to the third grade. This was later modified to allow the school inspector to permit instruction to continue in narrow cases. The policy was passed with the support of many English-speaking Catholics in Ontario.[38] The French fought their case all the way up to the Judicial Committee of the Privy Council in London, which in November 1916 upheld the validity of Regulation 17, stating that any constitutional guarantees were made to religious minorities, not racial groups, leaving no legal basis on which to claim discrimination against the French language. Many schools defied the regulation, and it was overturned in 1927 under the Conservative provincial government of Howard Ferguson.

In 1916 the Liberal provincial government of T.C. Norris in Manitoba enacted English as the official language, in contravention of the Laurier–Greenway compromise in 1896.[39] The original compromise had been meant to please English Canadians by giving no special status to French. This had the unintended consequence of making the administration of bilingual schools impractical following heavy immigration from non-English-speaking countries, such that there needed to be 13 different languages of instruction.[40] Pressures for English-only teaching emerged in Saskatchewan in 1918, when Liberal premier W.M. Martin passed a law restricting teaching mostly to English; French was limited to one hour a day after Grade 1.[41] The provincial elections in June 1929 in Saskatchewan were heavily defined by sectarian issues, with the Conservative Party members advocating raising issues about schools and immigration. The success of the Conservatives under James Anderson led to bans on teaching French in primary courses and the wearing of religious garb by teachers in classrooms.[42]

The end result of maneuvering on language policy was that French-language schooling was allowed in Quebec and in French districts in the Maritimes. Transitional French instruction was allowed in Ontario (after 1927) and Alberta. English was the only language of instruction in British Columbia, Manitoba, and Saskatchewan (after 1930).[43]

Catholic freedom as provincial autonomy

The uneven provision of Catholic and French schooling reinforced Quebec Catholics' belief that provincial autonomy was the surest way to protect Catholic freedom. Maximal protection of Catholic and French interests was not going to come from the national government. This belief in provincial autonomy was also bolstered by the fact that Catholics dominated Quebec, and could reliably control the provincial government. Partly because of this privileging of provincial autonomy, there has been a trend toward decentralization of power since Confederation. As other scholars of Canadian federalism have pointed out, at the time of Confederation the powers given to the central government were very substantial, particularly in comparison to Australian federalism.[44] The Civil War in the United States had persuaded Canadian elites of the desirability of a more centralized constitution with federalist aspects.[45] Under the original BNA Act the governor general could disallow provincial legislation, and had the power to appoint provincial lieutenant governors.[46] Moreover, the federal government had the power to assume control over policies "for the general advantage of Canada or for the advantage of two or more provinces" and residual powers not explicitly specified in the BNA Act were to be assigned to the federal government.[47]

Over time, however, Canada and Australia evolved in different directions. Events such as war and economic depression, which provide opportunities for centralizing governmental power, were similar in both countries. Yet the long-run pattern is that provincial autonomy increased in Canada, while centralizing tendencies were predominant in Australia. From 1867 to 1896, the number of times the Canadian federal government disallowed or reserved provincial laws steadily declined, and from 1874 to 1914 federal subsidies as a percentage of provincial revenues also steadily declined.[48] Federal expenditure as a proportion of total expenditures also dropped throughout the twentieth century.[49]

The comparisons among Canada, Australia, and the United States show that the privileging of provincial autonomy had nothing to do with the inherent qualities of Catholicism. Catholics in Australia, for instance, were comfortable with high levels of unionization and industrial arbitration. Similarly, Catholics in the United States, initially integrated into urban political machines, were a significant component of the New Deal coalition in the United States. Ultimately, Catholics in Quebec would also embrace notions of freedom that centered on using the state to assist individuals in a complex economy. But often the emphasis on provincial autonomy hindered other notions of autonomy and made cross-national labor coalitions more difficult. One of the results of the privileging of provincial identity was a hampering of social democratic movements. Canadian unionization rates lagged behind Australia and were fairly similar to the United States up until the mid-twentieth century. Up until the 1950s, strike rates in Australia were also much higher than in Canada.[50]

Interprovincial comparisons lend further weight to the hypothesis that a reconstructive labor movement was critical in improving Catholic–Protestant relations. As previously mentioned, descriptive representation of Catholics lagged in the Canadian western provinces (Figure 3.5). This is striking because the proportion of the Catholic population in these provinces was not that different from the proportion of the Catholic population in South Australia. Nor was the distribution of the Catholic population in the western electoral ridings significantly different. It may be thought that skewed distribution of the Catholic population played some role in the underrepresentation of Catholics As some have claimed in the context of majority-minority redistricting in the United States, the creation of majority black districts may actually hurt African American influence, since some of their votes are wasted when a safe seat is created. Skewed distribution of the Catholic population, however, did not cause underrepresentation of Catholics in the western provinces in Canada. The provinces with the greatest variance in the size of the Catholic population are the Maritime provinces and Ontario.[51] In the western provinces, however, the variance in the size of the Catholic population is fairly small. More importantly, the size of the variance is not that much greater than the variances in the states of Australia.[52] This pattern is relatively consistent from 1911 to 1961. What distinguishes Tasmania and South Australia from the western provinces in Australia is the presence of a labor movement bridging both Catholics and Protestants.

The inability to form cross-national labor organizations also does not stem from a lack of a labor movement within Quebec. The Knights of Labor, which embraced a radical agenda, lasted longer in that province than even U.S. affiliates.[53] As elsewhere in North America, craft unions eventually supplanted the Knights throughout Canada. Yet confessional unions also formed a small but significant proportion of the Quebec labor movement. Catholic syndicates were established, and the Confederation of Catholic Workers of Canada was founded in 1921, with 26,000 members.[54] With the official approval of the Catholic Church, these unions had Catholic chaplains who could review and overrule the decisions of the union if not in accord with Catholic doctrine.

Compared to other provinces in terms of numbers, Quebec's trade union movement does not appear to be distinctive. According to data in the 1940s, unionization rates tended to be higher in British Columbia than in the rest of the provinces. Quebec's unionization rates were not markedly different from the other provinces, with the Maritimes having slightly higher rates and Ontario slightly lower rates prior to the 1950s.[55] Strike frequency in Quebec was consistently below the national average from 1891 to 1950, though strikes in the province often included larger numbers of workers.[56] Hence it appears that the potential for working-class consciousness was at least comparable to that found in other provinces. Explanations of the failure of cross-national class coalitions have to be sought elsewhere.

Opportunities to establish a national labor or social democratic party were ripe in the 1920s when agrarian populist movements in the west elected several members of the independent Progressive Party to the Canadian House of Commons. There were also opportunities in the Depression era with the rise of the CCF. Labor and social democratic parties typically wanted greater concentration of national power to deal with complex issues of the management of the economy. As in the United States, left-leaning Protestant churchmen such as Woodsworth and Salem Bland also called for greater state control over the economy.[57] The biggest stumbling-block to cooperation among the provincial labor movement was the issue of appropriate federal power.

After World War I, the Liberal Party platform called for unemployment, sickness, old age, and disability insurance, but implementation stalled. Federal social legislation passed prior to World War II only in rare circumstances. In 1927 the Liberal Party only had 99 seats, and a block of Progressives (24 seats), independents (four seats), and Labor (two seats, including J.S. Woodsworth) could potentially keep the balance of power from the Conservative Party (with 116 seats). As a condition for support of the government, the Progressives and Labor demanded implementation of old age insurance. Quebec premier Alexandre Taschereau opposed the measure, arguing that it would detract from Quebec's autonomy. The bill passed, but with some leeway for provinces to interpret the conditions under which they would be eligible for federal funding. Full participation by all provinces in the program did not occur until 1936, and the program was fairly meager. Eligibility did not start until age 70, and benefit levels were means-tested. In setting benefit levels, some provinces were given leeway to assume that children would be providing some support for elderly parents, whether or not this was actually the case.[58]

There were elements, including labor organizations, in Quebec that would support the centralization of power in the federal government. The Confederation of Catholic Workers of Canada supported the Old Age Pension Bill in 1927.[59] The Montreal Trades and Labour Council called for compulsory education, which was eventually implemented in Quebec in 1943.[60] However, these voices were often drowned out by more conservative elements in Quebec that capitalized on issues of provincial autonomy.

In Quebec, the Depression at first seemed to open the door to greater social democracy. Left and right critics of 40 years of Liberal government in the province united under Maurice Duplessis and the Union Nationale, which initially campaigned on dismantling trusts and promoting a progressive social welfare agenda. During Duplessis's premiership, however, he did not fulfill these promises and continued to restrict growth of the state. The Quebec government passed the Act Concerning Communist Propaganda, better known as the Padlock Law, in 1937, which allowed the government to lock up any building used to further communism. Under the law, the government raided the CCF and other progressive organizations and suppressed the ability of unions to agitate effectively in the province until the law was declared unconstitutional in 1957.[61]

In the last years of the Conservative federal government of Bennett (1930–1935), federal unemployment legislation was passed, but it was struck down by the Canadian Supreme Court and the British Privy Council.[62] As with the old age pensions scheme in 1927, Quebec politicians were concerned about the prospect of enhanced federal power.[63] Under the subsequent Liberal federal government of MacKenzie King, a constitutional amendment was proposed to allow for a federal unemployment bill. Duplessis opposed the amendment and, since unanimity from the provinces was necessary for constitutional change, federal unemployment insurance was delayed.

Duplessis's Union Nationale lost in 1939, allowing the Liberal provincial government of Godbout to agree to the amendment in 1940. In 1944 the federal government also initiated family allowances, a universal program that would pay a sum for each child under the age of 16 attending school, though larger families would get progressively less for each additional child. Catholic political elites largely approved of family allowances, since it fitted in with Catholic principles of subsidiarity and the church's support of large families. Quebec's major complaint centered on the decline in the benefit for larger families, which some Catholics felt unfairly penalized large Catholic families.[64] The Liberals under Godbout also implemented reforms such as compulsory education, nationalization of Hydro Quebec, and extension of the vote to women.

World War II, however, doomed the Liberal provincial government in Quebec and the movement toward joining the other provinces on a social welfare agenda. At the federal level, King turned back on his election commitment in 1939 not to employ conscription to support the war effort and called for a plebiscite on the issue. In the subsequent referendum on conscription, Quebec voted overwhelmingly against, while the other provinces voted overwhelmingly for conscription. Anger in Quebec over King's support for the British Empire strengthened Quebec nationalists, who generally supported a more rural society and Christian corporatism.[65] Duplessis successfully depicted himself as a protector of Quebec's provincial autonomy and his party won control of Quebec's provincial legislature in 1944, and he would rule until his death in 1959.[66]

Much of the basis for Duplessis's support came from rural constituencies, though he also attracted some urban support.[67] The Duplessis government's suppression of labor unions continued in the 1950s. In 1954, the provincial government passed Bills 19 and 20, which allowed the government to decertify unions with communists in its leadership or public sector unions that engaged in strikes.[68]

While social democracy stalled in Quebec, the western prairies embraced both populist and social democratic alternatives in the form of third parties. The Cooperative Commonwealth Federation was founded in 1932, combining labor and agrarian parties in the west. Starting in 1936, the CCF controlled government in Saskatchewan for 20 years. The CCF came close to forming a government in Ontario in 1943, winning approximately one-third of provincial seats.[69] At the federal level, the CCF underperformed relative to their provincial strength, controlling only 29 seats in Parliament in 1945, 32 seats after by-elections in 1948. If the CCF had won that percentage of federal seats, plus some percentage of seats in the Catholic provinces (Quebec and the Maritimes), it would still not have been able to form a government, but it might have been able to influence the Liberal Party to tack in a more welfarist direction. However, the CCF found no support in Quebec or the Maritimes, underscoring the difficulty of forming a cross-national reconstructive coalition around class.

The CCF called for more centralization of power in the federal government to handle issues of social welfare. Although the CCF often stated that it was religiously neutral, Quebec bishops evaluating the CCF in terms of the Papal encyclical *Quadregesimo anno* deemed the movement "socialist" and condemned Catholic participation in the organization.[70] Montreal Archbishop Gauthier criticized the CCF late in 1933 because "it denied man's fundamental right to possess private property, incited to class war, and was inevitably materialistic in philosophy."[71] Archbishops Georges Gauthier and Jean Marie Rodrigue Villeneuve prohibited their congregants from supporting the CCF.[72] The timing of the emergence of the CCF most likely did not help. With communism established in the Soviet Union, the salience of anti-communism to the Catholic Church was greater than when Labor was working out its coalition with the Catholic Church in Australia at the turn of the century.

Catholic bishops in the western province were more circumspect in their evaluation of the CCF, leaving it up to individual Catholics to decide whether the CCF was appropriate or not. Catholic support for the CCF was weak. Protestants were more likely to be overrepresented in the CCF, and Protestants led the social gospel movement in Canada.[73] Given the Liberal Party's record of protecting Quebec's provincial rights, Catholics continued to vote for the Liberal Party. Among CCF MPs, a much smaller percentage claimed to be Catholic than among Liberal MPs.[74]

The power of the provincial issue to sap support for the CCF was even evident in Henri Bourassa, an independent French Roman Catholic MP from Quebec who supported socialist objectives. Bourassa declared that he could not initially support Woodsworth and the CCF because of too great centralization of power.[75] In time, some Catholics changed their opinion of the CCF. Father Georges-Henri Levesque, a social scientist in Quebec who reported to the bishops on the relationship between the CCF and Catholicism, evaluated the CCF negatively in 1933; but several years later he changed his mind.[76] In 1943 the Catholic Church in Quebec issued an ambiguous statement favoring government social redistribution, while at the same time denouncing communism and materialistic philosophies. Some interpreted this statement as approving of congregants voting for the CCF, while others saw it as a statement of principles which the CCF had to meet to gain approval from the church.[77] A couple of individual bishops continued to urge their parishioners not to vote for the CCF even after the Quebec church declaration.[78] To Andre Laurendeau the CCF appeared "with an English aspect."[79] Joe Burton was a rare Catholic CCF parliamentarian, elected to Saskatchewan provincial assembly in 1938 and the House in 1943.

The Catholic Church's circumspect attitude toward the CCF as well as the control in Quebec by conservative, more rural-oriented Catholics contributed to more conservative opinions on social welfare. Analyses of public opinion in the 1950s indicated that Catholics, as well as the French-speaking residents of Quebec and the Maritimes, were less likely to support social welfare programs than were other Canadians. The opposite was the case in the United States, with Catholics more likely than Protestants to support social welfare measures.[80]

Quebec's opposition to federal power helped scuttle further expansion of the federal welfare state at the end of World War II. Government commissions proposed ending the means test for old age pensions for those over the age of 70; providing a means-tested pension for those between the ages of 65 and 69; and expanding unemployment and health insurance. To pay for these programs, provinces would cede some of their taxing power over personal and corporate income to the federal government. As with unemployment insurance in the 1930s, Duplessis opposed the scheme. This, along with Ontario's fear that it would be subsidizing poorer provinces, was enough to shelve these plans for expansion of the welfare state.[81]

The dual effects of Depression and war led eventually to increases in the capacity of the federal government, with the establishment of unemployment insurance and family allowances.[82] Legislation similar to the Wagner Act passed in 1944.[83] At the provincial level, more radical measures were taken. Saskatchewan implemented public hospitalization insurance in 1946, which was later taken up by British Columbia and Alberta. These programs paved the way for later establishing Canada's single-payer health insurance system. Catholics in the 1930s and 1940s, however, were not such reliable partners in building the social welfare state in Canada.

Conclusion

Despite having an advantage in numbers and resources, Catholic representation in Canada lagged behind their population proportion up until World War II and beyond. The political opportunity of the Great Depression did not translate into Catholic gains in descriptive representation because Canadian Catholics, particularly in Quebec, favored provincial autonomy. This calculation that provincial autonomy mattered more was aided by the fact that Quebec was dominated by Catholics and also by institutional settlements in schools and language that showed the reluctance of the federal government to impose one standard on the nation, and left a patchwork of different compromises across the Canadian nation. A cross-national reconstructive movement centered around labor had less force in the Canadian context, thus leading to fewer opportunities for Catholics and Protestants to be bound around a broader, more encompassing identity. The situation is comparable to the South in the United States, where regional commitments to racial order stunted the ability of the labor movement to bridge religious tensions.

Although party politics placed Canadian identities in a "holding pattern," identity transformation did take place, but by forces stemming internally within each group, rather than as a result of cross-national coalitions between groups. The Quiet Revolution in Quebec in the 1960s led to the rapid secularization of social service provision and prefigured a dramatic drop in weekly churchgoing attendance rates. The Quiet Revolution also began to turn Quebec away from a philosophy that state intervention in social welfare should be minimal. This development formed the context in which new Christian coalitions around secularization could or could not form in the latter half of the twentieth century.

Notes

1. Allen Mills, *Fool for Christ: The Political Thought of J.S. Woodsworth* (Toronto: University of Toronto, 1991), 37.
2. Ibid., 47–48.
3. Ibid., 56.
4. Ibid., 49–50.
5. Ibid., 245.
6. Janine Brodie and Jane Jenson, "Piercing the Smokescreen: Stability and Change in Brokerage Politics," in Alain-G. Gagnon and A. Brian Tanguay, *Canadian Parties in Transition*, 3rd edn (Peterborough, Ontario: Broadview, 2007), 38, 43.
7. James Bickerton, Alain-G. Gagnon, and Patrick J. Smith, *Ties That Bind: Parties and Voters in Canada* (Toronto: Oxford University Press, 1999), 25–26.
8. Quoted in Herbert F. Quinn, *The Union Nationale: Quebec Nationalism from Duplessis to Levesque* (Toronto: University of Toronto Press, 1979), 20–21.
9. "An Embarrassing Situation," *New York Times*, August 9, 1893. Available at http://query.nytimes.com/mem/archive-free/pdf?_r=1&res=9403E1D81431E033A2575AC0A96E9C94629ED7CF.
10. Barry Weingast, "Political Stability and the Civil War: Institutions, Commitment, and American Democracy," in Robert H. Bates, Avner Greif, Margaret Levi, and Jean-Laurent Rosenthal, *Analytic Narratives* (Princeton, NJ: Princeton University Press, 1998), 156.
11. Hereward Senior, "Orangeism in Ontario Politics, 1872–1896," in Donald Swainson (ed.), *Oliver Mowat's Ontario: Papers Presented to the Oliver Mowat Colloquium, Queen's University, November 25–26, 1970* (Toronto: Macmillan of Canada, 1972), 145.
12. Ibid., 146.
13. Alan Cairns, "The Electoral System and the Party System in Canada," *Canadian Journal of Political Science* 1, no. 1 (1968): 61–62.
14. Provincial judges are also appointed by federal government.
15. Nelson Wiseman, "The Questionable Relevance of the Constitution in Advancing Minority Cultural Rights in Manitoba," *Canadian Journal of Political Science* 25, no. 4 (December 1992): 704.
16. Ronald Manzer, *Public Schools and Political Ideas: Canadian Educational Policy in Historical Perspective* (Toronto: University of Toronto Press, 1994), 58. These arrangements were ultimately deemed constitutional in *Rogers* et al. v. *the School Trustees of School District No. 2 of Bathurst* in 1896.
17. Wiseman, "The Questionable Relevance of the Constitution," 700.
18. Manzer, *Public Schools and Political Ideas*, 60–61.
19. From Irwin Widen, "Public Support for Parochial Schools: Why the Issue Has Reemerged," *History of Education Journal* 4, no. 2 (winter, 1953), 71; citation is to Paul Kinney et al., *Should Public Schools Do Church Work* (New York: National Liberal League, 1947). By 1925, one estimate has 200 communities in 24 U.S. states participating in such programs; 400 communities in 30 states by 1935; and nearly 2,000 communities in 47 states by 1947.
20. John L. Hiemstra, "Domesticating Catholic Schools (1885–1905): The Assimilation Intent of Alberta's Separate School System." Paper given at the Canadian Political Science Association Annual Meeting, Dalhousie University, May 30 to June 1, 2003, Halifax, Nova Scotia. Available at www.cpsa-acsp.ca/paper-2003/hiemstra.pdf (see 6–7).
21. Manzer, *Public Schools and Political Ideas*, 56–57.
22. Richard Johnston, Andre Balis, Henry E. Brady, and Jean Crete, *Letting the People Decide: Dynamics of a Canadian Election* (Palo Alto: Stanford University Press, 1992), 45–46.

23 Anthony Appleblatt, "The School Question in the 1929 Saskatchewan Provincial Election," *CCHA Study Sessions* 43(1976): 75–90. Available at www.umanitoba.ca/colleges/st_pauls/ccha/Back%20Issues/CCHA1976/Appleblatt.html.
24 Ibid.
25 See Mark McGowan, *The Enduring Gift: Catholic Education in the Province of Ontario* (Toronto: Ontario Catholic School Trustees' Association). Available at www.ocecn.net/catholic_education/enduring_gift.htm.
26 "Bilingualism Is a Religious Question," *Sentinel*; January 28, 1915, 1; "The French Tongue Necessary to Preserve Roman Catholic Faith," *Sentinel*, April 29, 1915, 5.
27 *Sentinel*, January 12, 1911, 1; "Must Quebec Select a Liberal Leader?," *Sentinel*, June 17, 1915, 1.
28 "Outside Pressure Will Do It," *Sentinel*, July 6, 1893, 1; *Sentinel*, January 17, 1929, 2.
29 R.S. Pennefather (ed.), *The Orange and the Black: Documents in the History of the Orange Order, Ontario and the West, 1890–1940* (Orange and Black Publications, 1984), 23.
30 Robert Choquette, *Language and Religion: A History of English–French Conflict in Ontario* (Ottawa: University of Ottawa Press, 1975), 174.
31 Roberto Perin, *The Immigrant's Church: The Third Force in Canadian Catholicism, 1880–1920* (Ottawa: Canadian Historical Association, 1998).
32 John Zucchi, "Introduction," in John Zucchi (trans.), *The View from Rome: Archbishop Stagni's 1915 Reports on the Ontario Bilingual Schools Question* (Montreal: McGill-Queen's, 2002), xxv.
33 Roberto Perin, *Rome in Canada: The Vatican and Canadian Affairs in the Late Victorian Age* (Toronto: University of Toronto Press, 1990), 19.
34 Ibid., 21–22.
35 Ibid., 21.
36 Terence J. Fay, *History of Canadian Catholics: Gallicanism, Romanism, and Canadianism* (Montreal: McGill-Queen's, 2002), 158.
37 Manzer, *Public Schools and Political Ideas*, 63–64.
38 As Fay has put it, the French "tended to see themselves as victims of an unparalleled provincial tyranny abetted by Irish Catholics" (Fay, *History*, 159).
39 Raymond M. Hebert, *Manitoba's French Language Crisis: A Cautionary Tale* (Montreal: McGill-Queen's, 2004), 13.
40 Wiseman, "Questionable Relevance," 713; Manzer, *Public Schools and Political Ideas*, 64.
41 James M. Pitsula, *For All We Have and Are: Regina and the Experience of the Great War* (Winnipeg, Manitoba: University of Manitoba Press, 2008), 244–247.
42 Anthony Appleblatt, "The School Question in the 1929 Saskatchewan Provincial Election," *CCHA Study Sessions* 43(1976): 75–90. Available at www.umanitoba.ca/colleges/st_pauls/ccha/Back%20Issues/CCHA1976/Appleblatt.html. Manzer, *Public Schools and Political Ideas*, 64.
43 Manzer, *Public Schools and Political Ideas*, 173–174.
44 Bruce W. Hodgins, "The Plans of Mice and Men," in Bruce W. Hodgins, Don Wright, and W.H. Heck, *Federalism in Canada and Australia: The Early Years* (Waterloo, Ontario: Wilfrid Laurier, 1978), 3–4; Bruce W. Hodgins, John J. Eddy, Shelagh D. Grant, and James Struthers (eds), *Federalism in Canada and Australia: Historical Perspectives, 1920–1988* (Peterborough, Canada: Frost Centre for Canadian Heritage and Development Studies, Trent University, 1989).
45 Richard Simeon and Ian Robinson, *State, Society, and the Development of Canadian Federalism* (Toronto: University of Toronto Press, 1990), 20. John MacDonald stated in 1864 that the problem with the United States Constitution "was that each state reserved to itself all sovereign rights save the small portion delegated. We must reverse this process." Quoted in Hodgins et al., "The Plans of Mice and Men," 3.
46 Simeon and Robinson, *State, Society, and the Development of Canadian Federalism*, 24.

47 Ibid.
48 Ibid., 53, 55.
49 Pradeep Chhibbers and Ken Kollman, *Formation of National Party Systems: Federalism and Party Competition in Canada, Great Britain, India, and the United States* (Princeton, NJ: Princeton University Press, 2004), 114.
50 For unionization rates, see George Sayers Bain and Robert Price, *Profiles of Union Growth: A Comparative Statistical Portrait of Eight Countries* (Oxford: Blackwell, 1980), 170. For strike rates, see Henry Stephen Albinski, *Canadian and Australian Politics in Comparative Perspective* (New York: Oxford University Press, 1973), 178–179. Cardinal Taschereau initially prohibited Catholics from joining the Knights, although the ban was lifted three years later under pressure from American bishops and the Archbishop of Montreal. See Education Committees of Confederation des Syndicats Nationaux and Centrale de l'enseignement du Quebec (trans. Arnold Bennett), *The History of the Labour Movement in Quebec* (Montreal: Black Rose, 1987), 52.
51 Data analyzed from Donald E. Blake, "Canadian Census and Election Data, 1908–1968," data deposited at ICPSR (ICPSR 39), http://doi.org/10.3886/ICPSR00039.v2.
52 Data on Australia are included in Appendix 4.
53 Paul Andre Linteau, Rene Durocher, and Jean-Claude Robert, *Quebec: A History, 1867–1929* (Toronto: Lorimer, 1983), 181. The Knights advocated for calling for public ownership of public services; progressive taxation; universal access to education; sexual, racial, and religious equality in the workplace, an eight-hour day, and an end to child labor. Education Committees, *The History of the Labour Movement in Quebec*, 52.
54 Bryan D. Palmer, *Working Class Experience: Rethinking the History of Canadian Labour, 1800–1991* (Toronto: McClelland and Stewart, 1992), 191–192.
55 Economics and Research Branch, Canada Department of Labor, *Union Growth in Canada, 1921–1967* (Ottawa: Information Canada, 1970), 80.
56 "Strikes in Canada, 1891–1950," in Gregory S. Kealey, *Workers and Canadian History* (Buffalo: McGill-Queen's, 1995), 351.
57 Robert A. Wright, "The Canadian Protestant Tradition, 1914–1945," in George A. Rawlyk (ed.), *The Canadian Protestant Experience, 1760–1990* (Montreal: McGill-Queen's, 1990), 145.
58 Bernard L. Vigod, *Quebec before Duplessis: The Political Career of Louis-Alexandre Taschereau* (Kingston: McGill-Queen's, 1986), 149–150; Dennis Guest, *The Emergence of Social Security in Canada*, 3rd edn (Vancouver: UBC, 1997), 74–78.
59 Simeon and Robinson, *State, Society, and the Development of Canadian Federalism*, 70.
60 Education Committees, *The History of the Labour Movement in Quebec*, 70.
61 Ibid., 129.
62 Daniel Beland and Andre Lecours, "Nationalism and Social Policy in Canada and Quebec," in Nicola McEwen and Luis Moreno (eds), *The Territorial Politics of Welfare* (New York: Routledge, 2005), 191.
63 Guest, *The Emergence of Social Security in Canada*, 90.
64 Beland and Lecours, "Nationalism and Social Policy in Canada and Quebec," 192.
65 Michael D. Behiels, *Prelude to Quebec's Quiet Revolution: Liberalism versus Neo-Nationalism, 1945–1960* (Kingston: McGill-Queen's, 1985), 88.
66 John Dickinson and Brian Young, *A Short History of Quebec*, 4th edn (Montreal: McGill-Queen's, 2008), 295.
67 Simeon and Robinson, *State, Society, and the Development of Canadian Federalism*, 138.
68 Alain G. Gagnon and Mary Beth Montcalm, *Quebec beyond the Quiet Revolution* (Scarborough, Ontario: Nelson Canada, 1989), 80.
69 Education Committees, *The History of the Labour Movement in Quebec*, 147.

70 Gregory Baum, *Catholics and Canadian Socialism: Political Thought in the Thirties and Forties* (New York: Paulist, 1980), 21, 52, 97–136.
71 Quoted in Teresita Kambeitz, "Relations between the Catholic Church and CCF in Saskatchewan, 1930–1950," CCHA, *Study Sessions* 46 (1979): 49–69. Available at www.umanitoba.ca/colleges/st_pauls/ccha/Back%20Issues/CCHA1979/Kambeitz.html.
72 Mills, *Fool for Christ*, 245.
73 Richard Allen, *The Social Passion: Religion and Social Reform in Canada, 1914–1928* (Toronto: University of Toronto, 1990), 154.
74 Hoffman notes that in 1964, only 11 percent of CCF MPs were Catholic. George Hoffman, "Saskatchewan Catholics and the Coming of a New Politics, 1930–1934," in Richard Allen (ed.), *Religion and Society in the Prairie West* (Regina: Canadian Plains Research Center, 1974), 88.
75 Baum, *Catholics and Canadian Socialism*, 110–111.
76 Ibid., 99–100.
77 Walter D. Young, *The Anatomy of a Party: The National CCF, 1932–61* (Toronto: University of Toronto Press, 1961), 210.
78 Ibid., 212–213.
79 Ibid., 214.
80 Mildred A. Schwartz, *Public Opinion and Canadian Identity* (Berkeley: University of California Press, 1967), 101.
81 Guest, *The Emergence of Social Security in Canada*, 132–133; Alvin Finkel, *Social Policy and Practice in Canada: A History* (Waterloo, Ontario: Wilfrid Laurier, 2006), 135–137.
82 Education Committees, *The History of the Labour Movement in Quebec*, 122.
83 Ibid., 127, 138.

7 Catholic standing in the latter half of the twentieth century

This book started with the example of *V for Vendetta* and the Guy Fawkes mask as a marker of the forgetting of Catholic stigma at the end of the twentieth century, evidence of the passage of Catholics into normality. The transformation in Catholic status involved not just the selective forgetting of the stigma of Catholicism, however. Also evident at the beginning of the twenty-first century was a focus on the celebration of Catholic identity, particularly from the conservative right. Two quotes in particular capture the dizzying transformation of Catholic valuation, with the border between the Protestant and Catholic becoming much fuzzier. Will Herberg, a conservative commentator for *National Review*, wrote in the 1960s that for Catholics, "Americanization has meant Protestantization."[1] By "Protestantization" Herberg meant that Catholics were now following their own individual consciences and being good democratic citizens, rather than adhering robotically to church doctrine. Political scientist Samuel Huntington agreed with this evaluation, noting that Catholics "do not like people referring to the 'Protestantization' of their religion," though "that is precisely what Americanization involves."[2] Yet just a little over three decades later, the *Washington Post* wrote an article analyzing the importance of Catholics to the George W. Bush presidency suggesting the reverse: it was Protestants who had been Catholicized. As the article put it, "If Bill Clinton can be called America's first black president [...] then George W. Bush could well be the nation's first Catholic president." Former U.S. Senator Rick Santorum called Bush "much more Catholic than Kennedy" and former Bush faith-based policy advisor John DiIulio deemed Bush a "closet Catholic."[3] As one former Bush speechwriter William McGurn put it, there were "more Catholics on President Bush's speechwriting team than on any Notre Dame starting lineup in the past half-century."[4]

The positive value placed on Catholicism and the "Catholicization" of non-Catholics was most evident in critiques launched against liberal Catholic politicians supporting abortion, gay marriage, and stem-cell research in the United States, Australia, and Canada. For instance, when Catholic Democrat John Kerry ran for the presidency in 2004, he did not have to issue a statement as John F. Kennedy did in 1960, or Al Smith in 1928, declaring his belief in the separation of church and state and his independence from the Vatican. Instead, Kerry came under attack by those who claimed he strayed too far from the doctrines of the

Roman Catholic Church. A few Catholic bishops declared that he should not receive communion because of his stance in support of abortion, and the Republican National Committee launched a website called "KerryWrongForCatholics.com."[5] As the media engaged in what comedian Jon Stewart deemed a "wafer watch" to see whether Kerry would be denied communion, Kerry remarked, "For John F. Kennedy, the challenge was to prove he wasn't too Catholic to be president. Mine was to prove I was Catholic enough."[6] Anti-Catholic Protestants had long maintained that Catholics were inherently slavish because they needed to be instructed from elite authorities as to the correct moral and spiritual readings of the Bible, while Protestants celebrated individual conscience. The historical irony of the Republican Party invoking papal authority to criticize Kerry has gone without much remark. The idea of "cafeteria Catholics" – Catholics following their conscience in deciding which of the church's doctrines to support – had once been celebrated by Herberg as "Protestantization" of the Church. Now it was a term of abuse flung by conservative Christians of all stripes against communicants like Kerry. Catholicism was not just something that had melted into the American mainstream, invisible because unremarkable. Rather, it was now positively valued.

Another potent sign of the transformation of the standing of Catholics is the respect the Pope has acquired in the evangelical imagination. The "culture of life," from one of John Paul II's encyclicals, has become a catchword for conservative Catholics and Protestants. As one official at the United States Conference of Catholic Bishops put it, "There are many Protestants who [...] have well thumbed copies of his encyclical on the gospel of life, and have read it more carefully than Catholics have."[7] One of those evangelical admirers, born-again George W. Bush, became the first U.S. president to attend the funeral of a Pope.[8] In another sign of evangelical approval, an unnamed Pope gets raptured up into heaven in the bestselling apocalyptic book series *Left Behind*, written by the evangelical Tim LaHaye.

These trends seem even more puzzling when one considers the sex scandals that have rocked the church. The evidence for the sexual molestation, assault, and rape of children, and the cover-up by the Catholic Church hierarchy, far outweigh the evidence for alleged Catholic abuses in convents in the nineteenth and early twentieth centuries. In February 2004, a report sponsored by the National Review Board of the Catholic Laity stated that $573 million had been paid to settle allegations against nearly 4,400 members of the clergy in the United States. More settlements have been paid since then, with dioceses in Tuscon and Portland declaring bankruptcy and several others in desperate financial straits.[9] The John Jay report conducted for the church calculated that 4 percent of the clergy in ministry from 1950 to 2002 had allegations of abuse made against them.[10] These abuses have been worldwide, as evident in Pope Benedict XVI's pastoral letter in March 2010 addressing scandals in Ireland and his more general apology on June 11, 2010 for the sex scandals perpetrated by the church.

A nineteenth-century anti-Catholic transported to the early twenty-first century would most likely have argued that the sexual abuses stem from the church's decision to maintain priestly celibacy and that the cover-up of the abuses is linked with the hierarchical, antidemocratic, and self-interested aspects of the church. But there has been little political attempt to stigmatize the Catholic Church other than from outspoken atheists like Christopher Hitchens and Richard Dawkins; no attempt to corner ordinary Catholics into a "with us or against us" position on crimes that have occurred within Catholic churches; and no politician seeking to shun connection or endorsement from Catholic Church officials, or mobilizing a political crusade to monitor Catholic priests' relations with children and prosecute priests accused of molesting children. President George W. Bush, for instance, stated that he was "confident the Church will clean up its business. […] I trust the leadership of the Church," and noted that the church was "an important part of our great country."[11] Instead of stigmatization, the opposite has often occurred. Catholics in some quarters are considered ideal Americans. As the non-Catholic *New York Times* columnist David Brooks put it, "If this country was entirely Catholic, we wouldn't be having a big debate over stagnant wages and low social mobility. The problems would scarcely exist."[12]

What these examples show is a reconstruction of religious identity on the right, with Catholics being brought together with Protestants under the broader umbrella identity as Christian conservatives. As will be shown in the following section of this chapter, political representation of Catholics from the 1960s to the beginning of the twenty-first century bears out these trends. Starting in the 1980s in the United States, Catholics began to be proportionately represented in right-leaning parties. Incorporation as Christian conservatives helped improve Catholic standing. One finds that not only have Roman Catholics achieved parity and equality of status overall, they have done better than one might have expected, at least in Australia and the United States. In particular, Catholics are overrepresented in political office much more in the United States than in Australia; there is less information available from Canada. Catholic voting behavior bears out these trends. The Catholic vote for right-leaning parties has been much more advanced in Australia and the United States than in Canada. The rest of this chapter will use these findings to question previous thinking on why the stigmatization of Catholics has disappeared and why valorization has sometimes appeared. Overall, explanations centered on assimilation, pluralism, and the changes that occurred in the Catholic Church during Vatican II have a hard time accounting for the timing and patterns of contemporary Catholic political incorporation into right-leaning parties in these countries.

Patterns of Catholic political incorporation

In the United States, Catholics are overrepresented across a broad range of political offices. Catholics, representing about 24 percent of the population of the United States, exceeded their population percentages in Congress, the Supreme Court, and state governorships. In the 109th Congress (2005–2006), Catholics represented nearly 30 percent of representatives of the House. Following Sonia

112 *Catholic standing: late twentieth century*

Sotomayor's successful nomination to the Supreme Court, Catholics constituted six of nine justices up until the death of Scalia in 2016. Catholics have been overrepresented among state governors since at least 2000 (see Figure 7.1) and were particularly well represented in 2004, when they constituted 40 percent of all governors. In recent years, most of this overrepresentation among governors has been concentrated on the Democratic side. In 2004 Catholics constituted eight out of 28 Republican governors (28 percent) and 14 out of 22 Democratic governors (63 percent), a proportion that easily exceeds the percentage that Catholics constitute among Democratic partisan identifiers.

Figure 7.2 shows that Catholics became overrepresented in the House in the 1980s. This was largely because Catholics, for the first time in U.S. history, reached population proportionality in the Republican House delegation, as may be seen in Figure 7.3. Although Catholics overall had achieved population proportionality in the House many decades earlier, this was largely due to overrepresentation within the Democratic Party. Starting with Reagan, Catholic representation in the Republican Party increased significantly.

In comparison, Australia also experienced Catholic overrepresentation, though not as widespread. In recent years, especially with the Liberal-National

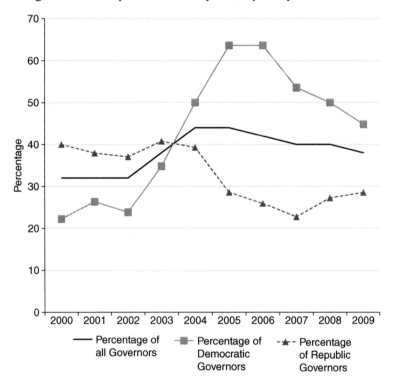

Figure 7.1 Percentage of Catholic U.S. Governors, 2000–2009.

Source: Governors' biographies at National Governor's Association website, via Internet Archive Wayback Machine.

Catholic standing: late twentieth century   113

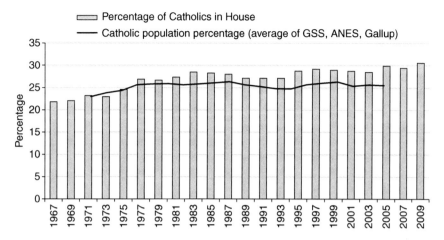

Figure 7.2 Percentage of Catholics in the U.S. House, 1967–2009.
Source: *Congressional Quarterly Weekly* and *Congressional Quarterly Almanac.*

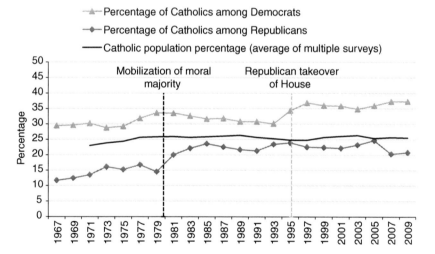

Figure 7.3 Percentage of Catholics in the U.S. House by party.
Source: *Congressional Quarterly Weekly* and *Congressional Quarterly Almanac.*

John Howard government from 1996 to 2007, there has been a resurgence of religion in political discourse, with a corresponding increase in the profile of Catholics. In 2007, with the Catholic proportion of the population at about 27 percent, the ministerial cabinet of the last Howard government included eight Catholics out of 18 (44 percent), an increase from six out of 18 in the previous Howard government (33 percent).[13] In addition, at the state level, Catholics have

114 Catholic standing: late twentieth century

become overrepresented among Liberal leaders in New South Wales in recent decades, with five of the last six being Catholics.[14]

Finding the religious affiliation of representatives in other Australian political offices is difficult, but there is evidence of Catholic overrepresentation. There have been eight Australian candidate studies conducted over the past few decades, which survey a sample of candidates running in the major parties for both Senate and House offices. Data on both party and religious affiliation are available from 1993 to 2007 (see Figures 7.4 and 7.5). The number of Catholic candidates running for the Liberal and National parties was lower than the actual percentage of Catholics in 1993, but since then it has slightly increased to approximately the proportion of the Catholic population in Australia. In comparison, the number of Catholic candidates running for the Australian Labor Party was about proportional to population in 1993 and 1996 (27.6 and 26.9 percent) but jumped to 39.1 percent in 2001, 36 percent in 2004, and 34.1 percent in 2007, which exceeds the percentage that Catholic voters constitute in the Labor coalition (32 percent among party identifiers and 31.6 percent of voters in 2001; 28.6 percent of Labor Party identifiers and 28.4 percent of Labor Party voters in the House in 2007).[15]

Catholic overrepresentation has also existed in Canada, though data limitations preclude conclusive characterization. Catholic prime ministers have

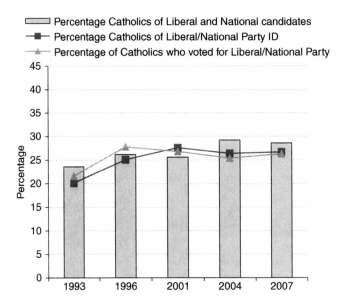

Figure 7.4 Percentage of Catholics among Liberal and National candidates in Australia, 1993–2007.

Source: Australian Candidate Studies.

Note
The surveys of candidates on which this figure is based represents a sampling of candidates to both the House of Commons and the Senate for the years 1993 ($n=411$), 1996 ($n=434$), 2001 ($n=460$), and 2004 ($n=508$).

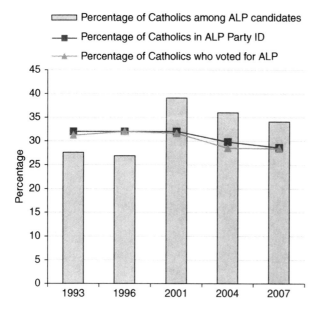

Figure 7.5 Percentage of Catholics among ALP candidates in Australia, 1993–2007.
Source: Australian Candidate Studies.

predominated in the latter half of the twentieth century. This probably reflects the fact that from World War II to the 1990s, the province of Quebec was one of the most important provinces in the Liberal coalition. At other levels of government, however, the pattern of Catholic overrepresentation is not present. When one looks at provincial premierships, Catholics are represented at about their population proportion of 45 percent. In 2006, for instance, five of the 12 provincial premiers were Catholic, i.e. around 40 percent. Recent data on the religious affiliation of members of the House of Commons are spotty, however. The data on religious affiliation from the *Canadian Parliamentary Guide* become increasingly unreliable in the late twentieth century, with the numbers not reporting religion becoming more numerous (See Figure 3.4). The data that do exist show proportionate representation of Catholics in the House of Commons up until about the mid-1980s. Another source of information about the legislature comes from candidate surveys, though these data are limited and do not carry through into the twenty-first century. A political candidate study in 1988 shows that Catholics were represented at about their population proportion in the Progressive Conservative Party and overrepresented in the Liberal Party, so although it is unknown which candidates were successful, it is possible that Catholics overall were overrepresented in Parliament, but at a time when the Progressive Conservatives were emphasizing conservative religious values.[16] In the 1990s, the Progressive Conservative coalition broke up, with the Reform Party

116 Catholic standing: late twentieth century

emerging as a conservative, more religious alternative in the western provinces. From the 1993 Canadian Candidate Study, Catholic representation among Progressive Conservative candidates decreased slightly to about 41 percent. In the Reform Party, Catholics comprised only about 16 percent of all the party's candidates, well below the Catholic population proportion in the western provinces, where the Reform Party fared the best.[17] Once religious issues became more prominent to parties on the right, Catholic integration was not as significant.

In the United States and Australia, at least, much of the gains in Catholic descriptive representation are correlated with greater comfortability of right-leaning parties with electing Catholic candidates. Analysis of the Catholic vote in the three countries shows a parallel increase in how readily Catholics have joined right-leaning parties. Figure 7.6 shows data for the Catholic partisan vote for the House of Representatives in Australia, the House of Representatives in the United States, and, for reference's sake, the House of Commons in Canada. For the purposes of this comparison, the Liberal, New Democratic, Bloc Quebecois, and Green parties in Canada are considered to be left-leaning.[18] Figure 7.7 shows that Catholics have moved into right-leaning parties more substantially in

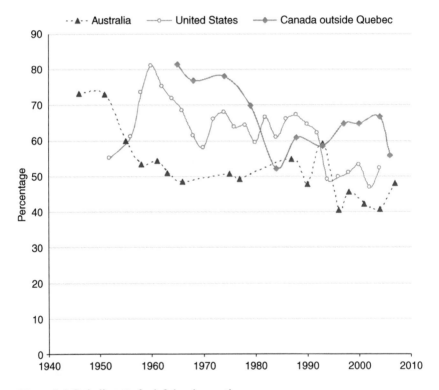

Figure 7.6 Catholic vote for left-leaning parties.

Source: American National Election Studies; Australian Election Studies; Canadian Election Studies. Reprinted with permission from Willie Gin, "Jesus Q. Politician: Religious Rhetoric in the United States, Australia, and Canada." *Politics and Religion* 5, no. 2 (August 2012).

Catholic standing: late twentieth century 117

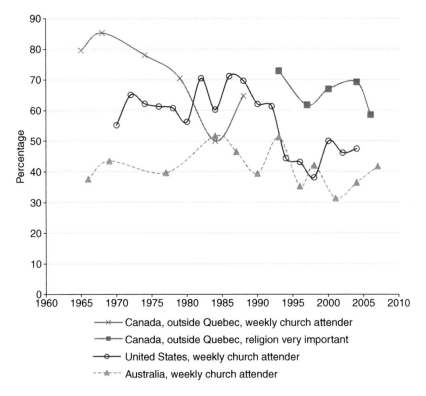

Figure 7.7 Catholic regular churchgoers, vote for left-leaning parties.

Source: ANES, AES, CES. Reprinted with permission from Gin, "Jesus Q. Politician".

Note
The CES stopped asking respondents about church attendance in 1993, and started asking a question about the importance of religion. The heavy line with open squares represents Catholics outside of Quebec who considered religion "very important."

Australia and the United States than in Canada. The same pattern holds if one looks at Catholics who are also regular churchgoers.

Evaluating alternative explanations

At the end of the twentieth century, Catholics became heavily overrepresented in the United States while being moderately overrepresented in Australia. This was in part driven by incorporation of Catholics into right-leaning parties emphasizing conservative values in response to opposing secularization. Such integration has occurred more deeply in the United States and Australia than in Canada. These patterns of Catholic standing and political incorporation do not simply continue the trends from the earlier period, when Catholic descriptive representation was largely driven by integration into center-left parties. Catholic

118 *Catholic standing: late twentieth century*

political incorporation had been far more advanced in Australia than in the United States, but at the end of the twentieth century that situation was reversed. Contemporary patterns show that other explanations based on demography, assimilation, mere coalitions, opportunities, and institutions cannot account for these new trends. Readers who are not interested in sorting through the details of these alternative explanations may skip ahead to Chapter 8 if they wish to see directly how the reconstructive coalition argument helps explain these new patterns.

Power resources

Catholic overrepresentation in the United States at the end of the twentieth century is unexpected because that is the country in which they constitute the smallest proportion of the population. At the start of the twenty-first century, Catholics comprise about 23 percent of the population in the United States, 27 percent in Australia, and 45 percent in Canada.

Perhaps part of the overrepresentation of Catholics in the United States stems from the overrepresentation of Catholics in higher income brackets. If one were to divide the population into household income thirds and look at the top one-third, Catholics in the United States constitute about 30 percent of all households in the top household income third in the first decade of the twenty-first century (see Figures 7.8, 7.9, and 7.10). By contrast, Australian Catholics have been

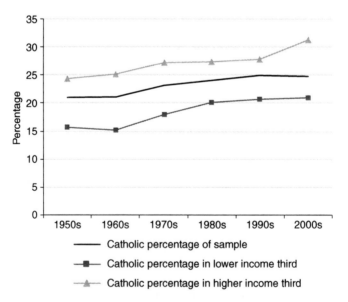

Figure 7.8 Catholic proportion in household income thirds: United States.

Source: ANES Cumulative Data File.

Note
Decade of the 2000s only includes up to 2004.

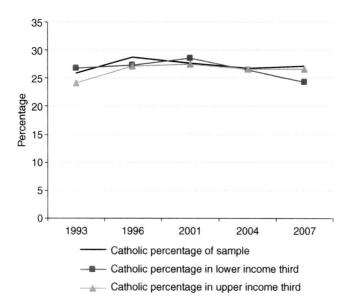

Figure 7.9 Catholic proportion in household income thirds: Australia.
Source: AES.

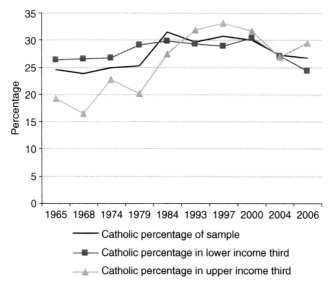

Figure 7.10 Catholic proportion in household income thirds: Canada, outside Quebec.
Source: CES.

represented at about their population proportion in all three income brackets since the 1990s. Canadian Catholics outside of Quebec were slightly underrepresented in the top household income third up until the 1990s, when they became about proportionally represented.

Although the overrepresentation of Catholics in the top one-third income bracket in the United States might be able to explain some of the overrepresentation in the House and the difference with Australia, it cannot explain the timing. Catholic overrepresentation in higher income brackets in the United States stems as far back as the 1950s (Figure 7.8), yet Catholic political overrepresentation in political offices is a much more recent phenomenon. In addition, Australian Catholics are overrepresented despite having no advantage in economic resources. This demonstrates that economic resources are not the prime factor driving the current overrepresentation.

Assimilation

One popular idea in explaining Catholic incorporation in the last half of the twentieth century is that Catholics have simply become assimilated and are no longer perceived as different from the rest of society. This perspective is limited in explaining the patterns of Catholic representation in the late twentieth century. For one, assimilation would suggest that Catholics would become represented at proportional levels, not overrepresented.

There are further considerations that suggest the limitations of an assimilation paradigm. One can break down the sources of tensions between Protestants and Catholics in the earlier half of the twentieth century. The sources of tension include the following:

1 The problem of church authority and Roman Catholic voters and politicians perceived as not being independent enough for republican self-rule.
2 Roman Catholic separate schools and attempts to acquire state funding for them, which led to perceptions of Catholics as promoting national disunity and separatism.
3 Perceptions that Roman Catholicism is associated with political illiberalism.
4 Perceptions that Roman Catholicism is associated with lack of economic prosperity.
5 Perceptions that Roman Catholicism is associated with immoral behavior, such as convent scandals and the oppression of women.
6 Doctrinal differences between Protestants and Roman Catholics, such as transubstantiation, the immaculate conception of Mary, and saint worship.
7 Violent conflicts between Protestants and Catholics in Ireland, as well as cases of religious oppression in countries where Roman Catholics are in the majority.

Many of the categories were perceived as inherently intertwined. For instance, exclusivist Protestants could argue that Catholic parochial schools contributed not just to separatism but also to intellectual, economic, and moral degradation. However, breaking down anti-Catholicism into its component dimensions is useful in examining in which areas tensions between Protestants and Catholics have been reduced.

One thing that has decisively changed is the association between Catholic and economic stagnation. As already mentioned, many Catholic ethnic groups in the United States are among the most prosperous, and nations such as Ireland with large Catholic populations have proven capable of having high and sustained economic growth. In general, the relationship between religion and economic success has become less clear, as non-Protestant countries such as Japan, South Korea, Taiwan, and now China and India, are proving to be economically dynamic.

Another decisive change occurred with Vatican II, which Pope John XXIII envisioned as an *aggiornamento*, an updating of the church. When Vatican II concluded at the end of 1965, the Catholic Church embraced greater democracy, allowing for experiments in liturgy, the use of vernacular in mass, and debate on contraception. One of the biggest surprises was the statement *Dignitatis Humanae*, which declared the church in support of freedom of conscience and religious liberty. The church also became more open to ecumenical exchanges.

These changes improved Catholic–Protestant relations. With economic progress, no longer could Protestants believe that Catholicism was inimical to capitalism. With Vatican II, no longer could Protestants simply declare the church to be against freedom. Dictatorships in heavily Catholic countries like Spain were replaced by democratic governments. Protestant evangelicals such as Billy Graham began to seek alliances with Catholics. Militant Protestant publications such as the Canadian *Sentinel* were phased out of existence, and Canadian lodges of the Orange Order shuttered their doors.[19]

There are good reasons, though, for not overestimating the effect of Vatican II on Catholic incorporation. Anti-Catholic discourse has always exaggerated the degree to which Catholics are mere automatons carrying out orders from the Vatican. Prior to Vatican II, for instance, many Roman Catholics in Protestant-dominated countries publicly declared their embrace of religious freedom.[20] This support paved the way for reform of the Catholic Church: the most vocal supporters of liberalizing changes at Vatican II were Catholic leaders from countries where Catholics constituted a minority.[21]

Another argument against the singular importance of Vatican II in transforming Catholic–Protestant relations relates to timing. In the United States, Catholics achieved proportionality in the Republican caucus in the House in the 1980s, well after Vatican II. The same occurred in Australia only in the 1990s. Even if Vatican II was an important "trigger," one would need to explore the factors that made eventual incorporation into right-leaning parties occur much later. Vatican II and assimilation may be a necessary but not a sufficient condition for the increase in Catholic representation in right-leaning parties.

In addition, after Vatican II, there was significant retrenchment in the Catholic Church. The encyclical *Humanae Vitae* attempted to outlaw the use of contraception in 1968, after two commissions of laypeople and clerics had advised the Pope to end the ban. Many Catholics simply ignored the encyclical.[22] John Paul II and Cardinal Joseph Ratzinger helped sweep away more liberal Catholic bishops and in some cases have reprimanded more liberal groups in the church.[23] John Paul II and Benedict XVI have continued to invoke authority on a wide variety of questions such as communism and moral issues. The recent "Doctrinal Note on Some Questions Regarding the Participation of Catholics in Political Life," issued as a political guide during the U.S. elections of 2008, clarified the church's position on freedom of conscience. Regarding religious liberty, the document states that the right to freedom of conscience is not based

> on the fact that all religions and all teachings, including those that are erroneous, would have more or less equal value. [...] The teaching on freedom of conscience and on religious freedom does not therefore contradict the condemnation of indifferentism and religious relativism by Catholic doctrine.[24]

Hence, though the church is publicly in favor of freedom of conscience and religious liberty, in practice it does more than merely advise its practitioners, and it considers some of its doctrines as inherently right. Kerry himself had invoked the right of religious conscience articulated at Vatican II as a reason for his stance on the legality of abortion, yet not only did conservative Catholics disagree, but also evangelical Protestants.[25] A number of priests have threatened Catholic politicians and voters to act or vote according to Catholic doctrine, or risk denial of communion or excommunication from the church.

In addition, the transnational Catholic Church has continued to support separate schools, and, as already mentioned, abundantly documented sex scandals among priests provide much more potential ammunition than the often fictitious "convent scandals" in the past for seeing the Roman Catholic Church as associated with immoral behavior. Doctrinal differences between Protestants and Roman Catholics remain, and some fundamentalist Protestants such as Bob Jones, Jr. and John Hagee in the United States continue to invoke the Pope as a Satanic force.[26] Lingering notions of Protestant providentialism may also still be found in academic discourse. As the scholar Samuel Huntington put it in 2004,

> Would America be the America it is today if in the seventeenth and eighteenth centuries it had been settled not by British Protestants but by French, Spanish, or Portuguese Catholics? The answer is no. It would not be America; it would be Quebec, Mexico, or Brazil.[27]

In summary, some of the same themes that were deployed against Catholics in the earlier part of the twentieth century could still be deployed against them in the latter part of the twentieth century. Perusing the list above, one could argue that the basis still exists for arguing against Catholicism on grounds that it is too hierarchical, promotes separatism and immorality, and espouses fundamentally different doctrines than Protestants. Even on economic grounds, a committed anti-Catholic may be able to conjure up some argument about how Catholic parties in Europe and their commitment to state welfare schemes might be crucial in explaining "Euro-stagnation." Hence, assimilation does not seem to be the most important factor in explaining why it is that the figure of the Catholic is invoked positively in political discourse.

Coalitions

In all three countries, significant proportions of Catholics were voting for right-leaning parties. As may be seen in Figure 7.6 and 7.7, the proportion of Catholics voting for left-leaning parties in Australia had already declined by the mid-century, followed by a smaller decline in the 1990s. In the United States, Catholic voting for left-leaning parties declined slightly in the 1960s after Kennedy, then more steeply in the 1990s. Catholics comprised a larger proportion of right-leaning parties in Australia than in the United States at the end of the twentieth century, but it is in the United States that one finds the most significant degree of Catholic overrepresentation. If merely being an electoral coalition partner transforms status, one might have expected the phenomenon of overrepresentation to occur in Australia first, then in the United States, but the reverse is true. The mere fact of coalition doesn't seem to explain differences in transformation of standing in Catholics.

Political opportunities

Might variations in political opportunities better account for the timing and inter-country patterns of Catholic representation observed? There is more convincing evidence here in terms of timing, but even this explanation is incomplete. The most obvious change in political opportunity is growing secularization. In all three societies there has been an expulsion of religion from a privileged position in the public sphere, providing a new opportunity for conservative Protestants to seek out conservative Catholics as allies. In the case of the United States, for much of its early history up until the mid-twentieth century, a moral establishment existed that excluded non-believers and smaller religions. Expressions of non-belief were punished by laws against blasphemy. Prayer and generalized religious instruction were allowed in public schools, a move criticized by some Catholics as covertly importing Protestant beliefs. Sunday closing laws discriminated against Jews, Seventh Day Adventists, and non-believers. Restrictions against contraception, abortion, and homosexuality were consonant with conservative Protestant morality.[28]

The foundations of this moral establishment were eroded over the course of the twentieth century. Increasingly the Supreme Court incorporated the religion clauses of the First Amendment into the Fourteenth Amendment, thus barring state governments from infringing religious freedom. Beginning in the 1960s, the Supreme Court struck down school prayer (*Engel* v. *Vitale*), school Bible

124   *Catholic standing: late twentieth century*

reading (*Abington School District* v. *Schempp*), anticontraception laws (*Griswold* v. *Connecticut*), antiabortion regulations (*Roe* v. *Wade*), and the criminalization of homosexuality (*Lawrence* v. *Texas*), upsetting conservative Protestants.

Moral establishments were also eroded in Australia and Canada. In Australia there was never a federal Sunday-closing law, though each state within Australia legislated for such laws. Many of these states now allow commerce on Sundays. In Australia each state also has its own separate abortion laws. State courts played a part in liberalizing abortion rights in some states, while legislatures led abortion reform in others.[29] With regard to gay marriage rights, though the federal Parliament has restricted the definition of marriage to one man and one woman, civil unions have been recognized in the states of New South Wales, Victoria, Tasmania, and the Australian Capital Territory, with those civil unions recognized at the federal level for the purposes of federal benefits.

In Canada, Protestantism did not occupy a privileged public position relative to Catholicism as a result of the status of the two groups as "founding peoples" of the Canadian nation. The allowance of Catholic and Protestant separate schools in some provinces reflected this compromise. However, there was still a "moral establishment" supporting religion and regulating a wide variety of behaviors. By the early 1970s, Canada considered itself more explicitly as a "multicultural" nation.[30] The adoption of the Charter and Rights and Freedom in 1984 further eroded the position of public Christianity in Canada, with courts insisting on greater separation of church and state.[31] Rulings against Sunday closing laws and prayer in schools followed.[32] In 1988 the Canadian Supreme Court ruled in *Morgentaler* to strike down federal regulation requiring women seeking abortions to seek the approval of abortion committees. The Canadian Supreme Court left it open to the legislature to devise abortion regulations absent the need for abortion committees, but the federal government has largely avoided the abortion issue, which has meant in practice that there is no legal regulation of abortion access throughout Canada beyond a requirement that a doctor perform the abortion. Canadian courts and legislatures have also been active in protecting gay marriage rights. Nine provincial courts supported gay marriage based on the Charter, leading to Prime Minister Paul Martin's decision to draft legislation at the federal level to affirm the legality of homosexual marriage in 2005.

Along with these transformations in public law, there have been significant religious transformations at the societal level. Both Australia and Canada have experienced significant declines in weekly church attendance.[33] All three countries have also experienced significant increases in the number of people willing to express no belief in God. Societal attitudes have changed as well. Statistics confirm increased consumption of pornography, an increase in premarital sex, divorce, single-parent families, and non-married families.[34]

The decline of the privileged position of Protestantism and Christianity in the public sphere in these three countries, led by the courts, legislatures, and societal developments, has had several consequences. First, it has made Protestants more receptive to the idea of authority. Christianity's devaluation in the public sphere made conservative Protestants more open to the idea that society was spinning out of control for lack of guiding core virtues and values. Sociological research seemed to lend support to the idea that greater authority is associated with more flourishing churches. In 1972 Dean Kelly argued in *Why Conservative Churches Are Growing* that stricter churches prompted greater church membership and attendance. Stricter churches were defined as espousing absolutism, conformity, and fanaticism, while less strict churches such as mainline churches were defined as espousing relativism, diversity, and dialogue. This thesis was echoed in Laurence Iannaccone's 1994 article, "Why Strict Churches Are Strong." Such research provided fuel to the argument that the problem was liberalization of attitudes and creeping relativism in liberal churches, thus strengthening the case for the need for authority.[35]

Conservative Protestant concerns over authority have been reinforced by splits within Protestantism. Wuthnow has documented how a split between liberals and conservatives became increasingly prominent within all denominations. During the New Deal era, liberal churches organized under the Federal Council of Churches that had a privileged position in the public sphere. Fundamentalist churches and evangelicals associated with the National Association of Evangelicals opposed greater state intervention in economy, the "social gospel" touted by the FCC.

In addition, the decline of the "moral establishment" along with an increase in the perception that the government has to be secular and neutral has meant that conservative Christian groups have more fully embraced a strategy in which public funds supplement vigorous Christian institutions in civil society. Although evangelicals have not fully embraced separatism in the way that fundamentalist Christians have, evangelicals have supported policies such as vouchers. When the "moral establishment" was strong and Protestants dominant in civil society, conservative Protestants could afford to oppose public funding of private religious institutions, such as schools.

In summary, secularization has occurred in all three countries, giving an opportunity for conservative Protestants to ally with conservative Catholics. Yet, despite this similar potential in all three societies, the relative success of conservative Christian coalitions incorporating Catholics and conservative Protestants has differed. Catholics achieved proportionate representation in the Republican Party in the United States in the 1980s, and in the Liberal–National coalition in the 1990s. Although Canadian Catholics were proportionately represented in the Progressive Conservative Party in the 1980s, Catholics did not achieve proportionate representation in the more religiously oriented Reform Party in the 1990s.

The larger size of the evangelical population in the United States may help explain why a Christian conservative coalition more quickly organized and called on conservative Catholics as allies, thus leading to Catholic overrepresentation. This may be part of the explanation, but it is not the full one. It does not take into account that there were other factors that made the coalescence of conservative Catholics and Protestants possible, in particular the transformation of the Jim Crow order in the South, which had previously made a left-leaning reconstructive moral coalition difficult. A brief comparison of Australia and Canada also shows that movement of conservative Catholics and Protestants together does not occur simply in response to the size of the religious population. The religious population is larger in Canada than in Australia, but Canadian Catholics did not constitute as much of a proportion of right-leaning parties as in Australia in the 1990s and early 2000s, as may be seen in Figures 7.6 and 7.7.

Political institutions

One reason the religious right combining Catholics and Protestants may have fared better in the United States compared to the other countries is that the political institutional structure may favor it. In a parliamentary Westminster system, political representatives are under much more pressure to adhere to the party's position. By contrast, in the United States, elections are much more "candidate centered." There is also much greater separation of powers in the United States, leading to more veto points. These include the separation of the executive from the legislature, and greater division between federal and state courts. In the United States, states play a larger role in the selection of state judges, and in many cases these judges are elected. In Canada and Australia, provincial and state judges are selected by the federal government. These multiple points of access in the United States may make it easier for the religious right, when confronted with the political opportunity of secularization, to sustain mobilization.[36]

These elements of political institutional structure may explain the difference between the United States and Australia, but they don't really explain difference between Australia and Canada when we look at the movement of Catholics toward right-leaning parties. Both countries share a parliamentary system, and have a similar system of appointed state judges. There are differences in federalism in the two countries. The criminal code is determined at the federal level in Canada while more of it is determined at the state level in Australia, so issues like abortion and pornography are under the sovereignty of the national government in Canada. However, it is not clear which situation leads to greater conservative religious mobilization. On the one hand, one could argue that in a system with multiple access points, the Christian right would be mobilized to a greater degree. On the other hand, one could argue that with fewer veto points there is greater conservative religious frustration and thus there should be more mobilization in the system with fewer veto points.[37]

Some might argue that the success of conservative religious movements in the United States is a result of a popular backlash against the judicially led transformation of society. The Supreme Court played a pivotal role in removing prayer and religious education from public schools in the 1960s and legalizing abortion in the 1970s. Supreme Court Justice Ruth Bader Ginsburg has suggested that legislative-led change may have sparked a less conservative backlash.[38] This explanation would not explain Australia and Canada however. Societal change in religion in schools and abortion has been led more by the legislature in Australia compared to the United States. In Canada, the Charter of Rights and Freedoms, enacted in the 1980s, has led to the more judicially led transformation of moral politics. However, it is in Australia where one finds greater relative success of conservative pan-Christian coalitions compared to Canada.

Contemporary reconstructive coalitions and Catholic standing

Patterns of Catholic representation do not neatly follow linear trends from the first half of the twentieth century. These divergences, as well as the phenomenon of overrepresentation, cast doubt on theories of incorporation that stress power resources, assimilation, Vatican II, mere coalitions, opportunities, and institutions. As in the first half of the twentieth century, the success of reconstructive coalitions helped determine changes in Catholic standing at the end of twentieth century. The reconstructive coalition explanation focuses on coalitions in which there is an identity that bridges minority groups with majority groups under the umbrella of a more embracing identity. Such a coalition, first, helps raise the standing of Catholics in the eyes of its coalition partners, and, second, it prompts competing coalitions to redouble their efforts to recapture the Catholic voters they once had. The post-World War II era presented new issues on which conservative Catholics could be united with conservative Protestants in reconstructive coalitions, particularly on conservative religious issues.[39] Whether this opportunity became an actual alliance between evangelicals and Catholics, however, depended on the centrality of Catholics to the movement and previous institutional legacies shaping the preferences of Catholics to enter into these reconstructive coalitions. The institutional conditions that helped make pan-Christian coalitions possible include elements such as preference voting, previous settlements on public funding of Catholic schools, and the presence of strong regional identities that can cross-cut the national significance of potential moral issues. In the United States, the South moved closer to the rest of the country, making a reconstructive moral coalition possible. In Canada, Quebec's distinctive position remained, making reconstructive moral coalitions more difficult. Chapters 8 and 9 will document in more detail the emergence of reconstructive coalitions in the three countries

Notes

1 Will Herberg, "Plight of American Catholicism," *National Review* August 27, 1968, 852–853.
2 Samuel Huntington, *Who Are We? The Challenges to America's Identity* (New York: Simon & Schuster, 2004), 96.
3 Daniel Burke, "A Catholic Wind in the White House," *Washington Post*, April 13, 2008, B02.
4 Ibid.
5 Michael Kranish, "GOP Urges Catholics to Shun Kerry," *Boston Globe*, September 26, 2004, A1.

6 Sasha Issenberg, "Kerry Says Religion Has Place in Politics," *Boston Globe*, November 2, 2004, A15.
7 Laurie Goldstein, "Schiavo Case Highlights an Alliance Between Catholics and Evangelicals," *New York Times*, March 24, 2005, 20. For information on a Greenberg Quinlan Rosner Research poll finding evangelicals admiring John Paul II more than Jerry Falwell or Pat Robertson, see "America's Evangelicals More and More Mainstream But Insecure," April 13, 2004. Available at https://web.archive.org/web/20080306034938/www.pbs.org/wnet/religionandethics/week733/release.html.
8 Jim VandeHei, "Freedom, Culture of Life United Bush and Pope," *Washington Post*, April 7, 2005, A19.
9 Jo Renee Formicola, "Catholicism and Pluralism: A Continuing Dilemma for the Twenty-First Century," in Barbara A. McGraw and Jo Renee Formicola, eds, *Taking Religious Pluralism Seriously: Spiritual Politics on America's Sacred Ground* (Waco: Baylor, 2005), 78–79.
10 Betty Clermont, *The Neo-Catholics: Implementing Christian Nationalism in America* (Atlanta: Clarity Press, 2009), 179.
11 Ibid., 171.
12 "The Catholic Boom," *New York Times*, May 25, 2007.
13 These eight were Tony Abbott, Kevin Andrews, Helen Coonan, Joe Hockey, Brendan Nelson, Peter McGauran, Malcolm Turnbull, and Mark Vaile. Christopher Pearson, "Catholics Flock to Cabinet," *The Australian*, February 3, 2007. Available at https://web.archive.org/web/20070331233244/www.theaustralian.news.com.au/story/0%2C20867%2C21160589-7583%2C00.html.
14 These were Nick Greiner, John Fahey, Peter Collins, Kerry Chikarovski, and John Brogden.
15 At the state level, according to at least one close observer of religion and politics in Australia, it is also unusual in recent decades for practicing Catholics to be the premier (Morris Iemma) and the deputy premier of the state Labor Party in New South Wales. John Warhurst, "Catholic Pollies Cover a Range of Ideologies," *The Canberra Times*, June 14, 2007, A19.
16 Andre Blais, "Accounting for the Electoral Success of the Liberal Party in Canada – Presidential Address to the Canadian Political Science Association, London, Ontario, June 3, 2005," *Canadian Journal of Political Science* 38, no. 4 (December 2005): 829.
17 From the 1991 Census, Roman Catholics comprised about 25 percent of the population in Alberta and Manitoba, and 30 percent in Sasketchewan. Obtaining religious affiliation in Canada since the 1990s has been extremely difficult. There was one candidate survey of those running for provincial office in British Columbia in 2009. In the Liberal Party, approximately 14 percent of candidates were Catholic, while Catholics constituted 17 percent of the provincial population in 2001, so there is no evidence of overrepresentation there. Survey conducted by the *Vancouver Sun*; information was formerly available at www.vancouversun.com/news/bc-election/candidates-survey.html (accessed 2009). Unfortunately, there is not much other data available on religious affiliation. This difficulty may in itself be a sign that religion in general is considered not as significant and that it is unnecessary to "signal" such information to the public. In comparison, one can note how eagerly John Howard in Australia remarked upon the number of Catholics in his cabinet.
18 There may be some concern about labeling the Liberal Party in Canada as left-leaning, particularly in the mid-twentieth century, though even back then that party supported state intervention in the economy through both national health insurance and equalization payments between the provinces. By the 1980s the Progressive Conservative Party began emphasizing more explicitly less state intervention, and this trend has increased with the Reform Party and its successors, the Alliance and Conservative Parties.

19 See Eric Kaufmann, "The Orange Order in Ontario, Newfoundland, Scotland, and Northern Ireland: A Macro-social Analysis." Available at www.sneps.net/OO/images/1-paper%20for%20Toronto%2006-graphs%20in.pdf, 16–17.
20 George Seldes, *The Catholic Crisis* (New York: J. Messner, 1939), 345.
21 Melissa J. Wilde, *Vatican II: A Sociological Analysis of Religious Change* (Princeton, NJ: Princeton University Press, 2007).
22 James Morone, *Hellfire Nation: The Politics of Sin in American History* (New Haven, CT: Yale University Press, 2003), 410–411.
23 David Van Biema, "Is Liberal Catholicism Dead?," *Time*, May 3, 2008. Available at www.time.com/time/nation/article/0,8599,1737323,00.html; Laurie Goodstein, "Vatican Reprimands a Group of U.S. Nuns and Plans Changes," *New York Times*, April 19, 2012, A16.
24 Congregation for the Doctrine of the Faith, "Doctrinal Note on Some Questions Regarding the Participation of Catholics in Political Life," Vatican website. Available at www.vatican.va/roman_curia/congregations/cfaith/documents/rc_con_cfaith_doc_20021124_politica_en.html.
25 See "The Politics of Communion," *Christianity Today*, June 1, 2004. Available at www.christianitytoday.com/ct/2004/june/10.24.html.
26 In recent political campaigns, George W. Bush's ties to Bob Jones, Jr. and John McCain's ties to Hagee were highlighted in an attempt to portray those candidates as anti-Catholic.
27 Huntington, *Who Are We?*, 59.
28 David Sehat, *The Myth of American Religious Freedom* (New York: Oxford University Press, 2011), ch. 1.
29 For an overview see Natasha Cica, "Abortion Law in Australia," Research Paper 1, 1998–1999, August 31, 1998. Available at www.aph.gov.au/About_Parliament/Parliamentary_Departments/Parliamentary_Library/pubs/rp/rp9899/99rp01; Karen Coleman, "The Politics of Abortion in Australia: Freedom, Church, and State," *Feminist Review* 29 (summer 1988): 75–97.
30 Gary Miedema, *For Canada's Sake: Public Religion, Centennial Celebrations, and the Remaking of Canada in the 1960s* (Montreal: McGill-Queen's, 2006).
31 Mark Noll, "What Happened to Christian Canada?," *Church History* 75, no. 2 (June 2006): 258.
32 See *R. v. Big M Drug Mart Ltd.* For school prayer in Ontario, see *Zylberberg v. Sudbury Board of Education* (1988); for British Columbia, see *Russow and Lambert v. Attorney General of British Columbia* (1989). For the decision preventing teaching of Christianity in school, see the *Elgin County* ruling in Ontario in 1990.
33 Willie Gin, "Jesus Q. Politician: Religious Rhetoric in the United States, Australia, and Canada," *Politics and Religion* 5, no. 2 (2012): 321.
34 Theodore Caplow, Howard M. Bahr, John Modell, and Bruce A. Chadwick, *Recent Social Trends in the United States, 1960–1990* (Montreal: McGill-Queen's, 1991); Lance W. Roberts, Rodney A. Clifton, Barry Ferguson, Karen Kampen, and Simon Langlois, *Recent Social Trends in Canada, 1960–2000* (Montreal: McGill-Queen's, 2005), 432–435; 145–148, 513–517; Kevin Andrews and Michelle Curtis, *Changing Australia: Social, Cultural, and Economic Trends Shaping the Nation* (Sydney: Federation Press, 1998), 29–49; Barbara Ann Sullivan, *The Politics of Sex: Prostitution and Pornography in Australia Since 1945* (Cambridge: Cambridge University Press, 1997), 125.
35 For critiques of the strict church thesis, see Shayne Lee and Phillip Luke Sinitiere, *Holy Mavericks: Evangelical Innovators and the Spiritual Marketplace* (New York: New York University Press, 2009), which notes that many of the most successful mega-churches are not strict in the sense advocated by Kelly and Iannoccone. Others have argued that the success of evangelical churches in the United States stems less from their strictness than from the tendency of evangelicals to have larger families, a

tendency that may be decreasing with increasing education and income. See Michael Hout, Andrew M. Greeley, and Melissa J. Wilde, "The Demographic Imperative in Religious Change," *American Journal of Sociology* 107, no. 2 (2001): 468–500.

36 Miriam Smith, *Political Institutions and Lesbian and Gay Rights in the United States and Canada* (New York: Routledge, 2008), ch. 1.

37 Dennis R. Hoover, "The Christian Right under Old Glory and the Maple Leaf," in Corwin E. Smidt and James M Pening (eds), *Sojourners in the Wilderness: The Christian Right in Comparative Perspective* (New York: Rowman & Littlefield, 1997), 207.

38 See, e.g., Emily Bazelon, "Backlash Whiplash," *Slate*, May 2013. Available at www.slate.com/articles/news_and_politics/jurisprudence/2013/05/justice_ginsburg_and_roe_v_wade_caution_for_gay_marriage.html.

39 Conservative religious morality is not the only reconstructive identity to emerge from the right during this period. The contemporary right in all three countries has also advocated larger umbrella identities around class, stressing a "productive" class of job creators and taxpayers versus a "parasitical" class of welfare cheats and tax takers. This has likely improved Catholic–Protestant relations, and the fact that Catholics have advanced more economically in the United States compared to Australia may explain the greater overrepresentation of Catholics in the United States compared to Australia. However, an emphasis on religious reconstruction is still warranted. When a producerist identity is coupled with a broader religious values identity, then reconstruction is likely to be more extensive. This may be seen in the data. Despite the fact that Catholics have been overrepresented in the top income third in the United States since the 1950s, a producerist identity did not lead to substantial Catholic representation among Congressional Republicans.

8 Realigning Catholicism and Protestantism at the turn of the twentieth century in the United States

If one were seeking examples of the integration of Catholics with evangelicals into the Republican Party, all one has to do is look at the 2012 Republican presidential primary, in which two of the three leading contenders for the nomination were Catholic. Rick Santorum, an Italian Catholic from western Pennsylvania, had made a name for himself as a staunch supporter of the rights of the unborn, heterosexual marriage, and the traditional family. Newt Gingrich had converted to Catholicism in 2009 and had just produced a documentary extolling Pope John Paul II's role in the fall of communism. In a gathering of 114 influential evangelical leaders prior to the South Carolina primary, 85 voted to endorse Santorum, while 29 endorsed Gingrich over the frontrunner, Mitt Romney.[1] Although Romney eventually won the nomination, early in the primary campaign evangelical voters tended to prefer the other two candidates. Prior to dropping out of the nomination battle in early April, Santorum received more votes from evangelicals than Romney. In the first 16 Republican primaries, Santorum won a plurality of the evangelical vote in nine of them; in states where evangelicals were over half the primary voters, Santorum won those states.[2] Santorum won the popular vote in a total of 11 states, despite being outspent by Romney.[3] Although evangelical preference for Santorum may have stemmed to some degree from Romney's Mormon background, Republican voters had already expressed their preference for Santorum over other evangelical candidates such as Tim Pawlenty, Michele Bachmann, Herman Cain, and Rick Perry. The 2012 primaries represented the culmination of a long process in which conservative Protestants could see a Roman Catholic as best representing their interests. To underscore the transformation of the politics of Catholicism and religion from 1960, Santorum noted during his campaign that he almost "threw up" when he read Kennedy's 1960 declaration that he would keep church and state separate in his politics.[4]

Romney subsequently chose Paul Ryan, a Catholic House representative, as his vice-presidential running mate (Obama's vice-president, Joe Biden, also happened to be Catholic).[5] Ryan, who became Speaker of the House in 2015, has become a leading figure among Republicans for his positions on cutting the deficit, and he has often emphasized Catholic teaching in explaining his positions on deficit politics. Santorum and Ryan's appeal to Republican evangelical voters marked another milestone in the growing coziness between conservative Catholics and other conservative Christians.

The closeness of conservative Catholics and Republicans over moral issues highlights the role of reconstructive coalitions in improving Catholic standing. The previous chapter showed that the timing of improvement in Catholic descriptive representation in right-leaning parties in the United States and Australia coincided with the rise of Christian conservative coalitions seeking to reinstate the predominance of religion in the public sphere. Two conditions turned this new political opportunity into a reconstruction of majority evaluations of Catholics: (1) the organizational and symbolic centrality of Catholics to this moral values coalition, and (2) the decline of Southern distinctiveness, which had impeded reconstruction of identity around class in the 1930s. This chapter further bolsters a reconstructive coalition theory of change by showing how Catholics were crucial partners in a variety of moral struggles, in many cases being the leaders or key figures in these movements. An important element of the reconstructive coalition theory is that such coalitions spark a rearticulation of identities into broader political identities, and this may be seen most dramatically in conservative ecumenical efforts like Evangelicals and Catholics Together in the 1990s.

Christian Über Alles? Pan-Christianity in the United States

The idea of a conservative "ecumenism in the trenches" uniting Protestants and Catholics can be traced back to conservative Protestants' confrontation with liberal and modernist theology. J. Gresham Machen, who split from the modernist northern Presbyterian Church to form the Orthodox Presbyterian Church, noted in the early twentieth century,

> How great is the common heritage which unites the Roman Catholic Church […] to devout Protestants today! We would not indeed obscure the difference which divides us from Rome. The gulf is indeed profound. But profound as it is, it seems almost trifling compared to the abyss which stands between us and many ministers of our own Church.[6]

Similarly, the Anglican C.S. Lewis, author of the popular Narnia children's books, advocated "mere Christianity" to describe the core doctrines that both Protestants and Catholics shared.[7]

Two factors prevented such a national coalition from emerging. The first was that it was not until the 1960s that the churches began to lose their privileged status in the public sphere, with court decisions affirming the right to contraception and banning prayer and religious teaching in public schools. Once this occurred conservative Catholics became central, both organizationally and symbolically, to conservative Christian movements. Second, strong regional identity and autonomy in the South helped prevent national moral coalitions from bringing Catholics and Protestants together. Once the institution of Jim Crow collapsed, national reconstructive coalitions became more likely.

The centrality of Catholics in the coalition

Features distinctive to Catholics made them well suited for conservative moral coalitions against perceived liberal permissiveness. First, there is a central authority in the Catholic Church that defines some core doctrines, so that there can be an appeal to doctrinal authority. For other churches there is no such central doctrinal position. Southern Baptists, for instance, conceive of their denomination as congregational, with the local church having much autonomy, even though there are national coordinating bodies such as the Southern Baptist Convention (SBC). Even when the SBC adopts an issue position, Baptists of different persuasions such as the mainline American Baptist Churches or the largely African American National Baptist Convention can offer differing interpretations of Baptist tradition. The same applies to the National Association of Evangelicals, which includes a wide variety of church traditions. As a result, it is often difficult to invoke the authority of the church to argue that there is a "correct position" on an issue.

One might argue that the significance of Catholic positions on various issues is overblown and feeds into old stereotypes about Catholics being subject to a foreign potentate. Even though there are core doctrinal positions espoused by the Roman Catholic hierarchy, there is often significant resistance within the laity to those positions. Most notably, much of the laity has ignored Catholic prohibitions of the use of contraceptives, and the overwhelming majority of Catholics use forms of birth control other than abstinence or the rhythm method. Even though the existence of a plurality of opinions around contentious issues within the Catholic Church is a sociological fact, much like it is for other denominations, the existence of "official" positions makes debates around Catholicism that much more contentious. Terms such as "cafeteria Catholics" imply that some Catholics are not genuine Catholics because they are picking and choosing what they want to believe rather than what the church espouses. Denial of or threats to deny communion have been issued to Catholics who are perceived as going against Catholic doctrine, highlighting the potential stigma Catholics may face if they veer from church doctrine.

The second reason the Catholic Church is central to these debates is because the issues that it has staked a position on typically split the left–right partisan divide. The church has relatively conservative positions on issues like abortion, same-sex marriage, and contraception, but it also has liberal positions on issues such as pre-emptive war, the death penalty, and immigration. One can argue about whether the church is closer to the left or the right. For instance, in 2012, the Vatican reprimanded the U.S. Leadership Conference of Women Religious, the most prominent group representing 57,000 nuns in the United States, for focusing too much on poverty instead of on abortion and gay marriage, and also diverging from positions held by the U.S. Conference of Catholic Bishops and supporting President Obama's healthcare reform.[8] Still, the church does not completely fall on one or the other side of the political spectrum. If the church consistently advocated positions favoring one party over another, there would be a reason for non-favored parties to stigmatize or otherwise ignore Catholics. Because the Catholic Church positions itself near a "symbolic median" between the left and the right, its positions may also be used by both conservatives and liberals to attack each other's policies.

The ascension of Pope Francis, following the unexpected resignation of Pope Benedict XVI in 2013, reaffirms the unusual position of the Catholic Church in domestic debates between the right and the left. Because Pope Francis has downplayed issues like abortion and gay marriage and put a greater spotlight on economic inequality, Democrats in the United States have seized on his comments as support for measures like extension of unemployment insurance. Even non-Catholics such as Bernie Sanders, a senator from Vermont with a Jewish background, have invoked the Pope's authority as support for left policies. Catholic Republicans like Paul Ryan have felt compelled to respond, saying that Pope Francis's remarks do not condemn Republican policies.[9]

Internet and print media confirm that Catholicism has attracted an unusual amount of discussion. Google search results for "Catholic swing voter" are nearly three times larger than "Christian swing voter." On the influential progressive blog Daily Kos, community members can create "diaries" on topics of interest, to which other community members can post comments. Diaries containing the word "Catholic" far outnumber any other religious denomination. From 2000 to 2013, over 18,000 diaries contained the word "Catholic," while only 12,000 diaries contained the word "evangelical," despite the fact that the size of the two populations in the United States are roughly similar.[10]

In some cases, the Roman Catholic Church's distinctive issue positions make it a privileged signifier in struggles over religious freedom and "permissiveness" in culture. The Catholic Church is largely out in front of other churches in advocating against the use of artificial contraception. Although other denominations advocate abstinence over birth control and wish to restrict the availability of contraception, most stop short of banning contraceptive use entirely. This has placed the Catholic Church at the center over recent struggles such as whether pharmacists should have a right of conscience to refuse to provide contraceptives or Plan B, a pill that can be taken after sexual activity to inhibit ovulation or prevent an egg from implanting in the uterus. The Vatican also advocates restricting priesthood to men. Although other churches adopt distinctive positions (one can think of the Amish, for instance), none is as large as the Catholic Church, nor has the Catholic Church's geographic spread.

A third reason that Catholics are central in contemporary debates about religion and morality is its institutional development. Partly because of the Church's commitment to a principle of "subsidiarity" (that there should be intermediary structures between the state and the individual) and partly because of the history of Catholic–Protestant conflict, the church has gone further than many other denominations in developing "parallel" institutions in the United States, Australia, and Canada. In both the United States and Australia, Catholic private schools are the most numerous of any religious or non-religious group.[11] In all three countries, Catholic hospitals are the largest religious hospital systems.[12]

In addition, Catholic institutions are major social service providers.[13] As a result, Catholic institutions are often featured in debates about the appropriate boundary between church and state. In all three countries, small-government conservatives have advocated shifting more of the provision of public services through private entities – in schooling through the use of vouchers, and in social service provision through subcontracting. Political mobilization concerning these issues often revolves around Catholic schools and institutions as a result.

These three features of contemporary Roman Catholicism are not that different from Roman Catholicism of the nineteenth and early twentieth centuries. What has changed is the context. In the nineteenth and early twentieth centuries, the existence of "official" Catholic issue positions was taken by exclusivist Protestants to mean that Catholics would not make good democratic citizens. In the late nineteenth and early twentieth centuries, though the Roman Catholic Church also positioned itself as an alternative to both communism and unbridled capitalism, Protestants often still tarred the church as essentially homogeneous. In addition, Catholic parallel institutional development was seen as dangerously separatist. What has changed is that these features of the Catholic Church have gained new meaning and have made Catholics symbolically and organizationally central to a conservative values movement as a result of transformations in the political environment.

The institutional transformation

In addition to distinctive features of Catholicism that make them symbolically and organizationally central to a moral values coalition, there were institutional changes that allowed a reconstructive coalition to flourish. Chapter 4 has already demonstrated how a reconstructive coalition on the left had little effect in transforming Catholic attitudes in the South during the mid-twentieth century. When the South was still tied to Jim Crow and a distinctive racial order based on an explicit racial caste hierarchy, this created important differences among religious groups. Many mainline Protestant denominations opposed Jim Crow segregation, and in 1958 the bishops in the United States Catholic Church issued a letter rejecting segregation by law, reflecting the church's stance on a common origin for all humans. Although different bishops moved faster than others in desegregating Catholic institutions, the official church stance put the Catholic Church at odds with southern white sentiment.[14] Southern difference also meant the defense of the state's rights against federal power. This limited the potential of national moral coalitions. Although moral coalitions succeeded on some issues such as prohibition, others ran aground of distinctive regional interests. For instance, the South was disproportionately opposed to the Child Labor Law in 1916 (subsequently overturned by the Supreme Court), as well as the attempt in the 1920s to pass a constitutional amendment against child labor.[15] White Christian southerners were overwhelmingly opposed to the extension of federal funding to public schools and also to the opening up of immigration, both of which ended up hurting the interests of certain fragments of the Catholic community.

The end of the order of segregation in the South reduced southern difference from the rest of the country. The South has become more similar to the rest of the country, for instance, in the way that class influences the vote. Looking at red and blue states, there is little difference among the poor in their support for the Democratic Party.[16] The rich in red Midwestern states vote like the rich in red southern states. Both are more likely than the rich in blue states to be influenced by conservative religious concerns.[17] Culturally, southern styles of religious worship have also become more widespread. As religious historian Mark Noll has put it, "Stripped of racist overtones, southern evangelical religion – the preaching, the piety, the sensibilities, and above all the music – became much easier to export throughout the country."[18] By the end of the twentieth century, the Southern Baptist Convention had spread to every state and was among the top four denominations in much of the areas directly contiguous to the South, including the Midwest, Southwest, Mountain west, and California.[19] Even cultural identification as "Southern" has spread beyond the states of the Confederacy. Counties in which the adjective "Southern" appears in businesses to a significant degree include parts of Kansas, Illinois, Indiana, and Ohio.[20]

At the same time as the South has begun to look like the rest of the country, the rest of the country has moved toward the South. For instance, with the end of legal ascription based on race, battles over racial equality center on issues like school desegregation, means-tested welfare, affirmative action programs, and incarceration policy. Conservative approaches to racial inequality focus on what King and Smith have called race-blind coalitions, which argue against using race in the determination of public policy. Racially conscious coalitions, on the other hand, would be more open to factoring in race in public policy to transform the unequal legacies of the past.[21] Catholics outside of the South could potentially find common ground with white southerners on such issues. McGreevey and Gamm, for instance, have argued that Catholics in the northern states have been heavily affected by struggles for integration.[22] Gamm has argued that because of the centrality of the ethnic parish to U.S. Catholic community life, Catholics could not easily flee from the movement of African Americans to urban areas in the North. Gamm argues that white Catholics thus struggled more intensely with integration during and after the Civil Rights movement, which may have left these Catholics more receptive to race-blind coalitions.

The decline of southern difference opened up new political opportunities for constructing cross-national moral coalitions. With the Democratic Party committed to ending the Jim Crow racial order in the South, Republicans such as Kevin Phillips strategized how to win over white southerners to the Republican Party. Republican politicians in the late 1960s were quick to sense the possibility of attracting Catholic voters. Nixon supported public aid for parochial schools, which was introduced in the Republican platform of 1968, and his administration submitted a brief in support of such aid during the Supreme Court case of *Lemon* v. *Kurtzman*, which adopted the "Lemon test" for determining whether such aid was constitutional.[23] Nixon subsequently pursued the idea of creating tax credits for parents sending their children to parochial schools. Although some members of his administration worried that seeking to attract Catholic voters on these issues might prompt a backlash from Protestants, Nixon's Catholic advisor, Patrick Buchanan, argued that the issue would "drive a wedge right down the middle of the Democratic Party."[24]

Conservative Catholic and Protestant alliances

Closer examination of particular moral issues demonstrates the ties that developed between conservative Catholics and Protestants. For instance, conservative Catholics mobilized more fully against abortion than other churches in response to legislative liberalization at the state level and the Supreme Court decision *Roe* v. *Wade*.[25] William Buckley's initial hesitancy to condemn abortion for non-Catholics spurred *National Review* editor L. Brent Bozell, a Catholic who believed that abortion should be illegal in all circumstances, to found a new magazine, *Triumph*, in 1966. Bozell helped organize the Society for a Christian Commonwealth (SCC) and Americans United for Life (AUL) in 1971, the latter as a cross-denominational group to attack abortion.[26] Catholics also spearheaded the National Right to Life Committee (NRLC).[27] Both the AUL and NRLC submitted briefs opposing abortion rights in *Roe*. Following the decision, the National Conference of Catholic Bishops issued "A Pastoral Plan for Pro-Life Activities" urging the mobilization of pro-life Catholics in every Congressional district. Recognizing the leadership role of the Catholic Church on opposing abortion, the evangelical Francis Schaeffer initially considered abortion to be primarily a Catholic issue and evangelical Jerry Falwell complained that "the voices of evangelical and fundamentalist leaders remained silent" compared to the Catholic Church.[28]

Although five of the justices deciding in favor of a right to abortion in *Roe* v. *Wade* were nominees of Republican presidents, Republican politicians made some efforts to mobilize a broad coalition against abortion. Hull and Hoffer note that abortion was a litmus test for the Republican Party in the late 1960s, when the New York state legislature debated abortion.[29] In 1971 Richard Nixon ordered military hospitals to roll back recent liberalizations in abortion access, and in 1972 he wrote a letter to the Archbishop of New York praising him and "tens of thousands of Catholics, Protestants, Jews, and men and women of no particular faith" for supporting the rights of the unborn.[30] Starting in 1976 the Republican party platform called for a constitutional amendment to restore the rights of unborn life.

Immediately after *Roe*, conservative Protestants expressed a variety of opinions on abortion. The AUL initially had a Unitarian chair who supported abortion in cases of rape and incest, a position that infuriated the Catholic Bozell.[31] The NAE opposed abortion for "personal convenience, social adjustment or economic advantage" but endorsed abortion to preserve the health and life of the mother.[32] In 1971 the Southern Baptist Convention (SBC) advocated allowing abortion in cases of "rape, incest, clear evidence of severe fetal deformity, and carefully ascertained evidence of the likelihood of damage to emotional, mental, and physical health of the mother." The SBC's position began to change in the late 1970s after more conservative factions within the SBC gained increased control. In 1980 the SBC opposed "abortion on demand" and in 1984 opposed all abortions except to save the life of the mother.[33]

By the 1980s conditions were ripe for a full-fledged conservative Catholic and Protestant alliance against abortion liberalization. Catholic anti-abortion activists, in particular, inspired evangelical and fundamentalist Protestants. A Catholic woman, Joan Andrews, broke into an abortion clinic in Florida and vandalized the clinic's equipment, leading her to serve a five-year prison sentence. In Christian alternative media like the 700 Club, Andrews became a cause celebre.[34] The evangelical Randall Terry, who founded the antiabortion group Operation Rescue in 1987 and led it until 1995, has noted that he was inspired by the Catholic John Ryan, founder of the Pro-Life Direct Action League, to engage in antiabortion activism. Since then, he has claimed to have led "tens of thousands of evangelicals and Catholics in pro-life activism" based on "Christian ethic of life and justice as defined by our historical and common Christian faith."[35] To preserve the pan-Christian coalition, he found himself "defending Catholics against ignorance and bigotry, and defending evangelicals against ignorance and bigotry."[36] Terry later even valorized the Catholic Church, converting because the church "had a much better sociology and better stability, coupled with a phenomenal theology of suffering." Evangelical antiabortion activists, he claimed, were more likely to drop out of the pro-life movement than Catholics owing to a weaker sociological and theological grounding.[37]

Issues other than abortion played a role in mobilizing evangelicals and Catholics. In the 1970s, the capacity of Catholics to represent conservative Christian morality was perhaps most evident with Phyllis Schlafly in her fight against the ratification of the Equal Rights Amendment (ERA), drafted to guarantee equal rights for women. Schlafly had become known in national politics by supporting the campaign of Barry Goldwater and writing several books on foreign policy in the 1960s. These works had a pan-religious theme because religion was needed to fight against the atheistic Soviet menace. Schlafly's work led her to leadership positions in the Illinois Federation of Republican Women and the National Federation of Republican Women. In the 1970s Schlafly again became more nationally known as a result of the campaign against the ERA. Against feminism, Schlafly effectively deployed a persona as a "supermom" who would prioritize her husband and her children above all, but still have time to work on books, run for Congress, pursue a law degree, and organize political campaigns. Schlafly dismissed liberals as unhappy misanthropists, stating, "I don't see that they have fulfillment, happy marriages, or the wonderfully successful children that I have."[38] Religion was central to the appeal which Schlafly made against the ERA. Schlafly described her opposition to the ERA as a "heavenly cause" and believed that God had made men and women different.[39] Schlafly argued that the ERA would shut down single-sex Catholic schools, force the ordination of women, and promote homosexual rights.[40]

As head of the STOP ERA movement, Schlafly helped convince conservative Protestants that Catholics were useful allies in the fight against secularism, even as more liberal Catholics groups, such as the Leadership Conference of Women Religious, endorsed the ERA. Schlafly noted,

> Our movement brought together [...] Protestants of all denominations, Catholics, Mormons, and Orthodox Jews. [...] At our meetings I taught them that, although they might be sitting next to someone who might not be saved, we could nevertheless work together in behalf of a political/social goal we all shared.[41]

One Catholic anti-ERA organizer in Oklahoma, where the ERA was defeated, noted,

> I was discriminated against at first. I was a Catholic and Republican, and that's about as discriminated as you can get. At that time, everybody around here was partial to the Methodists. But now they call me from every church.[42]

In 1975 when Schlafly reorganized STOP ERA into the Eagle Forum, the Forum claimed about 60,000 members. Opponents of the ERA were drawn heavily from churchgoing women.[43] The battle over the ERA also transcended regional identities. By 1974 33 states had ratified the amendment while 17 voted against. Only five more states were needed to ratify the amendment for it to become law. Although the majority of states opposing the ERA were in the South, Illinois became a particularly tense battleground, with a ratification vote occurring every year until the time limit for ratification expired in 1982.[44]

Catholics were less central, but still active, in early national mobilizations against LGBT rights. The passage of a gay rights ordinance in Metro-Dade County in Florida in 1976 sparked opposition from Protestants, Catholics, and Jews. The Protestant evangelical singer Anita Bryant became prominent in the mobilization, and her organization, Save Our Children, included Robert Brake, a Catholic, as its secretary.[45] Describing the struggle in her book (which was in part dedicated to the Catholic Archbishop of Miami Coleman Carroll), Bryant argued that the religious of all denominations "need to put our differences aside on major issues that confront us which attempt to spoil the family unit."[46] Immediately before the final vote on repeal of the ordinance, over 100 ministers representing Baptist, Catholic, Methodist, and Presbyterian churches took out an advertisement in the Miami News urging repeal of the gay rights ordinance.[47]

As the campaign against homosexual antidiscrimination statutes expanded to other cities and states, Catholic support was mixed. In Wichita, Kansas, for instance, Bishop James Malone sided with Save Our Children in advocating against a gay rights ordinance.[48] However, archbishops in St. Paul and Minneapolis, and in Milwaukee, supported antidiscrimination ordinances, and the Catholic bishop of San Francisco opposed Proposition 6, also known as the Brigg

Initiative, which sought to eliminate homosexuals from teaching in public schools.[49] In the 1980s, after Bryant and Save Our Children had faded from public significance, controversies over gay antidiscrimination bills continued. Catholic archbishops in New York and Chicago opposed antidiscrimination measures based on sexual orientation.[50]

Another issue uniting conservative Catholics and Protestants was the school voucher debate. Given that the Catholic Church operates the largest private school system in the United States, the church has played a major role in arguing for increased funding to private parochial schools in the form of vouchers. In the Supreme Court case *Zelman v. Simmons-Harris*, which considered the constitutionality of vouchers, the U.S. Conference of Catholic Bishops submitted a brief in support of the constitutionality of vouchers, along with briefs from the Southern Baptist Ethics and Religious Liberty Commission, Family Research Council, National Association of Evangelicals, American Center for Law and Justice (founded by Pat Robertson), and Focus on the Family.

Responding to these developments in abortion, feminism, LGBT rights, and religious schooling, conservative Catholics and Protestants started to go beyond single-issue groups and form more broadly based interest groups. One of the first explicitly Christian nationalist groups was the Moral Majority, a group with the goal to "defend the free enterprise system, the family, Bible morality, [and] fundamental values."[51] Although headed by an evangelical, Jerry Falwell, the Moral Majority included as founding members two Roman Catholics, Richard Viguerie, a pioneer in computerized direct mail, and Terry Dolan, founder of the National Conservative Political Action Committee. Another co-founder, Paul Weyrich, creator of the Heritage Foundation, had been raised as a Roman Catholic but had converted to the Greek Catholic Church. Falwell has claimed that one-third of the members were Roman Catholic.[52] In assembling this pan-religious group, Falwell stated that he was influenced by Francis Schaeffer's idea of "co-belligerency." In his 1970 book, *The Church at the End of the Twentieth Century*, Schaeffer argued that evangelicals needed to work with whoever was willing – non-Protestants, even non-believers – to realize evangelical goals. Co-belligerency as a concept was carefully distinguished from actual alliance because co-belligerency was seen as something temporary and episodic.[53] As Falwell told his pan-Christian coalition, "I know that under normal circumstances most of us wouldn't even speak to one another. But these aren't normal circumstances. We've got to work together to save this nation. Afterward we can go back to arguing among ourselves."[54]

The influence of the Moral Majority is debatable. At its height its leaders claimed four million members, smaller than the AFL-CIO (about 15 million members). The Catholic Church hierarchy never fully endorsed the Moral Majority, and in some cases clashed with fundamentalists, for instance, in the nomination of Robert Billings as assistant secretary of public education.[55] However, the Moral Majority did score some success in improving the image of Catholics among conservative Christians. Three of the four candidates it backed in senatorial races in 1980 were Catholic: Frank Murkowski in Alaska, Don

Nickles in Oklahoma, and Jeremiah Denton in Alabama, who became the first Republican senator in that state since the end of Reconstruction, a striking achievement given the low population percentage of Catholics in Alabama.[56]

After the Moral Majority disbanded by the end of the 1980s, the Christian Coalition was founded by Pat Robertson and led by Ralph Reed. The Christian Coalition later initiated the Catholic Alliance in 1995, a group specifically for Catholics. The Alliance never attracted a million members as its founders intended. The group later split from the Christian Coalition and was led by a Democrat.[57] Despite this setback, pan-Christian movements continued into the 2000s. In 2009, for instance, leaders of Christian conservatives from orthodox, evangelical, and Catholic traditions signed the Manhattan Declaration, affirming the sanctity of life, traditional marriage, and religious freedom as key principles.[58]

As a result of this co-belligerency, the status of Catholics improved among conservative Protestants. Catholic Republican candidates at the presidential level started to do better. The Christian Coalition endorsed the religiously moderate George H.W. Bush over the much more socially conservative Catholic Patrick Buchanan in the 1992 Republican primaries. Reed cited the need to be pragmatic about electability and building influence within the Republican Party. On the ground, however, many evangelicals were willing to support Buchanan. Pat Robertson claimed that in a poll of his own congregants, 79 percent preferred Buchanan over Bush.[59] Up through Super Tuesday, by which time Bush locked up the nomination, Buchanan was able to win between 20 and 35 percent of the vote even in states like Georgia, South Carolina, Florida, Oklahoma, and Texas (his worst showing was in Mississippi, with only 15 percent of the vote). Buchanan actually came within 2 percentage points of beating Bush in the precincts representing the fundamentalist institution Bob Jones University.[60] The Christian Coalition did not endorse any candidate in 1996, but again, many Christian conservatives seriously considered backing the Catholic Republican candidate Patrick Buchanan over the more moderate Dole and Gramm. Buchanan fared marginally better than in 1992, winning four states, and beating Dole by 10 percentage points in Bob Jones University precincts.[61]

A striking sign of the transformation of Catholics in Republican presidential politics has been attempts by Republican candidates to accuse other Republicans of anti-Catholicism. In the 2000 election, George W. Bush spoke at Bob Jones University, which has criticized Catholic doctrine. Bush's opponent, John McCain, issued robo-calls to Catholic voters calling Bush anti-Catholic for being associated with the university, even though pluralities in precincts associated with the university readily voted for the Catholic Buchanan in 1996. Bush later made public a letter he wrote to Cardinal John O'Connor, the Archbishop of New York, which stated that he should have "been more clear in disassociating myself from anti-Catholic sentiments" and should have taken the opportunity to reject anti-Catholicism during his speech at the university.[62] In 2008 McCain found himself on the other end of charges of anti-Catholicism after John Hagee endorsed him. Hagee had made controversial statements attributing Hurricane

Katrina to sin in New Orleans and calling the Catholic Church the "Great Whore" (a reference to the "whore of Babylon" that appears in biblical prophecy). McCain ultimately repudiated Hagee's endorsement. These incidents show that in national public discourse, being associated with such anti-Catholicism was considered problematic for Republicans.

Survey analysis confirms a steady improvement in the status of Catholics among evangelicals since the 1960s. In the American National Election Studies of the 1970s, southern difference in terms of "feeling thermometer" scores toward Catholics disappear. Controlling for a variety of factors, regression analyses show that in the 2000s being a Republican, conservative, or a church attender are associated with a higher probability of rating Catholics favorably.[63]

An improvement in the image of Catholics may also be seen in valorization of the Pope. In surveys of Americans conducted since 1948 of the men they most admire, Pope John Paul II appeared on top ten lists 21 times from 1948 to 1998, most among all popes, and fourth among all others, behind Billy Graham, Ronald Reagan, and Dwight Eisenhower.[64] This has partly to do with the fact that John Paul II had one of the longest tenures of living popes in the latter half of the twentieth century (around 27 years), but in terms of ranking on the list, John Paul II tended to rank between number 2 and number 4 on the top ten list, particularly in the 1980s, while it was more common for Pius XII, John XXIII, and Paul VI to rank between 4 and 10.

Many conservative Christians consider John Paul II the most significant Pope since the Reformation.[65] In the article announcing John Paul II as *Time*'s man of the year in 1994, Billy Graham stated that John Paul II will "go down in history as the greatest of our modern Popes. He's been the strong conscience for the whole Christian world."[66] Evangelicals have admired John Paul II for his writings on a "culture of life," which has provided an intellectual framework for Christians in opposing abortion, euthanasia, and stem-cell testing. Praise for John Paul II also stemmed from his association with the end of communism, as touted in a documentary *Nine Days that Changed the World* (2010), produced by former Speaker of the House Newt Gingrich. As an article in *Christianity Today* put it: "What other clergyman played any comparable role in bringing down communism, a godless system?"[67] One poll even found that evangelicals considered John Paul II more favorably than Jerry Falwell or Pat Robertson.[68] Both Bushes and Clinton attended the funeral of Pope John Paul II. By contrast, in 1978 only Carter's mother and his wife attended the funerals of Pope John Paul I and Pope Paul VI.[69] After John Paul II's death, George W. Bush stated succinctly, "All Popes belong to the world."

The valorization of Pope John Paul II by evangelicals is instructive in evaluating causes of the improvement of Catholic standing. John Paul II is held in much higher esteem than Pope John XXIII, who presided over Vatican II. If it were true that Vatican II was the most important event in transforming Catholic status, one would expect that John XXIII would be more valorized than John Paul II.

In summary, conservative Catholics and Protestants have organized together around a variety of moral issues, both at the grassroots level and at the elite political level. Although differences and tensions emerged, never before had there been such levels of cooperation on the right. This was also reflected in conservative Catholics and Protestants trying to articulate ways in which they were doctrinally similar.

Reconstruction of identity in the United States

A key element of the reconstructive coalition theory of change is that the previously exclusive majority begins to rearticulate their own identity to be more inclusive of the previously excluded minority. Efforts at co-belligerency by Catholics and Protestants haven't resulted in complete identity between the two groups. Surveys typically show that Catholics are somewhere in between mainline Protestants and evangelicals in their attitudes toward various moral issues beyond abortion.[70] Co-belligerency and coalition politics, however, paved the way for increased efforts to reconstruct identities in the United States. Evangelicals have not only looked to John Paul II's statements on the "culture of life" and his columns in the evangelical periodical *Christianity Today* for articulation of their views, but also to Catholic academics like Robert George at Princeton and Richard John Neuhaus.[71] Starting in 1994, individual conservative evangelicals and Catholics have engaged in dialogues called Evangelicals and Catholics Together, which have produced four joint statements. The first ECT was organized by Richard John Neuhaus, a former-Lutheran-turned-Catholic, in the 1980s, and Charles Colson, an evangelical who led Prison Fellowship Ministries. The first ECT document noted common enemies of both evangelicals and Catholics, including Islam and secularization. Recognizing that there were still significant differences between evangelicals and Catholics, the document called for less conflict so that other priorities could be articulated. Significant agreement was evident between evangelicals and Catholics in affirming the United States as founded as a Christian nation; criticism of the courts' "obsession with 'no establishment'"; resistance against a "culture of death" that affects the unborn, the aged, and the disabled; and support for "parental choice in education," a "vibrant market economy," "appreciation of Western culture," appreciation of "mediating structures in society" such as churches and family, and a foreign policy guided by moral concerns and spreading religious freedom. The document called for restraint in proselytizing in each other's communities, noting that there were so many non-Christians in the world that proselytization was not "theologically legitimate nor a prudent use of resources."[72]

The document was drafted by 15 well-known evangelicals and Catholics, and signed by another 25, including such southern evangelicals as Bill Bright, Pat Robertson, and Richard Land. The participants of ECT I wanted to go beyond mere toleration of each other in the pursuit of common goals. In a book defending ECT I, Colson explicitly argued that co-belligerency, or being "allies solely for tactical purposes" and holding one's nose in the face of a common enemy, was not enough. "Political alliances based on expediency can be fleeting" and "does not hold soldiers fast in their trenches during battle," Colson argued.

Instead, he believed that conservative Christians need to have "a theologically rooted alliance" and the transformation that was needed was not merely political (electing more representatives) but cultural transformation that relied on the best of all Christian traditions. As he put it, "Neither a Baptist worldview – and I am a Southern Baptist – nor a Lutheran worldview, nor a Catholic worldview is enough to present a comprehensive, universal Christian worldview."[73]

The reconstruction of identities envisioned by ECT I emphasized doctrinal similarity that was ignored before. These include believing in the deity of Christ, his death and resurrection as atonement for human sin, his eventual Second Coming, and the Bible as the revealed world of God. This differentiated the evangelical–Catholic alliance from potential evangelical alliances with Mormons, Jews, or Muslims, which would more likely be alliances of a tactical rather than reconstructive nature in Colson's estimation.[74] This shared theological content also meant that Protestants and Catholics could legitimately claim to be co-guardians of Western civilization. In contrast to earlier Protestants who denied any contribution of Catholicism to the advance of world civilization, ECT I affirmed that "Evangelicals and Catholics have made an inestimable contribution" to Western civilization. Because of this shared identity, supporters of ECT I re-envisioned how evangelicals and Catholics should approach evangelizing each other. Packer wrote that while ECT I does not prevent Protestants from proselytizing among Catholics, it does rule out the idea that "a Roman Catholic cannot be saved without becoming a Protestant or vice versa, and on this basis putting people under pressure to change churches." This in itself was a striking sign of acceptance of Catholics, given that some evangelical critics of Catholicism continued to deny that the church was "an acceptable Christian community."[75] Timothy George articulated a slightly different position in advocating that it was acceptable for Catholics to preach to evangelicals and vice versa because such preaching could reach nominal Christians in both camps who have not fully accepted Jesus as savior.[76]

ECT I attracted significant criticism and pushback from groups like Christians United for Reformation and the Alliance of Confessing Evangelicals. Richard Land and Larry Lewis later removed their names from the document, and both Colson and Bright claimed loss of financial contributions because of their support for ECT.[77] Still, the ecumenical discussions have continued. Further ECT statements sought to find more common doctrinal ground on issues of whether salvation is through grace or faith, and whether salvation comes from the Bible or through the interpretation of church authorities. ECT II reached consensus that justification proceeds by faith alone.[78] ECT III advocated that both individual readings of the Bible and readings mediated through tradition were important in understanding the Word of God, thus nudging evangelical and Catholics closer together. As Timothy George noted, "One need only look at syllabi from courses on spiritual formation in Evangelical seminaries, or read works of spiritual theology [...] to realize the way in which 'the Catholic tradition' is being mined and appropriated for Evangelical purposes."[79] Even though these positions from ECT are heavily debated within the evangelical community, as the scholars Noll and Nystrom point out, "however limited the number of evangelicals and Catholics [ECT] was speaking for, such cooperation on questions of doctrine and social practice would have been simply unimaginable less than a generation ago."[80]

Democratic reconstruction of secular identity

Reconstructive one-party incorporation of a minority group can spark change in competing parties. In Australia in the period from 1930 to 1960, center-right parties responded to the success of the Labor–Catholic electoral coalition by modifying their position on state aid to religious schools. Similar dynamics may be seen in the contemporary period. Faced with Republican success in attracting Catholic votes and in conservative Christians' success in advancing a religious frame in politics, Democrats engaged in their own reconstruction of public philosophy, seeking to balance secularism with appearing pro-religious. Catholic representatives have been increasingly important to the Democratic coalition (as seen in Figure 7.3) since the 1990s. One possible explanation is that Democrats are fielding more Catholic candidates, whether out of a perceived need to appear "more religious" as a result of a shift in the political discourse or because of Catholic candidates' advantages in socioeconomic standing. Another possibility is that the defections of conservative Protestants from the Democratic Party to the Republicans have made Catholic Democratic representatives more integral to the party.

The increased public importance of religion means that even though Catholics are no more a "swing voter" in U.S. politics than other groups, Catholicism still continues to play a central symbolic role in contemporary U.S. politics.[81] With Catholics now occupying important positions in the Republican Party, Democrats have responded by asserting that Republican goals are not consistent with Catholic social teaching. In 2012, during debates about the U.S. budget, the U.S. Conference of Catholic Bishops repeatedly wrote letters urging the protection of programs such as food stamps and housing assistance that support the basic needs of the poor, and that cuts should be aimed first at those programs that benefit the affluent. Paul Ryan, a Republican Catholic who chairs the House Budget committee, responded that his budget proposal which slashed these programs and provided for a lowering of taxes was influenced by his religious convictions. Media associated with the left echoed the Catholics' complaints about Ryan's budget plan. The progressive blog DailyKos, for instance, which had run articles criticizing the Catholic Church's position on contraception and often showed Republicans pictured in mitre hats, reported the Catholics' criticisms of the Ryan budget. The controversy showed how both sides could invoke Catholic Church positions as a way of justifying policy choices. The controversy further showed the ambiguity of the left as completely secular. Although the contraception controversy sparked heavy disapproval of the Catholic Church, a different issue, namely the budget, sparked approval of the U.S. Catholic hierarchy. Rather than ignore religion or assert that it does not matter, there is very little leeway for a left stigmatization of the Catholic Church, and the left generally vacillates between a neutral secularism and support for religious positions when those values overlap with progressive policy goals. As the left-leaning columnist for the *New York Times* Nicholas Kristof put it in a title for an op-ed criticizing the Catholic Church's recent crackdown on the Leaders of Catholic Women Religious: "We Are All Nuns" now.[82]

Conclusion

The timing of increases in Catholic descriptive representation in right-leaning parties in the United States correlates with the rise of contemporary conservative Christian coalitions. This coalition was aided by an institutional transformation – the end of Jim Crow – which made a conservative pan-Christian coalition easier to assemble. This moral values coalition has led to an increase in Catholic standing among conservative Protestants, in some cases leading to reconstruction of identity so that Catholics and Protestants are not simply tolerating each other, but are envisioned as falling under a similar identity. Chapter 9 shows how similar coalitions transformed Catholic status in Australia. Canada is also examined to show how institutional factors can delay the emergence of Christian conservative coalitions in response to the political opportunity of secularization.

Notes

1. Erik Eckholm and Jeff Zeleny, "Evangelicals, Seeking Unity, Back Santorum for Nomination," *New York Times*, January 15, 2012, A1.
2. Samuel G. Freedman, "Santorum's Catholicism Proves a Draw to Evangelicals," *New York Times*, March 24, 2012, A12; Paul Stanley, "Evangelicals React to Santorum's Decision to Suspend Presidential Bid," *Christian Post*, April 26, 2012. Available at www.christianpost.com/news/evangelicals-react-to-santorums-decision-to-suspend-presidential-bid-72992/.
3. Ben Adler, "Did Romney Buy the GOP Nomination?," *Nation*, April 25, 2012. Available at www.thenation.com/blog/167544/did-romney-buy-gop-nomination#.
4. Rick Santorum, "That Makes Me Throw Up," *USA Today*, February 28, 2012. Available at http://usatoday30.usatoday.com/news/opinion/story/2012-02-28/Rick-Santorum-Kennedy-faith/53293630/1.
5. Peter Roff, "Why Obama Supporters Question Ryan's Catholicism," *US News & World Report*, August 20, 2012. Available at www.usnews.com/opinion/blogs/peter-roff/2012/08/20/why-obama-supporters-question-paul-ryans-catholicism.
6. John Gresham Machen, *Christianity and Liberalism* (Grand Rapids: Wm. B. Eerdmans, 1923), 52.
7. Lewis was heavily influenced by Roman Catholics such as J.R.R. Tolkien and G.K. Chesterton. Joseph Pearce, "C.S. Lewis and Catholic Converts," *Catholic World Report*, November 19, 2013. Available at www.catholicworldreport.com/Item/2724/cs_lewis_and_catholic_converts.aspx.
8. Laurie Goodstein, "Vatican Reprimands a Group of U.S. Nuns and Plans Changes," *New York Times*, April 19, 2012, A16.
9. Sheryl Gay Stolberg, "Popular Voice in the Capitol? It's the Pope's," *New York Times*, January 6, 2014, A1.
10. Searches conducted December 16, 2013.

11 Since the mid-1980s, about one-fifth of all Australian schoolchildren attend Catholic schools; over half of all Catholic schoolchildren and one-tenth of non-Catholic schoolchildren attend Catholic schools. Geoffrey Sherrington, "Religious Schools Systems," in James Jupp (ed.), *The Encyclopedia of Religion in Australia* (New York: Cambridge University Press, 2009), 672. In the United States in 2011 there were over 5,600 elementary schools and 1,200 high schools, serving about 2 million students. Dale McDonald, *United States Catholic Elementary and Secondary Schools 2011–2012: The Annual Statistical Report on Schools, Enrollment and Staffing* (Arlington, VA: National Catholic Educational Association, 2012). Online summary available at https://web.archive.org/web/20120102140535/www.ncea.org/news/Annual DataReport.asp. In Canada in 2004, there were over 1,400 Catholic primary schools, and nearly 300 Catholic high schools serving approximately 730,000 students (about the same as in Australia, despite Australia's smaller Catholic population, but still quite substantial). Gerald Grace and Joseph O'Keefe (eds), *International Handbook of Catholic Education: Challenges for School Systems in the 21st Century, Volume 2* (Dordrecht: Springer, 2007), 885.

12 Catholic hospitals comprise about 13 percent of all hospitals in the United States and account for about 16 percent of all hospital admissions. See Catholic Association of the United States, "Fast Facts." Available at https://web.archive.org/web/2013 0501010735/www.chausa.org/Pages/Newsroom/Fast_Facts/. In 1993 in Canada, there were 100 Catholic hospitals in English Canada alone compared to 11 Salvation Army hospitals and 3 United Church hospitals; see Michel Martin, "Catholic Hospitals Strive to Maintain Religious Focus in an Increasingly Secular Country," *Canadian Medical Association Journal* 148, no. 1 (1993): 64–65. Available at www.ncbi.nlm.nih.gov/pmc/articles/PMC1488598/pdf/cmaj00302-0066.pdf. In 2009/2010, there were 1,326 hospitals in Australia, 74 of which were Catholic institutions. According to Catholic Health Australia, about 10 percent of all hospital beds and 13 percent of all aged care beds are in Catholic hospitals and institutions. For the total number of hospitals, see Australian Institute of Health and Welfare, *Australian Hospital Statistics 2009–10*, Health Services Series No. 40, Cat. no. HSE 107 (Canberra: AHW, 2011). On Catholic hospitals, see Catholic Health Australia and PriceWaterhouse-Cooopers, "inFORMATION: Growing and Sustaining Our Ministries, Final Report," July 16, 2010, 2, 13.

13 In the United States in 2011, the church operated over 1,500 specialized homes, 400 orphanages, and 3,600 specialized social service centers. *The Official Catholic Directory Anno Domini 2011* (Berkeley Heights: National Register Publishing, 2011), 2102. In Australia in 2006, there were 407 homes for the elderly or disabled, 164 orphanages, 210 family counseling centers, and 480 centers for education and social rehabilitation. "Numbers for Australia Catholic Church Released Ahead of WYD," Catholic News Agency, July 8, 2008. Available at www.catholicnewsagency.com/news/numbers_for_australian_catholic_church_released_ahead_of_wyd/.

14 John T. McGreevey, *Parish Boundaries: The Catholic Encounter with Race in the Twentieth-century North* (Chicago, IL: University of Chicago Press, 1996), 90. In 1950, just under 33 percent of diocesan seminaries, 20 percent of religious seminaries, and 12 percent of congregations were integrated. "Jim Crow Catholicism," *Time* 55, no. 8 (February 2, 1950). See also Fay Botham, *Almighty God Created the Races: Christianity, Interracial Marriage, and American Law* (Chapel Hill: University of North Carolina Press, 2009), 111–120.

15 On sectional voting on the Keating-Owen Act in 1916, see Hugh D. Hindman, *Child Labor: An American History* (Armonk, NY: M.E. Sharpe, 2002), 65–67.

16 Richard Johnston and Byron Schafer, *The End of Southern Exceptionalism: Class, Race and Partisan Change in the Postwar South* (Cambridge, MA: Harvard University Press, 2006). Andrew Gelman, *Red State, Blue State, Rich State, Poor State: Why Americans Vote the Way They Do* (Princeton, NJ: Princeton University Press, 2008).

17 Gelman, *Red State*, ch. 1.
18 Mark Noll, *God and Race in American Politics: A Short History* (Princeton, NJ: Princeton University Press, 2008), 156–157; Darren Dochuck, *From Bible Belt to Sunbelt: Plain-folk Religion, Grassroots Politics, and the Rise of Evangelical Conservatism* (New York: W.W. Norton, 2012); Darren Dochuk, "Evangelicalism Becomes Southern, Politics Becomes Evangelical: From FDR to Ronald Reagan," in Mark A. Noll and Luke E. Harlow, *Religion and American Politics: From the Colonial Period to the Present*, 2nd edn (New York: Oxford University Press, 2007); George Marsden, *Fundamentalism and American Culture* (New York: Oxford University Press, 2006), 237.
19 Kevin Phillips, *American Theocracy: The Peril and Politics of Radical Religion, Oil, and Borrowed Money in the 21st Century* (New York: Viking Press, 2006), 167–169.
20 Phillips, *American Theocracy*, 160–161.
21 Desmond King and Rogers M. Smith, "Racial Orders in American Political Development," *American Political Science Review* 99 (2005): 75–92.
22 McGreevey, *Parish Boundaries*; Gerald H. Gamm, *Urban Exodus: Why the Jews Left Boston and the Catholics Stayed* (Cambridge, MA: Harvard University Press, 1999).
23 Robert Mason, *Richard Nixon and the Quest for a New Majority* (Chapel Hill: University of North Carolina Press, 2004), 152.
24 Ibid., 153.
25 N.E.H. Hull and Peter Charles Hoffer, *Roe v. Wade: The Abortion Rights Controversy in American History*, 2nd edn (Lawrence: University Press of Kansas), 185–186; Scott H. Ainsworth and Thad E. Hall, *Abortion Politics in Congress: Strategic Incrementalism and Policy Change* (New York: Cambridge University Press, 2011), 4–5; James Risen and Judy L. Thomas, *Wrath of Angels: The American Abortion War* (New York: Basic Books, 1998), 19–21; Rosemary Nossiff, *Before Roe: Abortion Policy in the States* (Philadelphia, PA: Temple University Press, 2000), 6, 42, 47–48.
26 Carol Mason, *Killing for Life: The Apocalyptic Narrative of Pro-life Politics* (Ithaca, NY: Cornell University Press, 2002), 139–140.
27 Paul A Djupe and Laura R. Olson (eds), *Encyclopedia of American Religion and Politics* (New York: Facts on File, 2003), 300.
28 David Sehat, *The Myth of American Religious Freedom* (New York: Oxford University Press, 2011), 264.
29 Hull and Hoffer, *Roe v. Wade*, 189; Jerry Falwell, *Falwell: An Autobiography* (Lynchburg: Liberty House, 1997), 358.
30 Mason, *Richard Nixon and the Quest for a New Majority*, 154; Linda Greenhouse and Reva Siegel (eds), *Before Roe v. Wade: Voices that Shaped the Abortion Debate before the Supreme Court's Ruling* (New York: Kaplan, 2010), 158.
31 Mason, *Killing for Life*, 140.
32 Greenhouse and Siegel (eds), *Before Roe v. Wade*, 71–72.
33 SBC resolutions. Available at www.sbc.net/resolutions/default.asp.
34 Risen and Thomas, *Wrath of Angels*, 186–188.
35 Tim Drake, "From Operation Rescue to Operation Convert," National Catholic Register. Available at www.ncregister.com/info/email-a-friend/from_operation_rescue_to_operation_convert.
36 Ibid.
37 Ibid.
38 Carol Felsenthal, *Sweetheart of the Silent Majority: The Biography of Phyllis Schlafly* (New York: Doubleday, 1981), 129.
39 Ibid., 110, n. 8; Phyllis Schlafly, *The Power of the Positive Woman* (New York: Jove, 1978), 13, 15, 38, 72, 183–185, 219–221.
40 Schlafly argued that there was a connection between promoting gender equality and homosexual rights because limiting marriage to heterosexuals could be seen as discriminating on the basis of the gender of one's chosen partner (Schlafly, *The Power of the Positive Woman*, 112–115, 165–166).

41 Ruth Murray Brown, *For a "Christian America": A History of the Religious Right* (New York: Prometheus, 2002), 78.
42 Brown, *For a "Christian America,"* 96.
43 Donald T. Critchlow, *Phyllis Schlafly and Grassroots Conservatism: A Woman's Crusade* (Princeton, NJ: Princeton University Press, 2005), 219–221.
44 Ibid., 235.
45 Fred Fejes, *Gay Rights and Moral Panic: The Origins of America's Debate on Homosexuality* (New York: Palgrave Macmillan, 2008), 76–80, 94.
46 Anita Bryant, *The Anita Bryant Story: The Survival of Our Nation's Families and the Threat of Militant Homosexuality* (Old Tappan, NJ: Fleming H. Revell, 1977), 37.
47 Fejes, *Gay Rights and Moral Panic*, 127.
48 Howell Williams, "Homosexuality and the American Catholic Church: Reconfiguring the Silence 1971–1999," dissertation (Florida State University, 2007), 69.
49 Fejes, *Gay Rights and Moral Panic*, 170–171. Archbishop of Milwaukee Rembert Weakland later admitted that he was homosexual. Randy Shilts, *The Mayor of Castro Street: The Life and Times of Harvey Milk* (New York: St. Martin's Press, 2008), 243.
50 Michael Goodwin, "Bill on Homosexual Rights Sparks Emotional Debates," *New York Times*, November 21, 1981, 29; Williams, "Homosexuality and the American Catholic Church," 73.
51 Betty Clermont, *The Neo-Catholics: Implementing Christian Nationalism in America* (Atlanta, GA: Clarity Press, 2009), 42.
52 Michael Sean Winters, "How the Ghost of Jerry Falwell Conquered the Republican Party," *New Republic*, March 5, 2012. Available at www.tnr.com/article/politics/101296/falwell-gop-winters?page=0,1.
53 Sehat, *The Myth of American Religious Freedom*, 265–266.
54 As recounted in Macel Falwell, *Jerry Falwell: His Life and Legacy* (New York: Howard, 2008), 116.
55 Mary Hanna, "Catholics and the Moral Majority," *Crisis Magazine*, November 1, 1982. Available at www.crisismagazine.com/1982/catholics-and-the-moral-majority.
56 Alf Tomas Tonnessen, *How Two Political Entrepreneurs Helped Create the American Conservative Movement, 1973–1981: The Ideas of Richard Viguerie and Paul Weyrich* (Lewiston, NY: Edwin Mellen, 2009), 245–249; Myra Macpherson, "The Militant Morality of Jeremiah Denton," *Washington Post*, December 7, 1980, L1; Mary Hanna, "Catholics and the Moral Majority," *Crisis Magazine*, November 1, 1982. Available at www.crisismagazine.com/1982/catholics-and-the-moral-majority.
57 Mark Rozell, "Political Marriage of Convenience? The Evolution of the Conservative Catholic–Evangelical Alliance in the Republican Party," in Kristin E. Heyer, Mark J. Rozell, and Michael A. Genovese (eds), *Catholic and Politics: The Dynamic Tension between Faith and Power* (Washington, DC: Georgetown University Press, 2008), 27–28.
58 See the Internet Wayback Machine archived version of their website. Available at https://web.archive.org/web/20130302005551/http://manhattandeclaration.org/#0.
59 Daniel Williams, *God's Own Party: the Making of the Christian Right* (New York: Oxford University Press, 2012), 231.
60 Oran P. Smith, *The Rise of Baptist Republicanism* (New York: New York University Press, 1997), 118, 121.
61 Ibid., 124.
62 Brian Knowlton, "Republican Says Bush Panders to the 'Agents of Intolerance': McCain Takes Aim at Religious Right," *New York Times*, February 29, 2000. Available at www.nytimes.com/2000/02/29/news/29iht-bush.2.t_9.html.
63 Carin Robinson, "Doctrine, Discussion, and Disagreement: Evangelical Protestant Interaction with Catholics in American Politics," dissertation (Georgetown University, July 25, 2008), 47.

64 Frank Newport, David W. Moore, and Lydia Saad, "Most Admired Men and Women: 1948–1998," Gallup News Service. Available at www.gallup.com/poll/3415/most-admired-men-women-19481998.aspx.
65 Collin Hansen, "Pope Gave Evangelicals the Moral Impetus We Didn't Have," *Christianity Today*, April 2, 2005. Available at www.christianitytoday.com/ct/2005/aprilweb-only/32.0.html.
66 Paul Gray, "John Paul II: Empire of the Spirit," *Time*, December 26, 1994.
67 Uwe Siemon-Netto, "He Was My Pope Too," *Christianity Today*, April 4, 2005. Available at www.christianitytoday.com/ct/2005/aprilweb-only/16.0.html.
68 Bruce Nolan, "Pope's Funeral Spotlights Kinship between Catholics and Evangelicals," *Christianity Today*, April 8, 2005. Available at www.christianitytoday.com/ct/2005/aprilweb-only/54.0.html.
69 "Remarks on Presenting the Presidential Medal of Freedom to Pope John Paul II at the Vatican City State," June 4, 2004. Available at www.presidency.ucsb.edu/ws/index.php?pid=62973. For other comments on the Pope and communism, see also Jim VandeHei, "Freedom, Culture of Life United Bush and Pope," *Washington Post*, April 7, 2005, A19. On attendance of papal funerals, see Bruce Nolan, "Pope's Funeral Spotlights Kinship Between Catholics and Evangelicals," *Christianity Today*, April 8, 2005. Available at www.christianitytoday.com/ct/2005/aprilweb-only/54.0.html.
70 Mary Hanna, "Catholics and the Moral Majority," *Crisis Magazine*, November 1, 1982. Available at www.crisismagazine.com/1982/catholics-and-the-moral-majority.
71 Laurie Goodstein, "Schiavo Case Highlights Catholic–Evangelical Alliance," *New York Times* March 24, 2005.
72 "Evangelicals and Catholics Together: The Christian Mission in the Third Millennium," *First Things* (May 1994). Available at www.firstthings.com/article/1994/05/evangelicals-catholics-together-the-christian-mission-in-the-third-millennium-2.
73 Charles Colson, "The Common Cultural Task: The Culture War from a Protestant Perspective," in Charles Colson and Richard John Neuhaus (eds), *Evangelicals and Catholics Together: Toward a Common Mission* (Dallas, TX: Word Publishing, 1995), 37.
74 Ibid.
75 Mark A. Noll and Carolyn Nystrom, *Is the Reformation Over? An Evangelical Assessment of Contemporary Roman Catholicism* (Grand Rapids: Baker Academic, 2005), 157.
76 Timothy George, "Evangelicals and Catholics Together: A New Initiative," *Christianity Today* 41, no. 14 (December 8, 1997), 34–35.
77 Noll and Nystrom, *Is the Reformation Over?*, 156–157.
78 George, "Evangelicals and Catholics Together," 34–35.
79 Noll and Nystrom, *Is the Reformation Over?*, 165.
80 Ibid., 160.
81 Matthew J. Streb and Brian Frederick, "The Myth of a Distinct Catholic Vote," in Kristin E. Heyer, Mark J. Rozell, and Michael A. Genovese (eds), *Catholic and Politics: The Dynamic Tension between Faith and Power* (Washington, DC: Georgetown University Press, 2008), 93–112.
82 Nicholas Kristof, "We Are All Nuns," *New York Times*, April 28, 2012. Available at www.nytimes.com/2012/04/29/opinion/sunday/kristof-we-are-all-nuns.html.

9 The limits of pan-Christian coalitions in Australia and Canada

For Australia, one has to explain (1) why Christian conservative coalitions emerged later than in the United States, and (2) the fact that Catholic overrepresentation in Australia is not as significant as in the United States. In Australia one sees similar developments as in the United States. There is dramatic secularization, Catholics are central to a conservative Christian movement, and there are no major regional identities to impede national reconstruction. However, institutional factors delayed direct integration of Catholics into the Liberal and Country parties. The use of preference voting allowed conservative Catholics to organize separately into their own party for some time. In addition, the smaller size of the religious population also means that religion is not as salient in politics as it is in the United States. While Catholics are central to a conservative morals coalition, such a coalition is less relevant in politics in general.

The second half of this chapter looks at the situation in Canada. There is not enough evidence to observe levels of Catholic political representation, but the Canadian case is instructive in showing that institutional factors can hamper the construction of Christian conservative coalitions in response to the political opportunity of secularization. These institutional factors include previous state–church settlements that made it harder to build a Christian coalition around state aid to schools; the rapid secularization of Quebec; and provincial autonomy in Quebec.

The centrality of Catholics to moral values coalitions in Australia

Catholics are central in a reconstructive moral values coalition in Australia because of (1) the size of the religious population, and (2) splits within the Protestant Church. There has been significant secularization in Australia, prompting reaction from conservative religious elements. In Australia, churchgoing is far less frequent than in the United States, and Christian fundamentalism is not as strong as in the United States, both in terms of number of believers and in development of Bible colleges and televangelist media.[1] With Roman Catholicism currently the largest denomination in Australia, the need for conservative Protestants to ally with Catholics is even more pressing.

152 *Limits of pan-Christian coalitions*

Splits between liberal and conservative wings of Protestant churches reinforced this need to rely on conservative Catholics. Anglicans in Australia were the largest denomination in Australia up until the 1980s and have been the second largest denomination since then. Globally, debates on abortion, female priests, and homosexuality have nearly riven the international church into two, and these splits have been reproduced in Australia.[2] The third largest church in Australia is the Uniting Church, which in 1977 brought together most of the congregations of the Methodist Church of Australasia, the Presbyterian Church of Australia, and the Congregation Union of Australia. The Uniting Church appears closer to American mainline churches than it does to southern evangelical churches, and is thus not a reliable ally in the Australian culture wars. Like the mainline churches in the National Council of Churches in the United States, the Uniting Church has been more receptive to social justice issues rather than conservative morality issues. On issues like abortion and acceptance of same-sex behavior and marriage, for instance, the Uniting Church has charted a position between complete restriction and total freedom.[3]

Given that the second largest denomination in Australia is riven by the liberal–conservative division, and the third largest is also split and leans toward liberal politics, religious conservatives in Australia are that much more likely to rely on the Catholic Church as an organizational ally in the culture wars. In turn, conservative Australian Catholics such as B.A. Santamaria have often recognized the need for pan-Christian alliances to preserve moral order.[4] Conservative Catholics in Australia have often bemoaned the fact that their potential allies are not as strong as with conservative Catholics in the United States. As Cardinal George Pell put it, the Catholic Church in Australia has to be at the forefront for preserving Judeo-Christian values because even though "we have many religious allies [...] there is unfortunately no Australian parallel to the strength of Protestantism in the USA, especially in the southern states."[5]

The importance of Australian Catholics to the conservative Christian movement is evident if one looks at the actual composition of activists in particular moral struggles. In abortion politics, conservative Catholic politicians opposed abortion liberalization in the Australian states in the late 1960s and 1970s, and, at the federal level, attempted unsuccessfully to prevent public health insurance from covering abortions.[6] Brian Harradine, an independent Senator from Tasmania, was a key Catholic politician advocating abortion restriction in the 1990s and used his leverage as a key swing vote to successfully block the use of abortifacients like RU-486 from 1996 to 2006.[7] At the grassroots level, the Catholic Church helped fund the largely Catholic group Right to Life (RTL) and participated in other antiabortion groups dominated by non-Catholics, such as the Festival of Light (FOL) and Women Who Want to Be Women (WWWW).[8] Catholic antiabortion activists have also been highly visible in the movement's most sensationalistic actions. Margaret Tighe, a Catholic leader of RTL in Victoria, brought to Australia the confrontational tactics more common in the United States, such as picketing of clinics and active campaigning against pro-abortion candidates.

As in the United States, reaction against liberal feminism has motivated a conservative backlash. After the Labor government under Bob Hawke passed the Sex Discrimination Act (SDA) in 1984, which outlawed discrimination based on gender, marital status, and pregnancy, one of the most prominent opponents to the law was the group Women Who Want to be Women (WWWW). As with STOP ERA in the United States, WWWW was founded in 1979 by a Catholic woman, Babette Francis, who believed that feminism harmed the traditional family.[9] Issues dealing with homosexuality have also featured heavily in the Catholic Church. On the sanctioning of gay marriage, the Australian Catholic Church is firmly against, whereas other churches are more open to some kind of accommodation. Responses to the recent attempt to reverse the 2004 definition of marriage indicate the closeness between conservative Catholics and Australian Protestants on this issue. Over 50 Australian male church leaders of all denominations endorsed the document "Revising Marriage? Why Marriage is the Union of a Man and a Woman" in response to legislative efforts to overturn the Howard-era law defining marriage as heterosexual. The document was endorsed by most of the Catholic archbishops, along with representatives from all the major Christian faiths.[10]

As this brief review shows, conservative Catholics were active in leading, inspiring, or participating in Australia's "culture wars," just as in the United States. These issues have prompted the formation of Protestant–Catholic coalitions, much like the Moral Majority and the Christian Coalition in the United States. In the 1970s, Fred Nile, who grew up in the Revesby Congregational Church, directed the Festival of Light, the political arm of which was the Family Action Movement (FAM), later reorganized into the Call to Australia (CTA) Party. Both the FAM and CTA emphasized the protection of traditional family values, and at times used terms like the "moral majority," borrowed from the United States to suggest a broader pan-Christian identity.[11] The current landscape of groups seeking to re-establish the pre-eminence of Judeo-Christian Australia is fairly diverse, including the Australian Family Association (derived from B.A. Santamaria's National Civic Council) and the Australian Christian Lobby.

Representative of changed attitudes of evangelicals toward Catholics is Anglican Archbishop of Sydney Peter Jensen. Jensen has defended politicians invoking Catholic principles, stating:

> The Roman Catholic teaching on life and on the embryo and on abortion, all those sort of things, you may not agree with it but it actually is both profound and intellectually worked out. [...] I think the Roman Catholic Church is wrong about lots of things. But I never underestimate its capacity for thought.[12]

Jensen has also praised Pope John Paul II. Over 40 years ago, shortly after Vatican II, Anglican Archbishop Marcus Loane refused to greet or engage in any activities with Pope Paul VI when he visited Australia. After the death of

John Paul II in 2005, Archbishop Jensen declared the deceased Pope "the greatest heart in Europe has ceased to beat" and "one of the great men of history."[13]

Ecumenism in smaller trenches in Australia: the institutional and political context for coalition formation

Despite dramatic secularization, Catholic integration into right-leaning parties in Australia took time to develop. Rather than direct organizational integration into the Liberal and Country parties, conservative Catholics cooperated initially with conservative Protestants through the Democratic Labor Party. The institution of preference voting gives minor parties greater opportunity to flourish because votes for minor parties are not necessarily "wasted." These minor parties can direct their second-preference votes to the major parties. This allowed conservative Catholics to retain a separate party existence, and this was reflected in the low proportion of Catholics in the Liberal and Country parties. In 1949, the Menzies cabinet included only two Catholics, and in the Liberal/Country governments in the 1970s, Phillip Lynch claimed he was the token Catholic in the Liberal/Country governments of that time.[14] Substantial representation of Catholics in the Liberal Party did not occur until the 1980s, after the DLP had collapsed, and, as may be seen in Figure 7.4, only in the 1990s do Catholics achieve proportionality in the Liberal–National coalition.[15]

The second important feature of the Australian context is the lower rates of church attendance. Moral values issues like abortion have less potency because more Australians support abortion compared with the United States.[16] With lower rates of church attendance and affiliation in Australia, it has taken longer for the right-leaning parties in Australia (the Liberal and Country/National coalition) to converge on a platform emphasizing both economic liberalism and social conservatism. It was only in the 1990s that the Liberal–National Party aggressively emphasized conservative moral issues, which increased the salience of conservative Catholics to conservative Protestants. In the late 1980s and early 1990s, the Liberal Party had not yet fully embraced conservative Christian causes. During John Hewson's leadership of the Liberals, he emphasized economic rather than social issues. After losing the elections in 1993, Hewson remained committed to social liberalism embracing individual choice, stating, "I do not have any problem myself with issues that relate to women's rights or gay rights as they are called, to seeing abortion as a matter of choice for a woman."[17] Hewson, for instance, supported the annual Gay and Lesbian Mardi Gras in Sydney in 1994.

Others within the Liberal Party, such as John Howard, believed putting greater emphasis on moral politics would help make the coalition achieve greater electoral success. Howard and other religiously oriented Liberal members formed the Lyons Forum in 1992, which included Catholic members like John Herron (a senator from Queensland) and Kevin Andrews, along with other conservative Christians. The group has been described as akin to the Moral

Majority and Christian Coalition in the United States, though the group tends to emphasize family values rather than a religious identity.[18]

Hewson's loss in the 1993 elections paved the way for Howard to become leader of the Liberal–National coalition. His victory in the 1996 elections gave Howard an opportunity to emphasize traditional religious values and bring conservative Catholics and Protestants together. Recalling his own mother's anti-Catholic attitudes, Howard remarked, "I just thought it was stupid that people who were professedly Christian should be fighting each other as to who was the superior Christian."[19] Howard, who was raised a Methodist and has an Anglican wife, has stated, "I would just as easily go to a Catholic Mass, and their liturgy is not all that different"[20] The existing data from candidate studies show that it was only in the 1990s, with the success of Howard, that Catholics achieved proportionality within the Liberal–National coalition (see Chapter 7). With the Howard government, Catholics formed a substantial proportion of the cabinet for the first time.[21]

Analysis of religious rhetoric in the maiden speeches of Australian MPs shows the increase in religious rhetoric of the Liberal–National coalition. Among all freshmen parliamentarians in the House of Representatives in Australia, religious rhetoric has increased over the past few decades (see Figure 9.1).[22] Liberal and Nationalist party members have been more willing to use religious rhetoric than has the Labor Party.

One sees an overall increase in 1996, when the conservative Howard government assumed control of Australian politics. In that year ten out of 52 maiden speeches in the Australian House mentioned "God."[23] When the analysis is broadened so that speeches that contain two or more religiously inflected words, 19 out of 52 maiden speeches contained such rhetoric. As numerous commentators have pointed out, appealing to religious conservatives was a major strategy of the Howard government. Maddox believes that in prime ministerial utterances this was largely achieved through use of "coded" rhetoric and appeals to imagery of a 1950s Australia of "white picket fences" and family values. The strategy is perhaps similar to President George W. Bush's "coded" religious rhetoric with scriptural inflection, as when his speechwriters include phrases like "wonder-working power."[24] Yet, in the maiden speeches of parliamentarians, one finds a great deal of direct use of religious rhetoric.

In addition to greater reliance on religious rhetoric, the Liberal–National coalition passed several pieces of legislation favoring conservative notions of the family and morals. In his first year in office, Howard allowed a free-conscience vote that led to the banning of RU-486, a drug that can induce abortion in the early weeks of pregnancy. The Howard government also overturned a voluntary euthanasia law in the Northern Territory; outlawed cloning embryos for stem cell research; passed the Marriage Amendment Bill in 2004, which defined marriage as between a man and a woman; shifted more government services such as employment services and marriage counseling through faith-based providers; initiated the National Schools Chaplaincy Program in 2007 to publicly fund chaplains in schools as counselors; and reformed tax policy to benefit single-income two-parent families more than other families.[25]

156 *Limits of pan-Christian coalitions*

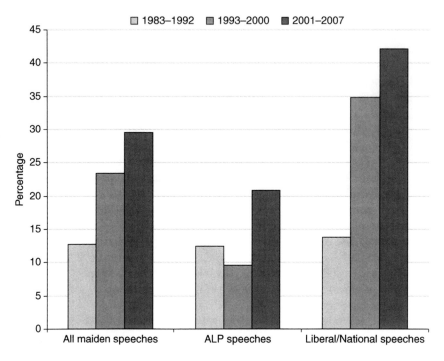

Figure 9.1 Percentage of Australian House maiden speeches with religious rhetoric.

Source: Australian Parliamentary Hansard. Reprinted with permission from Willie Gin, "Jesus Q. Politician: Religious Rhetoric in the United States, Australia, and Canada," *Politics and Religion* 5, no. 2 (August 2012).

Note
On the x-axis, each time period consists of three parliamentary sessions. There is substantial variation within each session, partially driven by the fact that some sessions have relatively fewer numbers of freshmen parliamentarians, which is why is makes sense to group sessions into blocks.

The success in reconstructing conservative Christian identity in the Liberal Party sparked counter-moves in the competing party, again showing how one-party reconstructive incorporation can have effects outside that party. To counter Howard's perceived success in attracting religious votes, Labor leader Kevin Rudd formed a discussion group on faith, religion, and values.[26] The use of religious rhetoric within Labor has also increased, as shown in Figure 9.1. As Labor MP Maria Vamvakinou, a Greek Orthodox, put it,

> I don't think the Liberal Party should be seen to have a monopoly on God. [...] Religion and faith are mainly private matters, but if I see an opportunity, in parliament or in public, I will speak more openly about my Christian beliefs.[27]

The greater receptivity of Labor to religious rhetoric has in turn led to greater valorization of Catholic social justice principles. Labor MP Luke Foley, for instance, has argued that Labor should use "language that is faithful to the Labor tradition but also faithful to Catholic social principles. [...] It disappoints me that often the religious voices in the public square today are predominantly right-wing conservative voices."[28] Signifying the pan-Christianity of the left, Rudd, who is an Anglican, took communion at Mary MacKillop Chapel, named after the Australian Catholic nun who was to be imminently canonized as a saint. As Australia's first Roman Catholic saint, Rudd extolled her as a model for all Australians.[29]

In addition to increasing its religious rhetoric, Labor has made some incremental moves to be more accommodating toward religion in public policy. At times, Labor members have provided some support for conservative moral issues. Some Labor members supported the Marriage Amendment Act in 2004. Since coming to power in 2006, Labor has increased support for private schools and extended and expanded funding for the school chaplaincy program.[30]

There are limits to the reach of religion inside the ALP. The Labor Party continues to direct second preferences to the Green party rather than to smaller family-values-based parties like Family First. Secularism and humanism remain important factions within Labor.[31] In 2010 Julia Gillard, an avowed atheist, replaced Rudd as head of the ALP and was successfully elected. The comparatively limited reach of religion in Labor demonstrates the limits of Christian right-style politics in Australia in general. Some of the legislation that Howard passed in his early governments has been undone or weakened. In 2006, bans on the abortion pill RU-486 and on cloning were overturned. More recently, there has been an attempt initiated by the Green Party to expand the definition of marriage to include same-sex couples. The Green Party introduced one bill that was voted down in the Senate in February 2010. Momentum, however, seems to be on the side of same-sex marriage proponents. In 2011, Labor included recognition of same-sex marriage into its party platform, though Gillard advocated keeping the traditional definition of marriage and voted against the unsuccessful 2012 bill that would have legalized same-sex marriage.[32]

The reversals of certain Howard-era policies reflect the relative weakness of the Christian right in Australia.[33] Even Liberal–National leader Tony Abbott, who is Catholic, carefully parsed the role of religion in politics in the 2010 election. In an address before the Australian Christian Lobby during the 2010 election, Abbott stated that religion does not "shape my politics" and asked that Christians vote for him not because he is Christian but because he is an "effective politician." In proving his party's effectiveness, he noted that the Howard government's achievements included more outsourcing of government services to churches; the growth of independent religious schools; encouraging more births through the government baby bonus; the implementation of government-funded school chaplains, and protecting religious freedom of conscience.[34] Abbott noted that these accomplishments should be praised because they are effective policy, not because they benefit churches. Although it is debatable how much Abbott is or is not using coded rhetoric to appeal to Australian Christians without offending secular Australians, it is clear that religious rhetoric is more carefully deployed in Australia compared to the United States. Even the eight questions the ACL asked of the candidates reflected a more modest role of the Christian right: the ACL, for instance, did not ask the candidates about abortion.[35]

Although the Australian Christian right is not as powerful as the Christian right in the United States, to the degree that it has been successful it has helped normalize Catholics to other conservative Australian Christians, contributed to the integration of Catholics into the right-leaning parties in Australia, and increased religious rhetoric in Labor during the Rudd years.

The institutional and political context of coalition formation in Canada

In Canada there has been ample opportunity for Protestants and Catholics to come together over socially conservative issues. Conservative Catholic and evangelical alliances should also be strong in Canada because on issues like abortion, female equal rights, and homosexual rights Canada has gone further than the United States in liberalizing social policy. With the *Morgentaler* decision in 1988, abortion access became completely liberalized throughout the country. In the realm of gender, feminists successfully mobilized to include two provisions for gender equality in the Canadian Charter of Rights and Freedom: Section 15, calling for no discrimination based on sex; and Section 28, which guarantees equal rights between men and women. As these clauses in the Charter have been interpreted by the courts they have sparked some change, including opening combat positions in the military to women beginning in 1989, well before the United States. In the realm of sexual orientation rights, the passage of Bill C-33 in 1996 established that discrimination cannot be based on sexual orientation and in 2004 gay marriage was legalized throughout the country, well before the United States. In terms of sheer magnitude of legislative and judicial liberalization and secularization of social policies, Canada easily surpasses the United States and Australia.

Conservative Catholics were instrumental in opposing these Canadian developments. Early antiabortion mobilization was primarily Catholic, with groups like Alliance for Life (the largest antiabortion group in the 1970s) and the Campaign Life Coalition.[36] It was only in the late 1970s and 1980s that evangelical groups became more active against abortion.[37] In response to feminism, Realistic, Equal, and Active for Life (REAL) Women formed in 1983; one of its founders was Gwendolyn Landolt, a Phyllis Schafly-like Catholic woman who curtailed her career in law to raise her five children. Opposing feminist causes such as state childcare, equal pay legislation, and homosexual rights, REAL Women described itself as a non-denominational organization with the goal "to promote and defend legislation upholding the Judeo-Christian understanding of marriage and family life."[38] Conservative Catholics also played a role in opposing gay rights in groups like the Defend Marriage Coalition, which includes the Catholic Civil Rights League, Campaign Life, REAL Women, and the Canadian Family Action Coalition.

Limits of pan-Christian coalitions 159

Participation in campaigns against secularization has brought Canadian Catholics and evangelicals closer together. A survey of leaders of Christian right interest groups in Canada demonstrated that many Protestant evangelicals had heard of Evangelicals and Catholics Together, and 70 percent approved of ecumenical discussions. Protestant evangelical leaders estimated that there were Catholics participating in their organizations, and three-quarters stated that they occasionally or frequently participated with Catholic groups on an issue-by-issue basis. Survey respondents stated a variety of reasons for increased warmth toward Catholics, including fighting a common enemy.[39]

While Canada's experiences with abortion, gender transformation, and same-sex marriage rights provide incentives for conservative religious to unite, there are also impediments that do not exist in the United States, helping explain why Catholic–Protestant electoral alliances have been comparatively delayed (see Figures 7.6 and 7.7). One reason is that Canadian Christians are not as conservative as in the United States. As numerous scholars have observed, Christian-right politics in the mold of the United States is not as strong in the Canadian context. Although the churchgoing population in Canada is large, fundamentalism is not as strong in Canada, and the evangelical population is also different.[40] Based on an Angus Reid survey in 1996, about one-third of the U.S. population could be described as evangelical compared to just 12 percent of the population in Canada.[41] Canadian evangelicals are less likely to believe that moral values are more important than other issues, are less likely to be economic conservatives, and are more likely to identify as center/liberal in partisan politics as opposed to right/conservative.[42] The composition of the Canadian evangelical population may also lend it a less conservative cast, with more Baptists in the U.S. Christian right than in the Canadian Christian right.[43] The evolution of the National Association of Evangelicals in the United States and its equivalent organization in Canada, the Evangelical Fellowship of Canada (EFC), demonstrates these differences. The EFC was formed in 1964 and its constitution ratified in 1965, much later than the formation of the NAE in the United States.[44] As late as 1976, it still had only a meager budget of $30,000 and did not have a full-time executive director until 1983. The EFC opened a lobbying office in Ottawa only in 1996.[45]

In addition to the weakness of conservative Protestantism in Canada, the institutional context contributed to slowing down the formation of conservative Christian alliances in Canada. As will be detailed below, previous institutional settlements contributed to: decreased incentives for coalitions around schooling; secularization in Quebec; and regional cleavages that make it harder to organize national politics around moral issues like abortion and same-sex marriage.

Coalitions around state aid to private schools

Contemporary political coalitions around state funding for schools have been affected by the past. In Australia and the United States there is a higher degree of overlap between Catholics and other conservative Christians on the issue of state aid to parochial schools. In Canada, because different choices were made in the past accommodating Catholic schooling, there is less overlap between Catholics and other conservative Christians on the issue.

Since 1963, when religious secondary schools in Australia started receiving government funding for science education and commonwealth scholarships were offered as tenable at private schools, state aid to religious and private schools was steadily expanded by both Labor and Liberal governments.[46] Even though the vast majority of private schools receiving state aid are Catholic, a substantial proportion of non-Catholic religious schools as well as non-religious schools receive such aid. In 2011, about one-third of all Australian students were attending private schools, with close to 95 percent of all private schools affiliated with some religion. Initially 80 percent of private school students were attending Catholic schools. By the 1990s this number was only 60 percent, and many other religious denominations benefited, including Islamic and conservative Christians. In 2006, it was estimated that four out of ten children of Christian fundamentalist sects were attending private schools.[47] Hence, the politics of increasing funding to Catholic private schools in Australia places Catholic school supporters in alliance with other religious denominations.

Supporters of more public funding of Catholic schools in the United States are also in a similar position to other churches. Since there are no specific privileges granted to the Catholic Church, any government decision on public funds going to private schools affects Catholic and Protestant schools. Constitutional battles to extend public funding reflect this. For instance, amicus curae briefs in *Zelman* v. *Simmons-Harris* supporting the constitutionality of school voucher programs included a wide range of religious groups.[48] Establishment clause jurisprudence also supports broad coalitions around religion. Although liberals and conservatives on the Supreme Court disagree on what the establishment clause in the Constitution means, all agree that aid has to be non-discriminatory for it to be constitutional.

The situation in Canada with regard to state aid to religious schools is different than in the United States and Australia. Prior to World War II, many provinces had separate Catholic and Protestant schools. In British Columbia and Manitoba there were no separate Catholic schools. The fact that some Catholic schools received funding prior to secularization in the latter half of the twentieth century meant that this was an issue on which conservative Catholics and Protestants could not as effectively mobilize together.

In the Maritimes and Quebec, experience with separate schooling convinced the public that such schools were not viable. New Brunswick, Nova Scotia, and Prince Edward Island allowed some public schools to be operated informally as Catholic schools, but the systems were deconfessionalized in the latter half of the twentieth century. Quebec's schools are no longer separated into public and religious schools but instead into English and French schools. There is still the option to take religious classes within both kinds of schools however, and there is partial funding for students who wish to go to private schools.[49]

Outside of the Maritimes and Quebec, the existence of fully funded separate schools likely means that the impetus to extend such funding to independent and private schools is not as vigorous. With the Catholic Church already receiving funding from the government, there is less incentive for Catholic groups to organize with other religious denominations to establish state schools for other religions. Such funding could potentially threaten the amount of funding Catholics receive. There is also less incentive for the Catholic Church to join movements to extend state money to private schools, since Catholics are already accommodated through state schools.

In Ontario, for instance, it was some time before the Progressive Conservative Party embraced public funding of religious schools. Premier William Davis opposed funding of Catholic high schools in the 1970s, then reversed course at the end of his premiership in 1984. This makes Ontario the only province in Canada that funds one religion's schools, but not others. In the 1990s Jewish groups and groups representing non-Catholic Christians argued that aid to only Catholic schools was discriminatory and that state aid should be extended to all religious denominations. However, public support for extending funding to all religious groups was unpopular in Ontario at the turn of the twenty-first century. In 2002, the Progressive Conservative government under provincial premier Mike Harris allowed tax credits for sending children to private schools, but this measure was repealed by the subsequent Liberal government in 2003. PC party leader John Tory advocated direct funding of private schools in 2007 but lost the provincial election. Public opinion polls did not record great support for the measure.[50] Catholic interest was also muted; during the election, the Ontario Conference of Catholic Bishops did not issue any statement in support or against extension of funding.[51]

Secularization and liberalization in Quebec

Another way in which historical institutional ordering has shaped contemporary politics is in influencing the religiosity of the population, particularly in Quebec. Prior to the 1960s Canada was the most religious of the three countries in terms of proportion of the population attending church on a regular basis. Since then, Canada has slipped behind the United States. The severe drop in Catholic churchgoing rates accounts for a large part of this change. Catholic churchgoing rates in Quebec have dropped more than Catholic rates in any other Canadian province, and more than Catholic rates in the United States and Australia. In Quebec, Catholic Church attendance fell from 83 percent in 1957 to 33 percent in 1990, a decline of 50 percentage points. During the same time period, Catholic attendance outside Quebec fell from 75 percent to 37 percent, a decline of 33 percentage points.[52] In comparison, from 1955 to 1992, Catholic attendance rates in the United States dropped from 74 percent to 45 percent, a decline of 29 percentage points.[53] In Australia in 1950, 62 percent of Catholics claimed to have gone to church within the previous week. On the eve of Vatican II, in 1960, this number had already declined to around 53 percent. The figure continued to decline to around 37 percent in 1981.[54]

162 *Limits of pan-Christian coalitions*

What is it about Quebec that has caused such a severe decline in churchgoing? One possibility is that Quebec experienced greater secularization. Secularization theory argues that modernity and greater pluralism lead to declines in religion. Pluralism supposedly increases the appeal of non-religious ideas because once people are exposed to more information and compare religions, they realize that religion is irrational.[55] Yet Quebec did not experience greater relative modernization or pluralism. Quebec has experienced economic growth, but has not fully caught up with Ontario.[56] Quebec has also not experienced greater relative pluralism. Although the foreign-born population in contemporary Quebec breaks previous historical records, in 2006 the foreign born in Quebec accounted for about 11.5 percent of the population, which is close to the foreign-born population in the United States and much less than the foreign-born population in Australia (around 20 percent), or even neighboring Ontario (with over 30 percent of the population being foreign born).[57]

Another prominent theory of religiosity is that a free market in religion sustains religious belief. The major proponents of this theory, Roger Finke and Rodney Stark, argue that people's religious preferences are typically diverse and organized like a bell curve.[58] Some prefer religions that are very demanding and are in high tension with the norms of secular society. Others prefer religions that are not so demanding and that are in low tension with the norms of secular society. Most are somewhere in between. Because a single religion cannot simultaneously appeal to all spectrums of the bell curve of religious preferences, state-sanctioned church monopolies will be inefficient and religious adherence will be low. Religious niches will be ignored, and the church will typically be lazy and inefficient in trying to attract new members. By contrast, where there is no established church, there will be more religious firms competing to attract adherents. Competition ensures that each religion is motivated to maintain its market share in the religious economy and that all niches within the spectrum of religious preferences are filled. From Finke and Stark's perspective, the Catholic Church in Quebec may have represented a quasi-established church, because the provincial government provided some aid to the church. The church's failure to adapt itself and appeal to as many people as possible caused the precipitous drop in church attendance there.[59]

Another possibility is that the decline of the Catholic Church in Quebec has resulted from the history of the political institutionalization of the church there. Catholic weekly churchgoing rates in Quebec were extremely high in the mid-twentieth century compared to Catholic rates in the United States and Australia, which suggests that religious monopolies or quasi-monopolies are not always bad in motivating religiosity. Sustained political conflict can reinforce religious identity, whether quasi-established or not.[60] The World Values Survey, for instance, shows that Ireland and Poland stand out among Catholic countries with the highest church attendance. Irish Catholics struggled against Protestant North Ireland, while Polish Catholics faced down communist government. Following the fall of communism and greater peace between Protestants and Catholics in Northern Ireland, attachment to religion decreased. Weekly churchgoing rates of

Catholics in Poland have declined, from about 70 percent in 1990 to about 60 percent in 2005. In Ireland, the decline has been steeper, from about 85 percent in the mid-1980s to about 65 percent in 2000 (see Figure 9.2). These countries seem to show that when political conflict overlaps religious identities, religious identities are enhanced. Quebec Catholics may have been particularly religious prior to 1960 because the intense cultural conflict between Protestants and Catholics mapped onto geographical and political boundaries.

Political disaffection since the 1960s may have played a role in the drop in church attendance in Quebec. Catholic control of the political institutions in Quebec may have meant that disaffection with politics translated into a simultaneous disaffection with the Catholic Church. In other systems where Catholics

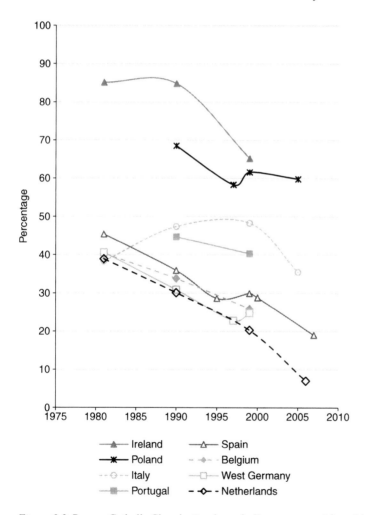

Figure 9.2 Roman Catholic Church attendance in European countries, at least weekly.
Source: World Values Survey Online Analysis.

164   *Limits of pan-Christian coalitions*

have not had as much control over the state, but where there was significant control over social welfare and education services given to the church, such as in the Netherlands and Germany, significant declines in Catholic churchgoing occurred as well (see Figure 9.2).

Whether the explanation for the drop in church attendance lies in the lack of a free market in religion or the dynamics of political blame in a society with an established or quasi-established church, rapid secularization has influenced contemporary Quebec politics in the direction of liberalization. Surveys show that Quebec Catholics not only have the lowest rates of attendance compared to Catholics from other provinces, but also skew to the political left, emphasize social justice to a greater degree, demand more lay participation in the church, and support abortion and same-sex marriage. A 2003 poll by Environics showed that 64 percent of Quebec Catholics supported gay marriage, compared to 51 percent of all other Catholics.[61] The liberalization of Quebec Catholics has decreased the potential pool of Catholics willing to sign up to a conservative values agenda. The World Values Survey confirmed that in 1990 Canadian French speakers (most of whom are in Quebec) are more accepting of homosexuality, divorce, and euthanasia than English-speaking Canadians, and that compared to ten other European countries and the United States, French-speaking Canadians rank behind only the Netherlands on a combined index of moral permissiveness.[62] Other research also confirms the liberalness of Quebec on moral issues.[63]

The more "liberal" attitude of the Catholic Quebec population is mirrored in the attitudes of that province's Catholic hierarchy. For instance, Quebec is home to one of the most controversial Catholic priests in Canada, Father Raymond Gravel, a former prostitute-turned-priest who supports abortion and gay marriage rights. In the 1970s and 1980s Quebec's Catholic bishops regularly advocated liberal positions on the ordination of women, the marriage of priests, sacraments for the divorced and remarried, abortion, and same-sex marriage.[64] During the papacy of John Paul II the ability of Quebec bishops to speak freely was curtailed, but while toeing official Vatican positions, Catholic bishops in Quebec have advocated subtly different positions, such as supporting civil unions for same-sex couples and their rights to adopt children.[65] The further one goes down the church hierarchy, the more willingness there is to challenge the "official" positions of the church. In 2006, for instance, 19 priests from Quebec representing a group called Forum Andre-Naud openly published a letter advocating acceptance of homosexuality within the Church. Although some U.S. priests also have similar beliefs, they have not been as public as Quebec priests.[66]

Liberal attitudes in Quebec also find expression in the dominant party and policy. Bloc Quebecois supporters are more liberal on moral values and economic issues than supporters of any other Canadian party in 2000.[67] The party also downplays religion in the public sphere. As a sign of the economic and moral liberalness of Quebec, Dr. Henry Morgentaler first began performing illegal abortions in the late 1960s in Quebec, and Quebec juries acquitted him of any wrongdoing. As early as 1975 the Parti Quebecois declared that it would not prosecute abortion providers in the province.[68] Quebec was the first province to include sexual orientation in antidiscrimination legislation.[69] In 1997 it became the first province to subsidize daycare through public daycare facilities, and in 2010 the province banned the teaching of religion in public daycare institutions.

Given the importance of Quebec in securing majorities in national politics, the secularization of Quebec has made conservative moral politics more difficult. By decreasing religiosity and contributing to the liberalization of Quebec Catholics' attitudes, the long-term effect of provincial autonomy has decreased the strength of this potential coalition.

Regional differences and constructing moral coalitions

More broadly, provincial and regional autonomy makes forming cross-national coalitions more difficult. The reason that cross-national conservative Christian coalitions have been more successful in the United States and Australia is that these regional impediments are less severe. In the earlier period of Catholic political incorporation, regional identities in the American South and in Quebec slowed down reconstructive coalitions with Catholics. In the contemporary period Quebec has remained distinctive, while the U.S. South has become less distinctive, making possible cross-national coalitions around conservative religion.

When Quebec was still highly religious, the limits to a cross-national religious coalition were clear. The mutual distrust between Protestants and Catholics prevented the emergence of an alignment that would feature conservative Protestants and Catholics allied together against liberal Protestants and Catholics. In addition, the vested interest of Quebec Catholics in preserving their provincial autonomy also stymied the building of a cross-national moral coalition. Conservative Protestants could not ally with conservative Catholics because of conservative Catholics' commitment to Quebec's provincial autonomy (much as northern conservative Protestants in the United States could not ally with southern conservative Protestants over disagreements on racial segregation).

At the same time, Quebec, being one of the more populous provinces, could not simply be ignored. Quebec has been akin to the "Solid South" prior to the Mulroney government. This in part explains the dominance of the Liberal Party during the post-war era, since Quebec constitutes about a quarter of all parliamentarians. Up until the emergence of the Bloc Quebecois in the 1993 elections, the Liberal Party gained most of its lead over the competing Progressive Conservative Party by drawing parliamentarians from Quebec.

Since the Charter of Rights and Freedom was adopted in 1982, the question of Quebec separatism has been one of the dominant issues in Canadian politics. The primacy of this question tamped down on public displays of religion. As Mark Noll has put it, "From 1980 onwards economic and political preoccupations have almost completely eclipsed all other contenders, including religion, in dominating Canadian public space."[70] The Progressive Conservative Mulroney government was able to take power in the 1980s due in part to its ability to appeal to voters in Quebec on constitutional issues of provincial autonomy, rather than an appeal to moral conservatism.

As already noted, over this time period Quebec has shifted from being one of the most morally conservative provinces to one of the most morally liberal, which poses additional dilemmas to the building of a cross-national conservative religious coalition. In votes on moral issues over the past decade, parliamentarians from Quebec and the Bloc Quebecois have been some of the staunchest supporters of liberal positions on moral issues. Hence, although the emergence of the Bloc Quebecois has changed the importance of Quebec, shifting the most important province electorally for the Liberal Party to Ontario, Quebec's votes in Parliament are still important, since the Bloc, as well as other legislators from Quebec, can still prevent moral legislation from passing.

Delayed party response in Canada

These institutional barriers have contributed to the longer time it has taken for the right in Canada to effectively organize a successful electoral coalition around these issues. From the 1960s to the 1990s, many in the center-right Progressive Conservative Party did not buy into conservative Christian politics. For instance, during the debates on the decriminalization of homosexuality and abortions with the approval of therapeutic abortion committees in 1968, the Progressive Conservative Party allowed MPs to vote with their conscience rather than follow the party line.[71] During the vote on Trudeau's abortion legislation, about 35 percent of Progressive Conservative members voted against it, while 55 percent were absent.[72]

Moral issues were also downplayed by the Progressive Conservative Party during the Mulroney government in the 1980s. Within Mulroney's Progressive Conservative governing coalition in the 1980s there were around 30 Catholic and evangelical members whom Mulroney labeled his "God Squad"; about 12 to 14 of these regularly attended a weekly pro-life caucus.[73] The small numbers reflected the low prominence of moral issues on the political agenda, sometimes with less than 2 percent of the population believing that abortion was the most important issue.[74] In 1989 the Mulroney government managed to pass Bill C-43 out of the House of Commons, which would have made abortion legal only when necessary to preserve the life of the mother. However, the bill died in the Senate, with two Progressive Conservative Party members helping to kill it.

In addition, there were many front benchers in the Progressive Conservative Party who supported gay rights. Justice ministers in the Progressive Conservative Party tried twice to introduce legislation to make discrimination based on sexual orientation illegal for employers, but were stymied by forces within the party that did not want to address the issue. In 1992, Progressive Conservative Minister of Justice Kim Campbell allowed gays and lesbians to openly join the military.[75] In *Veysey* v. *Correctional Services* (1990) and *Haig* v. *Canada* (1992), courts read sexual orientation into federal antidiscrimination law; the PC government did not attempt to challenge these decisions.[76]

The failure of the Mulroney government to emphasize moral issues contributed to discontent among the religious grassroots.[77] Disillusionment with Progressive Conservative policies in the western provinces contributed to its demise and to the rise of the Reform Party, which supported strengthening the family, but did not impose a party line upon individual MPs' decisions on abortion or gay rights.[78] The leader of the party, Preston Manning, noted, "There's a taboo in the House of Commons that you don't not talk about your deepest spiritual convictions and part of the reason is that people who open themselves up just get hammered."[79] The Reform Party instructed members that when voting on moral and religious issues they should follow the majority in their riding.[80] Although almost all Reform Party members voted against Bill C-33, the law preventing discrimination based on sexual orientation, many chose to cite reasons other than religious conviction for their votes.[81]

Because it has taken longer for right-leaning parties to decide how to bring together economic and socially conservative issues together, there hasn't been as clear a party choice for the Christian right, allowing other issues to motivate voter choice. Although the Christian right in Canada supported the Reform Party at nearly double the rate of the average voter, a small majority voted for the Liberal Party in 1996, in line with the average voter. In comparison, the Christian right in the United States tilted slightly toward Dole in 1996, out of line with the average voter.[82] Canadian Catholics have tended to stay with the Liberal Party in the 1990s, and French Catholics were virtually absent in voting for the Reform Party.[83]

The Reform Party eventually joined the Canadian Alliance in 2000. The evangelical Stockwell Day led the party, but failed to win government and was mocked for believing in creationism. Stephen Harper, who would eventually become prime minister in 2006, subsequently successfully challenged Day for leadership of the Canadian Alliance, emphasizing his own secularity and criticizing Day for mixing churches and politics.[84] Earlier in his political career, Harper worked to make sure that issues such as abortion and homosexuality should not appear on the Reform Party's platform, and he actively opposed a resolution defining marriage as between a man and a woman in the 1994 party convention.[85] Only in 2003 did Harper begin a shift to emphasize socially conservative issues on abortion, gay marriage, foreign policy, and law and order, and he helped orchestrate a merger of the Canadian Alliance with the Progressive Conservative Party to form the Conservative Party.[86]

The successful election of Harper in 2006 finally brought some form of Christian conservative politics to Canada, many years later than the United States and Australia. Harper's victory may have been aided by a backlash against the legalization of gay marriage. According to one poll, weekly Protestant churchgoers significantly increased their support for the Conservative Party in 2006 compared with 2004, partly on the strength of Harper's pledge to hold a conscience vote on the issue of same-sex marriage.[87] Yet Harper has been careful not to place too much emphasis on religion. Even during the elections in 2006, Harper did not highlight his evangelical background in the media, and many were unaware of this background until the publication of *The Pilgrimage of Stephen Harper* just months before the election. Prior to that, Harper's few public statements on the role of Christianity in his politics were ambiguous. For instance, he stated, "I won't say I always keep my faith and politics separate, but I don't mix my advocacy of a political position with my advocacy of faith." Harper instructed Conservative candidates in the 2006 election to avoid talking about same-sex marriage.[88]

Harper in office has often preferred a stealth strategy in advancing conservative religious goals. In terms of policy, these include raising the age of consent for sex from 14 to 16 years old and redirecting childcare funds from providers to families. Other moves have been more symbolic, such as appointments of religious conservatives.[89] Attempts to significantly challenge positions on gay marriage and abortion, however, have either failed or been avoided. The Conservatives held a conscience vote on gay marriage, but Harper did not push for overturning gay marriage, and the law stood. Harper has stated that he will not support any bill that reopens the abortion debate, and he has opposed several measures introduced by backbenchers to define fetal rights, including Roxanne's Law (C510), which attempted to criminalize coerced abortions; and Motion 312, which proposed further study on when life begins. Harper did vote to support the Unborn Victims of Crime bill (C484), which sought to increase penalties for criminals injuring the fetus of a pregnant woman, but the bill never made it to a third reading and died after the 2008 elections. The Harper government also prohibited its contributions to a maternal health fund for women in the developing world being used for abortion, but it has also continued to support international Planned Parenthood funding.[90] Even with control of the government, the legislative success of religious conservative elements in the Conservative Party has been limited.

Conclusion

In both Australia and Canada, the potential for pan-Christian conservative coalitions has existed. Conservative Catholics in both countries have been at the vanguard in mobilizing on particular issues like abortion, the status of women, and same-sex marriage. Yet these new political opportunities did not immediately become actual reconstructive coalitions between conservative Catholics and Protestants. Institutions shaped the way in which these coalitions formed.

In Australia, such a coalition did not become prominent and successful on the right until 1990, after the United States. Organizational integration of conservative Catholics into the Liberal–National coalition was delayed due partly to the preference voting system, which allowed the DLP to exist for some time. Organizational integration was also delayed because of the relative weakness of religion in Australia, so that the Liberal–National coalition did not start to emphasize religion until the 1990s. Once it did, however, Catholic standing increased.

In Canada conservative Christian political coalitions appear even later than in Australia, despite the fact that the religious population is larger in Canada and legislative and judicial secularization more advanced. The delay in the electoral success of conservative Christian coalitions occurred partly because of the institutional context. Previous political settlements between Catholics and Protestants contributed to difficulties in assembling Christian coalitions in state aid to religious schools, the liberalization of Quebec, and the persistence of Quebec in blocking the construction of national moral coalitions. Only in 2006 did a comparable "moral values" coalition appear to materialize in Canada.

Notes

1 Universities require charters, which has prevented the growth of Bible colleges in Australia. The licensing system for broadcasting has also limited the development of religious media. James Jupp, "Fundamentalism in Modern Society," in James Jupp (ed.), *The Encyclopedia of Religion in Australia* (New York: Cambridge University Press, 2009), 643–644.
2 Starting with Western Australia in 1992, most Anglican dioceses now accept the ordination of women, the prominent exception being the conservative Sydney diocese. See Anne O'Brien, "Of Faith and Feminism," *Australian Financial Review*, July 22, 2005, 11. The 2012 appointment of a gay priest to head a rural parish in Victoria sparked further criticism from conservative Anglicans.
3 Dean Drayton, "Uniting Church Calls for Compassion and Balance on Abortion Debate," February 3, 2005. Available at http://assembly.uca.org.au/component/k2/item/309-uniting-church-calls-for-compassion-and-balance-on-abortion-debate. For the Uniting Church on sexuality issues, see "Summary of Decisions on Sexuality in the Uniting Church." Available at https://web.archive.org/web/20140303194035/http://nsw.uca.org.au/church/sexuality-summary.htm; Barney Zwartz, "Gay 'Sacred Unions' Test Uniting Church Resolve," *Age* (Melbourne), June 28, 2010, News 9. On euthanasia, see Helen Pitt, "Uniting Church Divided on Outcome," *Sydney Morning Herald*, March 26, 1997, 6.
4 B.A. Santamaria, "Does Christianity Have a Future?," *Canberra Times*, December 24, 1988, 13.
5 Tess Livingstone, *George Pell: Defender of the Faith Down Under* (San Francisco, CA: Ignatius, 2004), 181–182.
6 "Unity in Fight against Abortion Wanted," *Canberra Times*, November 11, 1972; Karen Coleman, "The Politics of Abortion in Australia: Freedom, Church, and State," *Feminist Review* 29 (summer 1998), 83–84; John Warhurst and Vance Merrill, "The Abortion Issue in Australia: Pressure Politics and Policy," *The Australian Quarterly* 54, no. 2 (winter 1982), 125, 130.
7 Caroline de Costa, *RU-486: The Abortion Pill* (Salisbury, Queensland: Boolarong, 2007), 89–94.
8 Warhurst and Merrill, "The Abortion Issue in Australia," 132.
9 Ross Fitzgerald, *The Pope's Battalions: Santamaria, Catholicism, and the Labor Split* (St. Lucia, Queensland: University of Queensland Press, 2003), 330, n. 72; Babette Francis, "'Equal Opportunity' Legislation Threats Christian Teachings," Endeavour Forum website. Available at www.endeavourforum.org.au/old/ad2000_articles/equal.html.
10 The signatories originally appeared on the ACL website, though the link has disappeared (www.acl.org.au/2011/08/50-national-leaders-of-christian-churches-endorse-document-on-marriage). The Archbishop of Hobart, Adrian Doyle, did not appear as a signatory, though he has publicly criticized the Tasmanian House for voting for marriage equality. "Tas Gay Marriage Vote Disappoints Archbishop," CathNews, September 21, 2011. Available at https://web.archive.org/web/20130203120508/

http://cathnews.com/article.aspx?aeid=28368. Prior to the gay marriage vote in 2012, the Catholic Church in Australia distributed literature opposing legalization. See Meredith Griffiths, "Christian Leaders to Unite against Gay Marriage," ABC News, June 15, 2012. Available at www.abc.net.au/news/2012-06-16/christian-leaders-unite-against-gay-marriage/4074612.

11 Rodney K. Smith, *Against the Machines: Minor Parties and Independents in New South Wales 1910–2006* (Sydney: Federation, 2007), 85–86; Alan Gill, "Fred and Jerry Have Much in Common," *Sydney Morning Herald*, May 26, 1982, 7.

12 Monica Attard, "The Anglican Archbishop of Sydney, Peter Jensen," ABC Local Sunday Profile, August 8, 2010. Available at www.abc.net.au/sundayprofile/stories/2975337.htm.

13 Muriel Porter, "Anglicans Fall Under Papal Spell," *Age* (Melbourne), April 7, 2005, News, 21.

14 Tony Walker, "Liberals Form a Catholic Rump," *Australian Financial Review*, August 23, 2002, 75.

15 Joan Rydon, *A Federal Legislature: the Australian Commonwealth Parliament 1901–1980* (Melbourne: Oxford University Press, 1986), 39.

16 MDR Evans and Jonathan Kelley, "Attitudes toward Abortion: Australia in Comparative Perspective," *Australian Social Monitor* 2, no. 4 (October 1999): 87–89.

17 Marion Maddox, *God under Howard: The Rise of the Religious Right in Australian Politics* (Crows Nest, NSW: Allen & Unwin, 2005), 31, 35–36.

18 The slogan of the group, "The foundation of a nation's greatness is in the homes of its people," was derived from a speech by Catholic United Australia Party member Dame Enid Lyons, wife of Joseph Lyons. Maddox, *God under Howard*, 37. Members of the group often differ in defining the group as secular or religious (Maddox, *God under Howard*, 66–67).

19 Maddox, *God under Howard*, 110.

20 Tony Walker, "Liberals Form a Catholic Rump," *Australian Financial Review*, August 23, 2002, 75.

21 John Warhurst, "Religion in 21st Century Australian National Politics," Papers on Parliament No. 46, December 2006.

22 Electronic versions of maiden speeches from the Australian House of Representatives were collected for the parliamentary sessions, and keywords were searched for using standard word-processing software. A representative was coded as using faith-based rhetoric under two conditions: (1) the speech contained the word "God" (or a close correlate, such as a reference to "the Creator"); or (2) the speech contained two or more of the following words: Bible, pray, church, Christ, Christian, religious, religion, Catholic, spiritual, divine, or bless. Although each speech was not read in its entirety, each sentence and/or paragraph in which a keyword appeared was read to make sure that the usage was not colloquial. The criterion of two or more of the non-God keywords is meant to weed out colloquial usage. In speeches with the word "God," the vast majority were thanks to God. There were a few ambiguous cases ("Hughes is God's country; "My god, listen to this […]") which were coded as faith-based rhetoric. References to the anthem "God Save the Queen" were not coded as examples of faith-based rhetoric. See Willie Gin, "Jesus Q. Politician: Religious Rhetoric in the United States, Australia, and Canada," *Politics and Religion* 5, no. 2 (2012): 317–342.

23 Two of these are questionable, but even if they are left out that is still 8 of 52 using "God," and 17 out of 52 representatives using some kind of religious rhetoric.

24 David J. Kuo, *Tempting Faith: An Inside Story of Political Seduction* (New York: Free Press, 2006), 61.

25 Maddox, *God under Howard*, 235; Stephanie Peatling, "Revealed: The Battle Plan to Save Marriage," *Sydney Morning Herald*, January 9, 2006; Stephanie Peatling, "Family Centres a Step Closer," *Sydney Morning Herald*, April 5, 2006, 11; Peter Lavelle, "Making Allowances," *Sydney Morning Herald*, April 1, 2000, 128.

26 John Warhurst, "Religion and Politics in the Howard Decade," *Australian Journal of Political Science* 42, no. 1 (March 2007): 23.
27 Matt Price, "New Deity Dawns for Faithful Labor," *The Weekend Australian*, November 27, 2004, Local section, 4. As it turns out, Vamvakinou's maiden speech contained numerous references to religion.
28 Anna Patty, "MPs Moved by Heaven and Earth," *Sydney Morning Herald*, April 6, 2012, 8.
29 Kevin Rudd and Julie Bishop, "Our Nation Is Richer for Having Had MacKillop among Us," *Sunday Age* (Melbourne), October 17, 2010, 19.
30 Warhurst, "Religion and Politics in the Howard Decade"; Katherine Murphy and Dan Harrison, "School Chaplains to Stay," *The Age* (Melbourne), November 2, 2009, 5.
31 In 2000 Carmen Lawrence formed the Humanist Group in response to increasing religious rhetoric in Parliament (Warhurst, "Religion and Politics in the Howard Decade").
32 Phillip Coorey, "Labor Backs Gay Marriage," *Sydney Morning Herald*, December 3, 2011. Available at www.smh.com.au/national/labor-backs-gay-marriage-20111203-1oc4d.html; Simon Cullen, "Lower House Votes Down Same-sex Marriage Bill," ABC News, September 18, 2012. Available at www.abc.net.au/news/2012-09-19/same-sex-marriage-bill-voted-down/4270016. Gillard's relationship with religion has vacillated. In an interview with the ACL after displacing Rudd from power in 2010, Gillard noted that she was raised in a Baptist family and church, which gave her values that she carries today, even though she does not feel in her heart a belief in God. She also noted that those values help her respect others who do believe in religion. She also affirmed the importance of prayer in Parliament, continuing the school chaplaincy program, and not changing the 2004 Marriage Act (though the Labor Party under Gillard changed their platform to support same-sex marriage in December 2011, and Labor would allow members a conscience vote on the issue).In 2005 Gillard reversed her position to support gay marriage.
33 Rodney Smith, "How Would Jesus Vote? The Churches and the Election of the Rudd Government," *Australian Journal of Political Science* 44, no. 4 (2009), 613–637.
34 Tony Abbott, Address to the Australian Christian Lobby, Old Parliament House, Canberra, June 21, 2010. Available at https://web.archive.org/web/20130421130933/www.tonyabbott.com.au/LatestNews/Speeches/tabid/88/articleType/ArticleView/articleId/7435/Address-to-the-Australian-Christian-Lobby-Old-Parliament-House.aspx.
35 The subjects canvassed by the ACL were: social justice for indigenous people; prayer in Parliament; refugees; marriage; chaplaincy; sexualization of children; climate change, and negotiating with minor parties (such as Family First) in the Senate.
36 Dennis R. Hoover, "The Christian Right under Old Glory and the Maple Leaf," in Corwin E. Smidt and James M Pening (eds), *Sojourners in the Wilderness: The Christian Right in Comparative Perspective* (New York: Rowman & Littlefield, 1997), 198; James Harold Farney, *Social Conservatives and Party Politics in Canada and the United States* (Toronto: University of Toronto Press, 2012), 90.
37 Michael W. Cuneo, *Catholics against the Church: Anti-abortion Protest in Toronto, 1969–1985* (Toronto: University of Toronto Press, 1989), 12.
38 Kristin Blakely, "Women of the New Right in Canada," dissertation (Loyola University, Chicago, 2008), 123–124. Blakely does note that REAL Women considers itself secular, and that its use of religious rhetoric is less than a similar group in the United States, namely Concerned Women for America (Blakely, "Women in the New Right in Canada," 176). The Pro-family survey in 1986 of 1,200 members of REAL Women found that they were mostly Protestant and Catholic, 96 percent of whom attend church at least weekly. Lorna Erwin, "REAL Women, Anti-feminism, and the Welfare State," *Resources for Feminist Research* 17, no. 3 (1988): 147–149.
39 Dennis R. Hoover, "Ecumenism of the Trenches? The Politics of Evangelical–Catholic Alliances," *Journal of Ecumenical Studies* 41, no. 2 (spring 2004): 247–271.

40 John H. Simpson and Henry G. MacLeod, "The Politics of Morality in Canada," in Rodney Stark (ed.), *Religious Movements: Genesis, Exodus, Numbers* (New York: Paragon, 1985), 228.
41 There is no standard definition of "evangelical" but the results were determined by positive answers to a series of questions such as believing the Bible to be the word of God, considering oneself committed to Christ; and a willingness to evangelize others (Hoover, "Ecumenism of the Trenches?"). McDonald also estimates the Canadian evangelical population at around 10 to 12 percent. Marci McDonald, *The Armageddon Factor: The Rise of Christian Nationalism in Canada* (Toronto: Vintage Books, 2011), 18. Other researchers put the estimate of evangelicals in the U.S. as 18 percent compared to 9 percent in Canada. Lydia Bean, Marco Gonzalez, and Jason Kaufman, "Why Doesn't Canada Have an America-style Christian Right? Comparative Framework for Analyzing Political Effects on Evangelical Subcultural Identity," *Canadian Journal of Sociology* 33, no. 4 (2008), 914–915.
42 Hoover, "Ecumenism of the Trenches?"; see also Sam Reimer, *Evangelicals and the Continental Divide: The Conservative Protestant Subculture in Canada and the United States* (Montreal: McGill-Queen's, 2003), 130; Bean at al., "Why Doesn't Canada have an American-style Christian Right?," 915–916.
43 Hoover, "The Christian Right under Old Glory and the Maple Leaf," 208–209.
44 Stackhouse, "The National Association of Evangelicals, the Evangelical Fellowship of Canada, and the Limits of Evangelical Cooperation," *Christian Scholar's Review* 25, no. 2 (December 1995), 161–162.
45 Ibid., 167–168; Hoover, "The Christian Right under Old Glory and the Maple Leaf," 194.
46 Jennifer Buckingham, *The Rise of Religious Schools*, Centre for Independent Studies Policy Monograph 111, 2010, 7. Available at www.cis.org.au/images/stories/policy-monographs/pm-111.pdf.
47 Ibid., ix, 3, 9.
48 Groups submitting briefs included the U.S. Conference of Catholic Bishops, Southern Baptist Ethics and Religious Liberty Commission, Family Research Council, National Association of Evangelicals, American Center for Law and Justice (founded by Pat Robertson), and Focus on the Family.
49 Ronald Manzer, *Public Schools and Political Ideas: Canadian Educational Policy in Historical Perspective* (Toronto: University of Toronto Press, 1994), 165–173. See also Canadian Secular Alliance, "Public Financing of Religious Schools," 2009. Available at http://secularalliance.ca/about/policies/public-financing-of-religious-schools/; Jennifer Wilson, "Faith-based Schools," CBCNews.ca, September 17, 2007. Available at https://web.archive.org/web/20130531123551/www.cbc.ca/ontariovotes2007/features/features-faith.html.
50 Craig Offman, "Tory Risks Education Minefield on October 10," *National Post*, August 25, 2007, A1.
51 Lee Greenberg, "Catholic Bishops Hold Silence on Faith-based Schools Funding," *Ottawa Citizen*, September 1, 2007, A1.
52 Reginald Bibby, *Restless Gods: The Renaissance of Religion in Canada* (Toronto: Stoddart, 2002), 20.
53 George H. Gallup, Jr., "Catholics Trail Protestants in Church Attendance," Gallup Poll Tuesday Briefing, December 16, 2003, Washington, DC: Gallup Organization. Available at www.gallup.com/poll/10138/catholics-trail-protestants-church-attendance.aspx.
54 Vamplew, *Australians: Historical Statistics*, 438–439. Peter Kaldor et al. list the Catholic decline in monthly attendance rates from 76 percent in 1950 to 32 percent in 2000; P. Kaldor, J. Bellamy, R. Powell, K. Castle, and B. Hughes, *Build My Church: Trends and Possibilities for Australian Churches* (Adelaide: Openbook, 1999), 22.
55 Steve Bruce, *God Is Dead: Secularization in the West* (Oxford: Blackwell, 2002), 18.

56 H.V. Nelles, "Ontario 'Carries On,'" in Kenneth McRoberts (ed.), *Beyond Quebec: Taking Stock of Canada* (Montreal, Canada: McGill-Queen's, 2000), 32; Pierre Fortin, "Has Quebec's Standard of Living Been Catching Up?," in Patrick Grady and Andrew Sharpe (eds), *The State of Economics in Canada: Festschrift in Honour of David Slater*, Centre for the Study of Living Standards, 2001.
57 Tina Chui, Kelly Tran, and Helene Maheux, "Immigration in Canada: A Portrait of the Foreign-born Population, 2006 Census," Statistics Canada Catalogue no. 97–557, December 2007, 15.
58 Rodney Stark and Roger Finke, *Acts of Faith: Explaining the Human Side of Religion* (Berkeley: University of California Press, 2000).
59 This possibility was brought out by James Q. Wilson in a talk at the University of Pennsylvania, fall 2005. It also fits in with thinking about the advantages of "network power" versus concentrated sovereignty, as discussed in Michael Hardt and Antonio Negri's *Empire* (Cambridge, MA: Harvard University Press, 2000).
60 Bruce, *God Is Dead*, 31–35.
61 Solange Lefebvre and Jean-François Breton, "Roman Catholics and Same-sex Marriage in Quebec," in David Rayside and Clyde Wilcox, eds, *Faith, Politics, and Sexual Diversity in Canada and the United States* (Vancouver: UBC, 2011), 219–234. See also Solange Lefebvre, "The Francophone Roman Catholic Church," in Paul Bramadat and David Seljak, eds, *Christianity and Ethnicity in Canada* (Toronto: University of Toronto Press, 2008), 128.
62 Neil Nevitte, *The Decline of Deference: Canadian Value Change in Cross-national Perspective* (Orchard Park, NY: Broadview, 1996), 218; Neil Nevitte and Christopher Cochrane, "Value Change and the Dynamics of the Canadian Partisan Landscape," in Alain-G. Gagnon and A. Brian Tanguay (eds), *Canadian Parties in Transition*, 3rd edn (Orchard Park, NY: Broadview, 2007), 261.
63 Miriam Smith, *Political Institutions and Lesbian and Gay Rights in the United States and Canada* (New York: Routledge, 2008), 25.
64 Lefebvre and Breton, "Roman Catholics," 219, 221.
65 Ibid., 228.
66 Ted G. Jelen, "Catholicism, Homosexuality, and Same-Sex Marriage in the United States," in David Morton Rayside and Clyde Wilcox, *Faith, Politics, and Sexual Diversity in Canada and the United States* (Vancouver: UBC, 2011), 211.
67 Nevitte, *The Decline of Deference*, 218; Nevitte and Cochrane, "Value Change and the Dynamics of the Canadian Partisan Landscape," 261.
68 Ellen Anderson, *Judging Bertha Wilson: Law as Large as Life* (Toronto: University of Toronto Press, 2001), 227–228.
69 Smith, *Political Institutions and Lesbian and Gay Rights in the United States and Canada*, 49.
70 Mark Noll, *What Happened to Christian Canada* (Vancouver: Regent College Publishing, 2007).
71 Farney, *Social Conservatives and Party Politics in Canada and the United States*, 86.
72 Karen Dubinsky, *Lament for a "Patriarchy Lost?" Anti-feminism, Anti-abortion, and REAL Women in Canada* (Ottawa: Canadian Research Institute for the Advancement of Women, 1985), 10; citing Alphonse DeValk, *Morality and Law in Canadian Politics – the Abortion Controversy*, 1974, ch. 1.
73 Farney, *Social Conservatives and Party Politics in Canada and the United States*, 92.
74 Raymond Tatalovich, *The Politics of Abortion in the United States and Canada: A Comparative Study* (New York: M.E. Sharpe, 1997), 145.
75 Farney, *Social Conservatives and Party Politics in Canada and the United States*, 95–96.
76 Smith, *Political Institutions and Lesbian and Gay Rights in the United States and Canada*, 96.

174 *Limits of pan-Christian coalitions*

77 Bruce Wayne Foster, "New Right, Old Canada: An Analysis of the Political Thought and Actions of Selected Contemporary Right-Wing Organizations," dissertation submitted to Political Science Department (University of British Columbia, July 2000), 95.
78 Smith, *Political Institutions and Lesbian and Gay Rights in the United States and Canada*, 83.
79 McDonald, *The Armageddon Factor*, 105.
80 Hoover, "The Christian Right under Old Glory and the Maple Leaf," 201.
81 Farney, *Social Conservatives and Party Politics in Canada and the United States*, 109.
82 Hoover, "The Christian Right under Old Glory and the Maple Leaf," 203.
83 Hoover, "Ecumenism of the Trenches?"
84 McDonald, *The Armageddon Factor*, 33.
85 Ibid., 29–30.
86 Ibid., 34–35.
87 Ibid., 19.
88 Ibid., 17, 19–20.
89 Stockwell Day was appointed foreign affairs critic, and Jason Kenney, a Catholic, was appointed Harper's parliamentary secretary and liaison with religious groups.
90 John Ibbitson, "Behind Harper's Reluctance to Revisit Abortion Issue," *Globe and Mail*, April 23, 2011. Available at www.theglobeandmail.com/news/politics/behind-harpers-reluctance-to-revisit-abortion-issue/article580463/; "How the Abortion Debate Has Reared Its Head in Canada," CBCNews, April 26, 2012. Available at www.cbc.ca/news/canada/how-the-abortion-debate-has-reared-its-head-in-parliament-1.1200237; Meagan Fitzpatrick, "MPs Denounce Motion to Study When Life Begins," *CBC News*, April 26, 2012. Available at www.cbc.ca/news/politics/story/2012/04/26/pol-abortion-debate.html; Tonda MacCharles, "Conservative MP Blasts Decision to Fund Planned Parenthood," *Star*, September 28, 2011. Available at www.thestar.com/news/canada/2011/09/28/conservative_mp_blasts_decision_to_fund_planned_parenthood.html.

10 The Catholic past as prologue?
The future of ethnic, racial, and religious minority incorporation

This book began with Robert Putnam's question: Why can't we deconstruct our current tensions between majority and minority identities, just as we deconstructed Catholic–Protestant tensions before? The answer to Putnam's questions is that different coalitional possibilities can make for differences in transformation in minority standing. Whether reconstructive coalitions can form is dependent on the historical and institutional context. Each minority group encounters unique challenges in political incorporation, facing distinctive constellations of identities, institutions, and potential coalitions.

This book has not argued that the presence or absence of reconstructive coalitions determines everything about minority political standing. When reconstructive coalitions cannot occur, then transformations in minority standing may depend more on other factors, such as the minority group's power resources, the degree of assimilation with fragments of the majority group, or institutional opportunities. The remainder of this Conclusion considers how this perspective may illuminate the incorporation of other ethnic, racial, and religious minorities. Particular comparisons are made to Muslims in Western Europe, as well as Jews, Mormons, Latinos, and African Americans in the United States. In addition, the Conclusion considers how minority incorporation is related to political development and questions of religious freedom.

Beyond one-recipe-fits-all approaches to minorities

One implication of this book is a need to go beyond one-recipe-fits-all approaches to minority incorporation. Contemporary discourses often flatten the process of minority incorporation. Consider the idea advanced by *New York Times* pundit Ross Douthat that Protestant agitation and bigotry pressured Catholic minorities into assimilating. It is true that at Vatican II, for instance, representatives of nations where Catholics were a minority constituted the most vocal supporters of changing the church's positions on religious liberty. Countries in which Catholics were majorities felt less need to change the church, perhaps because, as Douthat has implied, Catholic minorities faced more pressure to conform to democratic norms.[1] Despite the seeming plausibility of this argument, the perspective of this book highlights several deficiencies. The first is that

Douthat's characterization of Catholic incorporation is, at best, only half right. It was not Catholics who solely moved toward the mainstream. Significant fractions of the mainstream met them halfway, adopting Catholic positions – first with liberal Protestants on social gospel issues, then with conservative Protestants on moral values issues. Future minority groups may not find themselves in a situation where fragments of the majority may be as keen to move toward the minority group.

Another implication of Douthat's argument is that assimilation of the minority is a good thing, and that pressuring minorities to conform is the best way to make minorities assimilate. Again, from the perspective of this book, Douthat's argument is incomplete. He does not inquire into what type of assimilation is desired. Australian Catholics achieved one kind of initial assimilation with the Labor coalition; Quebec Catholics achieved another kind of assimilation in which the Catholics in that province abandoned Catholicism or embraced much more liberal variants.

Depending on the kind of assimilation desired, different strategies may be more effective. Theorists such as Veidt Bader have suggested that granting minorities more autonomy, rather than pressuring them to conform and assimilate, may actually aid incorporation.[2] This debate is currently ongoing in the Netherlands, which historically provided social services and welfare provision along "pillarized" religious lines, with Catholics, Protestants, and secular liberals having their own schools, media, unions, and social service providers. With increased Muslim immigration to the country, many Dutch have wondered whether it was wise to extend the system of pillarization to Muslim immigrants.

Canadian Catholicism is instructive in this regard. In Quebec, Catholics were given the most autonomy of the three countries in this study to pursue their vision of what appropriate church–state relations should be. Looking at the long sweep of history, Catholics have experienced the most transformative change, with churchgoing rates plummeting and religious practice looking more like "believing without belonging."[3] Opinion polls show that moral and economic values in Quebec have been significantly liberalized. The strongest party in the province, the Bloc Quebecois, is significantly to the left on both moral and economic issues.[4] The Canadian Catholic experience suggests that recognition of difference, rather than homogeneous assimilation, can lead to significant transformative change in religion.

In other systems where Catholics have not had as complete control over the state, but where there was significant control over social welfare and education services given to the church, such as in the Netherlands and Germany, there have been significant declines in Catholic churchgoing as well (see Figure 9.2). Just as with religious establishment, situations of quasi-establishment as in Quebec seem to corrode churchgoing, whether due to making the church less responsive to its constituents' needs, or whether because such entanglement with the state tends to lead to a political backlash against the church.

Even if one were to accept the shaky terms of the contemporary "Muslim question" – that Muslim difference poses a problem to liberal democracy – how

The Catholic past as prologue? 177

to go about assimilating Muslims is an open question.[5] If one wants Muslims in liberal democracies to be secularized in the sense of adopting less fundamentalist versions of their religion or even becoming irreligious, the best answer may be to leave them substantial governmental autonomy so that they end up like Quebecois Catholics. Someone like Douthat may object and say that the best goal is not to get Muslims to become like Quebecois Catholics, but to adopt a version that emphasizes conservative family and work values. This highlights, however, the ambiguities in hoping for "assimilation" of minorities. That assimilation can take many forms, whether it be assimilation into a laborist identity, a Judeo-Christian identity, a religious identity that doesn't involve organized religion, a secular identity, or something else. Questions about minority incorporation are tied to political choices about what we want society to look like.

Once one more fully appreciates how minority incorporation is contextual and can produce different kinds of assimilation, one can reject more fully "model minority" discourses. It is often thought that if only the newest minorities could follow the example of successful model minorities, all problems of racial, ethnic, and religious tension could be resolved. In the context of the United States, Asian Americans, Jewish Americans, and other white immigrants have often been used to suggest that the problems of social, economic, and political integration which African Americans face is largely their own fault. If they just tried harder and assimilated mainstream values more, they could follow the path of previous groups.[6]

Many other scholars have criticized model minority discourses. In the Asian American case, such discourses often disguise differences among ethnic groups within the Asian American population and do not seek to understand the historical sources of why some Asian American subgroups have done better than others.[7] The move also glosses over the fact that Asian Americans are underrepresented in terms of descriptive political representation, despite high educational and socioeconomic attainment levels.

If there are any "model minorities" in terms of being overrepresented in descriptive representation, it is Jewish and Catholic Americans. It will be difficult, however, for future minorities to follow the script of these religious minorities, because those groups were politically incorporated when particular coalitional possibilities existed. Both groups' political assimilation occurred in contexts when fragments of the majority needed them for particular kinds of political projects, possibilities that have not been the same with regard to coalitions with other groups.

Comparisons with other minority groups

Given the ways in which Catholic political incorporation has been dependent on unique contextual conditions, this may make the claim that Catholic political incorporation can speak to other instances of minority political incorporation less plausible. Nevertheless, even though a universal "theory of political incorporation" may not be possible, comparing the processes involved in Catholic political

178 *The Catholic past as prologue?*

incorporation with the contemporary political incorporation of other minorities may at least provide a roadmap in outlining how the institutional context favors or disfavors reconstructive coalition formation between the majority and minority groups.

African American political incorporation

African Americans have not followed the path of Catholics. The wave election of 2008 which swept Democratic majorities in all branches of government did not translate into gains for African Americans, in the way that the Great Depression brought Catholics into office. At the outset of the 111th Congress, there were 42 African Americans in the House, all Democrats. African Americans were underrepresented relative to their population proportion (around 12 percent) and in the Democratic caucus relative to their share of Democratic voters (about 22 percent).[8] Only in a couple of Congresses has the percentage of African American House members in the Democratic caucus been about equal to African American's share of Democratic voters (see Figure 10.1).

There are limits to comparing Catholic incorporation to African American incorporation. African Americans have been subjected to much more intense stigmatization and institutional disenfranchisement. However, there is still utility in comparing Catholics with African Americans. The baseline against which

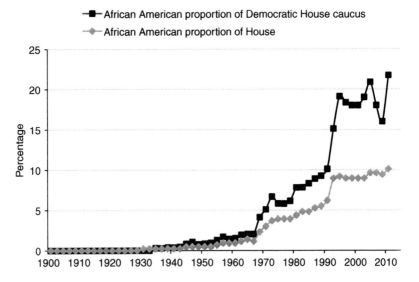

Figure 10.1 Percentage of African American representation in the House.

Sources: Jennifer E. Manning and Colleen J. Shogan, "African American Members of the United States Congress: 1870–2012," Congressional Research Service, November 26, 2012; Raffaela Wakeman, Norman Ornstein, Thomas E. Mann, Michael J. Malbin, and Andrew Rugg, "Vital Statistics on Congress." Available at www.brookings.edu/research/reports/2013/07/vital-statistics-congress-mann-ornstein.

The Catholic past as prologue? 179

African American descriptive representation should be measured is not proportionality, but overrepresentation in times of Democratic waves, as was seen in the Catholic case in Australia and the United States around the Great Depression. That African Americans have not achieved overrepresentation despite being a significant and loyal proportion of the contemporary Democratic Party throws their continued underrepresentation in government into even starker relief and highlights the failure of reconstruction within the Democratic coalition. This should prompt deeper questions about what institutional and coalitional configurations have prevented African Americans from following the path of Catholics.

African Americans have not been as organizationally central to coalitions in the way that Catholics have been to other reconstructive coalitions. Discrimination within labor unions limited the centrality of African Americans to the labor movement in the 1930s and continued well beyond.[9] In addition, African American influence in the working-class movement was suppressed by the failure to unionize the South and the institutions of Jim Crow. This helps explain why the initial decades of New Deal liberalism were not as transformative of African American standing as was Labor ascendancy in Australia for Catholic standing. In terms of a social conservative agenda, African Americans have not been as useful as Catholics to moral conservatives, even though polls have indicated that some African Americans hold conservative views on issues such as gay marriage. African American reluctance to join a moral values coalition stems from African American loyalty to the Democratic Party on class and race issues, rather than religious values issues. African American religious figures were not prominent in leading abortion clinic protests or the anti-ERA movement. By contrast, Catholics in the United States and Australia were not as limited in their affiliation to a moral values coalition; they had both experienced greater economic and political incorporation under a left-leaning government. African American symbolic centrality is also limited because there is no singular African American church that can deliver authoritative pronouncements on doctrine.

Compared to Catholics, coalitions with African Americans that have reconstructive potential have occurred only under rare circumstances. Klinkner and Smith argue persuasively in *The Unsteady March* that increases in African American standing typically followed major wars (Revolutionary War, Civil War, World War II, Cold War). These changes occurred partially due to a mobilizing effect on African Americans – changes in their consciousness and access to greater resources, leading to greater civil protest. African Americans were also needed in the war effort, and were thus more organizationally central (as soldiers and workers) and symbolically central (in showing that the United States is not as unjust as the countries which the United States is fighting). This can lead to some reconstructive articulation of identities, but clearly not as thoroughgoing as with Catholics.

One factor that may aid African American incorporation in the future is contemporary party polarization. Noel has argued that contemporary party coalitions have evolved to become more ideological. Parties at the turn of the twentieth century could afford to be less uniformly ideological because they could be patronage-based.[10] Contemporary parties are much more unified ideologically, according to Noel's data. This may mean that the terrain for reconstructive coalitions is much more favorable today. As the parties become more ideologically polarized, this may actually benefit minority groups like African Americans. There has been some preliminary research that ideological polarization has led Democratic partisans to move toward African Americans on issues such as police brutality and the Confederate flag.[11]

On the other hand, while party elites may be more ideologically cohesive, they may not have to be as ideologically cohesive in campaigning to the mass electorate because of the increased availability of data and advances in communication technology that have allowed the more precise targeting of individual voters. Widespread collection of data on individuals allows individual messages to be crafted to the particular voter's concerns, and these voters can be reached not just on mass communication platforms such as television and radio ads, but through smartphones, email, and web ads that only the potential voter will see. In 2012, the Obama campaign leveraged Facebook, for instance, to get Democratic supporters to mobilize undecided voters within their Facebook networks. Some theorists of technology and democracy worry that this increased use of technology to "microtarget" voters may be leading to siloes where individuals are trapped within "filter bubbles."[12] This is a factor that may undermine reconstructive coalitions as campaigns do not have to be ideologically consistent in making appeals to the electorate. This may limit the ability of the Democratic Party to spread one ideologically consistent position on African Americans to all of its party members.

Jewish and Mormon political incorporation in the United States

Comparisons with Jews and Mormons in the United States offer a further opportunity to examine the potential generalizability of the theory of reconstructive coalitions. American Jews were largely underrepresented in the House up until about 1970. Since then they have become highly overrepresented in the House relative to their population proportion (see Figure 10.2). What explains the difference with Catholics?

In comparison with Catholics, Jewish Americans are not as large a proportion of the population, constituting about 3.5 percent of the population around 1920. This has declined since the 1960s to about 2 percent of the population today. Jewish Americans were also heavily concentrated in the New York metropolitan area, with about half of all American Jews living there until the 1980s. These factors make Jewish Americans less likely to be organizationally central to either left- or right-leaning national coalitions, so reconstructive coalitions are not as likely to have as much effect. Jewish Americans may have been more symbolically central to the working-class movement, since they were often associated with radical labor politics in the first part of the twentieth century and the New Deal reinforced a Judeo-Christian identity as its basis. Perhaps, because of this particular mix of low organizational centrality but moderate symbolic centrality,

The Catholic past as prologue? 181

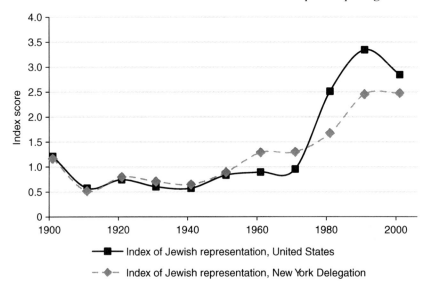

Figure 10.2 Index of Jewish representation in the House.

Source: American Jewish Year Book, 2001; Kurt F. Stone, The Jews of Capitol Hill: A Compendium of Jewish Congressional Members (Lanham, MD: Scarecrow, 2011); U.S. Census.

Note
The index is constructed by dividing the proportion of Jewish in the House by the proportion of Jewish in the population, so that a score of under 1 indicates underrepresentation and over 1 indicates overrepresentation. For the New York index, the Jewish population is taken from estimates of the Jewish population in the New York City metropolitan area, which includes areas in New Jersey and Connecticut. The Jewish population proportion is determined by dividng this by the New York population. Although imprecise, it gives a rough estimate of the index of representation in New York.

the evidence for increases in Jewish standing during the New Deal era is mixed. On the one hand, Gallup polls indicate a steady increase in those willing to vote for a Jewish candidate for president from 1937 to 1978, which is the same pattern for the public's willingness to elect a Catholic president.[13] On the other hand, it does not appear that the New Deal era significantly improved overall Jewish descriptive representation in the House. There is some increase looking only at the New York delegation, though it is unclear whether this is because of reconstructive coalitions or because of some other factor such as power resources.

More recent gains in Jewish descriptive representation do not appear to be driven by moral values coalitions on the right. Jews have some symbolic significance to conservative Protestants who read into the Bible predictions about the importance of Israel to the Second Coming. There has also been some rearticulation of identities on the right to suggest that stances against abortion, same-sex marriage, and secularization reflect a more general Judeo-Christian outlook. Gallup polls show continuing growth in approval of potential Jewish presidential candidates from 1980 to 2003.[14] However, Jewish Republicans remain a minority among all Jewish representatives, and Jews as a whole are much more unwilling to join the Republican coalition than Catholics. Public opinion polls show that Jewish Americans are much more likely to support abortion than any other religious group, including mainline Protestants and those with no religious affiliation.[15] Because of the lack of potential for widespread reconstructive coalitions with Jews, Jewish standing is likely to be more influenced by factors such as their levels of intermarriage and power resources.

Mormons' standing in the United States has not increased as much as Catholics', or even Jews'. Evidence that Mormons are more acceptable to the right includes the choice of Mitt Romney as the Republican candidate for president in 2012. However, survey evidence indicates that both Catholics and Jews are perceived more favorably than Mormons. The Gallup Poll, for instance, has asked whether respondents would vote for a Mormon for president. In 1967 about 75 percent of respondents indicated that they would. By 2007, when Mitt Romney first ran for the Republican presidential nomination, Gallup asked the question several times, yielding estimates from 72 to 80 percent. By this measure, Mormon standing has not changed very much in roughly 40 years. This number is less than the support for Catholics and Jews (over 90 percent of respondents indicated that they would vote for such candidates), but higher than for atheists (under 50 percent).[16]

A different question reveals much the same pattern of greater relative acceptance of Catholics and Jews over Mormons. The Religion and Public Life Survey in 2007 indicated that approximately 27 percent of Americans viewed Mormons mostly unfavorably or very unfavorably (compared with 9 percent for Jews, 14 percent for Catholics, 19 percent for evangelicals, 29 percent for Muslims, and 53 percent for atheists).[17]

The continued hesitancy to fully embrace Mormons is not related to the church's stance on the relation between religion and politics. The Doctrine and Covenants ratified by the general church conference in 1835 included statements supporting free exercise of conscience. Both Mormon and non-Mormon delegates to Utah's constitutional convention agreed on separation of church and state. In 1896 the Mormon Church declared in its Political Manifesto that the church was committed to separation of church and state. Moreover, Mormon Church leaders have claimed that the Declaration of Independence and the U.S. Constitution, including the clauses on religious freedom, were religiously inspired documents. Well before Vatican II, Mormons had embraced a commitment to religious liberty and the rights of minority religious groups, a stance informed by their own position as a minority religion.

As with Jews, Mormons currently comprise about 2 percent of the population, and they are heavily concentrated around Utah. Again, this factor limits the organizational centrality of Mormons to national reconstructive coalitions. In the 1970s and 1980s, Mormons were not at the forefront of moral values movements or the anticommunist struggle to the degree that Catholics were. Mormon votes are also already captured by the Republican Party, so there is no special need to appeal to their votes, while both Catholics and Jews have historically tended to

The Catholic past as prologue? 183

vote for the Democratic Party since the New Deal. These factors contribute to making Mormons less central to right-leaning moral values coalitions in the United States.

Muslim political incorporation in Western Europe

The prospects for increases in Muslim political standing appear dim, but not necessarily for reasons that might first come to mind. The global discourse of the War on Terror has cast suspicion on Muslims, but that alone should not determine Muslims' political incorporation. Catholics, too, had once been portrayed as an enemy to global civilizational progress. There are other factors that make it difficult for Muslims to be allied to various kinds of reconstructive coalitions.

Coalitional opportunities with Muslims are currently limited, partly because Muslims account for only a small percentage of the population. In 2005 Muslims constituted between 5 and 10 percent of the population in only France, the Netherlands, and Denmark. Elsewhere in Western Europe, Muslims comprised less than 5 percent of the population. Only on the periphery of the European Union (Bosnia-Herzegovina, Albania, Macedonia, and Turkey) do Muslims account for much higher population percentages.[18] In addition, the great ethnic diversity of Islamic immigrants may hamper their ability to act in a united fashion, limiting their organizational centrality.

But what if the European Muslim population continues to grow, as many demographers expect? Even then there are substantial obstacles. Muslim political incorporation into Western Europe resembles Catholic political incorporation into the United States in another respect. Both are instances in which the minority group grew gradually due to immigration and fertility, as opposed to in Australia and Canada, where Catholics comprised a substantial proportion of the population from the outset of those countries' histories. Based on proportion of the population alone, Muslim incorporation into Western Europe would most resemble Catholic incorporation into the United States from about 1850 to 1900. In the United States, direct attacks on Catholics at this time had the greatest chance of success. A flurry of Blaine Amendments passed at the state level largely before Catholics even exceeded 15 percent of the population, setting the institutional context which Catholics confront when they comprise a larger proportion of the population. One sees a similar dynamic at play in the passage of state-level Defense of Marriage Acts with respect to gay marriage. Many of these amendments have been rushed through because although gays are not growing as a group, public opinion in favor of gay rights and marriage has been trending toward greater acceptance. The institutions and policies adopted in this early phase when Muslim minority groups are still small may be critical in establishing the "facts on the ground" after Muslims increase their demographic and political influence.

The situation in the United States from 1850 to 1900 is not exactly the same as the situation facing Muslims in Western Europe today. There may be some factors favoring Muslim political incorporation in this early phase. Earlier accommodations of Christianity in Europe may have left constitutional legacies that make it hard in theory to deny extending similar accommodations to Muslims. In addition, the greater extensiveness of the welfare state and labor organization in Europe compared to the United States may be able to encourage more favorable economic, social, and political incorporation of Muslim immigrants. There is some research that such welfare institutions encourage the formation of trust across racial, ethnic, and linguistic boundaries.[19]

The greater institutionalization of the welfare state in Europe, however, may also hamper Muslim–labor coalitions. The left in Europe may be more concerned about preserving what they already have, rather than expanding the movement to encompass Muslim immigrants. As many scholars of social welfare have pointed out, the politics of welfare creation differ from the politics of welfare defense.[20] The former may require a broad base of allies, while the latter may not. The situation may be akin to that of Catholics in Ontario, who have state funding of religious schools, and so care less about whether other religious minorities get such aid. Countries in Europe may be encouraged to become more inclusive if globalization and capital mobility continue to erode labor and social welfare in Europe. Whether Muslims become central to such a campaign of protecting labor remains to be seen. They could, for instance, follow the path of African Americans, where labor unions excluded them from participation.

In addition, in countries like Germany and the Netherlands, there has been a tradition of extending state aid to churches. If Muslims become fully pillarized in the Netherlands or achieve public corporation status in Germany, the situation may play out as it did in Canada. There may be less incentive for Muslims to think in terms of a class identity as important, and therefore little need to reconstruct secular–Muslim relations. There is some evidence of this in the Netherlands' Catholic–Protestant past: when one looks at representation in the legislature, there has always been a slight underrepresentation of Catholics, just as in Canada.[21] Adding Muslims to the system of pillarization may help protect this system of welfare provision. In France, by contrast, where there is less of a tradition of extending state aid to churches, the incentive for Muslims to privilege the class basis of their identities may be greater.

What about a reconstructive coalition on the right? Opportunities for conservative Muslims to unite with conservative Christians are minimal because churchgoing in Europe is fairly low. In addition, an earlier history of accommodation of the Protestants and Catholics in countries like the Netherlands and Germany means that there is not so much motivation for Christians to mobilize against a "secular state."

Islam is different from Catholicism in that there is no equivalent to the Pope in the Islamic faith. Various nation-states with large Muslim populations are vying to be leaders of the global Muslim community, which makes entities such as the Organization of the Islamic Conference, composed of state representatives of the Islamic religious, fairly weak actors.[22] Casanova writes,

If there is anything on which most observers and analysts of contemporary Islam agree, it is on the fact that the Islamic tradition in the very recent past has undergone an unprecedented process of pluralization and fragmentation of religious authority.[23]

This may preclude the symbolic centrality Catholicism has achieved in debates over abortion, same-sex marriage, war, and welfare.

Latino political incorporation into the United States

In comparison to Muslims in Western Europe, the prospects for Latino political incorporation into the United States appear better. Unlike Islam, Latinos as a group have not been constructed as an enemy to global progress. Concerns about individual socialist Latin leaders (Chavez, Castro) and about the drug trade have not translated into a global discourse about inherent Latino inferiority or danger. But beyond this, there are other factors that make Latino political incorporation seem more promising.

Aspects of coalition formation that favor Latinos include the fact that they comprise about 14 percent of the American population, and are going to continue to increase their share. In addition, they are transforming the diversity of regions that have historically not been diverse in either racial or religious dimensions (e.g., the South and the Midwest). Latinos tend to be in a more economically precarious situation than the average American, so as a whole they have tended to vote for the Democratic Party.

On the other hand, there are factors which suggest that Latinos will not be as successful as Australian Catholics were in the 1930s. Latinos' actual numbers are reduced by low voter registration, which stems from many sources, including onerous registration requirements and disenfranchisement of felons. They are not in the same position as Australian Catholics were at the time of the Great Depression, when compulsory voting laws made it difficult for anti-Catholic Protestants to suppress Catholic votes. Like Catholics in the United States and Muslims in Europe they are an ethnically diverse group, which decreases their organizational unity. Cuban Americans, for instance, tend to support the Republican Party due to concerns over foreign policy in Cuba. In addition, the liberal–conservative divide in religion may also sufficiently split the Latino vote. Despite recent disillusionment of evangelicals with the second Bush administration, evangelicals are likely to remain highly mobilized and, as Wong has demonstrated, churches remain one of the most significant actors in voter mobilization in the United States. Wong has shown that the political attitudes of Latino Christians are somewhere in between "mainline" Christians and conservative evangelical Christians. On economics, labor, and possibly the environment, Latino Christians are closer to mainline Christians. On some other moral values issues, Latino Catholics and evangelicals appear closer to non-Latino Christian evangelicals.[24]

The main question confronting Latino political incorporation is whether they will remain affiliated with the Democratic Party, or become the focus of competition between both parties. Several academics have argued that an emerging Democratic majority will dominate politics in the early twenty-first century.[25] These scholars base their prediction in part on the growing size of Latino Americans and their propensity to vote Democratic. The other alternative is that divides within the Latino community will make Latinos follow the path of European Catholics in the United States. Although white Catholics still remain slightly more likely to vote Democratic, the shift over the twentieth century of major portions of the Catholic vote to Republicans helped make the conservative realignment from Reagan to the second Bush presidency possible.

Long-term reconstruction of identities is not likely from the right. Although prominent Republicans who are minorities include Bobby Jindal, Marc Rubio, and Nikki Haley, there is less incentive to push the boundaries of identity from this side of the political spectrum. Because minorities are generally economically disadvantaged, they will tend to form a small proportion of the Republican Party. The Republican base includes many who are actively opposed to Latinos on many public policy questions (immigration, education, etc.). Hence, prospects for Latino political incorporation will largely rely on the left. A class coalition provides the best prospects for advancing minority agenda while at the same time avoiding potential stigmatization (see targeting within universalism, Obama rhetoric).

The prospects for a reconstructive class coalition may not be as good as they were in the early half of the twentieth century in Australia and the United States. Globalization of the workforce has contributed to a significant decline of the labor movement in the United States over the past 30 years, and poses significant structural problems in re-energizing unionization rates. Yet in comparison with Europe, minorities may play a bigger role in the future union movement in the United States. Because unions have deteriorated so much in the United States, low-wage Latino workers form a much larger proportion of the labor movement compared to Muslims in Europe.[26] The high centrality of Latinos to the current labor movement in the United States helps explain contemporary unions' support for open borders and legalization of undocumented workers. By contrast, earlier union movements in the United States were heavily anti-immigrant.[27]

In addition, legacies of the incorporation of other races (including earlier rounds of incorporation of Latino minorities) may color attitudes toward contemporary Latinos. A concrete example of such earlier legacies affecting contemporary incorporation and coalitions are right-to-work laws. One problem facing union–Latino coalitions is that many states in which the Latino population is growing the fastest (as in the South) have adopted right-to-work laws that make union organization extremely difficult, and may inhibit the possibilities of labor–Latino coalitions. Other potential institutional and cultural legacies of earlier rounds of political incorporation include the passage of English-only laws, the growth of prisons, and widespread attitudes of white resentment at anything resembling transformative racial policy.

Diversity and political development

In addition to helping to see the incorporation of other minority groups in a different light, Catholic political incorporation may also shed light on issues of the relationship between minority political incorporation and political development in general. Just as there is no one model in which minorities incorporate and improve their standing, this book suggests that there is no one way in which diversity affects political development. The relationship is contextual.

For example, a substantial literature has developed arguing that greater racial, ethnic, and religious diversity is associated with more meager social welfare provision. Even if this is a general law, one can still wonder whether there are conditions that allow racially diverse liberal democracies to transcend this general law. The Australian Catholic case showed that a state with substantial diversity did not prevent the formation of a certain kind of welfare state – the wage earner's welfare state, relying on heavy unionization and pattern bargaining of wages, rather than a welfare state in which the government provides direct welfare benefits. Previous research indicates that the form of welfare provision matters in stigmatization. Direct means-tested payments tend to be highly stigmatizing, while more universalist programs where recipients may be seen to have worked and earned their benefits are less stigmatizing.[28] Under the conditions of a successful reconstructive coalition, the tendency of diversity to lead to weaker social welfare prospects may be mitigated. The outcome for social welfare may not depend only on overall levels of diversity, but also on whether a minority is successfully or unsuccessfully incorporated politically.

From the perspective of this book there is good reason to expect that in a state with a significant minority population the development of general institutions, policies, and political orders will be connected with the success or lack of success of minority incorporation. From a coalition perspective, transformative projects are intertwined. Rarely is it the case that a political project to increase minority standing can succeed alone. Minorities, almost by definition, lack the numerical strength to capture government in democracies. Hence, they are going to ally themselves with other transformative projects. Consider how Australian Catholic standing was intertwined with the success of the Labor movement, which ended up preserving a wage earner's welfare state, and possibly contributed to the entrenchment of compulsory voting. Successful minority political incorporation in Australia also led opposition parties to change, which led to fairly advanced provision of state aid to religious and private schools.

Sometimes the effect of minority incorporation on institutions and society can be unexpected. This is most clear in the case of Canada. Establishing separate schools for Catholics and allowing Quebec substantial provincial autonomy had an effect on building Christian conservative coalitions toward the end of the twentieth century. At the time when these policies were enacted, no one could have possibly foreseen that these developments would play a role in the abandonment of state religious schools in heavily Catholic provinces or that it would lead to dramatic secularization in Quebec.

To put this in the most general terms, civil society and political institutions are going to be mutually braided. One structure of civil society (diverse or not diverse) is not going to lead inexorably to one kind of political institutional structure (low or high welfare provision). Similarly, one kind of political institutional structure (e.g., parliamentary government) is not going to lead to one kind of outcome in civil society (low or high secularization). The combination of civil societal structure and institutional conditions is going to affect political development, leading to new kinds of civil societal structure and institutional conditions.

The development and meaning of religious freedom

Although not the primary focus of this book, some of the findings may also shed light on questions of religious freedom in liberal democracies. For example, some pluralist theorists suggest that greater religious diversity leads to more tolerant religious institutions. Others might argue that a state's tradition of church–state separation is the key factor in overall religious freedom. If the claim that there is no one way in which civil society structure or institutional structure is associated with political development is true, then both the diversity and church–state theses are thrown into doubt.

Mere religious diversity does not seem to be associated with overall religious freedom. While the early American republic included some institutionalizations of religious freedom, anti-Catholicism was also very strong in the early and mid-nineteenth century. Nominal diversity in the United States became less so as various Protestant denominations organized themselves in a broader Protestant identity rather than a "liberal Christian" or "conservative Christian" inclusive of Catholics.

It is also clear that separation of church and state does not by itself determine the levels of religious toleration and freedom. Civil society is not a neutral sphere and may be used to advance particular concepts of the essence of the nation under the cover of formal liberal democratic openness.[29] It often takes transformations in civil society (e.g., the appearance of reconstructive political movements) to make a nation more inclusive in its public law. This critique is not a new one. Whatever one may think of Marx's critique of capitalism and his political program of communism, Marx was a canny observer of the contradiction in liberalism in presupposing formal equality in terms of law and citizenship, but leaving in place inequalities in civil society. In Marx's *Critique of Hegel's Philosophy of Right*, Marx wrote, "Just as Christians are equal in heaven yet unequal on earth, so the individual members of the people are equal in the heaven of their political world, yet unequal in the earthly existence of society."[30] The insight of that remark is as appropriate to Protestant–Catholic relations as it is to relations between capital and labor. Protestants did not just support separation of church and state so that religious freedom would be available to all. Rather, many Protestants saw the sphere of civil society as one in which Protestantism would be uniquely able to succeed against Catholicism. Civil society was not a neutral sphere of tolerance, but was thought to be an active driver in the long-term dominance of Protestantism so long as Catholic interference through political machination was kept at bay.

Scholars such as Hamburger have argued that the history of separation of church and state was an anti-Catholic move meant to deny state aid to Catholic institutions. Hamburger argues that separation of church and state was not constitutional law, but was instead a perversion of it.[31] Some conservatives, in attempting to secure state voucher programs for religious schools, point to the passage of state-level Blaine laws as inherently anti-Catholic, as though any separation of church and state was inherently prejudicial and that real religious liberty lies in equal access to state funds. Yet this book suggests that the wrong lesson is being drawn from this history, because it focuses on making changes in formal church–state boundaries rather than understanding the mutual interplay between civil society and public law. Even if one takes Hamburger's controversial account of the meaning of the Constitution at face value, it was the dominance of Protestants in civil society that prompted a reading of the Constitution he dislikes. The causal order went from civil society to the Constitution, not the other way around. Hamburger doesn't question what configuration of resources and capabilities in civil society allowed such unequal influence in the first place. Why would one expect that these inequalities in influence would not continue if state funds were to be made available to faith-based groups? If unequal capacities as orchestrated through coalitions are the drivers of religious inequality, then there is no assurance that current coalitions will not be able to simultaneously assert an agenda that unduly privileges certain kinds of identities over others.

The experience of Muslims in the Netherlands and Germany underscores that a mere focus on formal delineations of church–state boundaries cannot guarantee religious equality. In both countries there has been no tradition of separation of church and state as there has been in the United States. In the Netherlands, Protestants and Catholics have historically been able to have their own schools, unions, and social service providers. Similarly, in Germany, churches that are recognized as public corporations can contract with the government to have the government collect additional taxes from the church's communicants and have the government provide funds to the churches to offer varying social services. However, Muslim immigrants in those countries have not yet been able to establish school and social service organizations in proportion to their population percentage; nor have they achieved public corporation status in Germany, for a variety of reasons.[32]

A narrow focus on formal church–state boundaries also tends to occlude the connection of religious freedom to other kinds of freedom. The relationship to other kinds of freedom can be either positive or negative, depending on how coalitions are articulated. It is untenable to privilege religious freedom without thinking how its development is associated with freedom in other domains. Given the connection between religious freedom and other kinds of freedom, there may not be easy answers to how best to balance these different kinds of freedom. Recognition of this, however, is an improvement over narratives that focus solely on religious freedom.

Attention to civil society opens up new possibilities for thinking about the content of religious freedom. The Australian experience shows the utility of a capabilities approach to religious freedom.[33] The Australian case in the first half of the twentieth century showed that when Catholic freedom was reconceived as laborers' freedom, this was fully consonant with an increase in the economic capacity of Catholic Australian workers to send their children to private religious schools. One can easily come up with other examples of how economic issues affect religious freedom. Lowering economic inequality, for instance, may make it easier for immigrant religious groups that have less wealth and status to assert their own voices in the public sphere and negotiate on equal terms in political coalitions, regardless of whether church and state are separate or not. Decreased economic inequality may also lead to less spending to "keep up with the Joneses," thus limiting materialism and promoting greater attentiveness to spirituality. Policies that assure living wages and increase the possibility of workers to take time off from work to attend to their families can increase the ability of parents to inculcate in their children their own religious values.

The capabilities approach may offer possibilities that narrowly delimited "rights talk" does not. The more that religious freedom is conceived in terms of rights, the more impossible religious freedom may seem, as such rights require the state to make judgments about what constitutes religion and the proper boundary between religion and state.[34] It is possible that emphasizing capabilities rather than rights in at least some domains of religious freedom may lead to less arbitrary distinctions about what constitutes religion and where the boundary between religion and state should be.

At this point, this book cannot offer a fully fleshed-out theory of what a religious capabilities approach might look like. No doubt there are issues and domains in which claims for religious freedom do not overlap with claims for economic equality and autonomy. And surely there is as much controversy over the proper division between economy and state as there is over church and state. Irreconcilability at the outer margins, however, should not be seen as a detriment to a capabilities approach but as a spur, because finding areas of commonality that do exist becomes all the more important in practical politics. Recognizing that increasing wages and reducing inequalities in wealth can help the religious in practicing, parenting, preaching, and proselytizing may help citizens better sort the costs and benefits of different kinds of coalitions, and spark alternative but realistic coalitional possibilities.

The future study of minority political incorporation

As a final implication of this book, it is hoped that it shows the utility of looking at minority political incorporation in a comparative manner. The comparisons made above provide only a preliminary roadmap to guide future inquiry. This book cannot claim to have unlocked all the secrets of minority political incorporation – an impossible task. But if one can see some value from looking at the political incorporation of one minority (Catholics), then how much more might be gained when one begins to look at other minorities and their impact upon each other and the majority? The time may actually be ripe for such comparative study – of outright domination, stigmatization, deadlock, normalization, and overrepresentation and valorization – to flourish. As more and more democracies become increasingly diverse, not only does the imperative to study minority political incorporation increase but also the capacity.

Notes

1 Melissa Wilde, *Vatican II: A Sociological Analysis of Religious Change* (Princeton, NJ: Princeton University Press, 2007), ch. 2.
2 See, e.g., Veit Bader, "Religious Diversity and Democratic Institutional Pluralism," *Political Theory* 31 (2003): 265–294; Veit Bader, "Legal Pluralism and Differentiated Morality: Shari'a in Ontario?," in Ralph Grillo, Roger Ballard, Alessandro Ferrari, Andre J. Hoekema, Marcel Maussen, and Prakash Shah (eds), *Legal Practice and Cultural Diversity* (Burlington, VA: Ashgate, 2009), 49–72.
3 This term was used by Grace Davies to challenge the secularization thesis; *Religion in Britain since 1945: Believing without Belonging* (New York: Wiley-Blackwell, 1994).
4 Bloc Quebecois voters, for instance, are the most left-leaning in terms of moral traditionalism (beliefs about abortion, divorce, homosexuality, prostitution, and euthanasia) and the free market. Interestingly, they are also heavily in support of policies encouraging two-parent families. See Neil Nevitte and Christopher Cochrane, "Value Change and the Dynamics of the Canadian Partisan Landscape," in Alain-G. Gagnon and A. Brian Tanguay (eds), *Canadian Parties in Transition*, 3rd edn (Peterborough, Ontario: Broadview, 2007), 261, 265.
5 There are substantial criticisms of the way the Muslim question is posed in the first place. Anne Norton, *On the Muslim Question* (Princeton, NJ: Princeton University Press, 2013).
6 For a recent example of this type of argument see Eugene Volokh, "How the Asians Became White," *Washington Post*, May 29, 2014. Available at www.washingtonpost.com/news/volokh-conspiracy/wp/2014/05/29/how-the-asians-became-white/.
7 For a critique of Volokh's argument that Asians are now white, see Jason T. Lagria, "No, Volokh: Asians is not the New White," *AAPI Voices*, June 6, 2014. Available at http://aapivoices.com/stem-aapi-not-white/.
8 Frank Newport, "Democrats Racially Diverse, Republicans Mostly White," Gallup.com, February 8, 2013. Available at www.gallup.com/poll/160373/democrats-racially-diverse-republicans-mostly-white.aspx.
9 Paul Frymer, *Black and Blue: African Americans, Labor, and the Decline of the Democratic Party* (Princeton, NJ: Princeton University Press, 2011).
10 Hans Noel, *Political Ideologies and Political Parties in America* (New York: Cambridge University Press, 2014).
11 Michael Tesler, "Donald Sterling Shows the Separate Realities of Democrats and Republicans about Race," *Washington Post Monkey Cage*, May 1, 2014. Available at www.washingtonpost.com/blogs/monkey-cage/wp/2014/05/01/donald-sterling-shows-the-separate-realities-of-democrats-and-republicans-about-race/; Michael Tesler, "Democrats Increasingly Think the Confederate Flag Is Racist. Republicans Don't," *Washington Post Monkey Cage*, July 9, 2015. Available at www.washingtonpost.com/blogs/monkey-cage/wp/2015/07/09/democrats-increasingly-think-the-confederate-flag-is-racist-republicans-dont/.
12 Eli Pariser, *The Filter Bubble: How the New Personalized Web is Changing What We Read and How We Think* (New York: Penguin, 2012).

13 David W. Moore, "Little Prejudice against a Woman, Jewish, Black or Catholic Presidential Candidate," Gallup News Service, June 10, 2003. Available at www.gallup.com/poll/8611/little-prejudice-against-woman-jewish-black-catholic-presidenti.aspx.
14 Ibid.
15 PewResearch Religion and Public Life Project, "Public Opinion on Abortion," July 2013. Available at https://web.archive.org/web/20151012053700/http://features.pewforum.org/abortion-slideshow/slide3.php.
16 Frank Newport, "Bias against a Mormon Presidential Candidate Same as in 1967," Gallup.com, June 21, 2012. Available at www.gallup.com/poll/155273/bias-against-mormon-presidential-candidate-1967.aspx; Justin McCarthy, "In U.S., Socialist Presidential Candidates Least Appealing," Gallup.com, June 22, 2015. Available at www.gallup.com/poll/183713/socialist-presidential-candidates-least-appealing.aspx.
17 "Public Expresses Mixed Views of Islam, Mormonism," Pew Research Center, September 26, 2007. Available at www.pewforum.org/2007/09/26/public-expresses-mixed-views-of-islam-mormonism/.
18 "Muslims in Europe: Country Guide," BBC News, 2005. Available at: http://news.bbc.co.uk/2/hi/europe/4385768.stm.
19 Marcus M.L. Crepaz, *Trust beyond Borders: Immigration, the Welfare State and Identity in Modern Societies* (Ann Arbor: University of Michigan Press, 2008).
20 Paul Pierson (ed.), *The New Politics of the Welfare State* (New York: Oxford University Press, 2001).
21 Data from the Netherlands and Germany (both of which have Catholic populations comprising 35 to 40 percent of the population) show that the Canadian representation levels are about the same as in those two countries. See Heinrich Best and Maurizio Cotta (eds), *Parliamentary Representatives in Europe: 1848–2000: Legislative Recruitment and Careers in Eleven European Countries* (New York: Oxford University Press, 2000).
22 José Casanova, "Catholic and Muslim Politics in Comparative Perspective," *Taiwan Journal of Democracy* 1, no. 2 (December 2005): 93–94.
23 Ibid., 100.
24 "Immigration, Religion, and Conservative Politics in America." Talk given at the American Politics Workshop, University of Pennsylvania, January 30, 2009.
25 Ruy Teixiera, "New Progressive America: Twenty Years of Demographic, Geographic, and Attitudinal Changes across the Country Herald a New Progressive Majority." Report for the Center for American Progress, March 11, 2009. Available at https://web.archive.org/web/20120714053519/www.americanprogress.org/issues/2009/03/progressive_america.html.
26 In addition, other areas of union strength in the United States, such as government workers, feature a high proportion of African Americans.
27 Daniel Tichenor, *Dividing Lines: The Politics of Immigration Control in America* (Princeton, NJ: Princeton University Press, 2002), ch. 5.
28 Theda Skocpol, *The Missing Middle: Working Families and the Future of American Social Policy* (New York: W.W. Norton, 2000), ch. 2.
29 Talal Asad makes a similar point in looking at the example of India. Even though the government is formally secular, there have been recurrent bouts of religious violence. Toleration in constitutional law does not automatically engender toleration in civil society. *Formations of the Secular: Christianity, Islam, Modernity* (Stanford, CA: Stanford University Press, 2003), 8.
30 Karl Marx, *Early Political Writings*, edited and translated by Joseph O'Malley, with Richard Davis (New York: Cambridge University Press, 1994), 17. Extract from *Critique of Hegel's Philosophy of Right*, 1843.
31 Philip Hamburger, *Separation of Church and State* (Cambridge, MA: Harvard University Press, 2002).

32 Stephen V. Mosnma and J. Christopher Soper, *The Challenge of Pluralism: Church and State in Five Democracies* (New York: Rowman & Littlefield, 2009), chs 3 and 6.
33 This is based in part on the capabilities approach developed by Amartya Sen. See his book *Development as Freedom* (New York: Knopf, 1999).
34 Winnifred Sullivan, *The Impossibility of Religious Freedom* (Princeton, NJ: Princeton University Press, 2007).

Appendices

Table A.1 Catholic proportion of population, Canadian provinces (%)

	1871	1881	1891	1901	1911	1941	2001
Alberta					16.6	19.1	
British Columbia		20.3	21.2	18.8	14.9	13.4	17.5
Manitoba		18.6	13.5	14.0	16.2	18.9	29.3
New Brunswick	33.6	34.0	36.1	38.0	41.2	48.2	53.6
Nova Scotia	26.3	26.7	27.2	28.2	29.4	32.7	36.6
Ontario	16.9	16.7	16.9	17.9	19.2	22.5	34.7
PEI		43.3	43.8	44.4	44.8	45.1	47.4
Quebec	85.6	86.1	86.8	86.7	86.1	86.8	83.4
Saskatchewan						18.3	22.4

Source: Census of Canada.

Table A.2 Catholic proportion of population, Australian states (%)

	1891	1901	1911	1921	1933	1947	1954	1961	1971	1981
NSW	25.8	26.0	25.5	24.3	24.1	25.5	27.0	29.2	30.4	30.7
VIC	22.2	22.3	22.3	21.4	21.6	22.6	25.5	29.2	30.5	31.5
QLD	23.8	24.3	24.8	23.9	25.3	25.6	26.6	27.7	27.5	27.4
WA	25.6	23.3	22.7	20.5	20.5	21.2	24.9	27.3	27.7	28.0
SA	15.4	14.7	14.8	13.9	14.3	14.3	17.8	21.1	21.9	22.2
TAS	18.2	17.9	17.7	16.9	16.9	17.3	18.9	20.4	21.1	21.3
NT			15.3	20.5	26.1	28.1	30.3	31.1	24.4	25.8
ACT					27.3	28.0	33.4	34.9	34.3	34.0
Total 1	22.9	23.0	23.0	21.9	22.3	23.2	25.3	27.9	28.7	29.2
Total 2	22.5	22.7	22.4	21.5	19.4	20.7	22.9	24.9	27.0	26.0

Source: Vamplew, *Australians: Historical Statistics*. The state data exclude those who answered "no reply" and "object to question" from the denominator. This could have some effect if most of those who don't reply or object are really irreligious. Total 1 excludes "No replies" and "Object to Question" from the denominator. Total 2 includes them. The contemporary figures for Total 1 do not seem to match up with other polls that indicate current Catholic population percentage as around 27 percent, which match better when the "no replies" are included in the denominator.

Table A.3 Catholic proportion of population, U.S. states (%)

State	1850	1860	1870	1890	1906	1916	1926	1952	1971	1980	1990	2000
AL	1.9	1.7	1.8	0.9	2.1	1.7	1.4	1.6	2.5	2.7	3.4	3.4
AK									16.4	9.8	8.2	8.7
AZ								24.6	23.1	17.9	17.9	19.0
AR	0.9	0.9	1.8	0.3	18.2	31.5	25.1	1.4	2.9	2.4	3.1	4.3
CA	16.2	19.0	35.9	13.0	2.2	1.3	1.4	22.1	19.7	20.1	24.0	29.8
CO			30.9	0.0	18.4	17.0	15.8	16.3	17.1	14.0	14.7	17.5
CT	3.8	12.6	13.0	20.5	14.9	12.1	12.7	37.3	43.9	44.7	41.8	40.3
DE	2.6	4.2	9.4	7.0	29.6	38.8	37.3	10.7	18.7	17.3	17.5	19.4
DC					12.5	14.2	15.9	13.6				
FL	2.9	3.9	3.7	4.3	2.7	2.9	3.2	5.4	13.5	13.9	12.4	16.2
GA	0.8	0.9	1.2	0.6	0.8	0.7	0.6	0.6	2.3	2.6	3.2	4.6
HA									25.4	21.8	21.0	19.9
ID				5.7	7.4	4.7	5.3	5.1	8.3	7.5	7.3	10.1
IL	4.9	9.1	10.7	12.4	17.8	19.3	19.2	26.9	32.1	31.5	31.6	31.2
IN	3.5	6.5	10.1	5.4	6.7	9.7	10.1	11.9	13.9	13.2	12.6	13.7
IA	2.9	6.8	7.9	8.6	9.3	11.3	11.8	14.3	18.7	18.5	18.7	19.1
KS		2.7	8.4	4.7	5.9	7.5	9.4	10.9	13.9	14.3	14.9	15.1
KY	3.9	6.4	11.9	5.0	7.5	6.8	7.0	8.7	10.5	10.0	9.9	10.0
LA	14.5	16.5	20.9	18.9	31.5	29.5	30.2	32.0	35.2	31.0	32.4	30.9
ME	1.5	3.5	5.4	8.7	15.8	19.7	22.2	25.1	27.3	24.5	21.5	22.2
MD	11.7	13.9	20.0	13.6	13.4	16.0	15.2	19.2	20.0	17.5	17.4	18.0
MA	5.4	11.7	17.7	27.5	35.0	39.1	40.2	48.4	51.7	53.0	49.2	48.7
MI	5.8	5.1	10.7	10.6	18.8	17.7	19.8	22.0	25.4	22.1	25.2	20.3
MN	1.0	14.8	15.0	20.9	19.8	18.6	19.2	23.2	26.2	25.6	25.4	25.6
MS	0.9	1.2	1.6	0.9	1.7	1.8	1.7	2.4	3.7	3.8	3.7	4.1
MO	6.5	7.0	11.7	6.1	12.0	13.3	14.7	15.0	16.1	16.3	15.7	15.3
MT				19.0	23.4	16.9	13.7	24.1	19.0	17.8	15.7	18.8
NE		2.8	3.0	4.9	8.9	10.9	11.6	15.5	19.6	21.2	21.2	21.8
NV			15.6	8.6	16.1	11.0	10.0	17.1	18.8	13.8	13.1	16.6
NH	0.7	3.7	5.6	10.6	28.5	31.1	32.3	35.6	36.0	31.0	26.8	34.9

continued

Table A.3 Continued

State	1850	1860	1870	1890	1906	1916	1926	1952	1971	1980	1990	2000
NJ	3.0	8.5	10.6	15.5	20.0	27.8	29.3	36.8	38.0	40.2	41.3	40.4
NM			117.6		46.5	51.7	44.5	43.6	35.8	34.2	30.8	36.9
NY	6.5	10.6	12.8	19.2	27.9	28.2	27.1	29.9	35.5	35.6	40.5	39.8
NC	0.2	0.5	0.5	0.2	0.2	0.2	0.0	0.7	1.4	1.6	2.3	3.9
NC				14.5	13.7	15.7	15.7	21.6	27.9	26.7	27.1	27.9
OH	5.8	10.6	11.3	9.2	12.5	16.0	15.7	19.2	21.2	22.5	19.7	19.7
OK					3.6	2.6	2.1	3.5	3.9	3.6	4.6	4.9
OR		6.7	5.8	9.6	6.5	6.8	6.4	7.3	10.2	12.2	9.8	10.2
PA	6.1	9.2	11.9	10.6	17.4	22.3	23.2	27.3	32.5	32.7	30.9	31.0
RI	7.8	21.4	22.2	28.0	40.4	45.6	50.4	58.9	63.6	63.7	63.1	51.7
SC	1.4	2.7	3.1	0.5	0.7	0.6	0.5	1.0	1.8	1.9	2.3	3.4
SC		1.0		7.8	12.4	11.8	14.6	17.0	20.3	20.0	20.7	24.0
TN	0.3		2.4	1.0	0.8	1.0	1.0	1.3	2.4	2.5	2.8	3.2
TX	4.9	3.3	3.2	4.5	8.9	9.4	10.6	18.2	18.0	16.4	21.0	21.0
UT				2.9	2.6	2.4	3.0	4.4	4.8	4.1	3.8	4.3
VT	2.0	5.0	12.7	12.9	23.5	22.1	25.1	30.3	32.7	30.6	25.6	24.3
VA	0.9	1.8	1.7	0.7	1.5	1.7	1.6	2.8	5.3	5.3	6.2	8.6
WA				6.0	9.0	7.8	8.3	11.2	10.7	9.2	10.8	12.2
WV				2.1	3.7	4.5	4.5	4.9	5.7	5.4	6.1	5.8
WI	10.3	12.3	14.5	14.8	23.0	24.0	23.6	29.6	33.7	32.8	31.8	31.6
WY				11.8	8.6	7.5	8.9	16.5	13.8	13.3	13.1	16.3
US	4.4	7.4	9.0	12.0	17.0	16.0	16.0	19.7	22.1	21.0		22.0

Sources: Obtaining reliable data on the population of Catholics in particular states in the nineteenth century is difficult, but one method to determine the number is based on the 1890 Census, which includes questions on four variables: church membership, church seating, church property, and church organizations. Because the 1850 to 1880 censuses included data on three of these variables (church seating, church property, and church organizations, but not church membership), the researchers Stark and Finke reasoned that they could find an equation which relates the three variables to church membership for 1890, then to use this equation to estimate church membership for the earlier censuses. Using the coefficients from their regression equation, I have calculated Catholic population percentages for each state from 1850 to 1870, and put these side by side with Census statistics from 1890 to 1926. One should interpret these numbers as having very high margins of error. For instance, the data for California in 1870 are almost certainly wrong because of the unusually high value of Catholic church property holding in that state. The 1890 to 1926 data are calculated from membership data assembled by the U.S. Census. The 1952 to 2000 data are from the American Religion Data Archive website.

Table A.4 Rough estimates of Catholic population percentage in Australian Electoral Districts, 1933

State	Electoral District	RC (%)	State	Electoral District	RC (%)
NSW	Barton	14.2	Victoria	Flinders	14.0
NSW	Calare	28.4	Victoria	Gippsland	16.0
NSW	Cook	27.2	Victoria	Henty	13.2
NSW	Cowper	18.8	Victoria	Indi	22.1
NSW	Dalley	21.1	Victoria	Kooyong	12.3
NSW	Darling	25.4	Victoria	Maribyrnong	18.3
NSW	East Sydney	30.1	Victoria	Melbourne	28.1
NSW	Eden-Monaro	26.4	Victoria	Melbourne Ports	22.7
NSW	Gwydir	23.9	Victoria	Wannon	19.6
NSW	Hume	27.8	Victoria	Wimmera	16.6
NSW	Hunter	14.8	Victoria	Yarra	24.9
NSW	Lang	18.4	Queensland	Brisbane	20.7
NSW	Macquarie	22.0	Queensland	Capricornia	21.7
NSW	Martin	17.0	Queensland	Darling Downs	23.8
NSW	New Castle	16.8	Queensland	Griffith	20.7
NSW	New England	20.2	Queensland	Herbert	28.2
NSW	North Sydney	17.2	Queensland	Kennedy	26.6
NSW	Parramatta	14.3	Queensland	Lilley	20.6
NSW	Reid	17.8	Queensland	Maranoa	23.7
NSW	Richmond	23.0	Queensland	Moreton	16.9
NSW	Riverina	25.2	Queensland	Wide Bay	16.0
NSW	Robertson	16.6	SA	Adelaide	14.8
NSW	Warringah	14.9	SA	Barker	9.7
NSW	Watson	28.1	SA	Boothby	10.3
NSW	Wentworth	25.4	SA	Grey	12.8
NSW	Werriwa	17.7	SA	Hindmarsh	12.7
NSW	West Sydney	26.2	SA	Wakefield	11.7
Victoria	Balaclava	16.8	WA	Forrest	15.1
Victoria	Ballarat	21.3	WA	Fremantle	16.1
Victoria	Batman	16.8	WA	Kalgoorlie	24.4
Victoria	Bendigo	21.2	WA	Perth	19.2
Victoria	Bourke	20.8	WA	Swan	16.5
Victoria	Corangamite	18.3	Tasmania	Bass	12.7
Victoria	Corio	20.4	Tasmania	Darwin	14.5
Victoria	Deakin	14.0	Tasmania	Denison	16.9
Victoria	Fawkner	15.7	Tasmania	Franklin	15.1

Source: Calculated from Census records of 1933; Glenn Rhodes, ed., *Commonwealth of Australia, 1901–1988, Electoral Redistributions*, Australian Electoral Commission and the Australian Surveying and Land Information Group, Department of Administrative Services, Commonwealth of Australia, 1989; Australian Electoral Office, *Commonwealth Electoral Maps, Proclaimed*, Canberra, 1983, microforms at the University of Sydney. There are errors in these figures, as electoral boundaries do not match up with the census boundaries, so census districts were assigned to electoral districts based on a best guess to closest fit.

Selected bibliography

Ainsworth, Scott H., and Thad E. Hall. *Abortion Politics in Congress: Strategic Incrementalism and Policy Change*. New York: Cambridge University Press, 2011.
Alba, Richard. *Blurring the Color Line: The New Chance for a More Integrated America*. Cambridge, MA: Harvard University Press, 2009.
Albinski, Henry Stephen. *Canadian and Australian Politics in Comparative Perspective*. New York: Oxford University Press, 1973.
Alesina, Alberto, and Edward L. Glaeser. *Fighting Poverty in the US and Europe: A World of Difference*. New York: Oxford University Press, 2004.
Alesina, Alberto, Reza Baqir, and William Easterly. "Public Goods and Ethnic Divisions." *Quarterly Journal of Economics* 114 (November 1999): 1243–1284.
Allen, Richard. *The Social Passion: Religion and Social Reform in Canada, 1914–1928*. Toronto: University of Toronto Press, 1990.
Anderson, Ellen. *Judging Bertha Wilson: Law as Large as Life*. Toronto: Published for the Osgoode Society for Canadian Legal History by the University of Toronto, 2001.
Andrews, Kevin, and Michelle Curtis. *Changing Australia: Social, Cultural, and Economic Trends Shaping the Nation*. Sydney: Federation, 1998.
Appleblatt, Anthony. "The School Question in the 1929 Saskatchewan Provincial Election." *CCHA Study Sessions* 43 (1976): 75–90. Available at www.umanitoba.ca/colleges/st_pauls/ccha/Back%20Issues/CCHA1976/Appleblatt.html.
Archer, Robin. *Why is There No Labor Party in the United States*. Princeton, NJ: Princeton University Press, 2007.
Asad, Talal. *Formations of the Secular: Christianity, Islam, Modernity*. Stanford, CA: Stanford University Press, 2003.
Australian Bureau of Statistics. *The Private Wealth of Australia and its Growth as Ascertained by Various Methods, Together with a Report of the War Census of 1915. Prepared under Instructions from the Minister of State for Home and Territories by G.H. Knibbs, Commonwealth Statistician*. Melbourne: McCarron, Bird, and Co., 1918.
Australian Institute of Health and Welfare. *Australian Hospital Statistics 2009–10*, Health Services Series Number 40, Cat. no. HSE 107. Canberra: AHW, 2011.
Bain, George Sayers, and Robert Price. *Profiles of Union Growth: A Comparative Statistical Portrait of Eight Countries*. Oxford: Blackwell, 1980.
Baum, Gregory. *Catholics and Canadian Socialism: Political Thought in the Thirties and Forties*. New York: Paulist, 1980.
Bean, Lydia, Marco Gonzalez, and Jason Kaufman. "Why Doesn't Canada Have an America-style Christian Right? Comparative Framework for Analyzing Political

Effects on Evangelical Subcultural Identity." *Canadian Journal of Sociology* 33, no. 4 (2008): 899–943.
Behiels, Michael D. *Prelude to Quebec's Quiet Revolution: Liberalism versus Neo-Nationalism, 1945–1960*. Kingston: McGill-Queen's, 1985.
Beland, Daniel, and Andre Lecours. "Nationalism and Social Policy in Canada and Quebec." In *The Territorial Politics of Welfare*, edited by Nicola McEwen and Luis Moreno, 189–206. New York: Routledge, 2005.
Bell, Derrick. *Faces at the Bottom of the Well: The Permanence of Racism*. New York: Basic Books, 1993.
Berggren, Jason D. "Jefferson Davis, Religion, and the Politics of Recognition." *White House Studies* 5, no. 2 (March 22, 2005): 231–242.
Best, Heinrich, and Maurizio Cotta, eds. *Parliamentary Representatives in Europe: 1848–2000: Legislative Recruitment and Careers in Eleven European Countries*. New York: Oxford University Press, 2000.
Beyer, Peter. "Religious Vitality in Canada: The Complementarity of Religious Market and Secularization Perspectives." *Journal for the Scientific Study of Religion* 36, no. 2 (June 1997): 272–288.
Bibby, Reginald. *Fragmented Gods: The Poverty and Potential of Religion in Canada*. Toronto: Irwin, 1987.
Bibby, Reginald. *Restless Gods: The Renaissance of Religion in Canada*. Toronto: Stoddart, 2002.
Bickerton, James, Alain-G. Gagnon, and Patrick J. Smith. *Ties That Bind: Parties and Voters in Canada*. Toronto: Oxford University Press, 1999.
Birch, A.H. *Federalism, Finance, and Social Legislation in Canada, Australia, and the United States*, Oxford: Clarendon Press, 1955.
Blais, Andre. "Accounting for the Electoral Success of the Liberal Party in Canada – Presidential Address to the Canadian Political Science Association, London, Ontario, June 3, 2005." *Canadian Journal of Political Science* 38, no. 4 (December 2005): 821–840.
Blake, Donald E. "Canadian Census and Election Data, 1908–1968." Data deposited at ICPSR (ICPSR 39), http://doi.org/10.3886/ICPSR00039.v2.
Blakely, Kristin. "Women of the New Right in Canada." Dissertation. Loyola University, Chicago, 2008.
Blum, Edward J. *Reforging the White Republic: Race, Religion, and American Nationalism, 1865–1898*. Baton Rouge: Louisiana State University Press, 2005.
Boix, Carles. "Setting the Rules of the Game: The Choice of Electoral Systems in Advanced Democracies." *American Political Science Review* 93, no. 3 (1999): 609–624.
Botham, Fay. *Almighty God Created the Races: Christianity, Interracial Marriage, and American Law*. Chapel Hill: University of North Carolina Press, 2009.
Brett, Judith. *Australian Liberals and the Moral Middle Class: From Alfred Deakin to John Howard*. New York: Cambridge University Press, 2003.
Brodie, Janine, and Jane Jenson. "Piercing the Smokescreen: Stability and Change in Brokerage Politics." In *Canadian Parties in Transition*, 3rd edn, edited by Alain-G. Gagnon and A. Brian Tanguay, 33–54. Peterborough, Ontario: Broadview, 2007.
Broome, Richard. *Treasure in Earthen Vessels: Protestant Christianity in New South Wales Society, 1900–1914*. St. Lucia, Queensland: University of Queensland, 1980.
Brown, Ruth Murray. *For a "Christian America": A History of the Religious Right*. New York: Prometheus, 2002.

Selected bibliography

Brown, Wendy. *Regulating Aversion: Tolerance in the Age of Identity and Empire*. Princeton, NJ: Princeton University Press, 2006.

Browning, Rufus P., Dale Rogers Marshall, and David H. Tabb. *Protest Is Not Enough*. Berkeley: University of California Press, 1984.

Browning, Rufus P., Dale Rogers Marshall, and David H. Tabb, eds. *Racial Politics in American Cities*, 3rd edn. New York: Longman, 1997.

Bruce, Steve. *God Is Dead: Secularization in the West*. Oxford: Blackwell, 2002.

Bryant, Anita. *The Anita Bryant Story: The Survival of Our Nation's Families and the Threat of Militant Homosexuality*. Old Tappan: Fleming H. Revell, 1977.

Buckingham, Jennifer. *The Rise of Religious Schools*, Centre for Independent Studies Policy Monograph 111, 2010. Available at www.cis.org.au/images/stories/policy-monographs/pm-111.pdf.

Buckley, Ken, and Ted Wheelwright. *No Paradise for Workers: Capitalism and the Common People in Australia, 1788–1914*. Melbourne: Oxford University Press, 1988.

Buice, David. "A Stench in the Nostrils of Honest Men: Southern Democrats and the Edmunds Act of 1882." *Dialogue: A Journal of Mormon Thought* 21, no. 3 (1988): 100–113.

Bureau of the Census. *Religious Bodies, 1906, Part I: Summary and General Tables*. Washington, DC: Government Printing Office, 1910.

Burgmann, Verity. "Capital and Labour." In *Who Are Our Enemies? Racism and the Working Class in Australia*, edited by A. Curthoys and A. Markus, 20–34. Neutral Bay, Australia: Hale and Iremonger, 1978.

Cairns, Alan. "The Electoral System and the Party System in Canada." *Canadian Journal of Political Science* 1, no. 1 (1968): 55–80.

Caplow, Theodore, Howard M. Bahr, John Modell, and Bruce A. Chadwick. *Recent Social Trends in the United States, 1960–1990*. Montreal: McGill-Queen's, 1991.

Carty, Thomas J. *A Catholic in the White House? Religion, Politics, and John F. Kennedy's Presidential Campaign*. New York: Palgrave Macmillan, 2004.

Casanova, José. "Catholic and Muslim Politics in Comparative Perspective." *Taiwan Journal of Democracy* 1, no. 2 (December 2005): 89–108.

Casey, Shaun A. *The Making of a Catholic President: Kennedy vs. Nixon 1960*. New York: Oxford University Press, 2009.

Castles, Francis G. *Working Class and Welfare: Reflections on the Political Development of the Welfare State in Australia and New Zealand, 1890–1980*. Sydney: Allen & Unwin, 1985.

Castles, Francis G. *Australian Public Policy and Economic Vulnerability: A Comparative and Historical Perspective*. Sydney: Allen & Unwin, 1988.

Chalmers, David M. *Hooded Americanism: The First Century of the Ku Klux Klan, 1865–1965*. Garden City, NY: Doubleday, 1965.

Chen, Anthony. "'The Hitlerian Rule of Quotas': Racial Conservatism and the Politics of Fair Employment Legislation in New York State, 1941–1945." *Journal of American History* 92, no. 4 (March 2006): 1238–1264.

Chhibbers, Pradeep, and Ken Kollman. *Formation of National Party Systems: Federalism and Party Competition in Canada, Great Britain, India, and the United States*. Princeton, NJ: Princeton University Press, 2004.

Choquette, Robert. *Language and Religion: A History of English–French Conflict in Ontario*. Ottawa: University of Ottawa Press, 1975.

Chui, Tina, Kelly Tran, and Helene Maheux. "Immigration in Canada: A Portrait of the Foreign-born Population, 2006 Census." *Statistics Canada Catalogue* no. 97–557 (December 2007): 15.

Cica, Natasha. "Abortion Law in Australia." Research Paper 1, 1998–1999, August 31, 1998. Available at www.aph.gov.au/About_Parliament/Parliamentary_Departments/Parliamentary_Library/pubs/rp/rp9899/99rp01.

Clermont, Betty. *The Neo-Catholics: Implementing Christian Nationalism in America*. Atlanta: Clarity Press, 2009.

Cohen, Lizabeth. *Making a New Deal: Industrial Workers in Chicago, 1919–1939*. New York: Cambridge University Press, 1991.

Coleman, Karen. "The Politics of Abortion in Australia: Freedom, Church, and State." *Feminist Review* 29 (summer 1988): 75–97.

Collins, William J. "The Political Economy of State Fair Housing Laws before 1968." *Social Science History* 30, no. 1 (spring 2006): 15–49.

Collins, William J. "The Political Economy of State-level Fair Employment Laws, 1940–1964." *Explorations in Economic History* 40, no. 1 (January 2003): 24–51.

Colson, Charles, and Richard John Neuhaus, eds. *Evangelicals and Catholics Together: Toward a Common Mission*. Dallas: Word Publishing, 1995.

Congregation for the Doctrine of the Faith. "Doctrinal Note on Some Questions Regarding the Participation of Catholics in Political Life." Vatican website. Available at www.vatican.va/roman_curia/congregations/cfaith/documents/rc_con_cfaith_doc_20021124_politica_en.html.

Connolly, James J. *The Triumph of Ethnic Progressivism: Urban Political Culture in Boston, 1900–1925*. Cambridge, MA: Harvard University Press, 1998.

Cramer, John. *Pioneers, Politics and People: A Political Memoir*. Sydney: Allen & Unwin, 1989.

Crepaz, Marcus M.L. *Trust beyond Borders: Immigration, the Welfare State and Identity in Modern Societies*. Ann Arbor: University of Michigan Press, 2008.

Critchlow, Donald T. *Phyllis Schlafly and Grassroots Conservatism: A Woman's Crusade*. Princeton, NJ: Princeton University Press, 2005.

Cuneo, Michael W. *Catholics against the Church: Anti-abortion Protest in Toronto, 1969–1985*. Toronto: University of Toronto Press, 1989.

Davies, Grace. *Religion in Britain since 1945: Believing without Belonging*. New York: Wiley-Blackwell, 1994.

de Costa, Caroline. *RU-486: The Abortion Pill*. Salisbury, Queensland: Boolarong, 2007.

Deforrest, Mark Edward. "An Overview and Evaluation of State Blaine Amendments: Origins, Scope, and First Amendment Concerns." *Harvard Journal of Law & Public Policy*, 26 (2003): 551–626.

Delorme, Rita H. "Recalling an Epic Battle: Bishop Keiley, Sisters, and the Catholic Laymen's Association versus the Veazey Law." *Southern Cross* (Roman Catholic Diocese of Savannah), July 20, 2006. Available at https://diosav.org/sites/all/files/archives/S8626p03.pdf.

Dickinson, John, and Brian Young. *A Short History of Quebec*, 4th edn. Montreal: McGill-Queen's, 2008.

Diner, Hasia R. *The Jews of the United States, 1654–2000*. Berkeley: University of California Press, 2004.

Djupe, Paul A., and Laura R. Olson, eds. *Encyclopedia of American Religion and Politics*. New York: Facts on File, 2003.

Selected bibliography

Dochuck, Darren. "Evangelicalism Becomes Southern, Politics Becomes Evangelical: From FDR to Ronald Reagan." In Mark A. Noll and Luke E. Harlow, *Religion and American Politics: From the Colonial Period to the Present*, 2nd edn. New York: Oxford University Press, 2007.

Dochuck, Darren. *From Bible Belt to Sunbelt: Plain-folk Religion, Grassroots Politics, and the Rise of Evangelical Conservatism*. New York: Norton, 2010.

Dolan, Jay P. *In Search of an American Catholicism: A History of Religion and Culture in Tension*. New York: Oxford University Press, 2003.

Dorrien, Gary. *The Making of American Liberal Theology: Idealism, Realism, and Modernity, 1900–1950*. Louisville: Westminster John Knox, 2003.

Drake, Tim. "From Operation Rescue to Operation Convert." National Catholic Register. Available at www.ncregister.com/info/email-a-friend/from_operation_rescue_to_operation_convert.

Dubinsky, Karen. *Lament for a "Patriarchy Lost?" Anti-feminism, Anti-abortion, and REAL Women in Canada*. Ottawa: Canadian Research Institute for the Advancement of Women, 1985.

Duncan, Kyle. "Secularism's Laws: State Blaine Amendments and Religious Persecution." *Fordham Law Review* 72 (December 2003): 493–593.

Economics and Research Branch, Canada Department of Labor. *Union Growth in Canada, 1921–1967*. Ottawa: Information Canada, 1970.

Education Committees of Confederation des Syndicats Nationaux and Centrale de l'enseignement du Quebec (trans. Arnold Bennett). *The History of the Labour Movement in Quebec*. Montreal: Black Rose Books, 1987.

Elliott, John H. *Building Bridges between Groups that Differ in Faith, Race, Culture*. New York: National Conference of Christians and Jews, 1947.

Elliott, Ward E.Y. *The Rise of Guardian Democracy; The Supreme Court's Role in Voting Rights Disputes, 1845–1969*. Cambridge, MA: Harvard University Press, 1974.

Erwin, Lorna. "REAL Women, Anti-feminism, and the Welfare State." *Resources for Feminist Research* 17, no. 3 (1988): 147–149.

Ethington, Philip J. *The Public City: The Political Construction of Urban Life in San Francisco, 1850–1900*. New York: Cambridge University Press, 1994.

Evans, M.D.R., and Jonathan Kelley. "Attitudes toward Abortion: Australia in Comparative Perspective." *Australian Social Monitor* 2, no. 4 (October 1999): 83–90.

Fairclough, Adam. *Race and Democracy: The Civil Rights Struggle in Louisiana 1915–1972*. Athens: University of Georgia Press, 1999.

Falwell, Jerry. *Falwell: An Autobiography*. Lynchburg: Liberty House, 1997.

Falwell, Macel. *Jerry Falwell: His Life and Legacy*. New York: Howard, 2008.

Farney, James Harold. *Social Conservatives and Party Politics in Canada and the United States*. Toronto: University of Toronto Press, 2012.

Farrelly, David G. "'Rum, Romanism and Rebellion' Resurrected." *The Western Political Quarterly* 8, no. 2 (June 1955): 262–270.

Fay, Terence J. *History of Canadian Catholics: Gallicanism, Romanism, and Canadianism*. Montreal: McGill-Queen's, 2002.

Fejes, Fred. *Gay Rights and Moral Panic: The Origins of America's Debate on Homosexuality*. New York: Palgrave Macmillan, 2008.

Felsenthal, Carol. *Sweetheart of the Silent Majority: The Biography of Phyllis Schlafly*. New York: Doubleday, 1981.

Field, Laurie. *The Forgotten War: Australia and the Boer War*. Carlton, Victoria: Melbourne, 1995.

Finke, Roger, and Rodney Stark. *The Churching of America, 1996–2005: Winners and Losers in Our Religious Economy*. New Brunswick, NJ: Rutgers University Press, 2005.

Finkel, Alvin. *Social Policy and Practice in Canada: A History*. Waterloo, Ontario: Wilfrid Laurier, 2006.

Fitzgerald, Ross. *The Pope's Battalions: Santamaria, Catholicism, and the Labor Split*. St. Lucia, Queensland: University of Queensland Press, 2003.

Fogarty, Ronald. *Catholic Education in Australia, 1806–1950*, vol. 2. Melbourne: Melbourne Press, 1959.

Foley, Patrick. "Catholics of the South: Historical Perspectives." *Catholic Social Science Review* 13 (2008): 77–90.

Foner, Eric. "Why is There No Socialism in the United States?" *History Workshop Journal* 17 (spring 1984): 57–80.

Ford, Patrick. *Cardinal Moran and the ALP: A Study in the Encounter between Moran and Socialism, 1890–1907 – Its Effects Upon the Australian Labor Party: The Foundation of Catholic Social Thought and Action in Modern Australia*. New York: Cambridge University Press, 1966.

Formicola, Jo Renee. "Catholicism and Pluralism: A Continuing Dilemma for the Twenty-first Century." In *Taking Religious Pluralism Seriously: Spiritual Politics on America's Sacred Ground*, edited by Barbara A. McGraw and Jo Renee Formicola, 61–86. Waco: Baylor, 2005.

Fortin, Pierre. "Has Quebec's Standard of Living Been Catching Up?" In *The State of Economics in Canada: Festschrift in Honour of David Slater*, edited by Patrick Grady and Andrew Sharpe, 381–402. Montreal: McGill-Queen's, 2001.

Foster, Bruce Wayne. "New Right, Old Canada: An Analysis of the Political Thought and Actions of Selected Contemporary Right-wing Organizations." Dissertation submitted to Political Science Department, University of British Columbia, July 2000.

Foster, Gaines M. *Moral Reconstruction: Christian Lobbyists and the Federal Legislation of Morality, 1865–1920*. Chapel Hill: University of North Carolina Press, 2002.

Fox, Cybelle. *Three Worlds of Relief: Race, Immigration and the American Welfare State from the Progressive Era to the New Deal*. Princeton, NJ: Princeton University Press, 2013.

Francis, Babette. "'Equal Opportunity' Legislation Threats Christian Teachings." Endeavour Forum website. Available at www.endeavourforum.org.au/old/ad2000_articles/equal.html.

Frazer, Andrew. "Parliament and the Industrial Power." *Parliament: The Vision in Hindsight*, edited by Geoffrey Lindell and R.L. Bennett, 93–148. Annandale, NSW: Federation, 2001.

Frymer, Paul. *Black and Blue: African Americans, the Labor Movement, and the Decline of the Democratic Party*. Princeton, NJ: Princeton University Press, 2007.

Frymer, Paul. *Uneasy Alliances*. Princeton, NJ: Princeton University Press, 2010.

Gagnon, Alain G., and Mary Beth Montcalm, *Quebec beyond the Quiet Revolution*. Scarborough, Ontario: Nelson Canada, 1989.

Gamm, Gerald H. *Urban Exodus: Why the Jews Left Boston and the Catholics Stayed*. Cambridge, MA: Harvard University Press, 1999.

Gelman, Andrew. *Red State, Blue State, Rich State, Poor State: Why Americans Vote the Way They Do*. Princeton, NJ: Princeton University Press, 2008.

Genovese, Eugene D. *The Southern Front: History and Politics in the Cultural War*. Columbia: University of Missouri Press, 1995.

Selected bibliography

George, Timothy. "Evangelicals and Catholics Together: A New Initiative." *Christianity Today* 41, no. 14 (December 8, 1997). Available at www.christianitytoday.com/ct/1997/december8/7te034.html.

Gin, Willie. "Jesus Q. Politician: Religious Rhetoric in the United States, Australia, and Canada." *Politics and Religion* 5, no. 2 (2012): 317–342.

Gladden, Washington. "The Anti-Catholic Crusade." *Century Illustrated Magazine* XLVII, no. 5 (March 1894): 789–795.

Gladden, Washington. "The Mischief of the A.P.A." *Century Illustrated Magazine* LII, no. 1 (May 1896): 156–157.

Gladden, Washington. "The Christian League of Connecticut." In *The Social Gospel in America 1870–1920*, edited by Robert T. Handy. New York: Oxford University Press, 1966.

Grace, Gerald, and Joseph O'Keefe, eds. *International Handbook of Catholic Education: Challenges for School Systems in the 21st Century, Volume 2*. Dordrect, NL: Springer Verlag, 2007.

Greenhouse, Linda, and Reva Siegel, eds. *Before Roe v. Wade: Voices that Shaped the Abortion Debate before the Supreme Court's Ruling*. New York: Kaplan, 2010.

Grieg, Alastair, Frank Lewins, and Kevin White. *Inequality in Australia*. Port Melbourne: Cambridge University Press, 2002.

Guest, Dennis. *The Emergence of Social Security in Canada*, 3rd edn. Vancouver: UBC, 1997.

Haddox, Thomas F. *Fears and Fascinations: Representing Catholicism in the American South*. New York: Fordham, 2005.

Hamburger, Philip. *Separation of Church and State*. Cambridge, MA: Harvard University Press, 2002.

Hanna, Mary. "Catholics and the Moral Majority." *Crisis Magazine*, November 1, 1982. Available at www.crisismagazine.com/1982/catholics-and-the-moral-majority.

Hattam, Victoria. *Labor Visions and State Power: The Origins of Business Unionism in the United States*. Princeton, NJ: Princeton University Press, 1993.

Hearn, Mark. *One Big Union: A History of the Australian Workers Union, 1886–1994*. New York: Cambridge University Press, 1996.

Hebert, Raymond M. *Manitoba's French Language Crisis: A Cautionary Tale*. Montreal: McGill-Queen's, 2004.

Herberg, Will. "Plight of American Catholicism." *National Review*, August 27, 1968, 852–853.

Hero, Rodney E., and Caroline J. Tolbert. "A Racial/Ethnic Diversity Interpretation of Politics and Policy in the States of the U.S." *American Journal of Political Science* 40, no. 3 (August 1996): 851–871.

Heyer, Kristin E., Mark J. Rozell, and Michael A. Genovese, eds. *Catholic and Politics: The Dynamic Tension between Faith and Power*. Washington, DC: Georgetown, 2008.

Hiemstra, John L. "Domesticating Catholic Schools (1885–1905): The Assimilation Intent of Alberta's Separate School System." Paper given at the Canadian Political Science Association Annual Meeting, Dalhousie University, May 30 to June 1, 2003, Halifax, Nova Scotia. Available at www.cpsa-acsp.ca/paper-2003/hiemstra.pdf.

Higham, John. *Strangers in the Land: Patterns of American Nativism*. New York: Atheneum, 1967.

Hill, Samuel S. *Religion in the Southern States*. Macon: Mercer, 1983.

Hill, Samuel S., Charles H. Lippy, and Charles Regan Wilson. *Encyclopedia of Religion in the South*. Macon: Mercer, 2005.

Hilliard, David. "Australia: Towards Secularisation and One Step Back." In *Secularisation in the Christian World*, edited by Callum G. Brown and Michael Snape, 75–91. Burlington, VA: Ashgate, 2010.

Hindman, Hugh D. *Child Labor: An American History*. Armonk, NY: M.E. Sharpe, 2002.

Hirst, John. *Australia's Democracy: A Short History*. Crows Nest, NSW: Allen & Unwin, 2002.

Historical Statistics of Canada. Toronto: Macmillan Co. of Canada Ltd., 1965.

Historical Statistics of the United States: Colonial Times to 1970, Part I. Washington, DC: Bureau of the Census, US Department of Commerce, 1975.

Hochschild, Jennifer L., and John H. Mollenkopf. "Modeling Immigrant Political Incorporation." In *Bringing Outsiders in: Transatlantic Perspectives on Immigrant Political Incorporation*, edited by Jennifer L. Hochschild and John H. Mollenkopf, 15–30. Ithaca, NY: Cornell University Press, 2009.

Hochschild, Jennifer, Jacqueline Chattopadhyay, Claudine Gay, and Michael Jones-Correa, eds. *Outsiders No More? Models of Immigrant Political Incorporation*. New York: Oxford University Press, 2013.

Hodgins, Bruce W. "The Plans of Mice and Men." In *Federalism in Canada and Australia: The Early Years*, edited by Bruce W. Hodgins, Don Wright, and W.H. Heck, 3–16. Waterloo, Ontario: Wilfrid Laurier, 1978.

Hodgins, Bruce W., John J. Eddy, Shelagh D. Grant, and James Struthers, eds. *Federalism in Canada and Australia: Historical Perspectives, 1920–1988*. Peterborough, Canada: Frost Centre for Canadian Heritage and Development Studies, Trent University, 1989.

Hogan, Michael. "The Catholic Campaign for State Aid to Non-state Schools in NSW and ACT." Doctoral dissertation, University of Sydney, 1977.

Hogan, Michael. *The Sectarian Strand: Religion in Australian History*. Ringwood, Victoria: Penguin, 1987.

Hoover, Dennis R. "The Christian Right under Old Glory and the Maple Leaf." In *Sojourners in the Wilderness: The Christian Right in Comparative Perspective*, edited by Corwin E. Smidt and James M Pening, 193–216. New York: Rowman & Littlefield, 1997.

Hoover, Dennis R. "Ecumenism of the Trenches? The Politics of Evangelical–Catholic Alliances." *Journal of Ecumenical Studies* 41, no. 2 (spring 2004): 247–292.

Hout, Michael, Andrew M. Greeley, and Melissa J. Wilde. "The Demographic Imperative in Religious Change." *American Journal of Sociology* 107, no. 2 (2001): 468–500.

Hull, N.E.H., and Peter Charles Hoffer. *Roe v. Wade: The Abortion Rights Controversy in American History*, 2nd edn. Lawrence: University Press of Kansas Press, 2001.

Hulsether, Mark. *Building a Protestant Left: Christianity and Crisis Magazine, 1941–1993*. Knoxville: University of Tennessee Press, 1999.

Huntington, Samuel. *Who Are We? The Challenges to America's Identity*. New York: Simon & Schuster, 2004.

Hutchison, William R. *Religious Pluralism in America: The Contentious History of a Founding Ideal*. New Haven, CT: Yale University Press, 2003.

Jacobson, Matthew Frye. *Whiteness of a Different Color: European Immigrants and the Alchemy of Race*. Cambridge, MA: Harvard University Press, 1998.

Jelen, Ted G. "Catholicism, Homosexuality, and Same-sex Marriage in the United States." In David Morton Rayside and Clyde Wilcox, *Faith, Politics, and Sexual Diversity in Canada and the United States*. Vancouver: UBC, 2011.

206 Selected bibliography

Johnston, Richard, and Byron Schafer. *The End of Southern Exceptionalism: Class, Race and Partisan Change in the Postwar South*. Cambridge, MA: Harvard University Press, 2006.

Johnston, Richard, Andre Balis, Henry E. Brady, and Jean Crete. *Letting the People Decide: Dynamics of a Canadian Election*. Palo Alto, CA: Stanford University Press, 1992.

Jupp, James. "Fundamentalism in Modern Society." In *The Encyclopedia of Religion in Australia*, edited by James Jupp. New York: Cambridge University Press, 2009.

Kaldor, Peter, J. Bellamy, R. Powell, K. Castle, and B. Hughes. *Build My Church: Trends and Possibilities for Australian Churches*. Adelaide: Openbook, 1999.

Kambeitz, Teresita. "Relations between the Catholic Church and CCF in Saskatchewan, 1930–1950." CCHA, *Study Sessions*, 46 (1979): 49–69. Available at www.umanitoba.ca/colleges/st_pauls/ccha/Back%20Issues/CCHA1979/Kambeitz.html.

Kaufmann, Eric. *The Rise and Fall of Anglo America*. Cambridge, MA: Harvard University Press, 2004.

Kaufmann, Eric. "The Orange Order in Ontario, Newfoundland, Scotland, and Northern Ireland: A Macro-social Analysis." Available at www.sneps.net/OO/images/1-paper%20for%20Toronto%202006-graphs%20in.pdf.

Key, V.O. *Southern Politics in State and Nation*. New York: Alfred A. Knopf, 1950.

Keyssar, Alexander. *The Right to Vote: The Contested History of Democracy in the United States*. New York: Basic Books, 2000.

King, Desmond, and Rogers M. Smith. "Racial Orders in American Political Development." *American Political Science Review* 99 (2005): 75–92.

Kinzer, Donald L. *An Episode of Anti-Catholicism: The American Protective Association*. Seattle: University of Washington Press, 1964.

Kleppner, Paul. *Continuity and Change in Electoral Politics, 1893–1928*. New York: Greenwood Press, 1987.

Kraut, Benny. "Jews, Catholics, and the Goodwill Movement." In *Between the Times: The Travail of the Protestant Establishment in America, 1900–1960*, edited by William R. Hutchison, 193–230. New York: Cambridge University Press, 1989.

Kuo, David J. *Tempting Faith: An Inside Story of Political Seduction*. New York: Free Press, 2006.

Landis, Benson Y., ed. *Religion and the Good Society: An Introduction to Social Teachings of Judaism, Catholicism, and Protestantism*. New York: National Conference of Christians and Jews, 1942.

Lee, Shayne, and Phillip Luke Sinitiere. *Holy Mavericks: Evangelical Innovators and the Spiritual Marketplace*. New York: New York University Press, 2009.

Lefebvre, Solange. "The Francophone Roman Catholic Church." In Paul Bramadat and David Seljak, eds, *Christianity and Ethnicity in Canada*. Toronto: University of Toronto Press, 2008.

Lefebvre, Solange, and Jean-François Breton. "Roman Catholics and Same-sex Marriage in Quebec." In *Faith, Politics, and Sexual Diversity in Canada and the United States*, edited by David Rayside and Clyde Wilcox, 219–234. Vancouver: UBC, 2011.

Levendusky, Matthew. *The Partisan Sort: How Liberals Became Democrats and Conservatives Became Republicans*. Chicago, IL: University of Chicago Press, 2009.

Lieberman, Robert C. *Shifting the Color Line: Race and the American Welfare State*. Cambridge, MA: Harvard University Press, 1999.

Linteau, Paul Andre, Rene Durocher, and Jean-Claude Robert. *Quebec: A History, 1867–1929*. Toronto: Lorimer, 1983.

Lipset, Seymour Martin. *Continental Divide: The Values and Institutions of the United States and Canada*. Toronto: C.D. Howe Institute and National Planning Association, 1989.
Lipset, Seymour Martin, and Gary Marks. *It Didn't Happen Here: Why Socialism Failed in the United States*. New York: Norton, 2001.
Livingstone, Tess. *George Pell: Defender of the Faith Down Under*. San Francisco, CA: Ignatius, 2004.
Lyons, Dame Enid. *Among the Carrion Crows*. Adelaide: Rigby, 1972.
Machen, John Gresham. *Christianity and Liberalism*. Grand Rapids: Wm. B. Eerdmans, 1923.
Maddox, Marion. *God under Howard: The Rise of the Religious Right in Australian Politics*. Crows Nest, NSW: Allen & Unwin, 2005.
Manzer, Ronald. *Public Schools and Political Ideas: Canadian Educational Policy in Historical Perspective*. Toronto: University of Toronto Press, 1994.
Manzer, Ronald. *Educational Regimes and Anglo-American Democracy*. Toronto: University of Toronto Press, 2003.
Marlin, George J. *The American Catholic Voter: 200 Years of Political Impact*. South Bend: St. Augustine's Press, 2004.
Marsden, George. *Fundamentalism and American Culture*. New York: Oxford University Press, 2006.
Martin, Michel. "Catholic Hospitals Strive to Maintain Religious Focus in an Increasingly Secular Country." *Canadian Medical Association Journal* 148, no. 1 (1993): 64–65. Available at www.ncbi.nlm.nih.gov/pmc/articles/PMC1488598/pdf/cmaj00302-0066.pdf.
Marx, Karl. *Early Political Writings*, edited and translated by Joseph O'Malley, with Richard Davis. New York: Cambridge University Press, 1994.
Mason, Carol. *Killing for Life: The Apocalyptic Narrative of Pro-Life Politics*. Ithaca, NY: Cornell University Press, 2002.
Mason, Robert. *Richard Nixon and the Quest for a New Majority*. Chapel Hill: University of North Carolina Press, 2004.
McCoy, Donald R. "The Good Neighbor League and the Presidential Campaign of 1936." *Western Political Quarterly* 13, no. 4 (December 1960): 1011–1021.
McDaniel, Colleen. *Catholics in the Movies*. New York: Oxford University Press, 2008.
McDonald, Dale. *United States Catholic Elementary and Secondary Schools 2011–2012: The Annual Statistical Report on Schools, Enrollment and Staffing*. Arlington, VA: National Catholic Educational Association, 2012. Available at https://web.archive.org/web/20120102140535/www.ncea.org/news/AnnualDataReport.asp.
McDonald, Marci. *The Armageddon Factor: The Rise of Christian Nationalism in Canada*. Toronto: Vintage Books, 2011.
McGowan, Mark. *The Enduring Gift: Catholic Education in the Province of Ontario*. Toronto: Ontario Catholic School Trustees' Association. Available at www.ocecn.net/catholic_education/enduring_gift.htm.
McGreevey, John T. *Parish Boundaries: The Catholic Encounter with Race in the Twentieth-century Urban North*. Chicago, IL: University of Chicago Press, 1996.
McKinney, Madge M. "The Personnel of the Seventy-seventh Congress." *American Political Science Review* 36, no. 1 (February 1942): 67–75.
McKinney, Madge M. "Religion and Elections." *The Public Opinion Quarterly* 8, no. 1 (spring 1944): 110–114.
McLean, Ian, and Sue Richardson. "More or Less Equal? Australian Income Distribution in 1933 and 1980." *Economic Record* 62 (March 1986): 67–82.

208 Selected bibliography

McRae, Kenneth D. "The Structure of Canadian History." In *Founding of New Societies: Studies in the History of the United States, Latin America, South Africa, Canada, and Australia*, edited by Louis Hartz, 219–274. New York: Harcourt, Brace & World, 1964.

McVeigh, Rory. "Power Devaluation, the Ku Klux Klan, and the Democratic National Convention of 1924." *Sociological Forum* 16, no. 1 (March 2001): 1–30.

Mettler, Suzanne. *The Submerged State: How Invisible Government Policies Undermine American Democracy*. Chicago, IL: University of Chicago Press, 2011.

Miedema, Gary. *For Canada's Sake: Public Religion, Centennial Celebrations, and the Remaking of Canada in the 1960s*. Montreal: McGill-Queen's, 2006.

Miller, Carman. *Painting the Map Red: Canada and the South African War, 1899–1902*. Montreal: Canadian War Museum and McGill-Queen's, 1993.

Mills, Allen. *Fool for Christ: The Political Thought of J.S. Woodsworth*. Toronto: University of Toronto Press, 1991.

Mink, Gwendolyn. *Old Labor and New Immigrants in American Political Development: Union, Party, and State, 1875–1920*. Ithaca, NY: Cornell University Press, 1990.

Minutes of the Proceedings of the General Assembly of the Presbyterian Church of Australia. Sydney, September 1964, Thirtieth Session.

Mol, Hans. *Religion in Australia: A Sociological Investigation*. Melbourne: Nelson, 1971.

Moore, Andrew S. *The South's Tolerable Alien: Roman Catholics in Alabama and Georgia, 1945–1970*. Baton Rouge: Louisiana State University Press, 2007.

Moreau, Joseph. *Schoolbook Nation: Conflicts over American History Textbooks from the Civil War to the Present*. Ann Arbor: University of Michigan Press, 2003.

Morone, James. *Hellfire Nation: The Politics of Sin in American History*. New Haven, CT: Yale University Press, 2004.

Mosnma, Stephen V., and J. Christopher Soper. *The Challenge of Pluralism: Church and State in Five Democracies*. New York: Rowman & Littlefield, 2009.

Nations, Gilbert O. "Rome in Congress." *The Protestant*, 1922.

Nelles, H.V. "Ontario 'Carries On.'" In *Beyond Quebec: Taking Stock of Canada*, edited by Kenneth McRoberts, 31–44. Montreal: McGill-Queen's, 2000.

Nevitte, Neil. *The Decline of Deference: Canadian Value Change in Cross-national Perspective*. Orchard Park: Broadview, 1996.

Nevitte, Neil, and Christopher Cochrane. "Value Change and the Dynamics of the Canadian Partisan Landscape." In *Canadian Parties in Transition*, 3rd edn, edited by Alain-G. Gagnon and A. Brian Tanguay, 255–275. Peterborough, Ontario: Broadview, 2007.

Noel, Hans. *Political Ideologies and Political Parties in America*. New York: Cambridge University Press, 2014.

Nolan, Bruce. "Pope's Funeral Spotlights Kinship between Catholics and Evangelicals." *Christianity Today*, April 8, 2005. Available at www.christianitytoday.com/ct/2005/aprilweb-only/54.0.html.

Noll, Mark. "What Happened to Christian Canada?" *Church History* 75, no. 2 (June 2006): 245–273.

Noll, Mark. *What Happened to Christian Canada*. Vancouver: Regent College Publishing, 2007.

Noll, Mark. *God and Race in American Politics: A Short History*. Princeton, NJ: Princeton University Press, 2008.

Noll, Mark A., and Carolyn Nystrom. *Is the Reformation Over? An Evangelical Assessment of Contemporary Roman Catholicism*. Grand Rapids: Baker Academic, 2005.

Norton, Anne. *On the Muslim Question*. Princeton, NJ: Princeton University Press, 2013.

Nossiff, Rosemary. *Before Roe: Abortion Policy in the States*. Philadelphia, PA: Temple University Press, 2000.
O'Brien, Anne. "Of Faith and Feminism." *Australian Financial Review*, July 22, 2005, 11.
O'Connor, John. "Catholic Senate and House, 1936." John O'Connor Manuscripts Collection, Collection No. LMC 1945, Box 25, Lilly Library, Indiana University, Bloomington.
O'Farrell, Patrick (ed.). *Documents in Australian Catholic History, Volume II: 1884–1968*. Melbourne: Geoffrey Chapman, 1969.
O'Farrell, Patrick. *The Catholic Church and Community: An Australian History*. Kensington: New South Wales University, 1985.
O'Farrell, Patrick. *The Irish in Australia: 1788 to the Present*. Notre Dame, IN: Notre Dame Press, 2000.
Official Catholic Directory Anno Domini 2011. Berkeley Heights: National Register Publishing, 2011.
"Official Pronouncements of the Churches in Australia Regarding State Aid." Special Committee's Report to the 1961 Sydney Diocesan Synod, MS 7645, Box 69, National Library of Australia.
Orren, Karen, and Stephen Skowronek. *The Search for American Political Development*. New York: Cambridge University Press, 2004.
Page, David P. "Bishop Michael J. Curley and Anti-Catholic Nativism in Florida." *Florida Historical Quarterly* XLV, no. 2 (October 1966): 101–117.
Palmer, Bryan D. *Working Class Experience: Rethinking the History of Canadian Labour, 1800–1991*. Toronto: McClelland and Stewart, 1992.
Pariser, Eli. *The Filter Bubble: How the New Personalized Web is Changing What We Read and How We Think*. New York: Penguin, 2012.
Pearce, Joseph. "C.S. Lewis and Catholic Converts." *Catholic World Report*, November 19, 2013. Available at www.catholicworldreport.com/Item/2724/cs_lewis_and_catholic_converts.aspx.
Pennefather, R.S., ed. *The Orange and the Black: Documents in the History of the Orange Order, Ontario and the West, 1890–1940*. Orange and Black Publications, 1984.
Perin, Roberto. *Rome in Canada: The Vatican and Canadian Affairs in the Late Victorian Age*. Toronto: University of Toronto Press, 1990.
Perin, Roberto. *The Immigrant's Church: The Third Force in Canadian Catholicism, 1880–1920*. Ottawa: Canadian Historical Association, 1998.
Perkins, Havery L. "State Aid to Denominational Schools." Report to Australian Council of Churches, 1961, 4–6, MS 7645, Box 69, National Library of Australia.
Pew Research Religion and Public Life Project. "Public Opinion on Abortion." July 2013. Available at https://web.archive.org/web/20151012053700/http://features.pewforum.org/abortion-slideshow/slide3.php.
Phillips, Kevin. *William McKinley*. New York: Times Books, 2003.
Phillips, Kevin. *American Theocracy: The Peril and Politics of Radical Religion, Oil, and Borrowed Money in the 21st Century*. New York: Viking Press, 2006.
Pierson, Paul, ed. *The New Politics of the Welfare State*. New York: Oxford University Press, 2001.
Pierson, Paul. "Increasing Returns, Path Dependence, and the Study of Politics." *American Political Science Review* 94, no. 2 (June 2000): 251–267.
Pitsula, James M. *For All We Have and Are: Regina and the Experience of the Great War*. Winnipeg, Manitoba: University of Manitoba Press, 2008.

Prendergast, William B. *The Catholic Voter in American Politics*. Washington, DC: Georgetown Press, 1999.
Prest, Wilfrid, Kerrie Round, and Carol S. Fort. *Wakefield Companion to South Australian History*. Kent Town, South Australia: Wakefield, 2001.
Putnam, Robert. *Bowling Alone: The Collapse and Revival of American Community*. New York: Touchstone, 2001.
Putnam, Robert D. "E Pluribus Unum: Diversity and Community in the Twenty-first Century." *Scandinavian Political Studies* 30, no. 2 (2007): 137–174.
Putnam, Robert D., and David E. Campbell. *American Grace: How Religion Divides and Unites Us*. New York: Simon & Schuster, 2012.
Quinn, Herbert F. *The Union Nationale: Quebec Nationalism from Duplessis to Levesque*. Toronto: University of Toronto Press, 1979.
Rauschenbusch, Walter. *Christianity and the Social Crisis*. New York: Macmillan, 1908.
Ravitch, Diane. *The Troubled Crusade: American Education, 1945–1980*. New York: Basic Books, 1983.
Reimer, Sam. *Evangelicals and the Continental Divide: The Conservative Protestant Subculture in Canada and the United States*. Montreal: McGill-Queen's, 2003.
Reitz, Jeffrey G. *Warmth of the Welcome: The Social Causes of Economic Success for Immigrants in Different Nations and Cities*. Boulder, CO: Westview Press, 1998.
Risen, James, and Judy L. Thomas. *Wrath of Angels: The American Abortion War*. New York: Basic Books, 1998.
Roberts, Lance W., Rodney A. Clifton, Barry Ferguson, Karen Kampen, and Simon Langlois. *Recent Social Trends in Canada, 1960–2000*. Montreal: McGill-Queen's, 2005.
Robertson, John. *J.H. Scullin: A Political Biography*. Nedlands, Western Australia: University of Western Australia Press, 1974.
Robinson, Carin. "Doctrine, Discussion, and Disagreement: Evangelical Protestant Interaction with Catholics in American Politics." Dissertation, Georgetown University, July 25, 2008.
Roediger, David R. *Working toward Whiteness: How America's Immigrant Became White – The Strange Journey from Ellis Island to the Suburbs*. New York: Basic Books, 2005.
Rosenstone, Steven J., and John Mark Hansen. *Mobilization, Participation, and Democracy in America*. New York: Macmillan, 1993.
Rosswurm, Steve. "The Catholic Church and the Left-led Unions: Labor Priests, Labor Schools, and the ACTU." In *The CIO's Left-led Unions*, edited by Steve Rosswurm, 119–137. New Brunswick, NJ: Rutgers University Press, 1992.
Rozell, Mark. "Political Marriage of Convenience? The Evolution of the Conservative Catholic–Evangelical Alliance in the Republican Party." In *Catholic and Politics: The Dynamic Tension between Faith and Power*, edited by Kristin E. Heyer, Mark J. Rozell, and Michael A. Genovese, 27–42. Washington, DC: Georgetown University Press, 2008.
Rydon, Joan. *A Federal Legislature: The Australian Commonwealth Parliament 1901–1980*. Melbourne: Oxford University Press, 1986.
Santamaria, B.A. *"State Aid" in Perspective*. Melbourne: Hawthorn, 1966.
Santamaria, B.A. "Does Christianity Have a Future?" *Canberra Times*, December 24, 1988, 13.
Schlafly, Phyllis. *The Power of the Positive Woman*. New York: Jove, 1978.
Schultz, Kevin M. *Tri-faith America: How Catholics and Jews Held Postwar America to Its Protestant Promise*. New York: Oxford University Press, 2011.

Schwartz, Mildred A. *Public Opinion and Canadian Identity*. Berkeley: University of California Press, 1967.
Sehat, David. *The Myth of American Religious Freedom*. New York: Oxford University Press, 2011.
Seldes, George. *The Catholic Crisis*. New York: J. Messner, 1939.
Sen, Amartya. *Development as Freedom*. New York: Alfred A. Knopf, 1999.
Senior, Hereward. "Orangeism in Ontario Politics, 1872–1896." In *Oliver Mowat's Ontario: Papers Presented to the Oliver Mowat Colloquium, Queen's University, November 25–26, 1970*, edited by Donald Swainson, 136–153. Toronto: Macmillan of Canada, 1972.
Sherrington, Geoffrey. "Religious Schools Systems." In *The Encyclopedia of Religion in Australia*, edited by James Jupp, 668–676. New York: Cambridge University Press, 2009.
Shilts, Randy. *The Mayor of Castro Street: The Life and Times of Harvey Milk*. New York: St. Martin's Press, 2008.
Simeon, Richard, and Ian Robinson. *State, Society, and the Development of Canadian Federalism*. Toronto: University of Toronto Press, 1990.
Simpson, John H., and Henry G. MacLeod. "The Politics of Morality in Canada." In *Religious Movements: Genesis, Exodus, Numbers*, edited by Rodney Stark, 221–241. New York: Paragon, 1985.
Skocpol, Theda. *The Missing Middle: Working Families and the Future of American Social Policy*. New York: W.W. Norton, 2000.
Skowronek, Stephen. *The Politics Presidents Make: Leadership from John Adams to Bill Clinton*. New York: Belknap Press, 1997.
Skrabec, Quentin R., Jr. *William McKinley, Apostle of Protectionism*. New York: Algora, 2008.
Smith, David T. *Religious Persecution and Political Order in the United States*. New York: Cambridge University Press, 2015.
Smith, Eric Ledell, and Kenneth C. Wolensky. "A Novel Public Policy." *Pennsylvania History* 69, no. 4 (fall 2002): 489–523.
Smith, Miriam. *Political Institutions and Lesbian and Gay Rights in the United States and Canada*. New York: Routledge, 2008.
Smith, Oran P. *The Rise of Baptist Republicanism*. New York: New York University Press, 1997.
Smith, Rodney K. *Against the Machines: Minor Parties and Independents in New South Wales 1910–2006*. Sydney: Federation, 2007.
Smith, Rodney. "How Would Jesus Vote? The Churches and the Election of the Rudd Government." *Australian Journal of Political Science* 44, no. 4 (2009): 613–637.
Sonensheim, Raphael. *Politics in Black and White: Race and Power in Los Angeles*. Princeton, NJ: Princeton University Press, 1993.
Spann, R.N. "The Catholic Vote in Australia." In *Catholics and the Free Society*, edited by Henry Mayer. Melbourne: F.W. Cheshire, 1961.
Stackhouse, John G. "The National Association of Evangelicals, the Evangelical Fellowship of Canada, and the Limits of Evangelical Cooperation." *Christian Scholar's Review* 25, no. 2 (December 1995): 157–179.
Stark, Rodney, and Roger Finke. *Acts of Faith: Explaining the Human Side of Religion*. Berkeley: University of California Press, 2000.
Stone, Kurt F. *The Jews of Capitol Hill: A Compendium of Jewish Congressional Members*. Lanham, MD: Scarecrow, 2011.

Stowell, Daniel W. *Rebuilding Zion: The Religious Reconstruction of the South, 1863–1877*. New York: Oxford University Press, 1998.

Streb, Matthew J., and Brian Frederick. "The Myth of a Distinct Catholic Vote." In *Catholic and Politics: The Dynamic Tension between Faith and Power*, edited by Kristin E. Heyer, Mark J. Rozell, and Michael A. Genovese, 93–112. Washington, DC: Georgetown University Press, 2008.

Streeck, Wolfgang, and Kathleen Thelen. "Introduction: Institutional Change in Advance Political Economies." In *Beyond Continuity: Institutional Change in Advanced Political Economies*, edited by Wolfgang Streeck and Kathleen Thelen, 1–39. New York: Oxford University Press, 2005.

Sugrue, Thomas J. *Sweet Land of Liberty: The Forgotten Struggle for Civil Rights in the North*. New York: Random House, 2008.

Sullivan, Barbara Ann. *The Politics of Sex: Prostitution and Pornography in Australia since 1945*. Cambridge: Cambridge University Press, 1997.

Sullivan, Winnifred. *The Impossibility of Religious Freedom*. Princeton, NJ: Princeton University Press, 2007.

Summers, Mark Wahlgren. *Rum, Romanism, and Rebellion: The Making of a President, 1884*. Chapel Hill: University of North Carolina Press, 2000.

Sussman, Lance J. "'Toward Better Understanding': The Rise of the Interfaith Movement in America and the Role of Rabbi Isaac Landman." *American Jewish Archives* 34 (April 1982): 35–51.

Tatalovich, Raymond. *The Politics of Abortion in the United States and Canada: A Comparative Study*. New York: M.E. Sharpe, 1997.

Teixiera, Ruy. "New Progressive America: Twenty Years of Demographic, Geographic, and Attitudinal Changes Across the Country Herald a New Progressive Majority." Report for the Center for American Progress, March 11, 2009. Available at https://web.archive.org/web/20120714053519/www.americanprogress.org/issues/2009/03/progressive_america.html.

Tesler, Michael. "Donald Sterling Shows the Separate Realities of Democrats and Republicans." Monkey Cage Blog, May 1, 2014. Available at www.washingtonpost.com/blogs/monkey-cage/wp/2014/05/01/donald-sterling-shows-the-separate-realities-of-democrats-and-republicans-about-race/.

Tesler, Michael. "Democrats Increasingly Think the Confederate Flag Is Racist, Republicans Don't." Monkey Cage Blog, July 9, 2015. Available at www.washingtonpost.com/blogs/monkey-cage/wp/2015/07/09/democrats-increasingly-think-the-confederate-flag-is-racist-republicans-dont/.

Tesler, Michael. *Post-racial or Most-racial? Race and Politics in the Obama Era*. Chicago, IL: University of Chicago Press, 2016.

Thompson, Roger C. *Religion in Australia: A History*. Melbourne: Oxford University Press, 1994.

Tichenor, Daniel. *Dividing Lines: The Politics of Immigration Control in America*. Princeton, NJ: Princeton University Press, 2002.

Ture, Kwame, and Charles Hamilton. *Black Power: The Politics of Liberation*. New York: Vintage Books, 1992.

Vamplew, Wray, ed. *Australians: Historical Statistics*. New South Wales: Fairfax, Syme, & Weldon Associates, 1987.

Verney, Douglas V. *Three Civilizations, Two Cultures, One State: Canada's Political Traditions*. Durham, NC: Duke University Press, 1986.

Vigod, Bernard L. *Quebec before Duplessis: The Political Career of Louis-Alexandre Taschereau*. Montreal: McGill-Queen's, 1986.
Walker, Kenneth F. "Australia." In *Comparative Labor Movements*, edited by Walter Galenson, 173–242. New York: Russell and Russell, 1968.
Warhurst, John. "Religion in 21st Century Australian National Politics." Papers on Parliament No. 46, December 2006.
Warhurst, John. "Religion and Politics in the Howard Decade." *Australian Journal of Political Science* 42, no. 1 (March 2007): 19–32.
Warhurst, John, and Vance Merrill. "The Abortion Issue in Australia: Pressure Politics and Policy." *The Australian Quarterly* 54, no. 2 (winter 1982): 119–135.
Watt, James T. "Anti-Catholic Nativism in Canada: The Protestant Protective Association." *Canadian Historical Review* 48, no. 1 (March 1967): 45–58.
Weingast, Barry. "Political Stability and the Civil War: Institutions, Commitment, and American Democracy." In Robert H. Bates, Avner Greif, Margaret Levi, and Jean-Laurent Rosenthal, *Analytic Narratives*. Princeton, NJ: Princeton University Press, 1998.
Widen, Irwin. "Public Support for Parochial Schools: Why the Issue Has Re-emerged." *History of Education Journal* 4, no. 2 (winter 1953): 58–72.
Wilde, Melissa J. *Vatican II: A Sociological Analysis of Religious Change*. Princeton, NJ: Princeton University Press, 2007.
Wilkinson, Ian R., Brian J. Caldwell, R.J.W. Selleck, Jessica Harris, and Pam Dettman. *A History of State Aid to Non-government Schools in Australia*. Department of Education, Science and Training, Commonwealth of Australia, 2007.
Williams, Daniel. *God's Own Party: the Making of the Christian Right*. New York: Oxford University Press, 2012.
Williams, Howell. "Homosexuality and the American Catholic Church: Reconfiguring the Silence 1971–1999." Dissertation, Florida State University, 2007.
Winter, James. "English Democracy and the Example of Australia." *The Pacific Historical Review* 35, no. 1 (February 1966): 67–81.
Winters, Michael Sean. "How the Ghost of Jerry Falwell Conquered the Republican Party." *New Republic*, March 5, 2012. Available at www.tnr.com/article/politics/101296/falwell-gop-winters?page=0,1.
Wiseman, Nelson. "The Questionable Relevance of the Constitution in Advancing Minority Cultural Rights in Manitoba." *Canadian Journal of Political Science* 25, no. 4 (December 1992): 697–721.
Wolbrecht, Christina, and Rodney E. Hero, eds. *The Politics of Democratic Inclusion*. Philadelphia, PA: Temple University Press, 2005.
Wong, Janelle. "Thinking about Immigrant Political Incorporation." Workshop on Immigrant Incorporation, Mobilization, and Participation, Campbell Public Affairs Institute, Maxwell School of Syracuse University, December 6, 2002. Available at https://web.archive.org/web/20060223172950/www.maxwell.syr.edu/moynihan/programs/iiwg/pdfs/Wong.pdf.
Woodward, C. Vann. *Tom Watson: Agrarian Rebel*. New York: Oxford University Press, 1963.
Wright, Robert A. "The Canadian Protestant Tradition, 1914–1945." In *The Canadian Protestant Experience, 1760–1990*, edited by George A. Rawlyk, 139–197. Montreal: McGill-Queen's, 1990.
Wuthnow, Robert. *Restructuring of American Religion: Society and Faith since World War II*. Princeton, NJ: Princeton University Press, 1988.

Wuthnow, Robert. *Red State Religion: Faith and Politics in America's Heartland*. Princeton, NJ: Princeton University Press, 2012.
Young, Walter D. *The Anatomy of a Party: The National CCF, 1932–61*. Toronto: University of Toronto Press, 1961.
Zanca, Kenneth J., ed. *American Catholics and Slavery: 1789–1866 – An Anthology of Primary Documents*. New York: University Press of America, 1994.
Zeitz, Joshua. *White Ethnic New York: Jews, Catholics, and the Shaping of Postwar Politics*. Chapel Hill: University of North Carolina Press, 2007.
Zucchi, John, ed. *The View from Rome: Archbishop Stagni's 1915 Reports on the Ontario Bilingual Schools Question*. Montreal: McGill-Queen's, 2002.

Index

Page numbers in *italics* denote tables, those in **bold** denote figures.

Abbott, Lyman 71
Abbott, Tony 157
Abington School District v. *Schempp* 124
aboriginal groups 9
abortion 21, 109, 124; African Americans 179; Australia 152, 154; Canada 158, 166, 168; Jewish Americans 182; United States 137–8
Act Concerning Communist Propaganda (1937) 101
African Americans 9, 15, 17, 22, 68, 80, 81, 177; political incorporation 178–80
Alba, Richard 36
Alberta: Catholic political representation 31, *32*; Catholic population proportions in electoral districts 100; language policy 98; separate schools 37, 95–6
Alliance for Life 158
Alliance of Confessing Evangelicals 144
American Protective Association 67; and Lyman Abbott 71; and southerners 79–80 and Washington Gladden 71
Americans United for Life 137
Anderson, James 98
Andrews, Joan 138
Andrews, Kevin 154
Anglican church: in Australia 152
anti-Catholicism 2
Appleby, R. Scott 3
ascription 9
Asian Americans 177
assimilation theory 14, 176–7; and Catholic political incorporation during Great Depression 34–7; and Catholics in latter half of twentieth century 120–3
Australia: Catholics and parties 51–61, 154–8; Catholics in cabinet 26–7, 113; Catholics in House 27–9, **29**, *33*, 112–14, **114**, 114–15; Catholic incorporation patterns 4–7, 25–6; Catholic voting 52, 59; compulsory voting 49–51; labor movement 47–8, 51–8, **54**, *55*; parochial schools **57**, 57–61; political development 187; political institutions 41–2, 126–7; religious conservative movements 151–4; secularization 124; wage earner's welfare state 47, 48, 187
Australian Christian Lobby 153, 157, 158
Australian Council of the World Council of Churches 60
Australian Family Association 153
Australian Labor Party 5, 46, 47; and Catholic voting **116**, 116–17; and Catholics 38; and religious rhetoric 155, **156**; and strength in state governments 56; and state aid to parochial schools 59–60, 160

Bachmann, Michelle 131
Bader, Veidt 176
Bailey Memorandum 70
Baptists 60, 159
Benjamin, Judah 78
Bennett, John Coleman 75
Biden, Joe 131
Bilbo, Theodore 69
Bill C-33 158, 167
Bill C-43 166
Billings, Robert 140
Blaine amendments 79, 183, 189
Blaine, James 65
Bland, Salem 101

216　Index

Bloc Quebecois: Catholic voting **116**, 116–17; 165; liberal attitudes 164, 166, 176
Bob Jones University 141
Boer War 36, 92
Bourassa, Henri 103
Bozell, L. Brent 137
Brake, Robert 139
Brigg Initiative (Proposition 6) 140
Bright, Bill 143
British Columbia: Catholic political representation 31, *32*; Catholic population proportions in electoral districts 100; language policy 98; state aid to parochial schools 94, 160
British Empire and anti-Catholicism 35–6, 40, 89, 92, 95
British North America Act 91, 92, 94, 95; centralized power 99; language policy 97
brokerage party 16, 66
Brooks, David 111
Brotherhood Day 73
Bryan, William Jennings 67
Bryant, Anita 139–40
Buchanan, Patrick 137, 141
Buckley, William 137
Burchard, Samuel D. 65
Burton, Joe 103
Bush, George H.W. 141
Bush, George W. 109, 110, 111; on John Paul II 142; religious rhetoric 155; speech at Bob Jones University 141

cafeteria Catholics 110, 133
Cain, Herman 131
Caldwell, Willie W. 69
Call to Australia Party 153
Callahan, Daniel 75
Calvert Association 73
Campaign Life 158
Campbell, David E. 3–4
Campbell, Kim 166
Canada: Catholics in legislature 30, **31**, *32*; Catholic incorporation patterns 5–7, 26, 114–17, **116**, 116–17; Catholic voting 93, 102, 103, 167; Catholics in ministries 27, **28**; labor movement 100–1, 102–3; language policy 96–8; parties and Catholicism 91, 166–8; political development 187–8; political institutions 41–2, 126–7; religious conservative movements 158–66; secularization 124; separate schools 92, 93–6; social welfare policy 101–2, 103–4; *see also* British North America Act
Canadian Alliance 167
Canadian Family Action Coalition 158
capabilities approach 190
captured minority 15
Carroll, Coleman 139
Carter, Thomas H. 67
Cartier, George-Etienne 91
Castles, Francis G. 47
catchall party 16, 66
Catholic Alliance 141
Catholic church: centralized doctrinal authority 133; contemporary Quebec 164; contraception 121–2, 134; freedom of conscience 121, 122; leaders in development of parallel institutions 134–5; left–right ideological positions 133, 135; LGBT rights 153; mobilization on abortion 137; Moral Majority 140; sex abuse scandal 110; violence 1, 11n3, 120
Catholic Civil Rights League 158
Catholic Federation 53
Catholic Interracial Councils 74
Catholic schools *see* parochial schools
Catholic Taxpayers Association 96
Catholics: abortion 137–8; in Australian cabinet 26–7; in Australian House 27–9, **29**, 31, *33*, 112–13, **114**, 114–15; in Canadian House 30, **31**, *32*, 115; in Canadian ministries 27, 28; in Canadian premierships 115; capabilities 190; ERA 138–9; income and wealth in Australia 34–5, 52; issue positions 133; LGBT rights 139–40; Liberal–National coalition 155; parochial schools 140, 160; power resources 118–20; Quebec 164; swing voter 134, 145; voting in Australia 52, 59; voting in Canada 93, 102, 103, 167; voting in United States 67–8, 70; in United States cabinet 27; in United States governorships 112; in United States House 29–30, **30**, *33*, 112, **113**; in United States Supreme Court 111–12; *see also specific parties, countries, provinces, and states* with Catholic *sublisting*
Catts, Sidney 80
Charter of Rights and Freedom 124, 165; Section 15 158; Section 28 158
Chifley, Ben 25; and Catholics 54; Catholics in cabinet 27
Child Labor Law (1916) 135
Christian Century 75

Christian Coalition 141, 153
Christianity and Crisis 75
Christians United for Reformation 144
church attendance: in Australia 151, 154, 161; in Canada 161; in Quebec 161, 176; in United States 161
Church of England, and Catholics 60; international Catholic comparison 162, **163**
church–state boundary 21, 41–2; and religious freedom 188–9; *see also* parochial schools
Civil War 78
clash of civilizations 2
class identity: Australian Catholics 46, 53; Canadian Catholics 100–4; parochial schools 58; United States Catholics 71–7; *see also* labor movement, unions
Cleveland, Grover 65
Clinchy, Everett 73
Clinton, Bill 109
cloning *see* stem-cell research
co-belligerency 143
coalition of convenience 10, 16
coalition theory 15; Catholics in latter half of twentieth century 123; political development 187
Colson, Charles 143–4
Commons School Act (1871) 94
Commonweal 73
communism 21, 103, 131; and John Paul II 142
compulsory voting: in Australia 46, 49–51, 187; and Protestants 50; in United States 50
Confederation of Catholic Workers of Canada 100, 101
Congregation Union of Australia 152
conscription crisis: in Australia 51–2, 54; in Canada 92
conservative moral movements 10, 16, 22, 123–6; and African Americans 179; Australia 152–4; Canada 158–68; and Jewish Americans 181–2; and European Muslims 184–5; and Mormons 182; United States 137–45
Conservative Party (Canada 1867–1942) 91, 101; language policy 98; separate schools 94
Conservative Party (Canada 2003–) 26, 167–8
convent scandal allegations 2, 80, 110, 120, 122

Coolidge, Calvin 68
Cooperative Commonwealth Federation 89–90, 100, 101, 102; and Catholics 103
Council for the Defence of Government Schools 60
Council of Public Instruction 95
Country Party (Australia) 4, 58–61, 154
courts 5, 96, 98, 101, 112, 123–4, 126–7, 132, 136, 137, 140, 143, 158, 160, 166
Cramer, John 58, 60–1
Crimean War 36
Critique of Hegel's Philosophy of Right 188
cues 17
culture of life 110, 142
Curtin, John 54

DailyKos 134, 145
Davis, Jefferson 78, 79
Davis, John W. 68
Dawkins, Richard 111
Day, Stockwell 167
Defend Marriage Coalition 158
Defense of Marriage acts 183
Democratic Labor Party (Australia) 58, 154
Democratic Party (United States) 4, 5, 25; African American political incorporation 178–9, **178**; Catholics 68, 70, 73–5; Pope Francis 133; wedge issues 136–7
Denton, Jeremiah 140
descriptive representation 4–6
Dignitatis Humanae (1965) 121
DiIulio, John 109
diversity: and political development 3, 7, 22, 187–8; as richness or evenness 39–40
divorce 164
"Doctrinal Note on Some Questions Regarding the Participation of Catholics in Political Life" 122
Dolan, Terry 140
Dole, Bob 167
Douthat, Ross 3, 175–7
Dredd Scott 78
Du Bois, W.E.B. 2
Duplessis, Maurice 101–2, 104

Eagle Forum 139
Edmunds Act (1882) 78
electoral coalitions 16, 17, 22
Elementary and Secondary Education Act (1965) 5, 82
Ely, Richard T. 71

218 Index

Engel v. *Vitale* 123–4
English Catholics (Canada) 26, 97
Episcopalian Church 71
Equal Rights Amendment 138–9
Equal Rights Association 92
established churches 162, 163–4, 176
Evangelical Alliance of Protestants 72
Evangelical Fellowship of Canada 159
evangelicals: appreciation of Catholics for anti-abortion mobilization 137; Canada 159; Pope John Paul II 142; size of population 125; support for Catholic candidates in Republican primaries 131, 141; support for Catholics 109–11, 142
Evangelicals and Catholics Together 132, 143–5; in Canada 159
euthanasia 155; Quebec attitude 164

faith-based services 155, 157
Falwell, Jerry 137, 142; influence of co-belligerency 140; and Moral Majority 140
Family Action Movement 153
Family First Party 157
Farley, James 27
Fawkes, Guy 1
Federal Council of Churches 60, 72, 125; on Al Smith 72; rejection by Southern churches 77
Federal Employment Practice Committee 74
federalism 22, 23; Canada 99–104, 165–6; United States 76–82, 135–6
feminism: Australia 153; Canada 158; United States 138–9
Ferguson, Howard 98
Festival of Light 152, 153
filter bubbles *see* microtargeting
Fine, John S. 74
Finke, Roger 162
Foley, Luke 156–7
Foraker, Joseph 67
Forum Andre-Naud 164
Francis, Babette 153
free-market theory of church attendance 162
French Catholics (Canada) 26, 35, 97; voting 167
Frymer, Paul 15, 18, 22
Fuller, George 37
fundamentalism 159, 160, 176

Gauthier, Georges 103
Geghan Law 79
George, Robert 143
George, Timothy 144
Genovese, Eugene 77
Germany 189
Gillard, Julia 157
Gingrich, Newt 131; on John Paul II 142
Gladden, Washington 71
God Squad 166
Godbout, Adélard 102
Good Neighbor League 73–4
Goodwill Committee 72
Goodwill movement 72, 73
Graham, Billy 121; on Pope John Paul II 142
Grant, Ulysses 79
Gravel, Raymond 164
Great Depression 41
Green Party (Australia) 157
Green Party (Canada): and Catholic voting **116**, 116–17
Gunpowder Plot 1

Haas, Francis J. 74
Hagee, John 122, 141–2
Haig v. *Canada* (1992) 166
Hamburger, Philip
Harlow, Bryce 81–2
Harper, Stephen 167–8
Harradine, Brian 152
Harris, Mike 161
Hartz, Louis 35
Hawke, Bob 153
Heflin, J. Thomas 69
Hepburn, Mitchell 96
Herberg, Will 75, 109, 110
Heritage Foundation 140
Herron, John 154
Hewson, John 154–5
historical institutionalism 14, 19–22, 47–51, 76–82, 91–8, 126–7, 135–7, 154, 158–66; Latino incorporation 186; Muslim incorporation 184
Hitchens, Christopher 111
Hoover, Herbert 25, 69
House of Commons (Canada) 5; Catholic representation 30, **31**, *32*
House of Representatives (Australia) 4; Catholic representation 27–8, **29**, *33*, 38, 112–13, **114**, 114–15
House of Representatives (United States) 4; African American representation 178–9, **178**; Catholic representation 29–30, **30**, *33*, 112, **113**; Jewish American representation 180–1, **181**

Howard, John 153, 154–5, 157
Humanae Vitae (1968) 121–2
Huntington, Samuel 109, 122

Iannaccone, Laurence 125
ideological coalition 10, 15–19, 21, 179–80; *see also* symbolic centrality
immigration: Catholics to United States 66
intercurrence 24n18; *see also* overlapping orders
Ireland, John 29, 67
Irish Catholic 3, 35; in Australia 29, 48; in Canada 97
Ives–Quinn bill 74

Jensen, Peter 153–4
Jesuit Estates Act (1888) 92
Jewish Americans 177, 180–2
Jewish Question 1
Johnson–Reed Act (1924) 69
Jones, Bob Jr. 122
Judeo-Christian identity 16, 73–5, 180–1

Kelly, Dean 125
Kennedy, John F. 6, 109–10; Bailey Memorandum 70; southerners 80–2, *81*
Kerry, John 109–10, 122
Key, V.O. 81
Kilby, Thomas E. 80
King, MacKenzie 101–2
Kingsley, Henry 48
Klinkner, Philip 179
Knights of Columbus 73
Knights of Labor 100
Know Nothing movement 66, 77, 78, 79
Kristof, Nicholas 3, 146
Ku Klux Klan 68; and Washington Gladden 71

labor movement 10, 16; African Americans 179; Australia 47–8; Australian Catholics 46, 51–8; Canada 99, 100; compulsory voting in Australia 49; Latino Americans 180; United States 66, 76–7
LaHaye, Tim 110
Land, Richard 143, 144
Landolt, Gwendolyn 158
language policy 96–8
Latino Americans 185–6
Laurendeau, Andre 103
Laurier, Wilfred 26, 37; separate schools 94–5
Laurier–Greenway agreement 95, 98

Lawrence v. Texas 124
Lawson, Henry 52
Left Behind 110
Lemon v. Kurtzman 136
Levesque, Georges-Henri 103
Lewis, C.S. 132
Lewis, Larry 144
LGBT rights: Australia 153; Canada 158, 166; Quebec 164–5
Liberal and Country League 56
Liberal Party (Australia) 4, 5; Catholic voting **116**, 116–17; Catholics 58–61, 65, 154; Catholics 93, 115; state-aid to parochial schools 160
Liberal Party (Canada) 6–7, 26, 101–2, 103; Catholic voting **116**, 116–17; Christian right voting 167; dominance of 165; language policy 98; Louis Riel 94; separate schools 94–5, 161
Lincoln, Abraham 78
literacy test 69–70; Southerners 80
Loane, Marcus 153
Lynch, John Joseph 97
Lynch, Phillip 58
Lyons Forum 154
Lyons, Joseph 25, 58

McAdoo, William G. 68
McCain, John 141; renunciation of Hagee endorsement 142
McCarthy, D'Alton 92
MacDonald, John A. 91; Catholics in cabinet 27
McGreevey, John T. 3
McGurn, William 109
Machen, J. Gresham 132
McKenna, Joseph 68
MacKillop, Mary 157
McKinley, William: Catholics 67; Catholics in cabinet 27
Macky, Dill 53
Maddox, Marion 155
maiden speeches 155, **156**
majoritarian electoral system 41; Quebec's power 90, 93
Mallory, Stephen 78
Malone, James 139
Manhattan Declaration 141
Manitoba: Catholic political representation 31, *32*; Catholic population proportions in electoral districts 100; language policy 98; Laurier–Greenway compromise 95; Manning, Preston 167; state aid to parochial schools 37, 94, 160

220 *Index*

Mannix, Daniel 25
Marriage Amendment Act (2004) 155, 157
Martin, Paul 124
Martin, W.M. 98
Marx, Karl 188
median voter theory 18
Menzies, Robert 4, 59, 65
Mercier, Honoré 92
Methodist Church of Australasia 152
Methodists 60
Métis 92
microtargeting 180
model minority 177
Montreal Trades and Labour Council 101
Moral Majority 140, 153
Moran, Patrick Francis 52
Morgentaler decision *see R* v. *Morgentaler*
Morgentaler, Henry 164
Morgenthau, Henry 27
Mormons 182–3
Morrill Act 1862 78
Mortalium Animus (1928) 73
Motion 312, 168
Motu Proprio (1917) 37
Mulroney, Brian 165, 166–7
Murkowski, Frank 140
Murphy, Frank 27
Muslims 2, 36, 176–7; political incorporation in western Europe 183–5, 189

National Association of Evangelicals 125, 133, 159; abortion 137; school vouchers 140
National Brotherhood Week 74
National Catholic Welfare Conference 73
National Civic Council 153
National Conference of Catholic Bishops 137
National Conservative Political Action Committee 140
National Council of Christians and Jews 73
National Council of Churches 152
National Party (Australia) 6, 154
National Right to Life Committee 137
National Schools Chaplaincy Program 155, 157
Nationalist Party (Australia) 25
Native Americans 9
Ne Temere (1908) 37
Netherlands 176, 184, 189
Neuhaus, Richard John 143
New Brunswick: Catholic political representation 31, *32*; Catholic population proportions in electoral districts 100; language policy 98; state aid to parochial schools 94, 160
New Democratic Party (Canada): Catholic voting **116**, 116–17
New South Wales: Catholic political representation 29, 31, *33*, 38, *55*, 56, 58; Catholics 53; and Protestant Federation 36–7
New South Wales Council of Churches 60
Nickles, Don 140
Nile, Fred 153
Nixon, Richard 70; abortion 137; southern strategy 136
Noel, Hans 17, 179–80
Noll, Mark 136
North-West Territories Act (1875) 95
Northwest Rebellion (1885) 92
Nova Scotia: Catholic political representation 31, *32*; Catholic population proportions in electoral districts 100; language policy 98; state aid to parochial schools 94, 160
normalization 12n15

Obama, Barack 133, 180
Obamacare 21, 133
Occupy Wall Street 1
O'Connor, John (archbishop of NY) 141
O'Connor, John J. 30
Old Age Pension Bill (1927) 101
one-party incorporation 18, 23; Catholics in Australia 51–2
Ontario: Catholic political representation 31, *32*; Catholic population proportions in electoral districts 100; Cooperative Commonwealth Federation 102; language policy 98; separate schools 91, 96, 161
Ontario Conference of Catholic Bishops 161
Operation Dixie 77
Operation Rescue 138
Orange Order 121
organizational centrality 21, 132, 133–5; African Americans 179; Catholics in Australia 51–2, 151–3; Catholics in United States 72, 134–5, 137–40; Jewish Americans 180; Latino Americans 186; Mormons 182; Muslims in Europe 183–4; *see also* symbolic centrality
Orren, Karen 20
overlapping orders 20–3
overrepresentation 6, 7, 14, 18–19, 21, 23, 34, 38, 56, 111, 177, 179

Padlock Law (1937) 101
parliamentary system 41, 126
Parkes, Henry 59
parochial schools 92–3; Catholic leadership in development of 134; comparison of Australia and Canada 57; effect on political development 187; evangelical support for state aid 125; state aid in Australia 58–61, 160; state aid in Canada 91, 93–6, 159–61; state aid in the United States 70, 140, 160
Parti Quebecois 164–5
parties *see specific parties*; *see also* one-party incorporation, two-party incorporation
Pawlenty, Tim 131
Pearson, Lester B.: Catholics in cabinet 27
Pell, George 152
Perkins, Frances 27
Perry, Rick 131
Phillips, Kevin 136
Planned Parenthood 168
Playford, Thomas 56
pluralist theory 39–40, 162, 188
polarization 15, 17, 179–80
political development 3, 7, 22, 23, 187–8
political incorporation 12n14
political opportunity theory 14, 20; Catholics during Great Depression 40–1; Catholics in latter half of twentieth century 123–6
political orders 20–1
polygamy 78
Pope Benedict XVI 110, 134
Pope Francis 5, 134
Pope John XXIII 121, 142
Pope John Paul I 142
Pope John Paul II 21, 110, 122, 131, 142, 153–4
Pope Leo XIII 52, 71
Pope Paul VI 142, 153
Pope Pius XI 73
Pope Pius XII 142
popes 9, 69, 110
power resource theory 14, 56; Catholics during Great Depression 37–9; Catholics in latter half of twentieth century 118–20
preferential voting 41, 154
Presbyterian Church of Australia 152
Presbyterians 60, 77
presidential system 41
Prince Edward Island: Catholic political representation 31, *32*; Catholic population proportions in electoral districts 100; language policy 98; state aid to parochial schools 94, 160
Progressive Conservative Party (Canada): Catholic representation 115–6; Catholic voting **116**, 116–17, 165; religious conservatism 166–8; state aid to parochial schools 161
Progressive Party (Canada) 100, 101
Protestant Defence Association 53
Protestant Federation 36–7
Protestant Protective Association 92
provincial autonomy: effect on political development 187; *see also* federalism
Putnam, Robert 3–4, 15, 175

Quadragesimo Anno (1931) 89, 103
Quebec 7; Catholic political representation 31, *32*; centralization of national power 90; Cooperative Commonwealth Federation 103; labor unions 100, 101–2; language policy 98; LGBT policy 165; Liberal Party 165; provincial autonomy and Catholic identity 90, 93, 99–104; secularization 161–5; separatism 165; social welfare policy 103–4; state aid to Catholic schools 91, 160
Queensland: Catholic political representation 31, *33*, 38, *55*, 56
Quiet Revolution 7, 104

R v. Morgentaler 124, 158
race 40; convergence of north and south in United States 136
Raskob, John J. 68
Ratzinger, Joseph 122; *see also* Pope Benedict XVI
Realistic, Equal, and Active for Life Women 158
reconstructive coalition 10, 15–19, 21–3, 24n7, 127, 175; African Americans 179–80; Australian Labor Party 52–8, 156–7; Canada 159, 166–8; conservative evangelicals and Catholics in the United States 132, 143–5; Democrats and reconstruction 145–6; Latino Americans 180; Liberal–National coalition 154–6; Mormons 182–3; polarization 179–80; social gospel in United States 71–6; targeted ads 180
Red River uprising 92
Reed, Ralph 141
Reform Party 115–16, 167
regional autonomy *see* federalism

Regulation 17, 98
Reitz, Jeffrey G. 48
religious freedom 188–90
Republican Party (United States) 6; abortion 137; anti-Catholicism 66–7, 79; Catholic representation 112, 125; Catholic voting 25, 65, 67–8, **116**, 116–17; Jewish Americans 181–2; Mormons 182; Southern strategy 136
Rerum Novarum (1891) 52, 89
"Revising Marriage? Why Marriage is the Union of a Man and a Woman" 153
Riel, Louis 92
Right to Life (Australia) 152
Robertson, Pat 141, 142, 143
Roe v. *Wade* 124, 137
Roediger, David 4, 40
Romney, Mitt 131, 182
Roosevelt, Franklin: Catholics in cabinet 27, 43n11; Catholics in judiciary 43n12; Goodwill movement 73–5
Roosevelt, Theodore: Catholics in cabinet 27, 68
Roxanne's Law 168
RU-486 152, 155, 157
Rudd, Kevin 156–7
Ryan, Abram 79
Ryan, John 74
Ryan, John (Pro–Life Direct Action League) 138
Ryan, Paul 131; defending budget 145; on Pope Francis' issue positions 134

St. Laurent, Louis 26
same-sex marriage 21; in Australia 153, 157; in Canada 158, 167–8; *see also* LGBT rights
Sanders, Bernie 134
Santamaria, B.A. 60, 152, 153
Santorum, Rick 109, 131
Saskatchewan: Catholic political representation 31, *32*; Catholic population proportions in electoral districts 100; Cooperative Commonwealth Federation 102; language policy 98; separate schools 37, 95–6
Save Our Children 139–40
Scalia, Antonin 112
Schaeffer, Francis 137; on co-belligerency 140
Schlafly, Phyllis 138–9, 158
school vouchers 140
Scott, Thomas Walker 96
Scudder, Vida 72

Scullin, James 25, 53–4; Catholics in cabinet 26–7; fit of Labor with Catholics 53, 58
secularization 7, 36; and state aid to parochial schools 59
Senate (United States) 41
Sentinel 97, 121
separate schools 21, 57–8
separation of church and state 131; *see also* church–state boundary
Sex Discrimination Act 153
Skowronek, Stephen 20
slavery 77–8
Smith, Al 25, 69, 109; 1924 religious liberty plank 68; Bailey Memorandum 70; southerners 80–1
Smith, Rogers 179
social capital 15, 16–17
social gospel movement 71–5, 125; in Canada 103
Society for a Christian Commonwealth 137
Sorenson, Theodore 70
Sotomayor, Sonia 111–12
South Australia: Catholic political representation 31, *33*, 38, *55*, 56
Southern Baptist Convention 77, 133; abortion 137–8; spread of 136
southern and eastern European Catholics 4; Australia 48; immigration restriction in United States 69
southerners (United States): Al Smith 25, 69, 80–1; Catholics 6, 76–82; decline of distinctiveness 132, 135–7; feeling thermometer scores on Catholics 142; John F. Kennedy 80–2
Stark, Rodney 162
state aid to parochial schools *see* parochial schools
stem-cell research 155, 157
Stephens, Alexander
Stewart, Jon 110
stigmatization 12n15
STOP ERA 139, 153
subsidiarity 102, 134
survivance 97
symbolic centrality 21; Catholics in Australia 151–4; Catholics in Canada 158–9; Catholics in United States 132, 133–5, 145–6; Jewish Americans 180; *see also* organizational centrality, ideological coalition

Taney, Roger 78

Taschereau, Alexandre 101
Tasmania: Catholic political representation 31, *33*, *55*
tariff 67
Temple of Religion 74
Terry, Randall 138
Tesler, Michael 17
Thompson, John 26; Catholics in ministry 91
Tighe, Margaret 152
Tiny Township case 96
toleration 16
Tory, John 161
Trudeau, Pierre 166
two-party incorporation 65–6; Catholics in Australia 58–61, 156–7; Catholics in United States 66–9, 145–6

Unborn Victims of Crime bill 168
Union Nationale 101–2
unions 47–8, 77; *see also* labor movement
United Australia Party 25, 41, 65
United States: Catholic incorporation patterns 4–7, 25, 109–11, 131–2; Catholics and parties 66–71, 73, 79, 141–2, 145–6; Catholics in cabinet 27; Catholics in Congress 29–30, **30**, *33*, 111, **113**; Catholics in governorships 112; Catholics in Supreme Court 111–2; as central in stories of Catholic incorporation 3–4; diversity and development 3; labor movement 77; political institutions 41–2, 126–7; religious conservative movements 132–5, 137–45; secularization 123–4; social gospel 71–6; *see also* southerners
Uniting Church 152
U.S. Conference of Catholic Bishops 133; school vouchers 140; United States budget 145

U.S. Leadership Conference of Women Religious 133, 146; on ERA 139

V for Vendetta 1
valorization 12n15, 21, 109–10, 138, 142
Vamvakinou, Maria 156
Vatican II 6, 121, 142
Veazey Act 80
Veysey v. *Correctional Services* (1990) 166
Victoria: Catholic political representation 31, *33*, 54–6, *55*, 58
Victorian Catholics Workers' Association 53
Viguerie, Richard 140
Villeneuve, Jean Marie Rodrigue 103

Walker, Frank 27
Walsh, Thomas 68
wage earner's welfare state 47, 48, 187
Watson, Tom 80
Weber, Max 2
Weigel, Gustave 75
Western Australia: Catholic political representation 31, *33*, 55
Weyrich, Paul 140
white Australia policy 47
Wilson, Woodrow 80
winner-take-all election system *see* majoritarian electoral system
Woodsworth, James S. 89, 101
World War I 36, 40; Australia 51–2; Canada 92; United States 72
World War II: African Americans 179; Australia 60; Quebec 102
Women Who Want to Be Women 152–3
Wuthnow, Robert 125

Zelman v. *Simmons–Harris* 140, 160

# Taylor & Francis eBooks

Helping you to choose the right eBooks for your Library

Add Routledge titles to your library's digital collection today. Taylor and Francis ebooks contains over 50,000 titles in the Humanities, Social Sciences, Behavioural Sciences, Built Environment and Law.

Choose from a range of subject packages or create your own!

Benefits for you
- Free MARC records
- COUNTER-compliant usage statistics
- Flexible purchase and pricing options
- All titles DRM-free.

Benefits for your user
- Off-site, anytime access via Athens or referring URL
- Print or copy pages or chapters
- Full content search
- Bookmark, highlight and annotate text
- Access to thousands of pages of quality research at the click of a button.

 Free Trials Available
We offer free trials to qualifying academic, corporate and government customers.

eCollections – Choose from over 30 subject eCollections, including:

Archaeology	Language Learning
Architecture	Law
Asian Studies	Literature
Business & Management	Media & Communication
Classical Studies	Middle East Studies
Construction	Music
Creative & Media Arts	Philosophy
Criminology & Criminal Justice	Planning
Economics	Politics
Education	Psychology & Mental Health
Energy	Religion
Engineering	Security
English Language & Linguistics	Social Work
Environment & Sustainability	Sociology
Geography	Sport
Health Studies	Theatre & Performance
History	Tourism, Hospitality & Events

For more information, pricing enquiries or to order a free trial, please contact your local sales team:
www.tandfebooks.com/page/sales

 The home of Routledge books

www.tandfebooks.com